PRAISE FOR *AMERICAN SCHISM*

"Those seeking to heal our divided nation should read *American Schism*. In an age of unreason, Seth David Radwell deftly conveys the history of our core values and shows us a reasoned way forward."

—**Ana Navarro,** CNN contributor

"*American Schism* is a vigorously written, deeply informed intellectual tour de force and a bracing call to *nonviolent* arms!"

—**David J. Garrow,** Pulitzer Prize-winning author of *Bearing the Cross*

"Almost every book I read about America these days makes me more pessimistic about the country's future. Seth Radwell's *American Schism* is a rare exception. Mr. Radwell shows that Americans have argued angrily about the meaning of the Enlightenment from the founding onwards. But he also shows that disagreements have not prevented them from forging creative consensuses. What might a new creative consensus look like? Mr. Radwell presents an admirable answer to this question—and demonstrates how long-standing American ideas about meritocracy and freedom can be reinvented and revitalized for a new and more diverse age."

—**Adrian Wooldridge,** author of *The Aristocracy of Talent: How Meritocracy Made the Modern World*

"With America facing an ever-expanding slew of challenges, the only bipartisan solution often seems to be blaming the other side. What this reflects, according to Seth David Radwell, is the divide between two distinct visions of the Enlightenment, one moderate and one radical, that has been present since the nation's founding and continues to shape our politics. Today the danger is that our divisions will cause us to abandon Enlightenment values–reason, tolerance and pluralism–altogether, retreating into a more primordial emphasis on loyalty to faction or political 'tribe' above principle and the common good. As a student of history and politics, and a committed political innovator, I wholly recommend Radwell's book as a vital foundation on which to build a better understanding of not just the problems of twenty-first-century America but of the solutions we require."

—**Katherine M. Gehl,** author of *The Politics Industry*

"For those of us who are anxious about the state of democracy in the US and beyond, Radwell's book is a salve. He diagnoses the sorry state of American democracy as our intellectual inheritance from the Enlightenment: many of our deepest divisions, he writes, are the result of earlier disagreements about how to interpret the Enlightenment project itself. But behind our current divisions, Radwell glimpses the prospects for a more hopeful future—one which requires re-committing ourselves to certain Enlightenment ideals. I find Radwell's vision compelling: historically nuanced, well-argued, and with a focus firmly on what we all have reason to hope is a better future together."

—**Sanford C. Goldberg,** Chester D. Tripp Professor in the Humanities and professor of philosophy, Northwestern University, professorial fellow, Arché Research Center, University of St. Andrews

"As the political polarization in our country deepens seemingly by the day, Seth David Radwell's *American Schism* could not come at a better time. In contrast to the widespread belief that our current state of affairs is unprecedented, Radwell shows that, in fact, its roots date back to the origins of this country in the form of 'The Two Enlightenments.' *American Schism* is a fascinating historical work, but Radwell also offers an optimistic look forward and a detailed road map for how we can restore our unity and greatness."

—**Whitney Tilson,** co-author of *Poor Charlie's Almanack, More Mortgage Meltdown, The Art of Value Investing,* and *The Art of Playing Defense,* and a well-known value investor and philanthropist

"An intriguing exploration of how past historical conflicts continue to play out in our present divisions."

—**Paul Loeb,** author of *Soul of a Citizen*

"It is not often that one encounters history powerfully combined with analysis of our present, deeply troubling reality in a way that compels us to reconsider and reset our own political notions . . . Seth David Radwell, with his engaging style, has done just that, escorting us from the America of the Enlightenment to the United States of today in a way that will cause a great many of us to rethink."

—**Jonathan Israel,** leading Enlightenment scholar and Professor Emeritus, Institute for Advanced Study, Princeton

AMERICAN SCHISM

HOW THE TWO ENLIGHTENMENTS
HOLD THE SECRET TO HEALING OUR NATION

SETH DAVID RADWELL

GREENLEAF
BOOK GROUP PRESS

This publication is designed to provide accurate and authoritative information in regard to the subject matter covered. It is sold with the understanding that the publisher and author are not engaged in rendering legal, accounting, or other professional services. Nothing herein shall create an attorney-client relationship, and nothing herein shall constitute legal advice or a solicitation to offer legal advice. If legal advice or other expert assistance is required, the services of a competent professional should be sought.

Published by Greenleaf Book Group Press
Austin, Texas
www.gbgpress.com

Distributed by Greenleaf Book Group

For ordering information or special discounts for bulk purchases, please contact Greenleaf Book Group at PO Box 91869, Austin, TX 78709, 512.891.6100.

Design and composition by Greenleaf Book Group and Sheila Parr
Cover design by Greenleaf Book Group and Sheila Parr
Cover images © iStockphoto / MicroStockHub, Shutterstock / Marian Weyo
Additional text permission credits on page 427

Publisher's Cataloging-in-Publication data is available.

Print ISBN: 978-1-62634-861-5

eBook ISBN: 978-1-62634-862-2

Part of the Tree Neutral® program, which offsets the number of trees consumed in the production and printing of this book by taking proactive steps, such as planting trees in direct proportion to the number of trees used: www.treeneutral.com

Printed in the United States of America on acid-free paper

21 22 23 24 25 26   10 9 8 7 6 5 4 3 2 1

First Edition

Dedicated to health care and frontline workers all over the world who have assiduously cared and provided for and sustained us during this pandemic.

"When populists argue that they offer a return to a purer form of democracy, they are in a sense right. However, Aristotle would caution that when you opt for this kind of democracy what you often get is demagoguery instead: an all-powerful leader who imposes their will without restraint, empowered by a supposed mandate from the people. The will of the people in its purest form leaves little room for the rule of law."

—**Julian Baggini***

---

*Julian Baggini, "Aristotle's Thinking on Democracy Has More Relevance Than Ever," *Prospect*, May 23, 2018, https://www.prospectmagazine.co.uk/philosophy/aristotles-thinking-on-democracy-has-more-relevance-than-ever.

CONTENTS

FOREWORD

It is a privilege to provide the foreword for Seth David Radwell's *American Schism*. It is not often that one encounters history powerfully combined with analysis of our present deeply troubling reality in a way that compels us to reconsider and reset our own political notions.

The consternation, pain, and exasperation that so many have felt during recent years in contemplating the present state of political deadlock in the United States, and the relentless degrading of political debate (and public debate about nearly everything else), is ubiquitous in every American city and locality. We see an unprecedented outpouring of horror, anguish, and anger everywhere, on both coasts and in every region in between. Since the United States has been an example to the rest of the world ever since its founding, it is scarcely surprising that this consternation is widely shared also abroad. But the range of evident response to the crisis remains distressingly wide. Some stick to their guns and shout louder than ever, some throw up their hands in despair, a few even resolve to emigrate overseas. But in addition, owing to the COVID-19 pandemic, among a great many suddenly with extra time on their hands, one of the chief reactions, and perhaps the most positive and fastest growing, is the impulse to read more about social and political issues—to investigate and think deeper. As Radwell shows in *American Schism*, some choose to fight *unreason* with *reason*.

Reading helps pass the time and brings solace. Sometimes, it brings more than mere consolation. While waiting for the pandemic to end and for something approaching the old normalcy to return, it also leads some to break old habits of thought and assumption, reconsider their own long-held views on the basis of fresh perspectives and new information, and start afresh in the public sphere having glimpsed what they hope will be a way out of the dark and gloomy thicket of dismay and exasperation. Reading *American Schism*, many will agree, provides just this kind of opportunity to place their own life experiences in the wider general social context, to get a grip on things, to sort out the many bothersome questions they have been struggling with.

It is undeniably true that every individual who succeeds in setting their own life on a new and better course during and after a time of crisis does so in part by thinking back on their key life experiences and pondering anew the mistakes he or she made, asking themselves what went wrong before. What is true of the individual turns out to be strikingly true also of society as a whole. It may be more unusual, and certainly more difficult, to analyze present difficulties and troubles in the light of key historical developments in the collective American past, but the reader of this book will soon appreciate that it is no less crucial and valuable an undertaking. Recollecting, reconsidering, and reappraising is the only way to find the best path out of the morass. Seth David Radwell, with his engaging style, has done just that, escorting us from the America of the Enlightenment to the United States of today in a way that will cause a great many of us to rethink.

Many Americans long to see America achieve a higher level of civic responsibility and awareness. All of us during the current crisis have thought about particular tensions in the republic's institutional framework. In recent times, the questions of the scope and competence of federal health agencies and whether Supreme Court judges should serve for life have grabbed nearly everyone's attention, even if only for brief moments. But how many, bringing the Enlightenment and its best traditions into the picture, have set out before our minds the entire array of what, fragmentarily and in particular instances, political scientists as well as many ordinary citizens envisage as much-needed, highly requisite, institutional changes? It is refreshing to see how Radwell has comprehensively unpacked American history and in short, sharp, and very clear sections laid it out in proper order for us to inspect so that nothing remains technical or unintelligible, and the complete panorama becomes a consistently exciting review.

Being presented with the whole range of key structural changes, advised by the best logic of the Enlightenment debates surrounding the American Revolution and Constitution, is, for whoever samples it, a truly thought-provoking experience. To line up in one's mind and visualize from the combined perspective of past and present the entire basket of desirable egalitarian changes makes an unforgettable personal experience for the individual and is a valuable contribution to our democracy.

Many today worry about the rapid growth of inequality in our society and wish for a greater collective effort and more funding to level up the educational playing field. Some see also the need for the education society provides to become less simplistically focused on vocational preparation and for civic and constitutional awareness to be nurtured along with a broadening of horizons. That is nothing new. Nor is the conviction that addressing healthcare, education, and other inequalities through reform can only occur under a comprehensive federal program. Most already understand that these goals are not achievable without substantial raising of funding levels and that such programs are impossible without increasing public spending, which in turn can only happen equitably by increasing the tax load on the wealthiest. Ever since the 18th-century Enlightenment, the democratic wing has consistently pressed for the richest element of society to be taxed more heavily in proportion to the less well off, the adoption of what was called "progressive taxation" for the organized good of society as a whole.

But the trend in recent decades has been the other way, and the undeniable fact is that since the 1950s and 1960s society has actually drifted backward instead of forward with respect to wealth distribution, educational equality, and progressive taxation, indeed a sobering reality. Do we have to be taught all over again a principle firmly established before 1800 and a key plank of the democratic program promoted by the Radical Enlightenment thinkers in Europe and their counterparts in the United States—Benjamin Franklin, Thomas Jefferson, Thomas Paine, Joel Barlow, and, later, Margaret Fuller, those who led the American Radical Enlightenment tendency—namely, that you cannot have genuine equality and equal rights for all and a successful democratic republic that truly promotes the common good without raising the general educational level, and you cannot raise the general educational level without introducing "progressive taxation"?

Such considerations have long been brewing in many minds. But joining our thoughts about these general points with the proposed institutional changes prominent in the news during the present phase of political upheaval and crisis in America—such as whether we should alter the presidential impeachment procedure, end life appointments for Supreme Court judges, and strengthen the scope and professionalism of federal health agencies, and then aligning these with the other changes leading experts recommend to modify or break what has been called the "two-party doom loop," is like pressing the reset button on some vast apparatus of insight and appraisal. It leads to appreciating how all these issues interconnect and then, also linked in with them, there is a need to reform electoral procedures for the House of Representatives, significantly enlarge the House to make it more representative of society as a whole, and drastically reduce the power and status of the Senate, the role of which, not a few consider, has become increasingly outmoded and obstructive.

And there is still more to add to the list: eliminating voter suppression, rooting out foreign electoral interference, introducing much-needed campaign advertising reform, and eradicating gerry-mandering. All need to be brought into the picture alongside removal of corporate so-called rights to political participation, which leads to general acceptance of the principle that business corporations and private foundations do not enjoy the rights of citizens under the American Constitution that they claim and some jurists assign them. And, finally, we learn to see why there is such an urgent need to abolish the present-day anomaly of the Electoral College so that in the future the American president is elected by popular vote, as surely he or she should be.

The full scope of this vast, bitterly contested scenario, relentlessly unfolding since the debates of the Enlightenment era, is positively arresting, providing an experience that will enrich and change the outlook of whoever seriously ponders *American Schism*.

—Jonathan Israel, Institute for Advanced Study, Princeton

Prologue

TWO CONFLICTING VISIONS
OF AMERICA

As I hunkered down at home to weather the global COVID-19 pandemic of 2020, I struggled to overcome the sense of shock at how suddenly and utterly our world had been turned upside down. But as I contemplated my state of mind, oscillating rapidly between depression, anxiety, and frustration, I sensed that well before the onslaught of the pandemic I had already fallen into a profound state of disillusionment. As the world came to a halt, the health crisis simply gave me the time and space to realize it. The root cause of this disillusionment was related to the shattering of an ideal image that I had, perhaps, clung on to for far too long.

How had it come to be that over the last four years my entire conception of the American credo had crumbled? My vision of America was firmly rooted in the ethos of both freedom *and* equality; my America was a place where everyone had a fair shot at building a rewarding and fulfilling life, where each individual could define their own idiosyncratic version of success, and where we collectively formed a country of shared values with mutual respect for individual differences. That vision felt unambiguously inconsistent with the America of 2020. Just how and when did my America disappear? Did my vision of America ever exist at all, or was it but a myth? If it did exist, how did it disintegrate so quickly in just a few years? Or was its ruin a slow process of decay that began undetected (by me) much earlier? I was determined to explore these questions, to understand the origins of my disillusionment. Professional responsibilities had distracted me long enough; one of the silver linings of the COVID-19 isolation was that I had ample time and liberated mental space for action. I therefore commenced a concerted and in-depth investigation, not quite knowing where it would lead.

The initial step for me was discovering how my original American "illusion" was constructed and then fortified in the first place. Sure, I had a superficial sense of this, but I was committed to more deeply exploring how the roots of this illusion were planted and nurtured. My image of the United States, firmly embedded in the "American dream," was that of a land of opportunity where, at the beginning of the last century, my grandparents arrived as immigrants with nothing, fleeing tyranny and religious persecution. I developed an early appreciation as a young boy for my ancestors' courage. The idea of definitively abandoning their European lives in the hopes of building a better future for their descendants seemed both bold and romantic; this was the stuff that filled novels and movies, and it left an indelible impression on me.

Growing up in the '60s and '70s, I became more and more enchanted by the American experience, a place where the circumstances of one's birth and heritage no longer portended a destined path. We were by no means wealthy, but our middle-income household was relatively stable, and the love of our extended family was plentiful. This "safe" environment provided a powerful contrast to the stories I heard from my grandparents when they described the social and political oppression and economic hardship of the old country. So, naturally, the American dream was quite seductive to me. America was a place where anyone and everyone had a shot, based on hard work and sweat and tears, of building a better life for one's family. An even and level playing field, so I thought. These ideals became deeply rooted in my consciousness.

I latched onto this view through much of my early life, despite a growing understanding and appreciation of our country's imperfections and an emerging awareness that my vision of the American dream was, in fact, not available to many people, especially African Americans and other people of color outside my White privileged lens. Yet despite my mounting recognition of these injustices, I still profoundly believed that our nation was a meritocracy where achievement brought rewards, and I set out to make my mark. I spent much of my twenties and thirties pursuing business endeavors here and abroad, and this core image was mostly reinforced. The inhabitants of other countries at times criticized the United States, punching holes in my narrative, but overall I confirmed that my account was widely shared globally. Our country was the envy of the world—very much admired, if also feared.

By the time I was a middle-aged adult, troubling events began to create cracks, chipping away at this storyline. While in the post-9/11 years there was intermittent additional erosion, it was only in the last four years that my idealized image entirely collapsed. I began wondering if everything I believed was but a veneer, merely "Mao style" propaganda meant to conceal a much darker reality. I had this creeping dread that perhaps I had been programmed, indoctrinated into believing a narrative meticulously and systematically built on falsehoods. Was everything I held dear but a smokescreen, a façade covering a much uglier hidden truth? Was the more accurate depiction that of a land stolen from Indigenous people and exploited through the horrors of slavery, always for the benefit of the few? Was the genuine truth of America a bitterly racist society, with deep-seated fear of the "other"? How could I reconcile that picture with the "extraordinary land of opportunity" view? During all the years that I had been living and

3

thriving in one America, had another American reality coexisted, one that I could not or chose not to see?

Wrestling with these two alternate narratives of our country began to weigh on me, more and more, eroding my core belief system. The angst created by these two conflicting visions began to feel maddening. Indeed, I felt like I was losing my ability to differentiate fundamental underlying truth from perception. Often in the daily dialogue, the concept of two information "bubbles," or even more frightening, two discrete and incompatible "realities" in America, would surface, so I knew I was not alone. Still, the nature of the bitter political discourse made it impossible to distinguish fact from myth. I had always enjoyed political debates among colleagues and friends with diverging points of view. Now, I dreaded such discussions, fearful of having lost my grounding, distrustful of my own perspective.

More than the bitter divisiveness in American society today, it was the apparent disappearance of "truth" that had become intolerable to me. If as a society we could no longer discern the difference between established facts or proven science and "fake news," my optimistic outlook for our country, in spite of all my prior transient disillusionments, was now thoroughly shattered. The normalization by our president of appalling behavior replacing civilized debate was troublesome, but it was the utter abandonment of the importance of empirical facts that weighed most heavily on me. Perhaps my feelings were best conveyed in George Packer's insightful piece in *The Atlantic* in March 2020. While discussing how the populace has reacted to the Trump era, he wrote:

> A third of the country locked itself in a hall of mirrors that it believed to be reality; a third drove itself mad with the effort to hold on to the idea of knowable truth; and a third gave up even trying.[1]

Naturally, I considered which third I fell in. For most of Trump's presidency, I would have put myself into Packer's second group.

However, it started to dawn on me over these last few years that while perhaps I was not slipping into insanity, I was quickly plummeting into Mr. Packer's third group.

In our popular discourse today, we often hear the idea of "two Americas." This is not new; at various times in our history, clashing visions for the soul of our nation vied for prominence, each competing to gain status and standing. For many years, although I conceded that there were undeniably contradictions, I refused to accept this notion of two distinct nations within our borders. I was mistaken. Indeed, it turns out that there *really are two different* Americas. But I am not referring to the red and blue Americas so much in the news today. We seem to talk incessantly about those two Americas. Or we talk about separate Americas based on socioeconomic class, race, or religion. Sometimes we divide our country based on its geography, such as an urban-rural split or a coastal-interior one. But what if we look beyond those factors and attempt to discover and categorize discrete Americas by the *differences in ideals and beliefs* of its citizens? No doubt differences in race, class, countries of origin, and geography are all factors connected to differences in ideals and beliefs. However, I believe the relentless focus on the most superficial manifestations of our differences is damaging and counterproductive—*we need to go deeper and explore fundamental ideas.*

A shallow approach invariably leads to the type of identity politics that dominate the political landscape in the United States today, fostering distrust and a passionate red-blue enmity. Furthermore, these identity battles, once they take on symbolic meaning, often become fully divorced from a more rational discussion of the meaningful and substantive distinctions in what we believe. Of course, symbols and core underlying beliefs are related and reinforcing. For many in America today, mask-wearing has become just such a political symbol. But in this case, as in many others, the symbol (of freedom from a government-ordered mask mandate) has overwhelmed the rational science-based argument that wearing a mask is an effective mitigation tool against further spread of COVID-19. Is wearing or not wearing a mask really about fundamental freedoms secured in our Bill of Rights or is this about common sense and good citizenship?

Contemporary political scientists and journalists have written extensively in recent years about how in-group and out-group dynamics have rendered the conflicts between our tribal or political identities more significant than our actual policy differences.[2] A well-documented phenomenon in the field of group psychology indicates how members of a group, even one weakly affiliated, will make nonrational choices and tolerate inferior outcomes in the service of the emotional satisfaction that results from "winning" against the opposing group. Furthermore, in any zero-sum setting, individuals in each group develop feelings of prejudice and anger toward the out-group, as well as pride and loyalty toward in-group members. (Sports fans are very familiar with the power of these in- and out-group impulses.) An additional related phenomenon is the linking of group status with individual self-esteem so that any attack on the group as a whole is perceived as an attack on the individual, which can motivate the respective person to take action to defend the group. The most salient takeaway from these findings in what is called "social identity theory" is that the roots of these feelings and behaviors are *based on primitive human drives* and not at all on *rational thought*. Because these common human traits must have been adaptive in our evolutionary history, the feelings and actions triggered as part of these experiences are to a large extent instinctually connected to our own survival mechanisms.

But today, these intergroup dynamics have hijacked our political discourse. The fact that Americans share so much in common has become progressively obscured by an almost obsessive focus on how we sort into socio-political in-group and out-group identities. Consequently, we are more susceptible to the primitive impulses associated with group behavior as a force operating independently of our individually developed policy positions. Whatever the actual content of the discussion, we tend to believe that our group's perspective is accurate and infallible. Furthermore, the political symbols described previously have become amygdala-related stimuli that induce emotional responses and discourage rational debate.

In *Uncivil Agreement: How Politics Became Our Identity* (2018), Lilliana Mason carefully explores and discusses these developments that are dramatically influencing our political discourse:

> While political enthusiasm is not usually thought of as problematic, it, along with anger, leads to increased political activity based not on policy goals but on knee-jerk identity-defense responses . . . Anger and enthusiasm are the primary emotional drivers of political action, and they are not drivers of thoughtful processing of information . . . [this] helps to explain how it is that partisans can grow increasingly divided even when their policy positions do not diverge . . . The group-based drivers of both anger and enthusiasm . . . [can] lead to relatively thoughtless political action.[3]

Our individual views on contested issues have become shaped by larger tribal identities, and rational policy debates have been replaced by tribal conflicts.[4] In sum, these tribal dynamics have *crowded out* coherent analysis and reasoned consideration in our political discourse. Unless we can individually distance ourselves from the pressures of the "mobs" that we ourselves create within our in-groups, we will fail in attempts to resolve our genuine policy differences. "The more people who feel angry, the less capable we are as a nation of finding common ground on policies, or even of treating our opponents like human beings."[5] Perversely, the same group behaviors that helped early humans survive now threaten our collective capacity to resolve pressing challenges. Allowing primal emotions to govern our political discourse is as ludicrous as attempting to resolve a nuanced and intricate disagreement through a WWE (World Wrestling Entertainment) match.

Without an appreciation of these forces at work, many of my friends and professional colleagues have marveled at this deterioration in our civic conversation over recent years. Together, we try to comprehend how and why our contemporary public discourse has collapsed; our basic communication model, *our collective discussion*, seems entirely broken. As many older Americans continue to shout at each other over social media and divide into increasingly polarized camps, a growing majority of younger Americans are becoming increasingly apathetic, convinced that the political establishment is deaf to their concerns and wholly incapable of solving tenacious and potentially devastating problems, like climate change and pandemics. When in recent history has our political dialogue been this fruitless? How have rational argument and passion been balanced in other eras, and why does that balance seem so out of whack now?

Some of my colleagues seem content to participate in the mayhem that is today's social media. I imagine they believe that the best prescription for shouting is more shouting, since commotion and hullabaloo seem to be what people want to hear. However, I contend that there is a better remedy in precisely the opposite approach—that of thoughtful analysis and painstaking reflection. Adding to the noise will not help; *we need to fight unreason with reason.*

* * *

It was in this spirit that I embarked upon an exploratory journey over the last few months, searching for a fresh and distinctive perspective on the recent corrosion of our civic life. As a voracious reader of both fiction and nonfiction, I delved into reading about the history of great ideas and events to investigate whether my American "illusion" was supported by actual facts that could be observed in historical episodes and socioeconomic trends.

My early findings from this journey quickly confirmed that none of the underlying conflicts that today manifest as an America "torn apart" are new. These battles reflect the fundamentally divergent visions of our country that emerged at our nation's founding and have been vying for prominence ever since. Furthermore, these conflicts are not the latest fad, a function of recent technological change, the result of nascent polarized information "bubbles," or a consequence of nontraditional White House leadership. On the contrary, they are as substantial as they have been enduring. But at the same time, new technology, information "bubbles," and a divisive president have all played major roles in propelling these divisions into the open and expediting a political sorting that diametrically and rancorously pits two sides against each other.

Not only are today's conflicts not new, but over the course of this expedition, I began recognizing parallel historical antecedents that made today's surreal world feel less exceptional and provided much-needed clarity. I began to detect direct longitudinal connections across numerous eras of our history and gain a more profound appreciation of disparate pieces that began to fit together into a coherent whole.

It quickly became apparent to me that I needed to return to the origins of the clashing visions that emerged at our nation's founding to acquire the more comprehensive and nuanced understanding that methodical historical exploration can bring. Consequently, the starting point of my investigation was to go back to the Enlightenment. Most Americans have at least some general sense that the founding principles that shaped the United States are rooted in the Enlightenment era. Typically, fleeting memories from a high school social studies class or recollections from a history book read long ago stay lodged in our brains. While I thought I was well versed in the Enlightenment, it became clear that only by reexamining my previous examinations of 18th-century thought and discovering more recent interpretations could I begin to gain greater clarity. I became convinced that extensive research would allow me to reorient the woes of the current world within a global historical context.

The first time I developed a deep understanding of the Enlightenment was during my years at Columbia College when I was immersed in its respected "core curriculum." Of course, over recent years, the core's in-depth exploration of the great thinkers influencing the development of Western civilization has been extensively criticized for its almost exclusive focus on "dead, White" European males. While there is patent validity to these critiques, it was via these humanities courses that I first developed a profound appreciation for the ideals of the Enlightenment and its emphasis on the vast potential of human capacity. Specifically, the concept that humans, through empirical observation and reason, could ascertain "truth in the universe" was personally awe-inspiring—especially so, given that this concept arose after centuries in which all aspects of daily life were dictated by religious dogma, the destruction of war, or the rules of rigidly stratified social hierarchy. I realized that not only was the very creation of our nation, the entire "American experiment," born out of these ideals, but also that these same ideals were responsible for a significant part of the technological and scientific advancement of civilization in subsequent centuries. For these reasons, despite its White, privileged, European, and male biases, I had forever since considered the Enlightenment as the transformational period most consequential for our modern world. Moreover, it was at this juncture, during my own collegiate enlightenment, that I began to channel my personal capacities into a deep dedication to the pursuit of objective truth in my own endeavors.

As part of my newly inspired investigative journey, I dusted off many of my old university texts that I had first encountered so many years ago. But I also immersed myself in more recent academic works of political history and analysis. I am particularly indebted to the esteemed academic Jonathan Israel for providing inspiration for this journey. Professor Israel is a highly decorated academic specializing in the Age of Enlightenment and philosophical history, among other topics. He is a member of the British Academy of Arts and Sciences and has been awarded numerous honors. His recent work, *The Enlightenment That Failed* (Oxford University Press, 2019), is a monumental tome of nearly 1,000 pages that is impeccably researched and annotated. This enormous work provides an incredible survey of the most important contributions to Western thought over the last 400 years. It was this work that initially motivated me to dig deeper and explore new sources and fresh paths of inquiry in the course of my present expedition.

My exploration did, in fact, reveal many surprises. At the highest level, I realized that the existence of two different Americas has rich historical antecedents. I discovered that throughout our nation's evolution, *two distinct Americas have always coexisted*. In fact, while both have always been present, at particular moments in a given era one would seemingly gain momentum or status. But much like a pendulum swinging back and forth, the farther the push in one direction in a given cycle, the more forceful the counterreaction in the next. It appeared that intervals of rapid progress toward a more ideal egalitarian society were inevitably followed by periods in which we were plunged back to a much darker reality.

Most surprising to me was that at the root of the two Americas was not *an* Enlightenment, but *two distinct* Enlightenments that were fiercely competing during the founding of our nation, as they have been ever since. At the same time as these conflicting Enlightenment influences were contending for prominence in the new nation, anti-Enlightenment counter-movements characterized by a subjugation of reason and empirical truth in favor of religiously inspired zeal were superimposed with unpredictable effects. Sometimes these anti-Enlightenment counterforces bubbled up from public sentiment and coalesced into popular movements; at other times, they were foisted on the general population from the top down by those in or seeking power as a tool of political expediency.

As I explored and learned, I was able to better define how my own personal vision of a country of meritocratic egalitarianism was flawed, as much a myth or illusion as a concept grounded in reality. Yes, the ideals underpinning my particular illusion were based on certain historical truths, but these specific truths were only half of the story. I needed to understand the other half, the elements underlying a much murkier side of our history; I needed to explore the roots of the glaring incongruities between the two nascent rival visions from the 18th century. What follows in the chapters ahead is an investigative tracing of the roots of these two discrete Americas, the means by which they have contested with each other, and their dynamic interplay with anti-Enlightenment movements over the last few centuries.

*   *   *

I am convinced that *reasoned analysis and sound historical perspective* can act as a salve for the wounded and irrational political discourse that is raging at present. It is due to this conviction that I believe my journey and explorations are worth sharing with readers. As long as our political identities are eclipsing our logical thinking, and emotional and nonrational impulses are crowding out lucid and cogent argument, we will continue to spin in circles, held hostage by our self-chosen mobs.

Collectively as a society, we can neither understand our present predicament nor forge consequential and enduring solutions to our most pressing problems without a more rational examination of the historical context of both, divorced from our triggered emotional states. So, while many of my fellow disillusioned citizens are searching for answers, looking to make some sense of the last four years of unbearably painful civic life and shattered public discourse, I fear their struggles will remain futile without the deeper and richer texture that an analytical perspective can bring. We intuitively understand that the seeds of our current dilemma were planted long before Trump came into office. These seeds took root perhaps a generation ago and have grown into mounting tensions among diverse American identities ever since.

Even aside from the current polarized environment in which emotions outstrip reason, I find it astonishing and disappointing that even in educated circles today, we seem completely blind to historical assessment. Since so many citizens have scant knowledge of history, most may not realize that their own beliefs, ideas, and opinions about how our society functions (or does not function) are founded on the basis of debates that unfolded centuries ago during the Revolutionary Era. Furthermore, understanding the nature of these debates is not only essential but, in fact, is a prerequisite for understanding today's quandaries, evaluating potential policy alternatives, and appreciating our democratic processes. How can we effectively debate the proper functioning of our civic society while lacking a basic understanding of the very principles upon which it is based? Somehow, in assigning blame for the acute ills associated with contemporary concerns, we deny ourselves the framework to truly comprehend how our differences have evolved. In short, in addition to our partisan bubbles, *we are caught in a time bubble* that inhibits any illuminating historical or longitudinal perspective.

Even for those who are more well-read or schooled in history or the humanities, or for nonacademics like myself, while we may recognize the importance of Enlightenment principles as foundational for our modern republic, we nonetheless are inclined to view the era as somewhat monolithic. Accordingly, we assume that a single uniform vision was largely responsible for our nation's birth. *This is not in the least bit the case.* On the contrary, there was a huge diversity of opinion expressed not only in declaring independence from the Crown, but more importantly, in determining what to construct in its wake.

Our Founders and the other great thinkers of the era posited and vigorously contested a large range of political solutions. But within this spectrum of Enlightenment views, two distinct polarities emerged that clashed on some of the most fundamental issues regarding the power structure of societies.

There is an explanation for why so many of our citizens lack this historical perspective—for all intents and purposes, they are never exposed to it. In recent generations, educational experts have shifted priorities in the mandated curriculum away from the social sciences. Furthermore, there are few accessible paths for many adult readers to *efficiently* acquire civic historical perspective precisely because the material is so mountainous. Many academics have dedicated their careers to interpreting and organizing the vast sea of material from the Enlightenment era and from subsequent periods and have added new viewpoints. Paradoxically, while such material is overflowing, it remains too often exclusively the purview of scholars and professors, written for academic purposes and rarely explored in the mass media. In fact, much of this material is *inaccessible* to us lay people, resulting in a tremendous knowledge gap in our contemporary discourse regarding the origins of many of our civic principles.

Given this context, I hope the following chapters might fill a needed gap by providing a more accessible history of the evolution of political thought from the founding of the nation to our contemporary times. My goal is to provide a more digestible rendering of this material and thereby open a more transparent window into how and why our society is organized the way it is. I am convinced that thoughtful historical analysis is not only highly germane to today's civic distress, but it can also provide a rational framework needed to overcome the lack of logical analysis in our contemporary political debate. At a minimum, I hope we will be better able to answer some simple yet still perplexing questions: Why do we appear to be stuck in neutral today, facing seemingly intractable problems? Must we make trade-offs between seemingly contradictory goals? Do we save our planet, or do we build a strong economy? Can we preserve our Bill of Rights without shouting at each other or shooting each other? We are in dire need of a rational approach in these times when facts seem discernibly subordinated to passions.

The content and tone of the debate manifest on today's social media platforms is fully indicative of this lack of historical analysis among citizens. Everyone seems to have a political opinion on every topic, and most, now enabled with a 21st-century global publishing platform, feel compelled to lob their content out into the digisphere without pause or reflection. The resulting debate is usually rife with aggressive or defensive opinions but lacking both factual data and historical analysis. Even when making reference to history, ideas are presented in purely one-dimensional and simplistic terms.

Examples of this naïveté are everywhere; many well-educated Americans think that our Founders were uniform in their views, which could not be further from the truth. Many young people feel that the core democratic foundation of our republic is solid and impregnable, having stood the test of time. In fact, our Founders had fundamental disagreements regarding the very model of what we call, in today's vernacular, a liberal democracy. In debating the optimal structure for the new American experiment, some of our Founders advocated for a broadly embracing democratic formula, while others called for a limited democracy, with strong guardrails to prevent what they saw as the dangers of mass democratic participation in the civic affairs of government.

Many United States citizens today seem to believe that liberty and equality are contradictory ideals—that one cannot have both. But history illustrates that these ideals can, in fact, be more complementary then competing. Enlightenment thinkers grappled with these same fundamental questions of political philosophy: Who gets a voice in civic affairs, and are all voices equally weighted? As a society, how do we determine the allocation of scarce resources? How do we evaluate the contributions of our citizens, and how do we distribute commensurate rewards? In today's public discourse, while we do not argue in these terms, these are the very questions that underlie some of our most tortured conflicts. Enlightenment-era debates on these issues often took place with illuminating clarity and simplicity. It is with the express purpose of encouraging readers to return to these original debates about the foundations of civil society that I have endeavored to write this book. I believe that by reflecting on these debates and investigating how they influenced later developments in our history, readers can better understand how their own contemporary opinions were originally molded and subsequently evolved. Moreover, perhaps they can challenge some of their own views anew.

The material we will cover in this book is as follows: First, I will present a summary of the overall argument that two contrasting Enlightenments not only existed but are at the root of the fundamental divisions in our society. I will then dive into the origins of the opposing principles starting with a brief overview of the pre-Enlightenment era, followed by an overview of the Enlightenment period itself, the era in which a sweeping departure in thinking indelibly shaped our modern society. In subsequent chapters, I will dissect these ideas in some detail, delineating rival schools of thought that emerged during the Enlightenment and putting forth a framework for describing and analyzing the consequences of their rivalry. I will then attempt to apply this framework to specific discrete periods of American history, including our current political era, to explore the consequences of the struggle. Finally, I will explore the issues at stake to distill core principles, to redefine the debate in more constructive terms, and productively advance the conversation within a logical construct. This last section will likely reveal clear and recognizable patterns and shed some light on the origins of the angst, the frustration, and the misdirected passion that we all feel every day. In addition, I will propose a set of priorities that I deem vital to address if we are to bridge our bitter divisions and reestablish a constructive civil discourse. In this last section, I offer a modest proposal (not in a Swiftian sense) for a course of action with the sole overarching purpose of rearticulating and recommitting to the democratic principles that I firmly trust most Americans hold dear.

But before we plow ahead, the reader deserves a definition of the overall concept behind this book's title. What exactly is the American Schism?

THE AMERICAN SCHISM

My vision of America as an unparalleled land of exceptionalism and opportunity, a level playing field where anyone who works hard can get ahead, is a myth. But this vision, this myth, is far from irrelevant. On the contrary, like most myths, it has elements of genuine truth blended with aspirational ideals. The ideals underlying my mythical vision have their origins in the 18th century and inspired two of the most consequential (and interrelated) events in modern history: the French Revolution and the birth of our country. Along with the 1917 Russian Revolution and the 20th-century World Wars and in-between era of fascism, the twin 18th-century revolutions arguably defined the modern era. The revolutions marked a demarcation point in Western civilization between a new modern society and a civic structure that, since the Middle Ages, had been organized almost exclusively around three immutable factors: hereditary rights, dogmatic religion, and brute force.

The reach of the American and French Revolutions extended far beyond the two sides of the Atlantic, with repercussions in all corners of the globe. Moreover, there is broad consensus that these two conjoined world-changing occurrences were made possible by the expansive development of thought in the period immediately prior and during those events—a development that we now call the Enlightenment (*Les Lumières*). It was during this period that the ideals of freedom, liberty, and equality were not only fiercely debated on a conceptual level but also inspired world-shattering events that shaped the modern world. Historians and political scientists of all stripes agree that democratic republics, or what we think of as open societies, owe a tremendous debt to Enlightenment thinkers.

But the Enlightenment was vast and encompassed a wide range of diverse ideas. *And here is where the American Schism originally formed.* America is not merely the product of one Enlightenment. America is the product of *two very different Enlightenments.* And at the founding of our nation, these two incompatible Enlightenments germinated into two rival and conflicting visions of our country—visions that have been at war ever since.

It is precisely because the gap between these two 18th-century visions were largely irreconcilable that we can validate the existence of *two separate Enlightenments*, each with its own set of prescriptions for modern society, each forming a distinct school of thought. As we will explore in detail throughout the chapters that lie ahead, the *Moderate Enlightenment*, while disseminating some of the most important advances of the age, fundamentally maintained much of the prevailing hierarchical inelasticity in society. In contrast, the *Radical Enlightenment* was the school of thought that more meticulously delineated an alternative to this rigid societal structure.

As a consequence of this split, the persistent gap between these two schools of thought has had colossal repercussions for civic life over the course of our subsequent history. At the same time, other societal dynamics and cultural forces that are profoundly opposed to Enlightenment principles altogether have implanted themselves and entwined with these two contending schools of thought, generating further complications and often surprising consequences. To understand and opine on the power structure of contemporary societies, one needs to grasp and appreciate these disparate tendrils and the interplay between them.

There has always been agreement that certain political thinkers of the Enlightenment were more "radical" than others. Accordingly, academics have advanced various schemas for best classifying or distinguishing among contrasting groups of ideas, or schools of thought. For example, many previous characterizations of the Enlightenment thinking used geography as the prime organizing classification: We frequently read about the British Enlightenment, or the French Enlightenment, or the Scottish, Dutch, or German Enlightenment. Since thinkers in all these countries made valuable and unique contributions to Enlightenment thought, country of origin can irrefutably serve as a viable distinguishing characteristic.

But Jonathan Israel has developed an organizing structure that is much more valuable—one that elucidates how individual and unique 18th-century strands of thinking coalesced, each forming a school of thought based on specific substantive elements of the central ideals posited by their proponents. Significantly, each of these schools has a discrete prescription for organizing civil society that vividly and substantially conflicts with the other. Moreover, in making explicit or implicit choices among these dissimilar prescriptions and their corresponding discrete power structures, subsequent civil societies have experienced the often violent consequences of the ensuing clashes. Exploring this array of material is not only relevant to understanding the past but is also required to grasp the origins and evolution of the American Schism, and the dynamics behind today's torment.

Ironically, the trend over the past fifty years has been to downplay the role of the Enlightenment. Postmodernist or Reconstructionist thought along with some currents of Marxist revisionism have argued that the impact of the Enlightenment was overemphasized, especially contrasted to the impact and the rise in influence of Marxist theology. Such intellectual stances are skeptical of a far-reaching grand narrative of history and instead tend to view power structures in society as relative, and certainly as nonconforming to Enlightenment philosophy. However, we deny the relevance of Enlightenment political and social philosophies at our own peril; indeed, differences between them have shaped the arc of modern history through all the following centuries and are at the root of the American Schism. But how did this schism form in the first place? Over precisely which issues did the split in 18th-century thought occur?

Prominent thinkers in the second half of the 18th century built off the solid foundation of their 17th-century counterparts, who adopted rational and empirical systems of philosophy. In fact, the great 17th-century thinkers had firmly established a clear shift in focus from faith-based concepts (in the centuries prior) to rationally derived ideas and empirically observed elements in our tangible world. Still others remained spiritual but endeavored to simultaneously understand and interpret the world through both faith-based and rational lenses. By the 18th century, the notion of science and discovery as a path to drive human progress forward was ascendant. Furthermore, the important concept of "reason" began being viewed as essential in decision-making and in advancing human civilization. In fact, these same notions exploded into intellectual and philosophical movements dominating ideas on both sides of the Atlantic—and the Enlightenment was born.

It was at this juncture that many thinkers turned to issues of political, social, and moral philosophy. And with these subjects came *vast disparities of thought* regarding the "rights of man" and the optimal power structures and governing principles of the social contract; these differences were the cause of the schism between the two Enlightenments. How exactly did these Enlightenment philosophies shape the political systems that followed? Can these same schools of thought clarify why we self-govern as we do and why other countries do so differently? And finally, can this framework help contextualize the nature of today's bitter political discourse, where agreed-upon facts are rare, but passionate conflicts are abundant? Can it help shed light on the conflicting visions of what the American experiment represents and the gaps between those visions? What contrasting beliefs underlying this rupture are still waging battle today? This book endeavors to elucidate these questions for those without a deep background in either political philosophy or history.

As we compare and contrast these concepts in the chapters that follow, we will see familiar terrain emerge, much like when fog dissipates from a mountainous landscape. Indeed, the discrepancies in beliefs underlying these 18th-century schools of thought are very much thriving today even if masked in a new contemporary vernacular. Moreover, the conflicts between these schools of thought are at the very root of the two incompatible Americas that are alive today, and they have been in continual rivalry over the course of our history as a nation. At times, they have locked horns in vigorous, yet reasoned and constructive debate, often with positive results. But equally as often, they have waged a ferocious war with tremendous violence and brutal consequences. Their interaction with Counter-Enlightenment ideas and movements during particular historical moments has also generated unpredictable outcomes, further muddying the picture. Most importantly, when we assess the vehement political debates of our present in light of the past, we can view our differences with the benefit of the arc of history. Within this context, we can be less riddled by passion and richer in insight. And with some newfound perspective, perhaps we will be able to more firmly ground our differing points of view in reason.

Part I

ORIGIN OF
THE AMERICAN SCHISM:
THE TWO ENLIGHTENMENTS

Chapter 1

EUROPE BEFORE THE ENLIGHTENMENT

To gain an appreciation for the features of the pre-Enlightenment era, let us briefly travel back in time to the late Middle Ages, a few hundred years before the 18th century. For almost a thousand years prior, societies around the world had been predominantly organized around three overarching themes: faith and superstition, heredity privilege, and brute force.

We all have some sense of the nature of daily life in the Middle Ages from its portrayals in film, TV, and books. For most people during these centuries, agriculture was the dominant way of life. Small groups of artisans and merchants were scattered in villages. Europe was persistently ravaged by war, usually in the name of the Roman Catholic Church (the Crusades spanned over four centuries) or in pursuit of imperial expansion, which required arduous battles between rivaling kings and noble lords. Of course, each part of Europe was unique; while France, England, and Spain were large kingdoms, smaller ruling entities held power over large territories in the area that now comprises Italy, Germany, and much of northern Europe. Importantly, the entire notion of the nation-state as we understand it today did not yet exist in Europe. The main identifying geographical characteristic was the region or village, not the nation—England did not become a sovereign country until 937, and Spain was not unified until 1490.

Before the emergence of industry, urban areas were mostly trading centers where mercantile activities were predominant. But in addition to having a higher concentration of merchants, these areas were also important seats of religious leadership and artistic centers. Thus, in preindustrial centuries, towns and small cities served as important crucibles for the development of thought where diverse segments of society could exchange new ideas, often with unanticipated results. In contrast, rural areas, dominated by an agricultural lifestyle supported by small villages and hamlets, were more tightly controlled by the local church, and religious dogma inhibited any nascent form of diversity in thought.

The Scientific Revolution is often cited as beginning with Copernicus, who published his famous theory proposing the heliocentric nature of our solar system in the late Renaissance of the early 1500s. In the centuries prior to that, influential thinkers concentrated on the spiritual realm, exploring concepts outside the dominion of the empirically observed or materialistic world. After Copernicus published his theory, scientific thinking and discovery exploded over the next few hundred years (through and beyond the Enlightenment). Faith-based pursuits continued to play a major role in daily life, and the dogma of organized religion provided the foundation of personal belief systems (as it does today). Yet the ascendancy of scientific discovery portended a sharp shift in the orientation of society.

All through the Middle Ages, as well as pre- and post-Renaissance, in most of Europe one's status in society was *predestined by birth*. There was virtually no concept of social mobility in the preindustrial age. European society was meticulously structured and rigid, with class structure determined mostly by the "birth lottery." Generally speaking, on the hierarchical top of society sat the nobility, those bestowed with affluence by their dynastic family line. Their wealth usually came in the form of land, but the associated authority and influence of "landed" people went well beyond capital.

Across most of Europe, the gentry, whether bloodline nobility or aristocracy, ruled over their local territory and ensured political, economic, and social stability in their dominions under the purview of the reigning monarch. Each kingdom followed its own hierarchy of titles, but whether a duke, count, earl, or some other designation, only this privileged class received a rich and comprehensive education. In the Middle Ages, with some exceptions (usually in religious circles), the populace was largely illiterate.

The second subdivision of society was the clergy. Originally, the Roman Catholic and Eastern Orthodox Churches had divided Europe, each dominating specific jurisdictions. Strict church doctrine guided the activity of local clergy, who were often tasked with mediating the inevitable conflicts between the kingdom or local nobility and the higher church authorities. Over the course of the Reformation, beginning in 1517, other church denominations emerged and gained prominence. But regardless of religious affiliation, in the late Middle Ages and throughout the Renaissance, the spiritual leaders—local priests and ministers—often represented the most influential local authority figures in the daily life of the local community. The focus on religion and faith remained central in education—the overarching goal of instruction was to inspire and support the pursuit of a spiritual life among the masses. Any additional secular education was usually confined to the routine skill training of an apprenticeship-oriented system.[1]

Subordinate to the nobility and clergy were the masses, most of whom were relatively poor with individual fortunes subject to local agricultural prospects and the whims of the local nobility or religious authority. Since this third group was by far the majority, most people were incentivized to conform to church teachings and to the local aristocratic desires to ensure some level of personal stability and familial protection. Except for those who joined the clergy, the most common path was the life of peasant or serf working on the land of someone more fortunate who collected rent (most often in the form of goods and services rather than hard money).

In most territories, an absolute monarch sat at the highest echelons of the nobility and had ultimate authority throughout the domain. As the centuries progressed, while nobles still retained some local control, the monarchs, through the military forces at their disposal, were increasingly able to force people into compliance with royal decrees. These monarchs surrounded themselves with the privileged nobility to bolster their power and thereby preside over the great royal courts of Europe. They wielded power beyond the sword, holding ultimate authority to bequeath favors and wealth to those in good service and to condemn to punishment those not in their favor. Importantly, monarchs viewed their own self-interests as their top priority in all endeavors.

At times, the ruling monarch might demonstrate genuine concern for the people in the kingdom, but examples of this were few and far between. Monarchs often pursued war for territorial expansion or other personal gain, often bestowing great power and status on brave warriors who did their bidding. But few of the undertakings in the royal sphere were in the legitimate interests of the people, despite proclamations of the opposite.[2]

During these centuries, most monarchies held absolute and total power over their dominions and are thus often referred to as "absolute monarchies." The important point is that with few (if any) checks on their power, these monarchies were frequently quite tyrannical. The monarch's power was ensured via two key alliances. First, in exchange for wealth and status, the influential nobility and aristocracy would maintain order in their individual territories. Individual nobles would accrue rewards based on demonstrable valor and devoted loyalty to the monarch. The intrigue and intricacies of royal courts, though often fascinating, were usually supercilious. In contrast, the plight of the masses was typically glum and often miserable.

In addition to the security and order provided by the noble hierarchy, the monarchy guaranteed its power via a second key alliance, this one with the clergy. In exchange for protection and privileged treatment, local clergy played a huge role in keeping the masses in line on behalf of the monarch. Tasked with using spiritual principles to assuage individual and community concerns, the most effective clergy kept the people docile. Submission to God and the monarchy went hand in hand. Since church dogma dictated that monarchical authority was divinely endowed, being obedient to the monarch was construed as demonstrating spiritual devotion and religious piety.

While cultures were extremely varied not only across kingdoms but often within sections of kingdoms themselves, a good part of Europe was loosely affiliated through the Holy Roman Empire. This empire was created in the ninth century by Charlemagne and allied separate territories for the common purpose of defending Christendom. Historians often correctly characterize the Holy Roman Empire as neither Holy, nor Roman, nor much of an Empire. In any case, there was an implicit collusion on a pan-European level between the monarchs and the church. Together, although not without conflicts between them, monarchs and the higher church authorities dictated the course of civil affairs with firm control over the masses. One great example of this collusion is provided by the Crusades, in which various monarchs, over many centuries, deployed their forces for the benefit of Christendom, in exchange for the Roman Catholic Church's sanction and broadening of their royal status.

It is true that there were frequent conflicts between the monarchies and the Roman Catholic Church when higher church authorities attempted to interfere in the domestic affairs of a kingdom. Monarchs were commonly admonished by the pope or other clergy members in the upper echelons of the church as a result of their bad behavior in international wars, alliances, and treaties. However, the clerical rule administered through the Holy Roman Emperor on behalf of the higher church authority was usually subordinated to the desires of the monarch through the means of effective diplomacy. Monarchs often deftly accomplished this subordination of church priorities by including in their cabinet the most influential church leaders in their local territory. For example, cardinals like Richelieu and Mazarin served in important political roles for Kings Louis XIII and Louis XIV, respectively. As chief minister, Mazarin was a vital part of Louis XIV's rise to prominent power in Europe. In England as well, alliances and disputes between archbishops and monarchs were quite consequential for the political affairs of Europe overall. The alliance of the monarchy with the authority of the church provided a domineering framework to successfully control the entire society within a kingdom. Both power and oppression were thereby solidified, often for extended periods.

Chapter 2

LES LUMIÈRES:
THE AGE OF REASON AND
SCIENTIFIC DISCOVERY

Much of this book's argument draws on concepts and ideas that were posited and debated during the Enlightenment era (17th and 18th centuries). Before we go into these in great detail, I owe the reader a justification for why I believe this particular period is so vital.

What was so important about the Enlightenment? How can I claim that its impact forever changed societies across the globe? A century ago, most scholars agreed with this assessment. The Enlightenment had been extensively studied across a wide range of humanities disciplines in prior generations, and its prominence and influence had been well-established in a broadly accepted narrative that the era did indeed lay the groundwork for the radical and enduring changes that would shape contemporary societies. This consensus narrative posited that not only did the Enlightenment usher in the modern era of human achievement but also directly spurred both the American and French Revolutions, thereby forging the modern political organizing paradigm.

From an American-centric point of view it is hard to overemphasize the importance of the American Revolution, but the French Revolution arguably provided a greater road map for what we refer to today as a free liberal society. As we will see in the chapters that follow, the American and French Revolutions were intertwined, both part of the overarching sweeping changes that became inexorable based on the ascendancy of Enlightenment thinking. However, as we will explore in depth throughout this book, the emergence of the American Schism resulted in the adoption of a hybrid aristocratic and democratic governing model on this side of the Atlantic, while the French Revolution set precedence by establishing the first secular democratic republic. As best explained by Professor Jonathan Israel:

> The French Revolution was qualitatively different from all known previous revolutions and also remains more fundamental for us than subsequent revolutions . . . for example, than the Russian Revolution. The reason consists in the Revolution's special relationship to the Enlightenment, and especially to the Enlightenment's republican, democratic and secularizing radical wing. It was especially foundational in that it fed into all later revolutions in Europe, Latin America, and Asia . . . introducing the social and constitutional principles that defined the modern political world. [The French Revolution was] the only democratic revolution thus far that conceived democracy as the pursuit of the majority's welfare, assigning governments the duty to promote the welfare of all as a society and combat economic inequality rather than just maintain order and defend property; it was the first sustained attempt to establish a secular, educated, welfare-oriented, human rights–based modernity. It sought maximization of social freedom combined with equal opportunities for all. All this affords the French Revolution a unique centrality in modern history and relevance to the challenges of our own time.[1]

Notwithstanding its sprawling legacy, the Enlightenment has always had its critics. In the 18th century, the Enlightenment was criticized by some conservative thinkers, including Edmund Burke, the Irish statesman and philosopher. Burke took issue with what he perceived as the Enlightenment's focus on individualism, the subordination of the collective morality of society to individual achievement.[2]

Furthermore, as we will explore in detail in subsequent chapters, a Counter-Enlightenment movement emerged in the late 18th century that was based explicitly on rejecting Enlightenment principles entirely, eschewing reason and rationality and returning to an emphasis on the spiritual realm. Counter-Enlightenment forces have posed significant challenges to Enlightenment ideals, at various times more so than others, up until today.

However, in the last fifty years a new critique of the Enlightenment has emerged via the inchoate intellectual tradition on the left, postmodernism, that has aggressively contested the conventional narrative of the Enlightenment's dominant influence on modern society. Since the mid to late 20th century, postmodernism has become a broad movement influencing many disciplines and fields of inquiry in the arts and humanities, including philosophy, historical and literary criticism, and architecture.[3] Overall, these schools of thought have deemphasized the importance of the Enlightenment in the development of modern society. While it is well beyond the scope of this book to explore in detail these various schools of 20th-century thought, which are quite interesting in their own right, two challenges posed by the postmodernist view must be confronted and debunked at the outset: first, its claim that the Enlightenment era was not as influential as many scholars had hitherto maintained, and second, its assertion that "objective truth" does not exist.

THE ENLIGHTENMENT PROVIDED THE FOUNDATION FOR WHAT FOLLOWED

The particular thrust of the postmodern interpretation that downplays the significance of the Enlightenment reflects a more general theme of postmodernist theory: namely, *maintaining skepticism toward all conventional views* in political and social discourse and ideology. Postmodernism contends, not unjustifiably, that established theories and narratives purporting to be universal are flawed since they reflect the perspective of historical actors in a particular place and time. In the case of the Enlightenment, this would be the "elite" strata of European societies most directly involved in the development of Enlightenment traditions.

Granted, Enlightenment thought (as well as many other intellectual traditions) and subsequent interpretations of it were dominated primarily (though not exclusively) by European White males and consequently reflect their biases. It is important to acknowledge the absence of other voices and perspectives; partiality must be placed in context. However, this does not reduce the substance of the contributions a priori. In fact, by adding additional perspectives to Enlightenment thought, postmodern thinking has extended, not diminished, the vitality of the 18th-century intellectual traditions. Because knowledge is cumulative, the layering of postmodern thought and its derivatives has undoubtedly made enormous additional contributions to the fields of philosophy, history, criticism, and the arts over the last fifty years. However, additional layers do not obviate the importance of their base foundation.

In addition, the idea that the influence of the Enlightenment must have been limited since only a small segment of the population debated its principles holds no water at all. While it is true that many of the thinkers of the period can be considered intellectual elites, these same thinkers posited concepts and systems applicable to the general public, including those who, in contemporary terms, we might describe as disenfranchised. The systems that were advanced in the fields of law, politics, and education, to name but a few, were intended to be applicable to all sectors of society, despite the sometimes condescending tone deployed by the philosophers of the period. Simply because some of these thinkers viewed the masses as less enlightened than themselves does not diminish the power or reach of the solutions they postulated.

While it is true that *direct* reading of Enlightenment thinkers was undoubtedly limited to the educated classes, these same readers were often the leaders of vast swaths of society who routinely interacted with the wider populace. Consequently, there is little doubt that the prominent ideas of men (and, unfortunately, only a few women) of letters of the period, often called *les philosophes*, had a spillover effect, absorbed first perhaps by politicians and men of affairs, and ultimately by the broader population.

Furthermore, the fact that the Enlightenment (like all philosophical movements) reflects the biases of the period does not negate the depth and breadth of its influence nor the significance and contemporary relevance of its contributions. It is incontrovertible that more recent schools of post-Enlightenment thought, principally Marxist theory, emerged as predominant influences starting in the 19th century and have continued to be influential up until the present day. The interplay between postmodernism and some strands of Marxist thought has encouraged a current trend among many contemporary academics and historians of applying a revisionist Marxist lens to the entire range of historical thinking and rebuking traditional interpretations and conventional narratives. It is in this context that some academics have more recently reevaluated the impact of the Enlightenment on modern society, diminishing the period's influence and instead attributing more importance to Marxist influences in shaping modern society. This line of thinking argues that since the fruits of the Enlightenment reached only a small subset of the population, represented by the educated elite, its influence must have been much less considerable and less relevant for the masses.

While there is unquestionably some validity to these arguments, from my reading of history, these interpretations are misguided, precisely due to the layering effect discussed previously. I agree with the many academics who find it hard to overemphasize the importance of the Enlightenment in shaping modern society. Not only were most of the governing mechanisms of the modern republic vigorously debated and defined during this era, but the moral and social underpinnings of Western civilization were interrogated through a secular lens outside the construct of a religious tradition for the first time perhaps since the pre-Christian era. Had there been no Enlightenment, subsequent schools of thought such as Marxism and postmodernism could not have developed as they have.

DOES OBJECTIVE TRUTH EXIST?

One of the foundations of Enlightenment thought is the claim that objective truth exists and can be discovered through empirical observation and rational thought. According to this view, reason and science provide accurate, objective, and reliable cornerstones of knowledge. As a result, science serves as an objective means of understanding the natural world, and its application can improve our lives. From an Enlightenment perspective, objective truth exists independent of human consciousness and can be known through the application of observation, experimentation, and reason.

The postmodern movement rejects these ideas via one of its principal tenets: the assertion that objective truth does not exist. For the postmodernist, everything is relative and fluid; subjectivity inherently contravenes objective interpretation. Accordingly, truth may exist independent of human consciousness, but we have no objective means of nailing it down. From this claim follow corollary notions: that clear boundaries between what is true and what is false do not exist; that reason and science are ideologies, simply myths created by humans; that reason itself is a specific Western tradition (ideology) competing with other traditions, like faith and other cultural means of knowing; that the "self" is a myth and largely a composite of one's social experiences and cultural contexts; and that there is no true definition of self or even gender. In the postmodernist view, we put on identities as masks or perform our "selves" exactly as do actors on a stage.[4]

The intent of this book is not to attempt to reconcile postmodern and classical thinking. This would be well beyond my capabilities. However, *objectivity in science and objectivity in political philosophy are two separate things.* Where the postmodern perspective is most helpful is in forcing an awareness of one's subjectivity in political conversation as in many other domains, mainly as it pertains to language and definition of terms, and not in denying the existence of objective truth itself. As Masha Gessen eloquently states: "When writers and academics question the limits of language, it is invariably an exercise that grows from a desire to bring more light into the public space, to arrive at a shared reality that is more nuanced than it was before the conversation began."[5]

Nonetheless, the premise of this book rests on my conviction that an empirical objective truth (i.e., the data) exists; furthermore, that postulating its existence does not contest the concurrent existence of subjective points of view (i.e., the interpretation of the data). Certainly, it is inarguable that outside the realm of the hard sciences, and especially in the field of political philosophy, postmodern thinking regarding nonobjectivity in philosophy is very much a part of our zeitgeist. We commonly accept the notion that idiosyncratic perspective encroaches upon individual interpretation. However, of late, a certain "lay postmodernism" more routinely reflected in our contemporary political discourse has had a pernicious influence on our public policy debates. Lay postmodernism has fostered a debilitating skepticism as well as a languid jadedness among many. Seemingly, many citizens today use this lay postmodernism to excuse their own apathetic approach to the pursuit of truth itself: After all, since everyone has their own truth, what is the point of its pursuit in the first place? Undeniably, these beliefs echo and reinforce our divisiveness, making consensus on policy issues quite difficult to achieve.

There is a great irony here; in many ways the lay postmodern perspective is essential for the survival of our democracy. For example, proactively inviting and embracing diverse viewpoints in our public dialogue is an obligation. We can no longer claim the mantle of a true democracy while allowing the dominance of White male viewpoints that crowd out other voices. As we will discuss later in this book, a citizenry of varied backgrounds and values presents challenges for a democracy, but the accompanying diversity of thought can be quite nourishing for the promulgation of innovative solutions. Furthermore, a democratic republic is necessarily based on a set of shared values. These common values can only be created by incorporating both objective scientific truth and the amalgamated set of subjective beliefs and values of its citizens.

On the other hand, when we allow lay postmodernism to invade the realm of science and reject the existence of objective scientific truth such as climate change or coronaviruses, we do so with great peril to our democracy. When we allow this lay postmodernism to justify our own "alternative facts," as frequently observed in contemporary news media, we do a tremendous disservice to the importance of the valuable aspects of the postmodern evaluation. Indeed, objective scientific truth is a required element of democracy, and embracing it is the only hope for reaching consensus on policy. Establishing a set of common values among a diverse citizenry is an arduous enough endeavor in itself, requiring broad and deep commitment. By maintaining that science is but an ideology, we erect additional obstacles to the realization of mutual understanding and thereby render the democratic form ever more difficult to attain and sustain.

THE ENLIGHTENMENT'S VAST CONTRIBUTIONS

From the point of view of substance, the themes explored during the Enlightenment ran the gamut, touching nearly all aspects of civilization. It was during this critical age that what today we would call human and civil rights took new shape, were delineated in detail, and were spiritedly contested. The pioneering perspectives of the Enlightenment period were prerequisites for the 19th- and 20th-century evolution of modern schools of thought and contemporary ways of life. This is partly because Enlightenment thinking was so expansive, encompassing exploration of the sciences and new advances in culture and the arts, and provided a more general recognition of the vast capacity of human potential. In modern parlance, we would say that Enlightenment thought was thoroughly interdisciplinary, which allowed its thinkers to make broad and wide-ranging inquiries into all facets of life.

Within this broad umbrella, one of the central foci of Enlightenment thought was *reason*, the idea that the human intellect could deduce truths based on observations and rational capacity. The implications of this idea were profound; discovery of objective features of the universe could lead to crucial advances in knowledge, and consequential benefits to humanity. But the Enlightenment was not limited to empirical discovery and reason; it also examined issues of morality and political philosophy. In these areas, some major themes were tolerance, liberty, natural rights, and social ethics. It was perhaps because of this eclectic range of inquiry that Enlightenment concepts were so sweeping, advancing so many aspects of what we today think of as modernity. Furthermore, much of this intellectual exploration was synergistic—ideas pinged from one area to another, which allowed for a larger accumulation of knowledge in total.

Perhaps the central distinguishing feature of the Enlightenment as a whole was its far-reaching departure from the authority of religion and spirituality that had been central in most prior intellectual traditions. Instead, the period was marked by an explosion of innovative thinking in the secular realm. Science and discovery became guiding principles of society, and a new sense of the formidable capacity and potential of the individual emerged. This was facilitated by advancements in technology that created a burgeoning class of people working in industry and business outside of agriculture, along with fresh notions about value creation.

Prior to the Enlightenment, the conventional belief was that gold, silver, and land were the sole sources of value in an economy. The notion that wealth was not fixed and that individuals could generate real sources of value and thus wealth through the creative and productive application of human ingenuity to the natural world was truly revolutionary. With this single groundbreaking notion, prospects for the future seemed suddenly brighter for many; despite not being born with or having any ability to legally acquire capital, the individual could create wealth through the capacity of human endeavor. It is perhaps difficult from our contemporary standpoint to appreciate what a liberating notion this must have been, an unshackling of the confines of what was thought to be a fully rigid society.

THE GENESIS OF THE ENLIGHTENMENT

So how exactly did this new movement surface? What were its antecedents and what formed its underpinnings? The foundations were laid in the early Enlightenment, with two important and at times conflicting philosophical developments of the 17th century.

In this earlier century, a new emphasis was placed on Rationalism, the school of philosophical thought that deems *reason* as the chief source and test of knowledge. More formally, Rationalism is defined as a methodology or a theory "in which the criterion of the truth is not sensory but intellectual and deductive."[6] One of the most salient assertions of the Rationalists was that reason was an *innate ability in all human beings.* In many ways, the development of Rationalism was a response to the centuries-old authority and dogma of the Roman Catholic Church.[7] In prior centuries, during the Inquisition, for example, church authorities fiercely dictated the mores of society. The power and influence of religious doctrine had been a constraint on free thinking, absorbing mental capacities in questions of faith as opposed to deductive discovery. Two of the principal fathers of this 17th-century Rationalist school were René Descartes (1596–1650) and Baruch Spinoza (1632–1677).

A second philosophical school of thought, Empiricism, also emerged during the subsequent period. John Locke (1632–1704), followed by George Berkeley (1685–1753) and David Hume (1711–1776), advanced the philosophical argument that knowledge of the world is based on personal experiences, chiefly sensory experiences. According to the Empiricists, human learning is based on developed capacities of observation and perception, implying that knowledge is not possible without experience.[8] The tradition of Empiricism was also greatly influenced by the prior work of Francis Bacon (1561–1626), a British philosopher and statesman, credited with first defining the scientific method as a means of observation and inductive reasoning. Because he tied observation into a formal approach of knowledge acquisition, Bacon is sometimes called the father of Empiricism.

In many ways these two schools of thought conflicted: How can knowledge be acquired based solely on experience, and at the same time, be derived from rational deduction? In Spinoza's famous *Theological-Political Treatise,* published clandestinely in 1670, the Dutch philosopher unmistakably foresaw the power of combining the tools of deductive reasoning and empirical observation:

Anyone seeking to persuade or dissuade people . . . must, to gain their acquiescence, deduce it from things already accepted, convincing them either by means of experience or reason. That is, one must convince them either by things which they know through their senses happen in nature or from clear intellectual concepts evident in themselves.[9]

While there were substantial conflicts between Rationalism and Empiricism, as Spinoza predicted, the two schools of thought also intermingled in the crucible of 18th-century society with catalytic effect. First, they contained an implicit individualism, a presupposition that each of us, as individuals, can arrive at the truth by ourselves, guided only by our faculties of observation and logic, without consulting the village priest. This notion of the autonomous individual attributed a potent and novel agency to human ability, which promised to expand the limits of human endeavor and break down the constraints on potential achievement. Further, this concept provided a formula for individual capacity to foster new endeavors and expand the frontiers of human enterprise. Combining what we can learn through empirical observation with what we can deduct from reason was a recipe for perpetuating a golden age of human discovery and achievement and for pushing the bounds of human aspiration across many diverse fields.

Scientific innovation had certainly occurred over the course of prior centuries, but this new Enlightenment formula of the late 17th and 18th centuries, which blended the power of reason with the science of experimentation, allowed thinkers to forge new ground in many disciplines. The results were explosive. Scientists like Galileo Galilei, Johannes Kepler, and, perhaps most importantly, Isaac Newton had a huge impact on their contemporaries. In fact, some historians consider the publication of Isaac Newton's *Principia Mathematica* in 1687 as the start of the Enlightenment period. Newton's discovery of a model of the physical world ascertained through observation was the epitome of what the Enlightenment was all about. The galvanizing effect of the interaction between Rationalism and Empiricism was that a much larger portion of society, even outside intellectual circles, embraced the notion of science, discovery, and reason as a path to drive human progress forward.

In addition to the advancement of science, the inspiring concept of the autonomous individual opened new horizons in the fields of social and moral philosophy. New ways of viewing society, morality, law, and the political process took hold among the educated classes on both sides of the Atlantic. Distinct geographic areas focused on different Enlightenment ideas,[10] but themes of reason, science, virtue, benevolence, tolerance, and liberty cut across not only the French and American Enlightenments, but also the British, Scottish, Dutch, and German Enlightenments. The question of how societies form and self-govern became a predominant focus of exploration. Historical assumptions regarding the structure of society were spiritedly contested.

Two questions were of great concern in this regard: Who held the power to govern, and on what authority was that power based? The belief that power was granted divinely by God exclusively to royal blood and nobility had been long established and unchallenged for centuries; now, this conviction was called into question. The great "social contract" thinkers of the time, such as Thomas Hobbes, Jean-Jacques Rousseau, and Locke, pondered what rights and freedoms people innately possess and preserve, and which of those rights need be relinquished to the state to create a secure society governed by law and order. These thinkers contrasted a "state of nature" in which they viewed people as equal before God (based on their Christian tenets) to civil society, which was created by humans for the sake of order, security, and for the protection of their property.

Compared to people in the state of nature, the social contract thinkers observed that the establishment of organized society inevitably required trade-offs; consenting to structured law and order entailed relinquishing certain freedoms associated with the state of nature. But other elements, such as security and stability, were clear gains. As part of this trade, social contract theorists pondered which rights and freedoms do people have to sacrifice and what are the communal benefits that the state must provide. Further, which rights are so unalienable, so unassailable, that the state must guarantee their preservation?

Most Enlightenment thinkers agreed that the absolute sovereignty that reigned through much of history was untenable precisely because it served to perpetuate a state of oppression and misery for the greater part of humanity and constrain human progress. Absolute monarchs left to their own devices would sacrifice the freedoms and livelihood of their subjects in personal quests for power. The resulting wars and famine were disastrous—the lot of most people was often wretched.

Interestingly, some members of the nobility and even select monarchs embraced particular Enlightenment principles. Referred to as "enlightened despots," these monarchs pursued some specific educational, social, and legal reforms. A prime example would be Frederick the Great of Prussia, who was a great military warrior early in his career. During his reign, he demonstrated genuine interest in making enduring improvements in society, such as in arts and education, for the benefit of the masses. Yet another example would be Catherine the Great of Russia, who reigned over what many consider to be the Golden Age of Russia in the 18th century.

As we will see in subsequent chapters, not all social contract thinkers condemned monarchy, but most advocated for restraining its power. They explored alternative governing structures that would improve conditions for the greatest number of people and recognized the concept of the "common good" or "common interest." They posed many questions regarding the power structure and governance of society: Which governing mechanisms could successfully check absolute power in a monarchy and thereby prevent the many abuses that had characterized the monarchies of prior centuries? Are other nonmonarchical forms of government superior in terms of benefiting the most people? Why are all societal powers held exclusively by the nobility, the clergy, and the landed gentry? What about the conditions of the masses?

Many of these thinkers described in detail how monarchies possessing an unquenchable thirst for strength and power had led to centuries of physical conflict resulting in mass death and destruction. This system of governance seemed counterproductive to the advancement of civilization. In addition, the growth of powerful monarchies was a self-reinforcing dynamic; power continued to accrue to the sovereigns most willing to wage war, the very same ones who were least concerned about the well-being of the masses. As a result of their success, such "imperial" monarchs reigned tyrannically over a greater number of people.

As they developed prescriptions for how societies could work more optimally, the social contract philosophers posited conflicting and often divergent solutions. It became increasingly evident over the course of the second half of the 18th century that the differences between the two groups of thinkers were not minor. They clashed on essential principles regarding the immutable rights of citizens and the obligation or imperative of government to preserve and even guarantee those rights. It was in this area that the Enlightenment diverged into the two dissimilar schools of thought that precipitated the American Schism and that we will explore in subsequent chapters: the *Moderate Enlightenment* and the *Radical Enlightenment*.

Chapter 3

THE MODERATE
ENLIGHTENMENT

As leading thinkers of the 18th century expanded into the fields of political and social philosophy, they amplified critiques of both contemporary and historical systems of government. In assessing the totality of the human condition, contrasting opinions emerged on how society might be more optimally structured for the benefit of all its citizens.

Given the prevailing governing structures of the time, special attention was naturally given to the problem of how best to control the abuses observed consistently under monarchical systems. However, the concept of checking unbridled monarchical power was not in itself new. Ever since the Magna Carta in 1215, philosophers and political figures discussed various systems that could effectually impose checks and balances on the excesses of monarchical power. So, in some sense, Enlightenment thinkers continued to reflect on this enduring historical question: What are the best methods to curb absolute monarchical power and advance the common interest or common good of society?

But Enlightenment thinkers expanded the query by considering what other forms of government might be superior for the benefit of citizens. Many of these thinkers explored the ideas of classic Greek and Roman philosophers, such as Aristotle, to discover their views on alternative forms of government. Many also revisited and reassessed the governing structures of the classical empires of bygone eras. As they answered these questions and posited concrete political philosophies, Enlightenment thinkers can be clearly differentiated into two discrete groups based on fundamentally conflicting philosophies: the Moderate Enlightenment and the Radical Enlightenment.

Moderate Enlightenment thinkers include many of the famous names most often encountered over the course of secondary and college-level education in the United States. These are the great philosophers most closely associated with the Enlightenment: Hobbes, Locke, Voltaire, Montesquieu, Rousseau, Immanuel Kant, etc. These larger-than-life figures were the "legitimized" great thinkers of the period, whom the French call *les philosophes*. They were quite often recognized and celebrated as such during their lifetimes. In posterity, they have become enshrined as the quintessence of great Enlightenment thinking.

While these philosophers were indeed critical of the ruling structures of their era and undeniably concerned with identifying optimal forms of governance for all citizens, they *rejected representative democracy* or a "government of the people" as the solution.[1] In fact, for many centuries the term "democracy" had quite a negative connotation and was associated with the tyranny of "mob rule" provoked by demagogues with malicious motives. Those in the Moderate Enlightenment school of thought abjured democracy because they thought manipulators would inevitably prey on the uneducated common citizens.

Irrespective of their rationale, one of the defining aspects of these thinkers' "moderate" characterization is exactly this foundational element: They *did not* advocate for a democratic system of government where all people are represented in the ruling structure. But wait, the reader might ask: Did not these Enlightenment heroes create the concept of the modern democratic republic? The answer is a definitive no. These thinkers did tackle questions of governance and citizens' rights, but the solutions they advocated may seem surprising to the 21st-century reader. How exactly did the Moderate Enlightenment group answer the fundamental questions of who should hold the power in society, who should govern, what rights must citizens yield to the governing authority, and what natural rights do people possess that cannot and should never be infringed upon by the governing group? The answers lie in the Enlightenment concept of the social contract described in the previous chapter.

The social contract model by which Enlightenment philosophers pondered the explicit and implicit agreements that form the basis of a civilized society involved trade-offs. Within the social contract, in exchange for the government providing a system of law and order to secure citizens' well-being, citizens are required to abide by those same laws and thereby relinquish some of their freedoms. But while many Enlightenment thinkers adopted the social contract model in espousing their political philosophies, they differed greatly on the details, specifically regarding these trade-offs.

Thomas Hobbes, one of the earlier British social contract theorists of the 17th century, famously characterized the human "state of nature" as one of savagery and lawlessness. In his renowned book *Leviathan* (1651), Hobbes explored in great detail the nature of the social contract and described the types of concessions required by citizens to create the system of law and order characteristic of a civilized society. Hobbes ultimately proposed that for civil society to avoid a *bellum omnium contra omnes*, Latin for "the war of all against all," a *strong central authority* must have ultimate control. In the end, Hobbes could not envision this happening effectively without a strong central monarch.[2]

The later social contract theorists proposed other points of view. They also accepted the proposition that in forming a civilized society, citizens must surrender some freedoms. One of the most compelling aspects of reading these theorists lies in their discussions regarding the fundamental nature of the rights of citizens. They acknowledged the premise that the government could legitimately restrict certain rights as part of the social contract, but *not all rights*. As a result of this construct, one of the most pertinent questions debated was: Which rights did citizens have to surrender to abide by the societal system of law and order and, conversely, which rights were so innate, so much a part of the human experience, that they were unassailable? In fact, because some civil rights are so fundamental, not only could the state *not impede* them, but, on the contrary, the social contract requires the state to *guarantee, uphold, and preserve* them.

One distinguishing feature of these Moderate Enlightenment thinkers was the preeminence given in their social contract frameworks to the concept of "property rights." In addition to guaranteeing the security and personal safety of citizens, one of the primary roles of government itself, according to the Moderates, was to allow its citizens to retain what was rightly in their ownership. Thus, for the Moderates, one of the primary trade-offs for entering a social contract was the notion that if citizens "play by the rules" and submit to the ruling authority, then that authority must guarantee that those same citizens will be able to retain what is rightfully theirs.[3] Consequently, social contracts required formal mechanisms, such as legal structures (i.e., contracts), not only to guarantee physical protection and well-being but also to secure citizens' property rights and to guarantee that citizens could retain what they possess without fear of expropriation.

In their detailed critiques of strictly heredity-based monarchical systems, the Moderates described how such ruling systems of government had failed to provide these basic property rights to citizens. At countless points in history, and even during their own contemporary times, particular monarchs or powerful nobles would seize land by royal decree. For example, during the reign of Louis XIV of France, continuous and seemingly random wars and social decrees such as the revocation of the Edict of Nantes (which had afforded protections to the Huguenots, French Protestants) threatened the stability of daily life and made the future intolerably unpredictable. Moderate Enlightenment thinkers viewed such instability, caused by the whims of monarchs, as threatening not only to law and order in society, but to the progress of civilization itself. The failure of government to ensure property rights was deemed incongruous with the advancement of a modern society, perhaps because the issue of property preservation was so close to the heart of Moderate Enlightenment thinkers themselves.[4] Thus, *guaranteeing property rights* was a fundamental impetus for the Moderates' ideal of the social contract.

What exactly was the solution that the Moderates advocated to deal with monarchies' failure to protect individual property rights? What system of justice and law and order did the Moderates espouse? In envisioning the optimal form of government, as mentioned previously, these thinkers *eschewed both representative and direct democracy*, believing it was unattainable. The vast majority of the populace was uneducated and therefore, according to the Moderates, unable to determine what was in their self-interest. They believed that because government was such a complex undertaking, most citizens, being illiterate and lacking formal education, could not even comprehend the issues involved, much less devise or support particular solutions. Nor were citizens able to evaluate appropriate candidates to advocate for their interests.

Instead of some form of representative democracy through which all citizens could choose leaders, Moderate Enlightenment thinkers believed that it was incumbent on the educated class of society (the enlightened, like themselves) to lead society *for the benefit of* and *on behalf of* all people.[5] Governing was viewed as a responsibility for the "enlightened" class.

The Moderates tended to support what today would be called an "aristocratic republic" in which groups of elite educated leaders (often based on land ownership) would hold broad and consequential powers to write and adopt laws. This group of powerful aristocrats would also have the authority to check the supremacy of a ruling monarch. Through what has been labeled a *constitutional monarchy*, these influential educated elites could protect the people from the whims of the monarch, balancing and checking sovereign power and ensuring that monarchical pursuits were not contravening the common good. This exact concept had been deployed eloquently in the English revolutions of the 17th century. In fact, ever since the Magna Carta in the 13th century, the English nobility had established some checks on the power of the monarchy, although those checks were enforced to varying degrees over the next four centuries.

The Moderate Enlightenment thinkers thus retained and vastly expanded these concepts, advocating for a nobility or landed aristocracy more broadly sanctioned to limit the power of the monarch through a more progressive framework of law and order. This ruling aristocracy would secure citizens' personal safety and property rights and prevent abuses of power from the monarch or other executive through the instrument of a constitution that would enumerate specific powers for each sector of society (e.g., ruling aristocrats, commoners). With the authority to propose binding laws and measures, the ruling aristocracy could both safeguard citizens' unalienable rights and keep the monarchy in check. While not all Moderates believed explicitly in a constitutional monarchy as the solution, the commonality across this group of thinkers is that they rejected any form of democratic representative government—the first key characteristic distinguishing the Moderate Enlightenment thinkers from their Radical Enlightenment contemporaries.

In addition to the Moderates' aversion to representative government, another common feature of their thinking was an implicit and often explicit sanctioning of the role of religion in the public sphere. Like all Enlightenment thinkers, the Moderates embraced science and discovery as fundamental to advancement; however, they also believed that faith-based systems upheld through religious dogma served a vital role in society. While they conceded that the Roman Catholic Church was vested with an enormous amount of power, most Moderates did not view the church as impeding the rights of the citizenry. On the contrary, the Moderates advocated sustaining the church's role in inculcating and upholding a societal moral code and providing education for citizens. After all, it was the church that ensured through its local administering mechanisms that the masses lived in accordance with a system of ethics.

Consequently, the Moderates envisioned that the church would remain a major "power player" in governance outside the nobility and the aristocracy, with its own hierarchical command structure. For centuries, the church had done the monarchy's bidding by keeping the masses in check. While the Moderates were often quite critical of Roman Catholic Church abuses of power, ultimately most Moderates endorsed the primary role that the church had been playing in civic society for centuries. Furthermore, for the Moderates, pursuits in empirical discovery and science did not conflict with the spiritual realm but needed to coexist with the church. In the next chapter, we will explore how this approach was a second point of differentiation between the Moderates and Radicals and contributed to a significant and lasting distinction between the two philosophical schools.

Chapter 4

THE RADICAL
ENLIGHTENMENT

The *Radical Enlightenment* school of thought had two primary distinguishing features that had colossal ramifications for the social contract envisaged by its adherents. Namely, unlike their counterparts in the Moderate Enlightenment school, the Radicals embraced the concept of democratic equality, and they insisted on a firm separation of the church and all faith-based endeavors from civic society. While seemingly straightforward, these two key points of demarcation meant that the Radical Enlightenment thinkers held a much more expansive view of a secular egalitarian society than the Moderate Enlightenment thinkers. Furthermore, and perhaps most importantly, these differences implied an unqualified rejection by the Radicals of the Moderates' view that only a small subsection of society could be enlightened. As Israel describes, for the Radicals

> only philosophical reason and its dissemination through society could defeat ignorance, error, and the ingrained popular prejudices nourishing tyranny that rendered society and politics hostages to villainy

and inherently irrational, unstable, and repressive. Enlightenment in their eyes was above all a process of eradicating prejudices, ignorance, and mistaken traditional views. Social harmony and stability depended, they believed, on forging rational laws, securing basic freedoms, and ensuring a viable constitution, besides laying an adequate basis in morality, social harmony, and civics to enable society to accomplish its goals, all of which were unattainable, they insisted, without extirpating credulity, intolerance, and religious authority.[1]

The starting point for the Radicals was their advocacy for a broader interpretation of unassailable *rights* that must be protected and secured by the social contract. The Radicals asserted fervently that individuals possess a much more encompassing set of *unalienable fundamental rights* beyond the rights to law and order and property rights that became the focus of the Moderates. For the Radicals, rights such as freedom, liberty, and the pursuit of well-being must not be obstructed or impeded but must be guaranteed by the state.[2]

The Radical Enlightenment thinkers' prescription for government was also unambiguously dissimilar from that of the Moderates. They believed that the only structural form of government that would allow for the safeguarding of this broader set of rights was *representative democracy* that mandated broad participation by the citizenry. The Radicals contended that unless all citizens have some form of representation, some "voice" as a part of the governmental mechanism, unalienable rights could not and most likely would not be preserved.

Radical Enlightenment thinkers deduced that as people naturally strive to improve their well-being and to make their future brighter, or to use a more common American phrase, "pursue happiness" within the confines of a social contract, they necessarily require "agency," some control and influence over the conditions of the society in which they live. Without this mechanism to participate in governing structures and thereby influence their shared surroundings, citizens would inevitably risk being subject to oppression and even tyranny. For the Radicals, the ability to contribute to the institutions of government, which both manifestly and profoundly impact the ability of citizens to achieve their human potential, was paramount.[3]

Furthermore, the Radicals firmly rejected the Moderates' position that, due to a lack of education, the masses could not possibly ascertain or advocate for their own self-interest. For the Radicals, this "excuse" was merely a specious justification for a government of and for the few. Based on this conviction, the Radicals coalesced around the principle that the only way unalienable rights could be protected, guaranteed, and secured in the long run was through a *democratic republic* in which all people have some voice in determining who has the authority to govern, as well as equal access to the institutions of government.

For the Radicals, unlike their Moderate Enlightenment counterparts, the right to freedom was inextricably linked to this more expansive notion of participation, which necessitated equality in voice and in access to governing mechanics (in addition to the notion of equality before and subject to the law). From a Radical Enlightenment point of view, freedoms and universal rights could not be sustained in the long term nor guaranteed in the absence of this form of equality incorporating some form of universal representation in the political arena.[4] Furthermore, this important concept of equality in access to political standing expressed in the enumeration of these rights reveals that it is the Radical Enlightenment that forms the basis of the democratic egalitarianism that has been so often heralded as a founding principle of the United States—a government of the people, by the people, and for the people. By fervently rejecting the structural hierarchy in government that would give one person or one class of people the right to arbitrarily exercise power over another, it was the Radical Enlightenment thinkers who stipulated the principle that was to become the bedrock of the American myth.

Radical Enlightenment thinkers did not prescribe representative democracy without acknowledging the significant barriers in its formation. They recognized that the challenges inherent in creating and sustaining a democratic republic would be substantial and enduring. They cogently understood that the most immediate problem was posed by the wide-ranging dearth of education among the masses. Traditional education of the masses focused primarily on spiritual matters and had created a tremendous pedagogic void in most people's understanding of the principles of civic society. The resulting educational gaps threatened to inhibit any form of direct democracy since most citizens did not possess the skills or training to fulfill governance or administrative roles in any way. But it also presented an enormous impediment for representative democracy, which requires an educated citizenry capable of evaluating candidates and discerning the abilities of potential representatives to advocate on their behalf.

Despite these considerable challenges, for the Radicals there was no viable alternative to democratic representation. The idea that citizens should choose their own representatives to advocate for their individual interests was a foundational element of the Radical Enlightenment philosophy, and thus, surmounting any obstacle to its realization was obligatory. Furthermore, many Radical Enlightenment thinkers argued that overcoming the hurdle of the massive education gap must itself become one of the state's governing imperatives. They argued that one of the most important roles of government was to assume prime responsibility for developing an educated citizenry. This idea represented a startling contrast to the role of government under a constitutional monarchy; in the latter, the state had no incentive to increase the education levels of the masses. In fact, in a constitutional aristocratic monarchy, educating the masses was seen as jeopardizing the concept of "government of the few," and could threaten the ability to maintain jurisdiction *over* the masses.

Accordingly, for a representative democracy to be successful in the Radical Enlightenment framework, in addition to securing the rights discussed previously, the government's role included a mandate to educate the citizenry. The Radicals appreciated that this implied a massive investment at all levels of education from early primary school through the secondary and university levels. However, from their point of view, educational investment would dramatically advance the well-being of all citizens and bring immeasurable benefits to society, albeit not immediately. By investing in education and building an appropriate educational infrastructure, the citizenry would gradually become more capable of discerning its own interests and thereby improve its capacity for evaluating potential representatives *over time*. At that era in history, since most education took place in religious settings, one of the principal missions of many Radicals was advocating for state-supported education outside the religious setting, free from religious dogma.[5]

This then leads to the second common feature of the Radical Enlightenment thinkers: They shared a strong conviction, unlike their Moderate Enlightenment counterparts, that religion or spiritual pursuits needed to be kept firmly separate from the state and *should not play any role* in civic affairs. In fact, these thinkers went to great lengths to condemn the role religion had historically played. They demonstrated, often in great detail, how over the course of prior centuries, organized religion had encroached into the realm of both education and governance with deleterious consequences for society. They depicted a tacit collusion between the church and the nobility designed to keep firm control over the masses, as discussed previously. This nobility-church complicity had successfully and unrelentingly kept the masses in a subordinate position for ages.

The Radicals' hostility toward church dogma was based on a number of factors. Many of these thinkers totally rejected organized religion, which they viewed as superstition. For them, embracing science, discovery, and reason as guiding forces for the advancement of human knowledge was in direct conflict and wholly irreconcilable with religious doctrine. Some but not all Radical Enlightenment thinkers were atheists, doubting or rejecting the spiritual realm entirely. However, many were not atheists but were firm and faithful believers. Nevertheless, irrespective of their personal beliefs, they firmly asserted that the faith-based realm was separate from state affairs and needed to be considered independent, outside of society's civic structure, and prevented from intervening in the affairs of governance.

Many Radical Enlightenment thinkers adhered to an intellectual movement of the 17th and 18th century called Deism. Deists accepted a creator or the existence of a supreme being on the basis of reason. Deism was sometimes labeled the "natural religion," since it rejected the concept of divine revelation and instead held that spiritual knowledge is innately part of all people. In any case, deists understood this supreme being as part of a separate dominion, not interfering in the worldly realm. They were vehemently opposed to the notion that God delegates authority exclusively to any individual church. This idea was also prominent in the works of Spinoza and the *cercle spinoziste*, a group of Spinoza's contemporaries.

One of the pillars of Spinoza's rational system was that it "transferred and institutionalized the state of nature's freedoms as basic human rights in political society and the common interest."[6] For Spinoza, God and Nature were one and the same, creating a system of beliefs based on reason "without reference to either revealed or divined truths accessed by mystical processes."[7] Whether personally atheists or deists, the Radical Enlightenment thinkers shared the conviction that a strong impermeable wall must separate the spiritual from the civic— what we today call separation of church and state.

In summary, the Radical Enlightenment prescription was for a representative democratic republic free from religious or superstitious forces. As Israel puts it, they combined a call for the "rejection of religious authority in the public sphere with a passionate democratizing republicanism and stress on universal and equal human rights."[8] In addition to ensuring law and order and preserving citizens' rights, as the Moderates demanded, Radicals also assigned to the republic an additional vital role of providing robust secular education for the population. Without an informed and aware citizenry, people would not be equipped to choose the representatives best able to advocate for their interests. Consequently, public education was an imperative requiring a strong mandate from government, and thus the Radicals advocated for a significant investment in education at all levels of society. In their wide-ranging vision of a new social order, it was the Radicals and not the Moderates who offered a "package of values sufficiently universal, secular, and egalitarian to set in motion the forces of a broad and general emancipation based on reason, freedom of thought, and democracy."[9]

Chapter 5

THE EMERGENCE OF
THE SCHISM IN EUROPE

Since the Enlightenment played out all across Europe, academics often refer to the British Enlightenment or the German or French Enlightenment. Yet while all Enlightenment thinkers were surely influenced by the specific local conditions within their countries, we can distinguish Moderates and Radicals *across* countries on the basis of their ideas rather than their geographies. Philosophical associations and social circles in each country (and often underground in the case of the Radicals) enabled a high degree of local interaction among thinkers. In addition, many Enlightenment thinkers were also exposed to, and in fact carefully reviewed material from, their international counterparts, which was often accessible in many languages. And many thinkers of the period had a significant amount of correspondence with other Enlightenment thinkers in other countries.

For purposes of illustration here, we will focus on comparing some of the key figures in the French Enlightenment and their specific political philosophies. (Space limitations prohibit a comprehensive review of a broader set of Enlightenment philosophers.) Much has been written about the influence of the British Enlightenment on the American Revolution.[1] While America's Founders were incontrovertibly influenced deeply by the British Enlightenment, the French Enlightenment arguably provided an equivalent degree of inspiration since developments in France vis-à-vis the *ancien régime* closely paralleled the colonists' grievances with the British Crown.

As mentioned previously, and as we will see in subsequent chapters, many Enlightenment thinkers (principally the Radicals) considered the French and American Revolutions as interconnected or conjoined as one overall movement rejecting the *ancien régime* and advancing the transformational concept of self-government. In Chapters 2 and 3, we briefly reviewed some of the thinking of Thomas Hobbes and John Locke. Now we will briefly review some of the most influential Moderates of the French Enlightenment, *les philosophes*.

THE EUROPEAN MODERATES

Voltaire, born as François-Marie Arouet, was a pivotal figure of the French Enlightenment, well known for his wit and his prolific output of plays, novels, and essays. Voltaire left behind more than 20,000 letters and over 2,000 books and pamphlets. Throughout his vast collection of writings, Voltaire frequently satirized religious dogma and parodied French *ancien régime* institutions, in addition to advocating for civil liberties for all classes of society.

One of Voltaire's great gifts was his skill in brazenly disparaging both the monarchy and the very aristocracy of which he himself was a part. With such abundant output, his material contains plenty of contradictions, especially in his latter works. In spite of such variation, consistent themes spanning much of Voltaire's work reflect the core principles of the Enlightenment, especially the enumeration of individual rights, or what we would today call civil rights: freedom of speech, the right to a fair trial, freedom of religion, etc. Because his writing was under constant risk of censorship by the domineering French Catholic monarchy, his use of satire or ironic literary devices served as an ingenious way to critique and express his views while eluding suppression by the authorities. Voltaire's acute knowledge of history allowed him to opine on myriad examples of the *ancien régime*'s abuse of civil rights. He was also harshly critical of the degree to which the church had a grip on the masses.

However, although Voltaire was intrepid in his writing to depict the aristocracy as corrupt, he was ultimately inseparable from this milieu. As an aristocrat himself, he would frequently rub shoulders with royal courts not only in France but all over Europe. Furthermore, he disparaged the masses as ignorant and superstitious and therefore incapable of self-government. Thus, when confronted with Radical Enlightenment viewpoints, expressly when the Radicals intensified their attacks on the monarchy and, most strikingly, began to link the church and the monarchy in a devious alliance, Voltaire got cold feet. He repudiated much of this radical thinking.

In the end, despite his scorn of the church and aristocracy, Voltaire continued to view both the royal court and the church as important pillars of the establishment. In effect, Voltaire believed these pillars were worthy of criticism, and perhaps due for reform, but not for dismantling. In this sense, while a brilliant and wide-ranging thinker, Voltaire's system was very much a "court" Enlightenment that ultimately affirmed the central governing role of the monarchy and the royal courts, albeit one needing the reforms that Voltaire tactfully advanced.

Interestingly, Voltaire very much embraced the monarchs who shared his beliefs, such as the "enlightened despots" Frederick and Catherine the Great, despite at the same time being disillusioned by their continuation of some of the same abuses of power so common in other monarchies. Moreover, while Voltaire may have had his own personal doubts about religion and was probably a Deist, he believed for the sake of social order that it was necessary for most people to remain under the church's guidance in order to escape a life of moral turpitude and for the ongoing expiation of their transgressions. Voltaire believed that the church needed "to retain guardianship over what he saw as the irredeemably ill-informed majority, by which he meant the nine-tenths of the population"[2] who could not be "enlightened." One of Voltaire's many legendary quotes is indicative of just how much Voltaire relied on the church to shepherd the masses: "*Si Dieu n'existait pas, il faudrait l'inventer.*" (If God did not exist, it would be necessary to invent him.)

Thus, in the final analysis, for Voltaire and his enlightened despots, the principles of the Enlightenment were applicable mostly to the relatively small group of educated and titled elites within whose circles they traveled. From the perspective of the social contract, Voltaire made important contributions along two dimensions: First, by wielding his impressive literary skills to sharply ridicule grossly unjust aspects of the *ancien régime*. Second, by highlighting what he believed were the essential and unalienable rights of citizens that required protection. Notwithstanding these contributions, the reforms he suggested in his writings unequivocally did not involve dismantling the *ancien régime*.

*   *   *

Montesquieu, born Charles-Louis de Secondat, was a skilled political philosopher and man of letters, in addition to serving as a legal scholar and judge. He is considered one of the greatest Enlightenment thinkers and was a strong advocate of the need to maintain a separation of powers in government to prevent the inevitable abuses that accompany states characterized by a concentration of power in any one part of the ruling structure.[3] His encyclopedic thinking and in-depth analysis on this subject provided an anchoring scaffold for the American Founders as they gave life to republican principles in writing the federal and individual state constitutions. As we will see in subsequent chapters, it was Montesquieu's principle of the balance of powers that most animated the writing of and ultimate ratification of our national charter. In fact, most scholars credit Montesquieu for creating the first thorough "separation of powers doctrine," aspects of which have been incorporated in government constitutions across the world ever since.

In his monumental work, *De l'esprit des lois* (*On the Spirit of the Laws* [1748]), which was originally published anonymously for fear of censorship, Montesquieu critiques monarchical and despotic political systems. He goes into great detail on the importance of political liberty, illustrating how *ancien régime* rule repeatedly fails to deliver this important element in its governing structures. Further, Montesquieu compares and classifies various societies going all the way back to the Roman Empire. It was via this far-reaching and comprehensive review that Montesquieu developed his theories of government.

Another important contribution of Montesquieu was his innovative thinking on the subject of criminal law. He expounds on what today we would call due process in criminal proceedings, stressing the presumption of innocence as a fundamental element of a fair and just society.

Montesquieu was "clearly attracted to aspects of radical thought"; however, with his frequent alignment with kings and courts, "his moderation became the dominant feature."[4] In many ways, Montesquieu provided the foundation for the mixed-government model that became the standard in 18th-century Britain after the Glorious Revolution, and to which many of the American Founders also subscribed.

* * *

Jean-Jacques Rousseau's *Discourse on Inequality* (1755) and *The Social Contract* (1762) are cornerstones of modern political and social thought. Rousseau is often credited with developing and advancing the concept of equality of all and for depicting a more positive view of the state of nature, in which each person is endowed with innate virtue outside their own self-interest. This was a distinctly more optimistic view than that expressed by Thomas Hobbes in his social contract work, *Leviathan*, mentioned previously.

While Rousseau is appropriately considered one of the most innovative and provocative social contract theorists, his prescriptions ultimately sustained the importance of the governing structures of his time. For example, perhaps because he believed that his positive view of human nature was a virtue endowed by God, Rousseau affirmed the importance of religion as playing a critical role as the guiding hand in society. In addition, Rousseau had little faith in the concept of representative democracy and negligible confidence in the notion of an expansive suffrage. In Israel's view, Rousseau's rejection of the concept of representation and his advocacy of a role for the church in civic governance place the philosopher in the Moderate Enlightenment camp.[5]

Nonetheless, Rousseau greatly advanced the social contract framework by discussing the relationship between the general will of the people as a whole and the specific governing structures vested with the authority to enforce law and order. Like most social contract theorists, Rousseau recognized that certain individual freedoms would be necessarily curtailed as part of the social contract. However, he believed that most individual freedoms were unassailable and required protection via the social contract. In fact, one of Rousseau's key principles of government was to afford the members of society a level of freedom that at least approximates the freedom enjoyed in the state of nature. Furthermore, Rousseau advocated that governing authorities' overall purpose was to serve his innovative notion of the "public good."

At the same time, Rousseau believed that existing laws and government institutions could be fundamentally corrupt and insisted that sovereignty, or the power to enact laws, remain in the hands of the people. One of Rousseau's most important contributions is his coherent and compelling argument that the government's right to exist and to govern can be granted only by the consent of the people.

In terms of where to vest the authority for enacting laws, however, Rousseau explicitly opted for society's educated elite and eschewed the concept of representative democracy. Although Rousseau advanced the concept of democracy for small states like his native Geneva, he felt that democracy was unworkable in a large, heterogeneous society. To a large degree, Rousseau believed the masses to be overly susceptible to the corrupt persuasions and tainted ideals of demagogues, who might seek to abuse their confidence. This is illustrated in one of Rousseau's most frequently cited statements: "The people cease to be free from the moment it chooses 'representatives' . . ."[6] Rousseau's model can best be described as an "aristocratic republic," with power in the hands of a privileged segment of "enlightened" society, those with titles and education representing the elite.[7]

Rousseau's writings, which at times incorporated Radical Enlightenment themes, were inarguably major contributions to the Enlightenment, principally his social contract theory. His influence on his Enlightenment contemporaries and leaders of the French Revolution during its many phases went unmatched. He was the "ubiquitous inspirer of the age . . . every part of the [French] Revolution made some claim on the heritage of Rousseau."[8] He was quite famous during his lifetime and was lionized after his death. Ironically, as we will review in subsequent chapters, the flag of Rousseau was waved by revolutionary leaders of all stripes. For example, his many writings on the subject of supreme equality would be used to justify Robespierre's coup and the beginning of the Terror phase of the French Revolution. It was perhaps because of Rousseau's great influence that he became a prime target for many of the Radicals who criticized his doctrines and advocated their own more sweeping solutions.

THE EUROPEAN RADICALS

The first real contrast to the thinking of the Moderate Enlightenment came as an underground movement that began stirring in France around the mid-1700s. The quintessential manifestation of this trend was a project started by Denis Diderot and Jean le Rond d'Alembert called the *Encyclopédie*. Started in the 1740s and enveloping a broad range of topics, its mission was to profoundly change the way people think. Since the church was the primary source of knowledge on most topics at that time and advanced exclusively those beliefs that were consistent with church dogma, the goal of the *Encyclopédie* was to broadly diffuse *secular material based on science and empirical data.*

The *Encyclopédie* illustrated the best practices of the sciences, the arts, manufacturing, and many other fields of inquiry. The bold mission of the project was to provide an all-inclusive summary of all human knowledge accumulated up until its time. In this vast undertaking, which took a good part of their lives, Diderot and d'Alembert strove for a widespread dissemination of valuable and practical knowledge and demonstrated that education and knowledge could be used by anyone to improve aspects of daily life.[9] Importantly, the material covered challenged religious doctrine and encouraged people to think for themselves outside the boundaries prescribed by the church.

As the *Encyclopédie* continued to spread more radical social and political ideas, it eventually got banned in France in 1759 by Louis XV and banned elsewhere in Europe by Pope Clement XIII. As Israel describes it, the *Encyclopédie* was "one of the greatest Enlightenment enterprises . . . a camouflaged *machine de guerre*, with subversive elements carefully buried, often inconspicuously, amidst a large mass of innocuous-seeming material."[10] In addition to writing thousands of pieces on a variety of topics himself, Diderot was able to gather contributions from a broad variety of thinkers and oversee the overall project.

Perhaps one of the most important contributions of Diderot is that he advocated for the idea that rational thinking based on empirical observation as illustrated throughout the *Encyclopédie* was not the exclusive purview of the elite in society, but on the contrary, was in the reach of the broader populace. He believed that the ability to think rationally was universal, provided that it was nurtured and developed by the state. This single but powerful concept alone provided a fascinating and important contrast to the Moderate Enlightenment thinking described previously. Montesquieu, as well as many of the other Moderates, viewed the masses disdainfully, believing them to be incapable of such abilities. For Diderot and the Radical Enlightenment thinkers, deficiencies in the nonelite classes of society were merely a result of lack of education and development. Diderot held the conviction that rational thinking could be commonly fostered and education widely disseminated should society resolutely choose to do so.

The Moderates noticeably viewed European society as more advanced than other "non-enlightened" societies. One of Montesquieu's doctrines indicated that moral and climatic contexts shaped the abilities of people in various parts of the globe. According to this theory, the innate abilities of people from diverse geographies varied based on the specific local environmental factors that were "fixed by the cosmos and irreversible."[11] Because of these variations, dissimilar geographies required distinct moral and legal codes. For example, for Montesquieu, African or Islamic societies required more stringent moral and legal codes based on the inferior abilities of individual inhabitants. This European-centric view of innate human rights and abilities was completely rejected by Diderot and many of the Radicals who believed that no innate deficiencies existed in such people; instead, they believed that the abilities of people in any given society were a function of the degree to which innate aptitudes were fostered and developed.

Early on, Diderot was closely associated with Rousseau, but their differences along Moderate/Radical Enlightenment lines of thought led to a rupture between the two. While Rousseau decidedly influenced Diderot, it was Diderot who asserted the principle "that all political authority comes from the hands of the people, a concept which removes all trace of divine-justification."[12] The implications of this statement were colossal. Recall that for centuries, monarchs (perhaps best epitomized by the "Sun King" Louis XIV) relied on the notion that the source of their power was divinely endowed; furthermore, this construct was sanctioned and continuously reinforced by the church authority itself. In addition, Diderot first advanced the concept of the public good, which he (not Rousseau) was the first to dub the "general will."[13]

* * *

A colleague and friend of Diderot, Paul-Henri Thiry, the Baron d'Holbach, was another great proponent of Radical Enlightenment ideals. D'Holbach was a philosopher, translator, and prominent social figure of the French Enlightenment, and while less known than some of his more celebrated contemporaries, he was remarkably influential in advancing the Radical Enlightenment school of thought and driving its more sweeping agenda.

D'Holbach was extremely critical of both religious authority and existing political structures and, notably, was one of the most prominent thinkers to explicitly link the abuses of the two realms into a coordinated system of oppression and domination. In his many writings he accused the monarchy and church of colluding to create a deplorable situation for most people, in which "most of humanity is kept in chains."[14] D'Holbach persuasively and unequivocally argued that monarchies are inevitably ruled in their own self-interests and that the church "despicably encourages tyranny to assure princes their power comes from God, deceit which had become one of the chief props of despotism."[15]

D'Holbach's theory of the persistent but tacit conspiracy between the monarchy and the church to subjugate the masses might have been informed by the writings of the Scottish empiricist David Hume (1711–1776). While usually considered in the Moderate Enlightenment camp along with his fellow empiricist John Locke (discussed previously), Hume was acutely critical of the role the church had played in quashing liberty, as evidenced by the following passage in one of his essays:

> In all ages of the world priests have been enemies to liberty. . . Liberty of thinking, and of expressing our thoughts is always fatal to priestly power . . . Hence . . . all princes, that have aimed at despotic power have known of what importance it was to gain the established clergy; as the clergy, on their part, have shown a great facility in entering into the views of such princes.[16]

Most Moderates espoused the view that the church was required to promulgate ethical principles. For d'Holbach, the church was not needed to provide society with a moral code. He strongly believed morality was universal in principle, and he proposed a secular universal moral code that he advocated for widespread adoption. He also advanced the concept of the "general will" or "common good" as the proper and sole objective of any political system.

But in addition to his beliefs, one of d'Holbach's greatest contributions was to describe in detail and in very practical terms *how to attain such a political system*. D'Holbach recognized that relying on monarchies and aristocrats for such a system was precarious, if not futile. Invariably, monarchs ruled for their own interests and were characterized by corrupt schemes and seizes of power and wealth. His condemnation of monarchy as corrupt was as absolute as his view of its desired power.

At the same time, d'Holbach was keenly aware of the danger of the tyranny of the mob in which people can be swayed by perfidious orators and clever manipulators. This tyranny of the masses could be so perilous, d'Holbach believed, that any type of direct democracy was a recipe for anarchy. He wrote, "In direct democracy, the people, sovereign in appearance, is generally the slave of perverse demagogues who flatter them and incite their passions, and thereby become tyrants."[17] Based on his conviction that the masses could not possibly self-govern, d'Holbach was firmly opposed to direct democracy. Ironically, in his writings from the 1770s, d'Holbach was incredibly prescient in his thinking; twenty years later during the Terror, Robespierre would use precisely these methods earlier described by d'Holbach to implement a tyrannical and violent purge.

But if d'Holbach condemned both monarchy and direct democracy, what solution did he advocate? How could a political system that would advance the concept of the general will be attained? In d'Holbach's prescription, representative democracy was the only valid form of government for a republic. Contrary to his Moderate Enlightenment counterparts, and in agreement with Diderot, d'Holbach fundamentally believed that both *morality and reason were well within* people's reach through a foundational level of education. Accordingly, his recommended blueprint for government relied on the masses being wholly capable of evaluating and choosing representatives whom they considered best able to advocate for their own interests. So even if the masses themselves were not sufficiently educated, d'Holbach deemed them entirely qualified to evaluate and assess in others the education, trustworthiness, and ability to advocate for the general will and the public interest. "Central to d'Holbach's political philosophy was the principle that government should be the sum of society's collective force deposited in the hands of those it judges best equipped to lead it to happiness . . . the best government is that that distributes well-being . . . to all members of society."[18]

One of the primary ways of doing this, according to d'Holbach, was to endow representative government with the means of properly educating the people through a national secular educational system. D'Holbach's prescription for what today we might call "a civically minded general education" was based on his astute recognition that education was a vital enabling force for democratic participation. D'Holbach envisioned that a robust educational system would progressively allow the citizens' choice of representatives to improve over generations as education became more widely promulgated. Over time, citizens would gradually improve in their ability to select advocates more capable of advancing their rational interests instead of those attempting to disingenuously inflame their passions.

In the final analysis, d'Holbach's vision for society was deeply rooted in the concept of *meritocracy*, where the state was responsible for leveling the playing field, providing equal opportunity to all citizens, and allowing people's individual capabilities and strengths to contribute jointly to the collective societal fabric. At the same time, d'Holbach recognized that society would still be stratified due to the variations in both natural abilities in and achievements of the citizenry. "Citizens should be equal in rights but not equal in influence or status. Those contributing most to the advantages society affords, society's wisest, most useful members, should be the best recompensed and receive the most tokens of distinction; but no meritocratic elite can or should ever be hereditary."[19]

The rise of socialistic ideas in the 19th century proceeded in an utterly different direction from the meritocratic ideals advocated by d'Holbach, who never advocated for the concept of "equality of outcomes." D'Holbach's vision of meritocracy has been quite close to the model we have embraced in the United States for the past century, if not longer, with arguably mixed results. Meritocracy is a critical Radical Enlightenment concept that has been assimilated into the idealized American myth discussed previously. For this critical reason, we will return to this concept in the third section of this book.

One of the most fascinating aspects of d'Holbach's work is his indirect critique of Rousseau. For example, Rousseau frequently argues that the main reason for humanity's ills is that it strays from a pure state of nature, in which all humans are equal, to corrupt societal structures founded on unlawful institutions. In contrast, d'Holbach attributes these ills to the fact that people were educated only in the church canon, which for him was superstition. For centuries, "Human reason remaining stunted in its infancy . . . [developed] into a system where the governing class holds power through superstition."[20]

Where for Rousseau people are equal by nature, for d'Holbach people are naturally endowed with different strengths and weaknesses, and thus not at all equal in all dimensions. Furthermore, people are born into dissimilar circumstances that accentuate these differences. For d'Holbach, it was the express purpose of the state "to offset the natural inequalities of wealth, strength and intellect [to ensure that] common rights, the common good and the general will become the collective force that corrects the imbalances."[21] According to Israel's research, d'Holbach was among the "very first to deploy 'universal and equal rights' as a political construct designed to correct the state of nature."[22] D'Holbach's influence on many other French thinkers of the time was profound, even if his ideas were not as broadly diffused internationally as others.

*   *   *

Marie-Jean-Antoine-Nicolas de Caritat, marquis de Condorcet, another French philosopher of this period, was greatly influenced by d'Holbach. In addition to being a great thinker in his own right, Condorcet was a major architect of the French Revolution. If d'Holbach was a leading champion of the tenets of egalitarian meritocracy, Condorcet dedicated his entire life to putting these tenets into motion during the Revolutionary era. He was one of the major formulators of the working mechanisms of the new governing regime from 1789–1793, and achieved immeasurable triumphs in this period before becoming a casualty of the Montagnards' coup of Robespierre and his colleagues. Condorcet was quite explicit in endorsing d'Holbach's views as the logical core that provided the suitable philosophical foundation for the principles of the French Revolution. These same principles formed the basis of the "Déclaration des droits de l'homme et du citoyen," one of the Enlightenment's most important proclamations.

Importantly, Condorcet also advocated for the concept of distributive justice, endowing the state with the power to formalize the concept of equal rights into concrete mechanisms that could counterweigh inequalities in natural abilities and circumstance.[23] Condorcet recognized that the greatly influential Rousseau did not firmly advocate for representative government and, in fact, shunned broad democratic participation.

Throughout Condorcet's life, from his early drafting of the Declaration of Rights to his primary authorship of the world's first democratic-republican constitution, his steadfast commitment to egalitarianism was his guiding light. Condorcet wrote frequently about the rights of women and consistently advocated for their political emancipation. Furthermore, his contribution to education reform was quite remarkable; Condorcet, perhaps more meticulously than any other Radical Enlightenment thinker, designed a wide-ranging education system because, like d'Holbach, he recognized that the democratic republic he envisioned necessitated an educated populace. For Condorcet and many of the other Radicals, in Israel's words,

A free society provides education for all its citizens, held Condorcet, identical for men and women . . . a democratic republic requires its citizens to be educated to understand and fulfill the requirements of their own liberty, their civic responsibilities, and duties, as well as contribute to the advancement of the nation's prosperity, and their own fulfillment and happiness as individuals. What is taught must therefore be unreservedly based on Enlightenment and science. Children from poor families must be given the opportunity to develop their talents on as equal a footing as possible with the help of the society. Universal education—that is, education of all citizens—is essential to society, and hence the responsibility of society.[24]

In the early 1790s, Condorcet wrote a detailed report for the French National Assembly on the required educational framework and implementation approach for a democratic republic, which marked a vast departure from the religious educational rigidity of the pre-Enlightenment era. Condorcet's plan specified the establishment of a national network of higher learning and educational institutions tasked with developing and training schoolmasters and instructors in all aspects of secular and civic education. Once empowered with a national army of secular educators, primary and secondary schools could then be established throughout France.

At the apex of the plan to develop a massive horde of educators of the people, Condorcet envisioned an Institute de France in Paris that would bring together "the most eminent scholars into a single organization at the Republic's heart, dividing them into three classes: (1) mathematical and physical sciences, (2) moral and political sciences, and (3) literature and fine arts."[25]

Condorcet's detailed road map was nothing less than a battle plan to create a broadly enlightened society at all levels. It epitomized the astute recognition among the Radicals that an *educational* revolution to change how people think was an essential accompaniment to the *political* revolution for which so many fought. Whereas most of the Moderates wrote off the abilities of the masses to become enlightened, for the Radicals, mass enlightenment was precisely the goal of a modern society. Significantly, it is in their differing assessments of how widely Enlightenment principles could be spread throughout society that Moderates and the Radicals had perhaps their most consequential disparity in views.

While Condorcet's plan was not immediately implemented, given the vagaries of the discrete phases of the French Revolution, it did ultimately form the basis of the French educational system, which Napoleon would later adopt and further develop.

In addition to Condorcet's focus on the educational needs of a modern society, perhaps his greatest contribution was his primary authorship of the world's first democratic-republican constitution, the 1793 French constitution. The reader may protest, saying that this was a few years *after* the ratification of the American Constitution. But as we will see in subsequent chapters, the 1787 U.S. Constitution, according to French Radicals, was remiss by not codifying all five ingredients indispensable to a republican democracy:

> Sovereignty of the people, equality of status, individual liberty, freedom of expression, and government for the common good, defined as what is best for society when everyone's interests are treated equally under the criterion of "reason" alone.[26]

For Condorcet, the American Constitution contained great defects with regard to these principles and lacked a fundamental grounding in the common good (*volonté générale*) and instead emphasized "guaranteeing property, inherited privilege, and in formal aristocracy, roughly on the British model."[27]

Precisely because the 1793 French constitution encompassed all five elements, in many ways it marked the culmination of the

Radical Enlightenment's achievements, despite the fact that it was overturned and replaced repeatedly in a cycle of revolution and restoration of the *ancien régime* that continued in France through the first half of the 19th century.

*　*　*

Together with Condorcet, Jacques Pierre Brissot (1754–1793) was the other principal actor in the political club called the Brissotins (sometimes called the Girondins) that in the 1789 French National Assembly publicly and adamantly rejected "constitutional monarchy on the British model . . . and fixed the Revolution's terms, concepts, principles and general direction."[28] The views of the Brissotins also epitomized the egalitarian nature of the Radical Enlightenment; they envisioned a broad set of protections for all types of people in society, including those we would today call "disenfranchised" (women, Protestants, Jews, people of illegitimate birth, etc.).

Brissot was one of the Revolution's most consequential leaders, using his newspaper to spread revolutionary fervor. Brissot insisted "on France's need to adopt an entirely new constitution, including a carefully formulated Declaration of the Rights of Man" and had great aspirations for exporting a new egalitarian order throughout Europe.[29] The Brissotins were also willing to tackle economic inequality through legal means, such as guaranteed provisions for society's most needy and progressive taxation structures.

The Brissotins were the true founders of the modern human rights tradition. They specified a much broader set of rights than the Americans did, incorporating the emancipation of Black people, women's rights, rights for the poor, and modern representative democracy.[30] Brissot himself was one of the foremost advocates for human rights. One notable contribution of Brissot was his conviction that enslaving people was immoral (slavery was instituted in some of France's overseas territories, although not in continental France itself). Brissot's condemnation of slavery was a vital part of his philosophy and led him to become an important advocate for its abolition.

* * *

Many additional voices contributed to the French Radical Enlightenment with numerous writings, pamphlets, and opinion pieces over the course of the 1780s and early 1790s. Many contained sweeping critiques of aspects of the *ancien régime* and were often published clandestinely and even anonymously. Interestingly, these diverse voices came from all parts of society that held power and influence: clergy, nobility, and civil society. While space limitations inhibit exploring their contributions, a few merit recognition.

Claude Adrien Helvétius (1715–1771) was a French philosopher and Freemason who was an early proponent of Radical Enlightenment ideals. In his famous book *De l'esprit (On Mind)*, first published in 1758, he presented a rival view to Montesquieu's renowned opus *Spirit of the Laws*. Helvétius argued strongly against Montesquieu's theory that climate influenced the character of nations. He proposed a radically egalitarian political philosophy in which he asserted all have an equal disposition for understanding and developing their capabilities. In essence, he regarded the human mind as a blank slate and believed that natural equality applied to all. Thus, the differences in national characteristics were not the result of innate differences between the people but rather a by-product of the systems of education and government. "No nation," wrote Helvétius, "has reason to regard itself superior to others by virtue of its innate endowment."[31] While Helvétius's work was condemned by the state and church authorities of his day, his work had a huge influence on the later Radicals such as Diderot, d'Holbach, Condorcet, and others and was precursor to many French revolutionary writings. Further, his work was translated into almost all the languages of Europe and became a frequent topic of discussion across intellectual and literary salons throughout the continent.

Emmanuel Joseph Sieyès (1748–1836), a Catholic *abbé* and son of a postal worker, expressed the desires and frustrations of common people in his important pamphlet *What Is the Third Estate?* (1789). He was involved in politics throughout the different periods of the Revolution and contributed on many constitutional committees, though he became more moderate in his later years and was an ally of Napoleon in his coup in 1799.

Constantin-François Chassebœuf, comte de Volney (1757–1820), from a noble family, advanced Radical Enlightenment ideals through his frequent publications in newspapers. One of the major themes in his writing, the importance of Enlightenment thinking in governance, was embraced by Thomas Jefferson, whom he came to visit in Virginia in June 1776. During this visit, Volney was shocked by the plight of the enslaved people and became a committed advocate to the power of education as a great liberator of all races. Volney was greatly influenced by both d'Holbach and Helvétius and was a vocal opponent of aristocratic power, often mocking Montesquieu and the British model's reliance on the aristocracy. He was involved in many stages of the Revolution and was a key proponent of spreading the Revolution through Europe and the Levant in the last years of the 18th century in what became known as the "General Revolution."

Honoré Gabriel Riqueti, comte de Mirabeau (1749–1791), was a key leader of the nascent stages of the French Revolution. His persistent attacks on absolute monarchy and resolute espousing of Radical Enlightenment ideals led him to become internationally known as one of the foremost voices of the Radicals. He had formidable oratory skills, which he used to promote Radical Enlightenment reforms in the incipient stages of the Revolution.

George Danton (1759–1794) was one of the foremost leaders of the French Revolution, although his legacy is indelibly scarred by his involvement in Robespierre's and Marat's coup, which led to the Reign of Terror. He ultimately tried to curb the Terror and ended up becoming one its victims, guillotined in 1794.

* * *

Before turning from the French Radicals, a few final comments are in order. The interaction among the French Moderate and Radical Enlightenment *philosophes* was complicated. They all knew each other and to some degree vied for status and attention within their social circles. In addition to Rousseau, Voltaire was in close contact with both Diderot and d'Holbach but created a definitive break with them after 1770 when "something like a mini civil war erupted among the *philosophes* over Voltaire's and d'Holbach's opposed positions."[32] According to Condorcet, this was the definitive break between the Moderates and the Radicals. Rousseau also broke with the Radicals around this time.

Another interesting and somewhat ironic point relates to d'Holbach's classification as a Radical. While d'Holbach advocated a dramatic restructuring of society and its institutions, he did *not* advocate "revolution" as the path to get there. D'Holbach deplored violence and was extremely wary of the concept of "a people's revolution." He feared that logic and reason of the most oppressed citizens would be eclipsed by "'charlatans' . . . promising to end the people's misery while, in reality, exploiting men's naïveté and 'superstition' to forge a fresh tyranny ever crueler and more 'superstitious' than that they rebelled against."[33]

Historians have at times incorrectly cast d'Holbach as a Moderate due to his resistance to revolution. Nothing can be further from the truth; the simple fact that d'Holbach did not advocate violence or revolution *as the means* of achieving the societal changes he sought does not render any less compelling the brilliance and weight of his revolutionary ideas. He was unquestionably a leading voice of the Radical Enlightenment. His courageous stance made him perhaps "the first theorist to follow Spinoza and Diderot in proclaiming in direct opposition to Hobbes, Locke, Montesquieu and, above all, Rousseau that neither security, property, [nor] spiritual care" should be the primary focus of the social contract, but instead universal equal rights and "le bonheur de la société."[34]

The split between the Moderate and Radical Enlightenment thinkers was of huge historical significance in France and (as we will see in subsequent chapters) in America. While at first the split was only polarizing, the schism became permanent after the storming of the Bastille in 1789. In the ensuing conflict, remaining neutral was not a viable option. The Moderates lined up in support of the existing monarchy (albeit with new controls), while the Radicals advocated for an entirely new system. "The Bastille's fall thus exacerbated but also clarified the long-standing rift between the two now openly competing Enlightenment wings."[35]

Chapter 6

THE DEVELOPMENT OF THE AMERICAN ENLIGHTENMENT

Now let us turn to the other side of the Atlantic. As stated previously, the French and American Revolutions were both part of a *titanic wave of change* that played out on two different continents. An in-depth examination of the views of our Founders will reveal that, as in France, the American Revolution was composed of two quite divergent schools of thought that at times came to consensus but more frequently exhibited sharp irreconcilable differences. Moreover, the same Moderate–Radical Enlightenment categorization becomes apparent when exploring the major distinctions in thought among our Founders and thereby serves as a useful framework to better understand the divergent impulses of the American Revolutionary Era. Thus, both the French and American Revolutions were essentially battlefields "between rival democratic and aristocratic variants of a single Atlantic revolution."[1]

The names discussed in the following will be very familiar to the reader; we all learned about these historical figures as early as first or second grade. We most likely continued to read or hear about them throughout the formative years of our education and perhaps even well into our adult lives. Yet I hope that exploring these familiar figures through the novel lens of the two opposing poles of Enlightenment thinking will provide an illuminating, clarifying, and perhaps even surprising perspective.

One of the fascinating aspects of the American Revolution is how the revolutionary undercurrent oscillated back and forth from Moderate to Radical and back to Moderate again, like a pendulum. In fact, the tidal shifts around our nation's birth provide an exemplary microcosm of the overall theme of this book. As we will explore, the fifteen-year period between 1775 and 1790 provides a fascinating contextual backdrop against which the tensions, impulses, and motivations underlying the two competing visions for the country are richly illustrated.

In the years leading up to the revolutionary conflict, despite an outpouring of protest, most colonists expected that their grievances against the Crown would ultimately be addressed without needing to resort to a complete break from England. Some of these protests, mostly boycotts, did grow increasingly boisterous in response to newly imposed British burdens like the Stamp Act (1765), which required colonists to place government-issued stamps on all printed matter as a mechanism to levy duties for the Crown.

As described in Bernard Bailyn's now classic analysis of the American Revolution, *The Ideological Origins of the American Revolution* (1967), the colonists developed a "logic of rebellion" not immediately, but gradually. As the effects of British actions accumulated (such as Parliament's vengeful enactment of the coercive actions of 1774) and progressively demonstrated to the colonists the reality of what was becoming a methodical assault on their liberties, support for rebellion grew. The revolutionary leaders increasingly began to suspect that a deliberate conspiracy was at play to eliminate colonial freedom and force the colonists' submission to the Crown's tyranny, in effect "enslaving the colonies, or bringing them under arbitrary government."[2]

Nevertheless, many loyalists proceeded with plans for reconciliation with the Crown. Radicals like Benjamin Franklin were among the first to propose independence in opposition to their loyalist colleagues. Franklin wrote in 1775:

> When I consider the extreme corruption prevalent among all orders of men in this old rotten state [Britain], and the glorious public virtue so predominant in our rising country, I cannot but apprehend more mischief than benefit from a closer union. I fear they will drag us after them in all the plundering wars which their desperate circumstances, injustice, and rapacity may prompt them to undertake . . . I apprehend, therefore, that to unite us intimately will only be to corrupt and poison us also.[3]

Of course, from the British perspective, the situation looked utterly different. As the world's leading hegemonic empire solidified its power, Britain's costs of administering and securing her spreading domain increased markedly. England's financial problems were particularly acute in the aftermath of the Seven Years' War, a global conflict between the British and French Empires that played out across many territories. Although Britain skirmished with the French on many continents and eventually emerged as the leading colonial power, the massive accumulation of wartime debts represented an immense burden for the Crown. Consequently, the only viable solution for Britain was to extract greater financial returns from her overseas assets through the imposition of taxes and duties.

As the appeal of revolt amplified among the colonists, the revolutionary leaders were put in a delicate situation because they faced homegrown peacekeeping challenges in addition to dealing with British tyranny. True, the revolutionary leaders' primary focus was developing and coordinating an effective response to the Crown's aggressions; however, at the same time, colonial leaders had to maintain civic law and order *within their own territories* while sustaining their individual influential and powerful leadership positions.

The need to balance these two loci of activity became particularly grave after the Stamp Act, which had a broader and deeper reach than previous duties and consequently provoked the most furious reaction yet seen. The colonial leaders were also irate at this hefty Crown imposition, but at the same time, they had to rein in the public response and keep it from turning into anarchy. In Massachusetts, "subversive local cliques . . . like the Sons of Liberty, [started] pillaging and wrecking" property.[4] These violent actions concerned Massachusetts' ruling elite, like brewer Sam Adams, his cousin John Adams, and John Hancock, a leading merchant and patriot.

Paradoxically, in many ways the political structure of the Thirteen Colonies closely resembled the aristocratic model in place in England. Long-standing colonial governments were controlled by powerful families that had been ruling for decades. In the Virginia Assembly, for example, since the establishment of the colony, Benjamin Harrison I, Benjamin Harrison II, and Benjamin Harrison III, IV, and V had all served in governing positions. "These were men with a century of governing behind them. America was already old before she got a chance to be 'born' from an idea."[5]

One of the resulting ironies of this established family-controlled rule is that the same colonial leaders who began to coalesce around their grievances against "tyrannical treatment" from the Crown were hardly egalitarian in the administration of their own colonies. As a result, these colonial ruling "aristocratic" elites had to strike a fine balance between criticism of authoritarian rule by King George and the maintenance of law, order, and firm jurisdiction in their own backyards. As we will see, this tension between the elite political leaders in the colonies and the common people was in fact an antecedent to a more manifest and enduring political division between the moderate and radical revolutionary leaders that would follow. From the perspective of the colonial leaders, the need to balance their rebellious spirit toward the Crown with the more conservative decorum within their own dominion was quite challenging. The tension inherent in this balance motivated many of the colonial aristocrats to critique with some anxiety the more populist, antiaristocratic expressions of the soon-to-be Radicals.

In any case, at the start of the American Revolution in 1774–1775, "hardly anyone intended to replace the highly elitist political systems in the Thirteen Colonies with more democratic and representative legislatures and constitutions."[6] The objections of the colonists, as illustrated in the writings of John Adams, were firmly contextualized within the existing British Parliamentary governing framework.[7] Ever since England's Glorious Revolution in the late 17th century, Britain was transformed from a near absolute monarchy to a more progressive constitutional monarchy. Accordingly, a new British constitution was adopted that established clear lines of authority preventing abuses and limiting any overreach by the monarch without explicit approval from the aristocratic elite (today's House of Lords).

English Enlightenment thought underpinning the new British constitution had evolved all through the English Civil Wars and Commonwealth period. For example, political writers from the early 18th century such as John Trenchard (1662–1723) and Thomas Gordon (1691–1750) wrote searing critiques of British politics, advocating libertarian ideals. Many of their works had reached the colonies and were quite widely distributed. "The writings of Trenchard and Gordon ranked with the treatises of Locke as the most authoritative statement of the nature of political liberty."[8] Many of Trenchard's and Gordon's themes, such as repudiation of the British monarch's use of standing armies to intimidate the populace throughout the British empire, undoubtedly stuck a chord with the colonists as their own conflict with the Crown escalated.

It was from this point of view, with deep knowledge and appreciation of the multifaceted issues underpinning the development of Britain's own constitutional monarchy, that the aristocratic leaders of the colonies enumerated their grievances in the mid-1770s. The major Enlightenment thinkers reviewed in the previous chapters provided the colonial leaders with philosophical and conceptual frameworks for governing (along with the classical Greek and Roman texts with which they were unarguably familiar). But also, the prolific writings on British historical events in the 17th and early 18th centuries provided a more textured landscape of practical considerations upon which John Adams and the other leaders were forced to maneuver. The consequence of this blend of influences was that initial colonial complaints were not formulated with an eye toward independence, but instead attempted to redress specific injustices resulting from Britain not abiding by the spirit of its own mixed-government constitution on the colonial side of the Atlantic.[9]

Thus, in the mid-1770s, while Adams and many other colonial leaders were striving for a higher level of autonomy for the colonies, they were doing so fully under the auspices of this existing British constitution, which had well-defined provisions for governing the remote parts of the British Empire. This was the colonial leaders' *existing frame of reference*. Interestingly, in interpreting the writings of John Adams, many modern readers have confounded references to "violations against the Constitution," believing Adams was referring to the Constitution of the United States, which of course had not yet been written. In fact, Adams was referring to violations against the British constitution that had been established after the 1688 Glorious Revolution. Similarly, in Adams's writings, many mentions of "The Revolution" referred to the same English Glorious Revolution, not the American Revolution, as many modern-day readers suppose. Therefore, since colonial leaders had the British mixed-government model as their frame of reference, the accusations against the Crown for which they demanded redress emphasized a failure *to apply the principles* of Britain's *own* constitutional monarchy to the American colonies.[10]

Adams was also patently inspired by the Enlightenment writings of

Locke and Montesquieu. As the American Revolution progressed, his vision for what needed fixing was based on the concept that the established elite political leaders in the colonies (a group of which he was part) could self-govern and replicate the very "English gentry republicanism" on the other side of the ocean. Many of the colony leaders, Adams's peers, were of a similar mindset, striving for more autonomy from Britain with a vision of developing a colonial mixed-government model with a Montesquieuian separation of powers.

While expressing their repugnance at the development of Britain's stance vis-à-vis the colonies, the elites in this colonial ruling class were also cognizant of their need to ensure that the popular protests associated with the grievances against British actions (mainly of the agricultural and mercantile class) did not boil over into chaos. Colonial leaders were quite concerned lest they replace the tyranny of a man (the king) with the tyranny of a mob. As the great historian Carl Becker has written, the American Revolution was as much about "who should rule at home" as it was about "home rule" (independence from Britain).[11]

However, this more moderate approach for redress within the existing stability of the colonial structure was about to be considerably challenged by voices advocating for a more dramatic and expansive solution. At this same point in 1774–1775, three radical leaders emerged and coalesced around a much more sweeping and what would become consequential point of view, forever changing the course of world history.

First, in an anonymously published tract, entitled *A Summary View of the Rights of British America*, a thirty-one-year-old unknown plantation owner from Monticello, Virginia, justified "resorting to armed resistance when in the face of the British 'unwarrantable encroachments.'"[12] It was in this document, for the first time, that Thomas Jefferson argued that the British Parliament had no *right* whatsoever *to exercise authority* over the colonies. In 1774, this was a very radical idea, quite contrary to popular opinion. This document made Jefferson known among the colonial leaders and demonstrated his persuasive writing talents, which would allow him to become "the pen" of the Revolution. Based on his remarkable abilities, Jefferson was appointed to be the drafter for the Continental Congress and was given what would turn out to be very important writing assignments.

As a very well-read Enlightenment thinker, Thomas Jefferson was to follow this debut by becoming one of the three leading voices of the radical wave in subsequent years. Thus, while Jefferson, like Adams, was an avid proponent of Enlightenment thinking, his prescriptions contrasted profoundly with those of Adams. Adams and Jefferson were "each iconic of a different type of Enlightenment . . . transforming political thought into a warring duality pervading the entire political and social arena—a struggle between 'aristocratic' and democratic republicanism."[13]

THE AMERICAN MODERATES

John Adams

By 1774 when the First Continental Congress met to coordinate the colonies' resistance to British policies, discontent was fomenting across all of the diverse strata of society throughout the colonies. Most of the representatives at the Congress were loyalists and Moderates who were developing an "appropriate" but measured response. For Adams, as mentioned previously, the grievances could have been resolved satisfactorily by extending the fruits of the British Glorious Revolution to her colonies.

This sense of caution was shared broadly among Adams's peers at the Congress; both John Jay representing New York and John Dickinson representing Pennsylvania were hesitant to take any sweeping course of action.[14] Adams quickly assumed a leading role at the Congress, urging the representatives to chart a carefully measured course of action. Throughout the revolutionary period, from the early revolution and into its later stages, Adams was incontrovertibly a leading voice, wielding the influence afforded by his great reputation to advocate for a more moderate course of action.

At this point, an important clarification is in order: In the vast library of material surrounding the American Revolution, Adams is frequently referred to as a "Radical." Of course, choice of words is often relative. In the 1770s, a great many colonists, including those in elite circles as well as many common people, were intent on remaining loyal to the British Crown. Therefore, Adams was indeed a Radical when compared to the loyalists among his peers. However, in the context of our analysis here, based on the vision of government he promoted and later sought to realize as president, Adams categorically merits classification as a proponent of Moderate Enlightenment ideals. Notwithstanding this classification, Adams eventually supported the break with Britain and the call for independence. However, at the same time, he unequivocally rejected the notion of "broad suffrages, equality . . . and Condorcet's democratic republicanism."[15]

For Adams, well grounded in Enlightenment theory and influenced by recent British history, society "consisted of three social orders, each with its own rights and privileges, and each embodying within it the principles of a certain form of government: royalty, whose natural form of government was monarchy; the nobility, whose natural form was aristocracy; and the commons, whose form was democracy."[16]

For Adams and many of his colleagues, all three governmental forms tended to enlarge their own powers at the expense of others and therefore needed to be carefully checked lest they encroach and become abusive and oppressive forces. For centuries, absolute monarchies had degenerated into tyranny, but there were also dangers in aristocratic or oligarchical rule. Moreover, democracies were specifically prone to dangerous mob rule since the uneducated common people were so easily swayed by demagogues who, by stirring public passions and fears, were able to camouflage their own self-interests and their unquenchable and malevolent desire for power. It was within this frame of reference that the balance of power explicitly designed in the mixed-government model advocated by Locke and Montesquieu was so appealing to Adams.

Adams would stay true to this model for much of his career. His proposed government paradigm prescribed the need for a sharing of powers *within government,* so as to avoid concentrating power in the hands of potential abusers; at the same time, it was also carefully restrictive regarding *access to government.* Adams was chiefly concerned about the negative influence of democratic forces and wanted to keep property ownership a prerequisite to suffrage, effectively excluding most people from access to the vote.

Even within Adams's "balance of powers" governing structure, his moderate stance further revealed itself when he advocated for bicameralism, a legislative structure with a more powerful aristocratic upper house controlling the whims of the lower house. Most importantly, Adams remained steadfastly reluctant to endow common people with any governing authority. He deemed it imperative "to preserve and institutionalize a republic's hereditary aristocracy, to balance both executive powers, on the one hand, and the people on the other."[17]

A crisp portrait of Adams's Moderate Enlightenment stance surfaces in his philosophical position vis-à-vis the Radicals of his time. These latter revolutionaries criticized all forms of monarchy, even constitutional monarchy that incorporated solid guardrails to check overreach by the monarch. In addition, the more radical view of the balance of powers advocated certain prescriptions that were divergent from those of the Moderates. First, the Radicals advocated for a powerful unicameral body that was representative of the people; second, in the Radicals' model, the executive power was relatively weak. In Adams's prescription, precisely the reverse was true.

One can also noticeably detect antagonism in Adams's many comments and writings about the Radicals. In criticizing Thomas Paine, Adams wrote that Paine had "a better hand at pulling down than building."[18] Adams was deeply concerned that the type of democratic scheme posited by the Radicals would lead to an unmanageable state, bordering on chaos.

In April 1776, Adams anonymously published his *Thoughts on Government*, in which he asserted that the goal of government was "to attain the desired ends—the happiness and virtue of the greatest number of people." His justification for opposing unicameralism was unequivocal: "A single assembly is liable to all the vices, follies and frailties of an individual."[19] At the same time, Adams articulated in this document a clear separation of powers among the executive, legislative, and judicial branches of government.

The influence of Adams's political thought was immediately apparent and quite widespread in the colonies; his writings were referenced extensively as each independent colony went through the process of drafting a new state constitution in the early days of the Revolution. Adams was by no means the most conservative among his colleagues. A wide range of views percolated among the diverse group of colonial leaders. For example, John Dickinson advocated for endowing the executive with even stronger power, while others wavered on the very notion of a permanent break with Britain at all.

In the face of these more conservative points of view, Adams unambiguously came to support both the act of declaring independence from Britain and the formation of a new independent republic. The structure of the republic he envisioned, however, was "elitist," governed by an aristocratic class. Additionally, in Adams's view, the new republic needed a robust executive, which in some ways resembled a restricted monarch. Finally, Adams's ideal government was not widely participatory; his vision gave limited influence to nonaristocratic voices whom Adams most likely viewed as unlikely to contribute to the act of governing or ascertaining and advocating for the general will of the people. Nonetheless, his principal contributions during the early founding of the nation are undisputable. Adams was indeed a great patriot with a distinguished career in public service, albeit with a style many of his fellow Founders described as often stubborn and cantankerous.

Before finishing up our brief review of John Adams, one important point should be noted. John Adams was quite consistent in his Moderate Enlightenment viewpoint over the course of his entire political career. He maintained his elitist stance restricting political participation to White men with property. On the other hand, there was one important dimension where, at least in theory, Adams was more progressive than some of his radical contemporaries; namely, Adams condemned slavery and never enslaved a single person in his life. In this aspect, Adams was closer in position to the French Radical Enlightenment thinkers, such as Brissot and Condorcet (discussed previously), who firmly rejected slavery. Unfortunately, however, this personal conviction never sufficiently influenced his advocacy. Adams, despite being opposed to slavery, did not support abolitionism unless it was done in a gradual way with "much caution and circumspection."[20]

Alexander Hamilton

The other most prominent Moderate who played a monumental role in the nation's founding was Alexander Hamilton. As recounted in Ron Chernow's groundbreaking 2004 biography and brought to life through the popular Broadway musical, Hamilton's contributions are remarkable as much for their practical ingenuity as for the expansiveness of their scope. Hamilton had a very modest upbringing. He was born out of wedlock in Nevis in the Caribbean and served as an assistant to a Caribbean merchant before coming to New York. Based on these nonaristocratic roots, it may seem somewhat surprising that

Hamilton became, along with Adams, a leading proponent of the elitist "aristocratic" Moderate Enlightenment camp among the Founders.

For four years, Hamilton served as Washington's chief aide-de-camp in the Revolutionary War, providing on-the-ground tactical support for combat efforts. In this position, his responsibilities were quite broad, encompassing intelligence, diplomacy, and combat, even if this latter duty occurred less frequently than Hamilton desired. In addition to his considerable intellectual skills, Hamilton staunchly yearned for military service to demonstrate his courage. His desire to achieve "revolutionary glory" as a complement to his academic leadership indicates both the breadth and depth of his ambitions.

When the war was drawing to a close, Hamilton assumed the role of, in today's vernacular, "project leader" for the building of a new nation. From financing the Revolutionary War, creating the nascent nation's first banks, to the subsequent building of the Treasury Department, Hamilton designed and implemented the entire set of financial foundations that would prove to be the critical prerequisite for the flourishing of what would eventually become an industrial nation. These contributions alone would suffice to designate Hamilton as one of the nation's preeminent Founders.

Incredibly, Hamilton's fierce problem-solving abilities and steadfast leadership were also on display in many other domains. Hamilton's mathematical and financial dexterity was likely honed during his training as a merchant in the Caribbean as a young man. Indubitably, prerevolutionary experiences were formative in his development of the practical expertise required for designing robust solutions and building enduring institutions. Hamilton's formal education at Kings College in New York (now Columbia University) and his subsequent practice of law added to this already rich portfolio of skills.

When the Thirteen Colonies first united to declare independence from Britain, they codified their union in the Articles of Confederation (drafted at the Second Continental Congress in 1777, ratified in

1781). It quickly became evident to the Founders, however, that the Articles of Confederation would require modification in several areas. The greatest weakness related to the lack of any defined role for a central government in areas where coordinated efforts across the colonies, soon to be states, were essential; raising funds, regulating interstate affairs, and conducting foreign policy provide just a few examples.

While recognizing these weaknesses in the design of the original Articles of Confederation, Hamilton also appreciated how multifaceted the development of adequate solutions would prove to be. This profound understanding motivated Hamilton to play a major role in developing and ratifying the new blueprint for the nation, the Constitution. Hamilton, along with James Madison, revealed remarkable diagnostic and analytical capabilities in shaping the essential components of what would become the U.S. Constitution. Hamilton's diplomatic skills, which enabled him to fashion practical compromises and build pragmatic solutions in "the room where it happens," were instrumental in the advancement of the early nation.

But perhaps as impressive was Hamilton's astute anticipation for the need to garner broad acceptance among the influential colonists for the end product to ensure ratification. It was at this juncture that Hamilton embarked on the Federalist Papers project, originally entitled *The Federalist*, because he accurately predicted the need for a "marketing brochure" to sell the concept of the Constitution to the individual states.

Through his supervision of the Federalist Papers, Hamilton served as both a creative problem solver through his substantive contributions and a chief trailblazer in overseeing the overall endeavor. The centrality of his role in *The Federalist* is indicative of his leadership as much as his sharp intellect. Not only did Hamilton write most of the material, but he recruited the other participants and oversaw the publication. (Some historians argue that the most influential contributor to *The Federalist* was James Madison due to the central importance of many of the papers he authored.)[21]

In terms of concrete results, Hamilton's impact is difficult to overstate. Instead of further delineating his contributions, which have been documented extensively elsewhere, a focus on Hamilton's political philosophy and its relationship to the split between the Moderate and Radical Enlightenment schools of thought is most germane to our purposes here.

Despite the modest roots of his childhood, it is unquestionable that Hamilton was a child of the Enlightenment. He provides an exemplary and quintessential illustration of the capacity of an individual to overcome modest beginnings and subsequently make immense contributions to society.[22] As reviewed previously, a key aspect of the Enlightenment was the concept of the autonomous individual—the notion that human capacity could be unleashed for the progress of civilization. In this spirit, a profile of Hamilton provides a rich illustration of how the Enlightenment encouraged the individual acquisition of knowledge, expertise, and competencies to unbridle the vast human capacity and realize its potential.

Hamilton's Enlightenment heritage can be described as the embodiment of the *competence* or *expertise* model. In the postwar environment, the monumental challenge of building a new nation required a significant amount of analytical capacity, practical know-how developed through experience, and considerable leadership talent, all qualities that Hamilton demonstrably possessed. As corroborated by the examples given, Hamilton understood that an exceptionally high level of aptitude and honed expertise were undeniable qualifications for success in creating and governing the new nation. Further, in Hamilton's view, this level of exceptionalism could be provided only by an educated and "enlightened" set of individuals, which in Hamilton's era translated into the educated and seasoned class of elites in whose circles he traveled.

An important word of caution is in order here, as words and labels can often be as confounding as they are helpful. Such is the case with the word "elite," which can mean many different things depending on the context in which it is deployed. (As we will see in subsequent chapters, this term had distinct connotations at various points in our history.) In Hamilton's case, because he was not born into a "titled" family, he could not be labeled "an aristocratic elite." On the contrary, Hamilton's elitism was very much self-made, based on his capabilities, ambitions, and concrete achievements. It was an elitism enabled by social mobility and meritocratic advancement and would become a model for Americans at numerous points throughout our history.

In the Revolutionary Era, Hamilton viewed the educated elite as being the only stratum of society that could adequately handle the complexities and architect the essential and practical solutions required to govern effectively. In other words, Hamilton was reluctant to put apprentices on the task; given the gravity of the circumstances, Hamilton demanded the best and the brightest. For Hamilton, these requirements justified his Moderate Enlightenment stance based on his conviction that the elite governance model was the only way to get the job done.

Hamilton, while a firm believer in the importance of guaranteeing unalienable rights for all citizens, believed like Adams that governing should be left to the capable. In fact, based on this competence model, Hamilton wanted to take the concept of self-government entirely out of the Constitution. Instead, Hamilton advocated that political power be given to the *well-qualified*, who were usually the rich and well-educated. This idea frequently isolated Hamilton from some of his fellow revolutionaries who were insistent on a more democratic model of government. Furthermore, as in the English model, Hamilton advocated for a strong executive to lead the government, an "elected" monarch.

In the late 18th century, Hamilton's leadership of the Federalist Party advocating for a centralization of power in the form of a strong federal government was clearly based on these ideals. Furthermore, this model was in direct contrast to Jefferson's Democratic-Republicans—a party grounded in a firm belief in the decentralization of power, in which individual citizens were free from an overly assertive central power and characterized by a more egalitarian model of local self-government. Interestingly, the Federalists became the party of the Northeast, and Democratic-Republicans became the party of the South. As events early in our nation's history played out, Hamilton's coalition with John Adams and their Federalist model ultimately won the tug-of-war with Jefferson's Democratic-Republicans and brought George Washington over to the Federalist camp.

In the final analysis, Hamilton's moderate stance was perhaps less ideological and more pragmatic. While Hamilton was irrefutably republican, he placed less value on consideration of the opinions of a broad range of people; instead, he concentrated governing and decision-making among experts whom he viewed as the most capable—and he set the bar quite high. At the same time and perhaps ironically, given his rise to a position of influence and achievement from quite humble beginnings, Hamilton's life was a genuine case study of social mobility, one in which he himself personified the benefits of broadening participation in government to include the manifold and cultivated talents of those outside the class of the traditional hereditary elites.

THE AMERICAN RADICALS

Thomas Jefferson

In many ways, Thomas Jefferson, more than any other of our Founders, inspired an enduring vision of what an "enlightened," free, and modern society could become. Over the course of his remarkable career, Jefferson was to become "the most consistent, unambiguous, democratizing republican among the Founding Fathers."[23] As the primary author of the Declaration of Independence, Jefferson created perhaps the most concise yet consequential political document in recent history, one that thoroughly embodies Enlightenment principles.

Jefferson's vision was grounded in his expansive belief in human potential and his ultimate confidence in the ability of common people to embrace a free society.[24] For Jefferson, the only prerequisite for participation in government was for citizens to "enlighten" themselves by resisting religious authority and unleashing their own individual capacities.

Jefferson was extensively well-read in a broad array of philosophical texts, including the Greek and Roman classics and pre-Enlightenment thinkers in addition to both Moderate and Radical Enlightenment thinkers from his era. As discussed previously, one of the foremost distinguishing principles of the Radical Enlightenment (as compared with the Moderate Enlightenment) was the need for a clear and impermeable separation of church and state. The interference of religious dogma in civic society was a "hot button" issue for Jefferson. Even before his national reputation was established, Jefferson worked indefatigably in Virginia for years to pass a law prohibiting religious authority from intruding into political society. Throughout his career he maintained that liberty required freedom not only *of* religion, but freedom *from* religion.[25] Jefferson's struggle to ensure this principle in his native Virginia took decades. In 1779, a major bill he wrote ensuring such freedoms at the Virginia state level was resisted by the state's powerful local religious forces. Unwavering, Jefferson persisted until he finally succeeded many years later in passing Virginia's Law of Religious Freedom (1786).

In Jefferson's early career, back in the mid-1770s, he quickly came to believe that the political forces that would become the American Revolution were expansive in possibility and had the potential for immense impact, not only in America but in Europe as well. From the start, Jefferson saw the Revolution as being about much more than just achieving independence from Britain; he believed in the concept of an American republic, which he would work tirelessly to create.[26] For Jefferson, "independence from England was only the initial political manifestation . . . as the last vestiges of feudalism and monarchy were destroyed and swept into the dustbin of history."[27] Through all the twists and turns in Revolutionary America, Jefferson held on to this ideal of a democratic society in which each citizen was free to pursue their own destiny and achieve their individual potential. Furthermore, he had high aspirations for this republic to serve as the "world's prime exemplum of modern democratic political and social principles."[28]

Remarkably, on top of serving as arguably the greatest "thinker" of the American Revolution—his primary role in writing the Declaration is well appreciated and was unarguably one of his most significant roles—Jefferson also played a significant role in the French Revolution, commencing with his relocation to France in 1784. At this point, Jefferson's main official responsibility, serving as the United States' minister to France, was to maintain this key alliance, which was essential for the new independent American nation. But through Jefferson's extracurricular activities, he became an influential colleague of and collaborator with the French Radicals discussed in the previous chapter, namely Condorcet, Brissot, Volney, and others who were at the heart of the French Revolution. He was centrally involved in the debates regarding the drafting of the "Déclaration des droits de l'homme et du citoyen," a document second in impact perhaps only to the American Declaration eleven years earlier. Jefferson also meticulously developed strategies and planned tactics with the leading French revolutionaries. This sequence of events helps explain why, for Jefferson, the American and French Revolutions were both part of the same movement, intricately intertwined throughout.

When the Bastille fell in 1789, Jefferson and his radical entourage in Paris felt that the Revolution they had commenced in 1775 in the colonies was vindicated as part of what was now a worldwide movement to end despotic regimes. In his autobiography, Jefferson expressed his profound optimism that the "appeal to the rights of man," which he believed had started in the United States and then spread to Europe, would extend worldwide, at which point the "condition of the civilized world will be greatly ameliorated."[29]

*　*　*

In so many ways, the character and ideas of Thomas Jefferson are enigmatic. For more than two hundred years, generations of Jeffersonian scholars have scrutinized all the bewildering contradictions in his life and in the political thinking he championed. Because of the depth and breadth of Jefferson's many paradoxes and ambiguities, the Jefferson legacy has been subsequently arrogated by many notably contrasting American presidents. For example, Andrew Jackson, Franklin Delano Roosevelt, and Ronald Reagan (to name but a few) all self-identified as Jeffersonian heirs but espoused utterly incongruent political philosophies. Yet each nonetheless claimed that his own philosophy was derived from the Jeffersonian canon. This phenomenon provides a good indication of just how difficult it can be to make cogent sense of the world of Thomas Jefferson. Any attempted summary here would fail to do justice to all the important nuances.

However, a few overall themes exist and are central to the schism that emerged in Revolutionary America; most Jeffersonian scholars would concur that these themes were manifest in myriad ways over the course of Jefferson's long career. Moreover, fully understanding and appreciating the American Schism necessitates their elucidation.

First, the "pure republicanism" fundamental to Jefferson's political philosophy was inextricably linked to the Enlightenment principle of the expansiveness of individual human capacity. Central to Jefferson's vision of the idyllic republic was a societal environment in which the individual could flourish, free from constraining authorities such as the church or an imposing central government. Accordingly, Jefferson was always wary of any form of power exercised against individual will. In his vision, a government was necessary to enforce the social contract and guarantee inviolable individual rights, but at the same time, government was a necessary evil, forever prone to abuse and corruption. For Jefferson, the more decentralized and defused government was, the better. For example, a local government close to the people was preferable to a far-removed central government (as with the British Crown).

A corollary of this basic philosophy was that the expansive activist government role prescribed by other Radical Enlightenment thinkers (as described previously) was noticeably eschewed by Jefferson. He harbored a more "acute sensitivity toward the explicit exercise of government power than any other member of the revolutionary generation."[30] Most importantly, whereas both Moderate and Radical Enlightenment thinkers would embrace various forms, structures, and required objectives of government, the Jeffersonian principles of minimalist government and its subordination to the predominance of individual liberty would become forever rooted in the American psyche.

Second, Thomas Jefferson was an idealist who refused to let pragmatic concerns encroach upon his quixotic endeavors to create his sublime republic. While the unique blend of Jefferson's romantic idealism and Radical Enlightenment thinking was indispensable in the Revolutionary Era, as we will see, it was to become more problematic when forging the practical compromises necessary to govern the young nation. For Jefferson, the "gap between 'what ought to be' and 'what the world allowed' constituted the central dilemma."[31]

Third, and perhaps most importantly, Jefferson personally embodied the American Revolution's most glaring contradiction—the one that would turn out to be our most lurid and heinous ongoing nightmare. While he opposed slavery in principle, often vehemently in his early career, and recognized its flagrant contradiction to Radical

Enlightenment principles, he failed to channel his considerable abilities to its abolition and failed to personally refrain from its practice. As Americans, we are all forced to live with the following perplexing and almost inconceivable incongruity: It was Thomas Jefferson, the owner of enslaved people, who provided the foundation for the "entire history of liberal reform in America . . . a process of discovery, with Jefferson's words, of a spiritually sanctioned mandate for ending slavery, providing the rights of citizenship to blacks and women, justifying welfare programs for the poor and expanding individual freedoms."[32]

As a consequence of all these contradictions, in our contemporary world, there is a justifiable tendency to qualify Jefferson's contributions and differentiate "the hero" Thomas Jefferson from the brutal plantation owner who held people in slavery, which he certainly was. This particular contradiction merits further discussion: There is no doubt that Jefferson actively participated in the institution of slavery, and that fact alone justifies condemnation. However, Jefferson's political philosophy regarding slavery was, in fact, quite ambiguous, "oscillating between outright condemnation of slavery as incompatible with republican values and equally outright procrastination when pushed to offer practical remedies to end it."[33]

As we will explore further, Jefferson's "self-evident truth" that "all men are created equal," contrary to popular belief, was *not* meant to be limited exclusively to White men. On the contrary, a preponderance of historical evidence exists that indicates that the concept Jefferson was conveying was intended to encompass all of humanity.

Contemporary reevaluation of historical figures is a constructive aspect of both history and political analysis. But at the same time, "latter-day moral judgments are notoriously easy to render from the comfortable perch that hindsight always allows."[34] The hypocritical characterization that we today ascribe to Thomas Jefferson with respect to slavery is founded less in duplicitous thoughts or concepts and instead has its roots, to a much more significant degree, in the vast chasm between those ideas and Jefferson's personal actions and public leadership with respect to slavery. If Jefferson's famous phrase reflected his genuine belief that "all men are created equal" (I will be returning to the support for this hypothesis in a subsequent chapter), it is unquestionably more difficult to speculate on Jefferson's intended timetable for the realization of this ideal. Even today, the remaining unsolved mystery remains: When, exactly, did Jefferson think that the ideals expressed in the Declaration would become reality, not only in Monticello, but in the entire country overall?

Many Jeffersonian scholars have defended Jefferson by pointing out that many of his writings indicate that he knew slavery was immoral and atrocious, and further, that he believed that abolition in the United States was necessary and inevitable. It is undeniable that his political writings express such beliefs. Some of the same historians justify his lack of definitive action based on the fact that dismantling or demolishing the deeply established institution of slavery presented an extraordinarily complicated set of problems. More recent research is more skeptical, stressing Jefferson's failed attempts at various junctures later in his career to at least prevent slavery from being extended to new territories (further discussed next and in a subsequent chapter).

Some facts are inarguable. Jefferson did personally design elaborate plans for manumission via the emigration of emancipated people to a new nation in which they could be free. Due to the accumulated hatred and bitterness resulting from the institution of slavery and its brutal practices, Jefferson believed that any system that attempted to both dismantle slavery and establish coexistence among the races would be impossible to peacefully achieve. The experiment in nearby Saint-Domingue (present-day Haiti) corroborated Jefferson's beliefs.

In 1789, at the beginning of the French Revolution, slavery was abolished in Haiti. American newspapers carried sensationalized reports of formerly enslaved people murdering enslavers and other inhabitants of the island. United States citizens at this time were terrified of the prospects of such an outcome on American soil. In this context, Jefferson developed an intricate plan that called for the liberation of enslaved people via their mass emigration and settlement in a new separate nation in which they would be free. His justification for the separation of the races was based on his belief that the effects of living through decades of slavery would make it impossible for formerly enslaved people to forgive their White oppressors, and that such people would need to find their own home.

Admittedly, Jefferson's proposed solution of deportation and colonization seems peculiar, perhaps even offensive, to modern-day ears. But it must be remembered that this was Jefferson's ancestral success formula for freedom. Fleeing one's native land to escape oppression in search of self-determination was exactly the model employed by Jefferson's ancestors in their quest to establish colonies in the New World. Furthermore, achieving independent sovereignty from an oppressive mother country was not only a historical legacy but was the goal of Jefferson's own lifelong endeavor—breaking away from Britain.

Despite Jefferson's personal distaste for religion, the biblical Exodus story was a dominant metaphor that remained powerfully entrenched in the American psyche, perhaps because of the parallels between the Hebrews' emancipation and the American independence story. Just as the biblical story involved flight from Egypt and establishment in a new land, so did the colonial history itself necessitate fleeing from England to establish a new land in which to enjoy freedom and liberty. Against this backdrop, Jefferson's search for a solution predicated on this model can be better understood. Liberation, along with planned deportation and colonization, must have appeared to be a preferable solution to what Jefferson considered the only other option, which he viewed as leading to an inevitable race war on American soil.

As Jeffersonian scholars acknowledge, Jefferson's views on race are complex and difficult to decipher. It remains fiercely debated as to whether Jefferson's reasoning for separation of the races was based on his belief in the relative inferiority or superiority of specific races, or on his desire for a practical solution that would allow the new colony of emancipated people to flourish while keeping the peace in the existing colonies.

In any case, the many fiercely debated Jeffersonian contradictions will likely never be satisfactorily reconciled. To our modern eyes, that such an innovative and gifted thinker like Thomas Jefferson, endowed with a firm Radical Enlightenment mindset, could also be a notorious enslaver and abuser of enslaved people will remain one of history's most perplexing challenges. Thus, in recent decades, it has become more common to condemn Jefferson for the gap between his vast intellectual and public contributions and both the way he conducted his private life and his failure to become an active abolitionist in his public life. Perhaps such condemnation is deserved. Nonetheless, I also believe that stressing Jefferson's contributions in this regard is important. Since this raises interesting questions that merit deeper analysis, unfortunately well beyond the scope of this book and best left to the professional Jeffersonian historians and scholars,[35] I can only conclude this brief overview with some hopefully provocative questions.

How do we evaluate and reevaluate historical figures who have made huge contributions while also being complicit and even participating in a system characterized by egregious and widespread atrocities? For the moral philosopher with absolute, nonrelative guideposts, this question undoubtedly poses an irresoluble paradox. But at the same time, history is rife with leaders who have made vast contributions to our collective world but who were also heartbreakingly flawed characters. Perhaps these paradoxical inconsistences have more to do with the ever-puzzling nature of the human psyche and are appropriate subjects for a different but still worthwhile exploration.

Nonetheless, in the case of our particular heroic figure in question, Jefferson's tragic flaw rose to Shakespearean dimensions in the latter part of his life. As we will explore in a subsequent chapter, over the course of his long career and notably as president, he allowed numerous concrete opportunities to lapse—opportunities in which definitive action could have made a difference, if not in unconditionally abolishing slavery, then certainly in preventing its expansion.

In sum, despite all the intricate and fascinating yet puzzling aspects of Thomas Jefferson as a historical figure, for our purposes here, from the perspective of his overarching vision and unique intellectual contributions, Jefferson's impact cannot be overlooked or even overemphasized. Jefferson was a prime advocate of Radical Enlightenment principles despite both his personal moral failings and his own aristocratic comportment. Inarguably, when it came to his professed Radical Enlightenment ideals, a crippling blindness or lack of courage ultimately prevented Jefferson from practicing what he preached. Yet his vast contributions both to the birth of the nation and to the defining aspects of the American credo cannot be overlooked or underestimated. As one notable Jeffersonian, Joseph Ellis, wrote in *American Sphinx* (1998): "The best and the worst of American history are inextricably tangled together in Jefferson, and anyone who confines his search to one side of the moral question is destined to miss a significant part of the story."[36]

Thomas Paine

In his early years, Jefferson's influence in the colonies was limited to the educated elite circle of leaders who were exposed to his initial writings. So how exactly did some of these more radical revolutionary ideas get diffused more broadly and reap the requisite public support? Much of this role fell to Thomas Paine, who is appropriately credited with taking this undercurrent of revolution and bringing it to the common people. In January 1776, his pamphlet *Common Sense* appeared anonymously in Philadelphia, the most populous city in the colonies, and spread like wildfire. The principles of the American Revolution finally found in one publicly accessible document "its most powerful expression in the most widely read, reprinted and discussed of all the pamphlets of the Revolution."[37]

As *Common Sense* got rapidly disseminated across the colonies, Paine's words more than any others convinced colonists that American freedom would not be attainable without more aggressive action. "Members of Congress might have been philosophers, reading Locke and Montesquieu. But ordinary Americans read the Bible, Poor Richard's Almanack and Thomas Paine."[38] Through his words, Paine helped common people see a few steps ahead of their current predicament; merely resolving the current set of expressed grievances was not sufficient. The colonists' freedom could "never be secure under British rule" due to two major British constitutional errors—monarchy and hereditary rule—that "made bad rulers even of capable individuals by breeding arrogance, and by separating them from the rest of mankind whose interests they needed to know well."[39]

Paine was able to successfully argue that the colonists' dire situation was not a result of a particularly stubborn king but was in fact *systemic* due to the very design of the British mixed-government system. While Jefferson was persuasive with his colleagues and perhaps on the ground in Virginia, throughout the colonies it was Paine who "decisively tilted the balance, against hesitation and compromise . . . summon[ing] Americans to fight for their independence, more equality, and new constitutional principles."[40]

From a contemporary perspective, it is difficult to appreciate how fresh and radical Paine's thinking was in his day. For most colonists, Paine injected a completely novel concept: Beyond the already radical notion of a total break with Britain, Paine actually *offered a vision of a new republic* as part of the solution for the colonists' predicament. Moreover, he asserted an equally radical concept that the people's rights and the common good could and should be *the prime objective* of that republic. Hitherto, arguments and passionate sentiments advocating for a break with the Crown had rarely been discussed in the colonies or in Britain.

Prior to the mass dissemination of *Common Sense*, most colonists greatly feared the idea of a break with the Crown, not because they were exceptionally enamored with the old regime, but because they had no clear conception of what would supersede it. Consequently, Paine was able to persuade more colonists to embrace revolution and overcome their fears of independence by *providing a vision of a better governing structure* for the New World. Thus, *Common Sense* consolidated all "the arguments together and used them not to persuade Congress, which was already moving apace toward Independence, but the people whose support Congress needed."[41]

Paine's radical denunciation of Britain's mixed-government model was most likely greatly influenced by the work of Diderot and the other French Radicals. Paine was well connected to French intellectual and political circles where these concepts were already an essential part of the debate in France by the 1770s. Of prime importance to highlight here is that Paine advanced a goal of the Revolution that was *in direct conflict* with the Moderates of the era. Instead of tinkering with the existing mixed-government model, he promoted something categorically innovative. Further, he explicitly recognized and pointed to the contradiction between the two Enlightenment camps, carefully delineating the fundamental and stark differences between the Radicals and the Moderates. For Paine, on both sides of the Atlantic, "the two kinds of republicanism, democratic and aristocratic . . . were fundamentally divergent, at odds, and irreconcilable."[42]

Writing later in retrospect, Paine wrote that "the independence of America would have added little to her own happiness, and been of no benefit to the world, if her government had been formed on the corrupt models of the old world."[43] *Common Sense* served as the animating vehicle that carried this erudite philosophy to the common citizen, decisively compelling "artisans, farmers, and shopkeepers, for elite and people alike . . . to support the move toward a total break, and full independence and a republican future."[44] As most historians agree, it was Paine's now legendary pamphlet that united the average citizens and political leaders behind the idea of independence, transforming what had been a colonial squabble into the American Revolution.

The influence of *Common Sense* was paradoxically dramatic in an additional manner. While tens of thousands of colonists who read Paine's words began to thirst for a new governing model, many moderate patriots were appalled by those same words. Many of the colonial ruling elite, those endowed with the formal authority at the Constitutional Congresses, were Moderates who were trepidatious that *Common Sense*, in particular, might lead to popular uprisings. They feared that Paine's words might stir chaos and provoke lawlessness among the colonists, which would threaten the ruling elites' control of their home turfs and perhaps even threaten their privileged ruling position. By staking out his radical vision, Paine helped define the same break between Moderate and Radical Enlightenment thinkers in the United States as had emerged in Europe.

As Paine's ideas gained popularity, the opposition of the Moderates also solidified. As a consequence of this tug-of-war, some of the foremost leaders of the Revolution repudiated Paine altogether. John Adams, who distrusted Paine early on, was particularly bothered that Paine's plan of government was "so democratic, without any restraint or even any attempt at any equilibrium or counterpoise that must produce confusion and every evil work."[45] Many of the eventual signers of the Declaration of Independence, including Adams, "detested *Common Sense* for its revolt against English constitutional traditions and principles as epitomized by the mixed government model of Montesquieu . . . by early 1776, very few among the American leadership went as far as Paine."[46]

But in terms of the Spirit of '76, as Thomas Jefferson noted, no one else promoted the "Rights of Man" so accessibly. Unquestionably, Paine played important roles in the revolution both in the United States and in France. Furthermore, Paine's vision brought the radical

Spirit of '76 to a wider audience of colonists, including White work-ing-class American men, who yearned for political participation; women, who hoped for political rights and suffrage; and enslaved people, who dreamed of freedom. As in the case of the French Radicals and firmly in contrast to the Moderates, Paine's vision for the repub-lic encompassed an expansive democratic egalitarianism reaching all colonists across all strata of society.

In the post-revolutionary years, Paine would continue to have a voice, albeit a controversial one, in the formation of the young coun-try. In addition to *Common Sense*, *The Rights of Man*, published both in France and the United States in 1793, was widely read. In many respects, *The Rights of Man* captured the essence of Jefferson's vision of the exis-tence of a forceful and persuasive mandate to free the individual from the intrusion of any abusive power, be it from the church or the government. However, during this period of the adoption of the new Constitution, the tide of antirepublicanism was on the rise, which made the reception of *Rights of Man* quite divisive. Provocateur to the bone as always, and not willing to mince words, Paine would continue to up the ante.

In his *Letter to George Washington* of 1796, Paine vociferously criti-cized Washington and the Federalist policies. Paine considered the 1787 Constitution an abandonment of the republican values of the Revolution (which we will explore in depth in a subsequent chapter). But unfortu-nately, in this later era, Paine was swimming against the tide. At the very same time, Washington was being deified and American opinion was moving to the right in support of the Federalists' policies, leading to a precipitous decline in Paine's popularity.

While Paine did return to America during Jefferson's administration and published *To the Citizens of the United States*, attempting to rekindle the earlier and more radical flames of 1776, he was broadly attacked due to the now established, less radical, and more religious environment. In this later work, he admonished his readers that "retreat from the princi-ples of '76 meant erosion of America's example to the world. Insidious efforts were being made to claw back freedom of expression [and] block democracy."[47] As the political winds continued to drift to the right in these later years, Paine's increasingly bitter criticism of the citizens' abandonment of republican principles left him further isolated. The fact that only twelve people attended his funeral in 1809 is a heartbreaking indication of the tragic fall from fame of such a previously influential man.[48]

Benjamin Franklin

Perhaps the American Moderates would have had their way in counterbalancing Paine's influence if not for a third major radical voice that surfaced in Philadelphia at this time. Benjamin Franklin was iconic in multiple ways of both the Radical Enlightenment and the American Revolution.[49] Outside of the political arena, Franklin's earlier contributions to science were quite significant and gained him much respect on both sides of the Atlantic. Franklin combined an empirical orientation and a fascination with the manipulation of and experimentation with physical mechanisms. This scientific mindset, as part of the "cult of Isaac Newton," along with his vast political contributions, make Franklin an exemplary personification of the Enlightenment and perhaps the most underappreciated of the Founders. If Leonardo da Vinci was the archetypal "Renaissance Man," Benjamin Franklin was undeniably the quintessential "Enlightenment Man."

What was so extraordinary about Franklin is that, unlike many of the other leaders of the Revolution, he was a wholeheartedly self-made man lacking any formal education (he stopped attending school when he was ten). Despite his own dearth of formal schooling and reliance on self-education, he was a strong advocate of public education later in life as an entrepreneur and political leader.

Two well-defined aspects of Franklin's radical side were his rejection of conventional religion from a young age and his fundamental belief in and advocacy for an egalitarian approach to realizing "the common good." The combination of these attributes with his astonishing leadership and diplomatic skills made Franklin seem destined to play a central role in the Revolution. In today's parlance we would call Franklin, in addition to his brilliance as a thinker, the rainmaker of the Revolution. It was Franklin who met with Paine in London and encouraged him to come to the United States. Moreover, it was Franklin's deep immersion in the Radical Enlightenment philosophical circle in Paris, starting in 1776, that perhaps had the broadest impact on both the American and French Revolutions.

Franklin, with his nonelitist persona, "shunning aristocratic attire and manners," became extremely well known in France as the symbol of the egalitarian themes sweeping the continent. He also sparked the same sentiment in the colonies, providing an outburst of enthusiasm for the American Revolution. Furthermore, he laid the diplomatic groundwork that empowered France to become such a vital strategic and tactical ally in the pending armed conflict with the British. As part of the most influential salon of leading thinkers in Paris, Franklin undoubtedly contributed to the nascent and evolving ideas of Condorcet, d'Holbach, and some of the other French Radicals discussed previously, thus contributing to the subsequent French Revolution, thirteen years after his arrival in Paris.

One of Franklin's important contributions from the perspective of his political philosophy was how he "persisted in rejecting bicameralism on principle, deeming it a pernicious vestige of the aristocratic British past."[50] From our modern-day perspective, as we witness the tragic decline of the Senate as an effective institution, with its reliance on antediluvian murky tactics like the filibuster, we cannot help but think how prophetic Franklin was in his thinking.

Finally, Benjamin Franklin made an astonishing assortment of wide-reaching practical contributions that together form the basis of a modern civil society. His strong conviction that the diffusion of knowledge was a powerful and requisite tool for the advancement of civilization drove him to pursue construction of the necessary infrastructure to achieve it. He was a lifelong proponent of freedom of the press, starting from his days as a young man printing his own newspaper when he first arrived in Philadelphia. He recognized the importance of the free press for sharing empirical observations and disseminating information throughout the world. For similar reasons, Franklin largely created the U.S. Postal Service, based on the astute reflection that a progressive society required a reliable and efficient delivery structure for interpersonal communication as a means of both sharing ideas and conveying emotions. He also created lending libraries to promulgate secular learning. But in addition to his incredible talent in spearheading these innovations, Franklin was also an expert in propaganda, though he was cleverly understated relative to the more brazen Thomas Paine.

Before the Revolution, in 1754, Franklin's famous woodcut, JOIN or DIE, propagated the notion that the colonies would need to unite for common defense. Given the significant disparities across the colonies at this time, Franklin possessed an early intuition that their political future portended the need for united action of some kind. He also sensed that given how diverse the colonies were at the time, "mass communication" was to play a fundamental supporting role by stressing the common unifying themes among colonists who were dispersed both geographically and ideologically.

Franklin honed his publicity skills throughout his entire adult life and was accomplished in the art of subtlety. Much as Diderot's remarkable work on the *Encyclopédie* allowed the inconspicuous diffusion of republican ideals concealed within a widely read "reference book," so did Franklin's *Poor Richard's Almanack* and then *La Science du bonhomme Richard*. Both of these works were influential publicity tools that did the same job on both sides of the Atlantic. The wide audience that Franklin reached with these ingenious vehicles represented another side of Franklin's communication skills and another method by which he was able to widely diffuse Enlightenment principles to the masses.

Franklin stayed in France from 1776 through 1785, becoming the archetypal example of the muscle of the American Revolution. Internationally, he became the "icon of the [American] revolution to such an unparalleled degree that his was the only name regularly placed alongside Washington's in accounts."[51] Franklin was so revered, such a cult figure in France, that the French National Assembly declared "'three days of public mourning' upon his death."[52]

Sadly perhaps, most Americans at the time were unaware of his towering reputation overseas. Even today, most Americans fail to grasp the enormous contribution he made not only in ensuring America's independence but also in creating a model and the tools for a more egalitarian country. Finally, his ability to evolve and demonstrate new moral ground through the wide range of his public activities validates what a remarkable and rare individual he was. While he was an enslaver early in his life, he eventually realized that slavery was a vile institution that was altogether inconsistent with the principles of the Enlightenment and revolution and, in his later years back in the United States, he became an avid abolitionist up until his death.

THE AMERICAN RADICALS IN LOCKSTEP

The triumvirate of Franklin, Jefferson, and Paine led the transformation from "a colonial squabble" into what became the American Revolution. All three were considerably absorbed in and influenced by the Enlightenment thinking emerging throughout Europe, especially in France, England, and Scotland in the mid-18th century. But an important commonality particular to this triad distinguished them from their more moderate counterparts; namely, an alignment with the French Radical Enlightenment. All three were immersed in and inspired by the documents written by their radical French counterparts.

Jefferson, Paine, and Franklin all spent much time in France and were intricately enmeshed in Parisian intellectual circles, albeit at varied points in time.

In 1784, after the Revolutionary War but before the Constitution was written, Franklin and Jefferson, along with Adams, formed a joint diplomatic team together in France. For all three, maintaining the support of America's first ally was of primary importance, but Jefferson and Franklin also continued their work on what would become the next chapter of the transformational era, the French Revolution.

In any case, this shared alignment with the French Radicals no doubt played a significant factor in the shaping of their successful alliance. This is the most likely explanation for why all three men believed at a profound level that the American and French Revolutions were intertwined, a spearhead representing a monumental and progressive step forward for Western civilization.

While not always together geographically, the triad aligned philosophically in the early days of the American Revolution. They concurred on specific key revolutionary elements based on ideals that had roots in the Radical Enlightenment: separation of powers in governance, representative democracy, separation of church and state, the protection of a broad set of human rights, etc. But as important, they also shared *a higher aspiration* for the entire colossal undertaking of the day; their paradigm for the new nation envisaged an *extensive transformation of society* characterized by a decreased emphasis on any form of dogmatic religion and a departure from the aristocratic hereditary-based rule of their era. While the American Revolution could achieve success only with a broad set of contributions from many of our Founders, it was this triumvirate who were the true visionaries of a different type of modern society, which they were determined to help forge.

For these Radical Enlightenment thinkers, independence from Britain was necessary, but not sufficient. Equally important was the nature of its replacement. And for Franklin, Jefferson, and Paine, the only viable answer was the establishment of a democratic republic that guaranteed freedom of the press, expanded secular education, and secured basic equal human rights for all (with the obvious and glaring exception of African Americans and Native Americans). The gap between their prescriptions for the new republic and those of the American Moderates was reflected in the "internal split over whether the Enlightenment meant reforming the existing social, legal and institutional order while leaving the main structure intact, or whether correcting abuses meant replacing the old institutions, laws, and practices with an entirely new structure."[53]

* * *

Before we proceed (in Part II) to review how the American Schism, the rupture between the Radical and Moderate Enlightenment schools of thought, played out over the course of the next few centuries in America, there is one more 18th-century force that also emerged at this time and merits review. This movement, the *Counter-Enlightenment,* was not so much a discrete school of thought as it was the *wholesale rejection* of Enlightenment philosophies and their implications for society. While in the late 18th century the impact of this movement might have seemed short-lived, a transitionary development, the exact opposite came to fruition. Not only did the Counter-Enlightenment significantly influence the political dénouement of both the American and French Revolutions, but its influence would persist as a powerful and dynamic force over the course of the next centuries. In fact, while Moderate and Radical Enlightenment impulses and principles are both alive and conflicting in contemporary America, the Counter-Enlightenment continues as a yet ever-present third force aggressively superimposing itself on the first two.

Chapter 7

COUNTER-ENLIGHTENMENT AND POPULISM

Frequently over the course of history, powerful ideological, philosophical, social, or cultural movements provoke backlash or contrarian opposition that can coalesce into a veritable counter-movement. If a particular group or school of thought, especially one advocating societal change, becomes prominent or quickly gains considerable influence, frequently those with firmly held opposing viewpoints come together with an organized response. Commonly, the explicit purpose of the reactionary group is to undermine and arrest the momentum of the initial movement. And if the originating movement mobilizes sufficient resources and thereby gains thrust, often the counter-movement will ratchet up its own efforts in lockstep. Many of the major issues that prompted activism in the history of our country have encountered these types of counter-movements. This phenomenon has no doubt been facilitated over the course of American history by our society's relatively high degree of freedom of expression, one of the foundational benefits of a liberal society.

Such a counter-movement emerged and gathered steam in the 18th century to specifically challenge the spread and influence of Enlightenment thinking. What we now call the *Counter-Enlightenment* was a movement driven by influential leaders who opposed the ideas advocated by Enlightenment thinkers and became prevalent in both Europe and the United States at about the same time. Its explicit intent was to confront and defy the prescriptions put forward by Enlightenment thinkers.

Unsurprisingly, this counterforce was composed of precisely those conservative elements of society that felt most threatened by Enlightenment principles. The two primary societal groups that converged in the Counter-Enlightenment in France were *the clergy and the nobility*, which in French revolutionary times were commonly referred to as the First and Second Estates (the Third Estate referred to commoners). Since members of both the church and the nobility recognized how the Enlightenment exposed and jeopardized their positions of authority over the masses, outspoken leaders in both these groups purposefully united in a joint assault with the express purpose of neutralizing its destabilizing and revolutionary ideas.

The intent of these Counter-Enlightenment reactionaries was to leverage their positions of influence in society to instill anxiety among the masses relating to the impact of progressive changes of the era, thereby thwarting the far-reaching transformations heralded by the Enlightenment movement overall. One recurrent and quite successful Counter-Enlightenment tactic was to portray the thinkers of the Enlightenment, *les philosophes*, as condescending elites who were disdainful and contemptuous of the masses.

Notably, since Radical Enlightenment thinkers represented the greatest threat to the status quo in both countries, they were naturally the Counter-Enlightenment's predominant targets. As discussed previously, because the Moderate Enlightenment thinkers in general were more charitable to religious doctrine, and more importantly, willing to endorse the intermingling of church and state and to sanction the church's authority in governance, the Moderates were less frequently beleaguered, and even at times supported the Counter-Enlightenment impulse in their own opposition to the Radicals. On the other hand, as we reviewed, because the Radicals vehemently condemned the intrusion of religious authority into affairs of state, they became a prime target of Counter-Enlightenment critique.

The propelling engine of Counter-Enlightenment forces in France came from the Roman Catholic Church, which had been tied to the French state for centuries. The French clerical authorities greatly feared that they would suffer a dramatic loss of influence in a society structured around Radical Enlightenment prescriptions. To resist this development, the church repudiated any Enlightenment themes that rejected church doctrine and personally attacked Radical Enlightenment thinkers for their antagonism to the church, at times accusing the Radicals of heresy.

It is important to remember that in most of France outside Paris, the entirety of agricultural life of rural France was organized around the Roman Catholic Church—it was the keystone of daily life. Consequently, in addition to the powerful influence of officials in the higher echelons of the Roman Catholic Church, the local church or parish leaders had enormous sway in their communities due to close generational ties to the local citizens. Furthermore, church leaders opining on current events was a well-established trend. Authoritarian religious leaders had used the pulpit for centuries to provide weekly critique of and commentary on social developments and political events. And, following the invention of the Gutenberg printing press in the 15th century and its subsequent dissemination, the clergy also had access to the local press and had powerful relationships with local agricultural and mercantile interests. Thus, the clergy as a group possessed a veritable army of influential local leaders ready to preach from their pulpits.

The Counter-Enlightenment emerged on both sides of the Atlantic but with significantly different consequences. In France, its repercussions would be tragic.

COUNTER-ENLIGHTENMENT IN FRANCE: THE REIGN OF TERROR

Many proponents of the Counter-Enlightenment movement in France were quite renowned in society. This group initially included members of the aristocracy and popular leaders of the church and, subsequently, respected thinkers who targeted the elite *philosophes* precisely when the initial hopes for the revolution were waning and citizens were beginning to confront the harsh reality of the conditions on the ground.

By the 1790s, the early stages of the French Revolution had already resulted in significant societal changes. The king and queen, Louis XVI and Marie Antoinette, were imprisoned to await an uncertain fate after attempting to flee, while the newly established constitutional monarchy teetered due to vehement disagreement among disparate political factions. This instability caused economic conditions in the country to deteriorate rapidly. For commoners, both in rural France and in cities, the promises of the Revolution were seemingly going unfulfilled. Not only did the present situation appear precarious for the masses, but the outlook for a better future seemed even more grim.

Against this backdrop, the *philosophes* provided a convenient target for disparagement and vilification from many sides. The masses, who had no time or luxury to sit in cafés thinking, writing, and debating, were counseled by clergy and royalty that the new *philosophes* were not only haughty and condescending but fractious, and some were even seditious. Influenced by these proponents of Counter-Enlightenment thinking, many of the poor and uneducated began to increasingly associate their dismal and deteriorating lot in life with the changes being introduced by Enlightenment thinkers.

As trusted local clergy began opportunistically stirring fears based on the uncertainty of the turbulent times, Counter-Enlightenment impulses became more prevalent, mainly in rural France. The public swiftly embraced Counter-Enlightenment thinking and turned against the *philosophes* precisely because the Enlightenment was universally identified as the cause of the turmoil. Furthermore, the Counter-Enlightenment narrative, as it became more widespread, was to become both a sharp political knife and a blunt fear-producing hammer. It was through the weaponization of growing popular concerns that the French Revolution metamorphized into its tragic phase, the Reign of Terror (1793–1794).

In 1792, following the declaration of the French Republic by Condorcet, Brissot, Mirabeau, and the leaders of the Radical Enlightenment group, the misery and economic distress associated with food shortages plaguing rural France were spreading to Paris. By 1793, economic suffering was quite intractably widespread throughout all of France. Coincidentally, the intensification of these dire conditions paralleled the rise in Counter-Enlightenment voices.

A conniving faction of perfidious revolutionary leaders in Paris recognized a political opportunity to seize control of the situation by capitalizing on the suffering of the poor. Headed by a coalition of populist leaders, this segment broke off in a decisive split and formed a new party, *Le Montagne* (the Mountain, also known as the Montagnards), and carefully orchestrated demonstrations of support from the poor working classes, at the time referred to as *les sans-culottes* (without knee-breeches, a symbol of equality). The poor working classes were infuriated that the Revolution's promised improvements had failed to materialize (due to the collapsing economy, the lives of the *sans-culottes* had in fact markedly deteriorated).

Led by Maximilien Robespierre, Jean-Paul Marat, George Danton, and their Montagnard "henchmen," the Montagnards, being the astute politicians they were, seized the opportunity, directly and emphatically tying the *miserable* plight of the masses with the "pretentious" Radicals in what was effectively a coup d'état. The seeds had already been sown for their coup by the same Counter-Enlightenment arguments that church leaders and royalists had been advancing since the Revolution's early stages. With their path already paved, it was quite easy for Robespierre and his allies to depict their political rivals as a highbrow intellectual movement, which they derided as "*la philosophie moderne*," and held responsible for the public's woes.

Truth be told, Robespierre and company genuinely disdained their rivals as scholarly elites who looked scornfully down on the masses. "Robespierre in any case detested Condorcet, Brissot, and the intellectuals leading the democratic-republican Revolution . . . oppos[ing] them on every issue."[1] In any case, the Montagnards further denounced the Radical Enlightenment leaders for rejecting the church, thereby ingratiating Robespierre's clique with the clergy.

Robespierre's co-conspirator Jean-Paul Marat became a fierce champion of the masses and defiantly rejected Enlightenment principles as elitist and inimical to the interests of the masses. Marat characterized the approach that Enlightenment advocates posited as highfalutin and pompous. By tenaciously and convincingly subordinating reason to the will and emotions of the people, Marat became a prime proponent of Counter-Enlightenment thought. He appealed to the least educated and advocated a popular chauvinism that for him was the prime goal of the Revolution. Moreover, he doggedly called for using totalitarian measures, including censorship and the abandonment of freedom of expression, to support his populist view, and strove to ultimately create a "dictatorship of the most uncompromising kind to rescue the people."[2] (Marat was quite an interesting historical figure. He was initially a physician by training before becoming swept up by the Revolution. He was the leader of what became known as the September Massacres, a horrific killing of many political prisoners in the name of the Revolution. After he was assassinated in 1793, he became a martyr for the *sans-culottes*.)

Once in power, the Montagnards' campaign deployed a relentless authoritarian populism to mobilize the masses against the intelligentsia. Even as this campaign became increasingly violent, the Montagnards for the most part retained the support of the clergy. Despite the bloodshed, the religious leaders undoubtedly viewed the Montagnards' movement as the best vehicle to restore the dominant role of Roman Catholic Church dogma in daily life. In addition to traducing the intellectuals, the Montagnards found a most symbolic scapegoat to hold accountable for the problems of the masses. As a symbol of its power, this group insisted on the execution of King Louis XVI while Condorcet's Democratic-Republicans were forming a plan for him to seek exile in the United States.

One of the most ironic and seemingly contradictory aspects of the Terror was that Robespierre was able to disguise his true intentions by brandishing the banner of Rousseau, by then a celebrated French hero. However, as he and his allies rallied the *sans-culottes* into a mob-like frenzy, he started a relentless anti-intellectual purge of all his political rivals. This campaign not only suppressed free speech and freedoms of the press but also targeted some of the Enlightenment's leading thinkers. Many were sentenced by Robespierre's Committee on Public Safety as traitors and subsequently executed. By bringing so many of his rivals to the guillotine, Robespierre was able to further consolidate his power. These same actions also silenced a whole class of intellectuals and competent leaders whom Robespierre successfully terrified until his arrest by the National Convention and his own death by guillotine in July 1794. In a little over a year, more than 17,000 were executed during the Terror as "enemies of the Revolution."

Robespierre's hypocrisy in using Rousseau to justify his coup of the Revolution, and the later purging (and guillotining) of many intellectuals, still astounds today. Israel's concise summary of the Terror is worth including here as he clearly distinguishes between the progressiveness of the previous stages of the French Revolution and the dictatorial violence of the Terror:

> A very different kind of French Revolution then rapidly evolved during the summer and autumn of 1793 into the unconstitutionality, repression, horror, organized popular coercion, and bloodshed of the Terror . . . The French populist authoritarianism generated by Marat and Robespierre was not in any way an offshoot of the democratic republican Revolution of 1789–93 but an entirely separate and fiercely antagonistic social, cultural and political trend . . . Enlightenment intellectuals, both moderate and radical . . . rejected the Montagne and denounced the calls for dictatorship and systematic election-rigging, intimidation and elimination of all criticism and muzzling of the press.[3]

Interestingly, it took some time for the true nature of the Terror to become transparent in the United States. Jefferson, who was back in the United States, initially had trouble distinguishing between the horrifying news from abroad and the usual anti-French slander often propagated by the American Moderates, who had always been more hostile to the French Revolution. But once the true nature of the Terror became clear, both Moderate and Radical Enlightenment thinkers in the United States denounced this calamitous turn in the French Revolution.

Regarding this tragic history, an important clarifying point is in order, once again because of quite confusing conventional labeling. Terms are not only relative, as we discussed previously, but also are inclined to stick based on the context in which they first arose. For much of recent history, Robespierre and the Montagne were labeled by the intelligentsia as "Radicals," and some of our Radical Enlightenment thinkers, such as Condorcet, were called "Moderates." But with the benefit of hindsight, these labels are not only unfortunate but are quite misleading, since Condorcet, Paine, Brissot, Franklin, Jefferson, and the entire Radical Enlightenment entourage advocated systematic sweeping change to create a more egalitarian and free society (certainly as contrasted with the ideals of the Moderate Enlightenment thinkers). The Montagnards, on the contrary, were those who tried to impede these advancements and assert an authoritarian regime curtailing freedom of expression and individual liberty.

By rejecting the core values of the Enlightenment with a virulent anti-intellectualism and a repressive totalitarian approach, in retrospect, as Thomas Jefferson and so many others have said, the Montagnards were the Revolution's great betrayers—their systematic violation of human rights was utterly antithetical to what both Moderate and Radical Enlightenment thinkers advocated. Furthermore, the social force that put the wind in the Montagnards' sails was incontrovertibly the Counter-Enlightenment, which was enabled by the formation of a political alliance between the conniving yet redoubtable Montagnards and the clergy, working in concert to target the intellectual elites of the French Revolution. Thus, the Terror, in addition to its campaign of violence, both rejected Enlightenment ideals and restored the church to the dominant role it had held in the prerevolutionary era.

* * *

Revolutionary clamor in France was far from settled after the Terror ended. When the dictatorship of Robespierre and the Montagne fell in 1794, a French constitution with a two-chamber legislature and an executive committee, the *Directoire*, was instituted. After some shuffling, a group called the *Ideologues* eventually rose in prominence and successfully reinstituted the Radical Enlightenment principles in a new phase of the Revolution. Many of the *Ideologues* were Radical Enlightenment thinkers (including Volney and Sieyès, mentioned previously) who had been imprisoned or forced to emigrate during the Terror. So while Condorcet, Brissot, and many others became casualties of the Terror, their remarkable contributions were revived by their former colleagues. The goal of the *Ideologues* was to restore the secular Enlightenment to "its proper place as the veritable guide of a humanity bolstered by democracy, human rights and the world revolution."[4]

It seemed that a stable republic might endure in France despite all the chronic upheaval. By 1797, the French Republic was reimposing core republican values from above by firmly repressing both royalism and popular authoritarianism. But during this period, royal opposition and instability grew until the 1799 coup that led to Napoleon's consolidation of power and his subsequent self-declaration as emperor in 1804, marking an end to the 18th-century revolutionary period in France.

The French Revolution was really three separate revolutions, each characteristic of a specific predominant force of the late 18th century. The democratic-republican revolution from 1788–1793 was the most important, despite its successive defeats. This was the revolution firmly rooted in the Radical Enlightenment, best embodied in Condorcet's 1793 constitution. The subsequent authoritarian populist revolution (1793–1794) was characterized by tremendous violence and repression and in many ways was a precursor to 20th-century fascism. This phase was plainly rooted in anti-intellectual Counter-Enlightenment impulses. Next, a constitutional monarchism inspired by the Moderate Enlightenment was established following a brief reemergence of the democratic orientation of the *Ideologues*. This final phase invoked Montesquieu and the British model with a strong executive in Napoleon. Eventually, this third revolutionary phase founded on Moderate Enlightenment impulses was terminated by Napoleon himself at the onset of his dictatorship and self-declaration as emperor.

* * *

In the next section of the book, we commence a more detailed review of a series of discrete episodes in United States history in which the gulf between the Moderate and Radical Enlightenment schools of thought resurfaced and stubbornly divided society as the American Schism endured. In that upcoming section, we will first return to the Revolutionary Era and further examine the dynamics that emerged following the writing of the Declaration of Independence. This twelve-year period is remarkably illustrative of our overall theme; we will see that the pendulum that the Radicals had succeeded in swinging to their side in 1776 came swinging back to the Moderate side with considerable momentum by 1788. In fact, the great rupture that developed between the two sides of the American Schism at that time would persist through the end of the century.

But in the last decade of the 18th century, a powerful Counter-Enlightenment force would also emerge in the United States, much as it did in France. This force would manifest as a dynamic superimposition on the already existing split between the Moderate and Radical Enlightenment ideals in the nascent country. Furthermore, this specific episode demonstrates striking parallels to our discussion of the Terror. For this reason, we breach the chronology (for which I ask the reader's indulgence) to discuss this fascinating period in this chapter.

COUNTER-ENLIGHTENMENT IN THE UNITED STATES: THE SECOND GREAT AWAKENING

Following the ratification of the U.S. Constitution, the already established divide between the Moderates and the Radicals revealed itself in the first two dominant political parties in the country—the Federalists (Washington, Adams, Hamilton) and the

Democratic-Republicans (Jefferson, Madison, Monroe). In fact, as the number of contentious issues left unanswered by the Constitution multiplied, the split only became further polarized. (For simplicity, going forward I will refer to the Democratic-Republicans as simply "Republicans.") It became clear as their divisions mounted that the two political parties interpreted the significance of the American Revolution in conflicting ways, which prompted further sorting as both camps competed for influence among the leading patriots of the young nation.

Adams, Hamilton, and Jefferson, all serving in President Washington's cabinet, had different interpretations of the tumultuous stages of the French Revolution as well. Although it would take years to fully grasp the dreadful nature of the Terror phase, the Federalists at this time unequivocally deemed the French Revolution a failure. However, it would require the benefit of a bit more perspective before the events in France would relinquish their illusionary allure for Jefferson and his fellow Republicans.

Thus, in the early 1790s, while the Federalists condemned the French Revolution, the Republicans continued to view it as conjoined to the American Revolution, and they considered France to be the sister republic of the United States. Once again, this bitter disagreement became a concrete manifestation of the split between the Moderate and Radical Enlightenment thinkers. "The irresolvable dispute about the French Revolution's significance in American politics was thus an extension of the clash of theories and interests in the American Revolution itself, and ultimately a collision over the future of America's own constitutional principles."[5]

Most importantly, the repercussions of the deepening schism were significant, fundamentally impacting the "optimal governing prototype" envisioned by each of the two parties. The Federalists viewed the English mixed-government model consistent with Moderate Enlightenment ideals as the targeted framework, while the

Republicans firmly advocated a democratic republic rooted in Radical Enlightenment principles. For the Federalists, an active central government was indispensable to guide the overall success of the nation and resolve the inevitable conflicts among the various states. However, the very notion of a powerful central government conflicted with Jefferson's pure republicanism. For Jefferson, Hamilton's prototype represented another version of the British Crown, "the latter-day apparition of a political dragon he thought he had slain in 1776."[6]

These philosophical differences created acrimony as both camps vied for dominance. The conflict escalated further when Hamilton convinced Washington to dissolve the entire French alliance in 1793 and to adopt a pro-British posture, against Jefferson's fierce objections. This ultimately led to the Jay Treaty in 1794, in which the Federalists built a rapprochement with Britain to settle many of the outstanding issues from the Revolutionary War. For Jefferson, America severing its alignment with France signified a shattering loss since it also represented the repudiation of the entire democratic-republic model and, for Jefferson personally, a betrayal of those whom he viewed as his revolutionary colleagues overseas.

These events first forced Jefferson's resignation from Washington's cabinet and into semiretirement in Monticello, and then back into a more active role in furthering the agenda of the Republican Party as rivals to Hamilton's Federalists. "As Jefferson saw it, the Jay Treaty was a repudiation of the Declaration of Independence, the Franco-American alliance, the revolutionary movement sweeping through Europe and all the political principles on which he staked his public career as an American statesman."[7]

The entrenched conflicts between the two parties could not be resolved merely by a cluster of men arguing in a crowded room. On top of the intellectual sparring between their political philosophies within the leadership circles, both the Federalists and the Republicans faced the formidable political problem of amassing support among the citizens of the new country, who were taking more and more interest in the affairs of their new government.

Initially, both political parties relied on the press to attempt to sway public opinion. At this time, social class and geography were the determining factors in public support; the Federalists were the party of the established traditional ruling elite, more concentrated in the Northeast, and the Republicans were the party of the laborers and farmers, more concentrated in the South. But these divisions were very fluid, and the Federalists recognized that they were struggling to gain popular support among the common people across all geographies precisely because of the elitism intrinsic in their governing philosophy.

The fact that the Federalists had difficulty relating to common citizens was hardly surprising since they prescribed government by well-educated privileged elites, with the masses largely excluded (consistent with Moderate Enlightenment principles). Moreover, the Federalists recognized that unless they could chart a course to overcome this obstacle, their political future would be greatly jeopardized. The ever-astute Jefferson was also aware of this political dynamic and believed that ultimately the common people would reject Adams's and Hamilton's elitist stance and support the more egalitarian democratic republicanism promoted by Jefferson's party.

This was a time of increasing popular political involvement at the grassroots level. The word "democracy" began to be used more in the press, and democratic societies began to arise. For a while, it seemed that Jeffersonian democracy was winning the ideological argument among the people, with public opinion tilting against the Federalists. Furthermore, the Federalists had already lost a significant amount of support in the early 1790s due to their financial policies, which were viewed as onerous for working people.

However, the Federalists were able to turn the political tide by devising and effectually deploying new political strategies crafted precisely to exploit the nature of the nascent political character blossoming across the American landscape. The political dynamics that resulted from the two parties' fierce battle in the arena of public support are worth delineating in some detail, specifically because they established important and long-lasting precedents for the dynamics at play in political jockeying in subsequent American history: Namely, the juxtaposition between democratic movements and popular religious revivals both arising bottom-up from common citizens on the one hand, and the weaponization of these trends by political leaders endeavoring to curry favor from the populace on the other.

As we will see, rhetorical tactics deployed by political leaders intending to commandeer popular movements would become an American tradition. Over the course of our history, this type of political maneuver has repeatedly allowed partisan leaders of all types to accumulate and consolidate their own electoral power and diminish the influence of their political rivals. The first Federalist strategy to build support at this juncture was to portray, for political gain, the bottom-up democratic movements of the era as both subversive and perilous to the young nation.

As news from the other side of the Atlantic was reaching America, many of the democratic movements of the period were characterized by a degree of protest and even lawlessness. By the mid-1790s, many Americans had heard of the bloodshed in France and were justifiably horrified; they were fearful that the democratic protest movement on this side of the Atlantic might take a similarly violent turn. The Federalists sensed an opportunity to capitalize on the increasing public anxiety and began associating the violence in France with the democratic protest movement in America. They forcefully deployed scare tactics, proclaiming that the unrest emerging from popular democratic movements was a precursor to a Terror like the one that had erupted in France. As American citizens were navigating an uncertain future, many feared that the carnage in France would indeed reach American shores. While the tactics deployed by the Federalists were at best shrewd and more likely duplicitous, overall, the Federalists' efforts proved quite successful, resulting in a marked decrease in popular support for Jeffersonian democracy.

To rouse fear among American citizens, Washington and Hamilton made public spectacles of using force to stamp out these "rebellions." One such protest that did escalate into violence became known as the Whiskey Rebellion. Not only did the Federalists strong-arm the protesters, but with a masterful political stroke they successfully connected the Whiskey Rebellion to a broader group of other democratic movements that had sprung up around the country, despite the fact that most of these latter movements were relatively peaceful. Jefferson was both cognizant of and outraged by what he viewed as unlawful manipulation and the encroachments on the freedoms of assembly and expression. For Jefferson and Madison, Washington's attack on the democratic societies expressing popular discontent was an attack on the core principle—the unalienable right of the people to express their voice—of the American Revolution itself. (Trump's threatened crackdown and fearmongering with respect to the mostly peaceful protests of the Black Lives Matter movement in 2020 provides a striking parallel.)

In addition to spinning the upsurge in the democratic sentiment for their own political advantages, the Federalists supplemented their appeal to fears of violence by tapping into yet another broad bottom-up movement from this era, the Second Great Awakening. This concurrent resurgence of devout piety would have a momentous impact on the religious tenor of the new nation.

At the end of the 18th century, many Americans were becoming fatigued by the constant state of change since the Revolutionary Era. The highly polarizing environment of the young nation and the prospect of interminable change were indisputably anxiety provoking. Beginning in Kentucky and Tennessee, and then spreading rapidly, the Second Great Awakening, a broad Protestant revival, brought a much-needed comforting blanket of spiritual faith to huge swaths of people and counteracted the high level of socio-political uncertainty experienced in the previous decades. Consequently, it attracted many converts to new Protestant denominations, especially Methodists and Baptists. While the Presbyterians also gained members, the numerical strength of the Baptists and Methodists grew relative to those of the denominations that were dominant in the colonial period—Anglicans, Presbyterians, and Congregationalists.

The Federalists, sensing that a large and growing part of the population were adopting more pious views, quickly allied themselves with this new movement to further their political ends. Recognizing that they could effectively use religion as a wedge issue to stem the growing support of their political rivals, they labeled Republicans as "anti-Christian" and embraced the religious upsurge. What made this strategy remarkably easy to implement was the fact that the entire country was well aware of Jefferson's antireligious stance and his antagonism toward strict religious doctrine.

In this endeavor, the Federalists found an important rhetorical asset in the orator Noah Webster. As the "Father of American Scholarship and Education," Webster was a powerful speaker with a grounding in religious Calvinist doctrine. He was emblematic of the resurgence of religion that characterized the Awakening. Hamilton hired him as the editor of the Federalist newspaper, which became, in addition to a medium for publishing his famous speeches, a powerful vehicle to preach to the American people. Webster advocated for Christian principles to become more central in American life and warned the public of the perils of the Terror in France. By blaming the disastrous outcome of the French Revolution on a dangerous move away from religion, Webster helped shift public opinion dramatically away from the "blasphemous" Republicans and toward the religiously tolerant Federalists.

The Federalist strategy of appealing to religion proved so effective not only due to Webster's service as a commanding general of potent rhetoric, but also because the Federalists had a well-trained "army" at their disposal waiting to go to battle. Pious authorities all across the nation responded to the Federalists' provocation and mobilized massively against Jefferson and Madison's party, portraying it as being antireligious. Following Webster's lead, preachers all over the country fell in line, emphatically differentiating and delinking the French Revolution from the American Revolution. The former was portrayed as an anti-Christian bloodbath, the latter as a noble and spiritually ordained endeavor.

The growing influence of Webster and other religious leaders starkly demonstrated that appeals couched in religious language could be a powerful political weapon, of service to the Federalist strategy of delegitimizing popular democratic movements, which were deemed destabilizing and violent. Indeed, a major theme in the newly embraced Federalist narrative was to contrast the French Revolution, which had abandoned religion, with its purported acceptance in the American Revolution. Preachers of the movement insisted that by embracing a nationalist Protestant conception of "American Identity," the colonists had avoided the fate of their French counterparts and successfully created a new American nation. Further, this surge in religious influence planted a new seed of "American exceptionalism," which quickly created

> widespread revulsion against the religiously subversive texts of Paine
> and the radicals . . . and a growing impulse within American society
> and culture in the late 1790s toward anti-*philosophisme*, anti-republi-
> canism, and anti-cosmopolitanism blended with resurgent organized
> religion to verge on becoming the new American mainstream.[8]

With this overall plan, the Federalists deftly outmaneuvered their Republican opponents, derailing grassroots democratic movements and recasting the American Revolution within a storyline of divine inspiration.

This episode in post-revolutionary America is particularly notable for the manner in which it considerably distorted Americans' understanding of their own history, which to some extent persists even today. The Federalists' political tactics created a *revisionist* view of the recent revolution, only two decades old. John Quincy Adams and other influential Moderates of the time insisted that the "Revolution's essence was the blending of liberty with Bible-based Christianity" and created a "new religious mythology of the Revolution."[9] Suddenly, the Revolution seemed to assume a divinely inspired religious aspect, one that did not at all accord with the actual events on the ground.

A famous painting commemorating George Washington depicts him handing the Constitution down to the people in the form of tablets etched in stone, as if God had granted it to him as a holy gift, much like the biblical Ten Commandments had been handed by God to Moses. The implication that the Constitution was a "sacred text" utterly belies the intensely secular debates that unfolded during its writing and ratification. It also conveys the erroneous notion that the Constitution was rigid when in fact the Framers intended the precise opposite; they envisaged the Constitution as a living and evolving national charter.

Moreover, the notion that the Founders were divinely inspired was an utter misrepresentation. On the contrary, most of our Founders (including the Moderates) were "long-standing adversaries of instituted religious authority," even if they were privately men of faith. Furthermore, the separation of church and state had been codified in the Bill of Rights of the Constitution and had been reaffirmed by the 1797 Treaty of Tripoli, which specified in unambiguous terms that the country was not founded in any sense on the Christian religion.[10]

Interestingly, the Founders were relatively silent regarding their private religious practices. Washington was an Anglican, but he was also a Freemason. Throughout his public life, Washington was very private and noncommittal regarding his faith, yet at Washington's funeral in

1799, he was eulogized as a new Moses, "the instrument of God, the very tool of divine providence."[11] "If the Revolution's most fervent adherents . . . were typically long-standing adversaries of instituted religious authority and theology . . . the Federalist press and the pulpit . . . succeeded in replacing the historical record with a popular mythology of the Founders' commitment to conventional religious notions."[12]

There was also a corresponding reinterpretation of other historical events of the time. The pivotal role played by France in the success of the American Revolution, both intellectually and financially, was stricken from the record. This was especially unfortunate because in the prior decades, as France enthusiastically supported the American patriots (both when France was officially a monarchy under Louis XVI and again when she declared herself a republic), many Americans jubilantly embraced French culture. In contrast to the gratitude felt by the American public vis-à-vis France in the 1770s and 1780s, the new ideology took root and changed the portrayal of America's first ally. The new narrative depicted the French as holders of radical views, "a menacing contagion" spread in America "via clandestine channels by the same malignant conspirators responsible for the French Revolution's irreligion."[13] Based on the espousal of this new narrative, attitudes toward France soured considerably. This posed a problem for the Federalists, as America was a young country in need of support. Accordingly, the Federalist government, in need of strong allies at this stage, turned back toward Britain, establishing a rapprochement with the "mother" country. The public mood soon followed.

It is also instructive to compare and contrast how Counter-Enlightenment forces in this era were mobilized in the United States and in France. On both sides of the Atlantic, self-interested political actors found ways to advance Counter-Enlightenment philosophies and link them to populist concerns in order to discredit the Radical Enlightenment movement and associate it with a demonist, antireligious philosophy. The local church authorities in both countries were utilized as armies to rapidly disseminate this view among the citizens, reinforcing religious dogma and warning the public of the menace of "cosmopolitan lifestyles." In both countries, Counter-Enlightenment thinking was channeled into a populist fervor that expressly rejected Enlightenment principles such as reason and secular pursuits as being inimical to religious faith and linked to "subversive" elites. This rejection rallied passionate anti-intellectualism against the new ideas that had recently prompted dramatic changes in society.

It is not surprising that linking the anxiety related to change and uncertainty to the radical forces that first initiated that change became a very effective strategy on both sides of the Atlantic. The tone of this groundswell in both countries was emotional, appealing to traditional religious dogma and rejecting rational argument. Notably, in both cases, the fuse ignited among the masses subsequently caused great collateral damage to society overall. In the case of France, this counter-movement rejected the influence of all Enlightenment thinkers, leading to the Terror and the persecution and execution of many *philosophes*. In addition to tremendous violence, French society became authoritarian, dismissing recently acquired freedoms of speech, the press, etc.

Fortunately, in the case of the United States, the consequences were less extreme. On this side of the Atlantic, the Moderate Enlightenment camp (i.e., the Federalists) took advantage of Counter-Enlightenment sympathies to gain the upper hand politically without fomenting violence. Nonetheless, the *fear of such violence* was deployed as a powerful political tool. In reaction to these fears, as in France, the subsequent period in America saw parallel and significant clawbacks of freedoms that had been deemed so cherished just two decades prior. The charge that America was "being contaminated by intellectual subversion" was used by the anti-Jeffersonian caucus in Congress to pass the Alien and Sedition Acts in the late 1790s. These undemocratic acts, which suppressed free speech and liberty in the name of law and order and the protection of the country from traitors, were signed by President Adams with broad Federalist support.

Given the liberties that Americans had died for just two decades earlier, the enactment of these repressive laws is astonishing and marked "the advent in America for the first time of an institutionalized, systematic repression of radical views."[14] Like most authoritarian acts, it was sustained by populist passions and fear. These acts also had the secondary effect of tolerating and even encouraging criticism of foreigners, and charges against Americans of seditious collaboration with foreigners were legally sanctioned and pursued.

At this point in time, many began to view immigration as a serious threat to the new nation. This resulted in concrete anti-immigration measures: The waiting period for immigrants to become citizens was extended, and immigrants, even those who were citizens, could be surveilled and deported. These measures deeply divided American public opinion, and many journalists were arrested and convicted for the opinions they expressed.

Eventually, the Federalists may have outplayed their hand; the Alien and Sedition Acts became increasingly unpopular and spurred anti-Federalist sentiment, which led to Jefferson narrowly winning the presidency in 1800 and the Federalists losing their controlling grip on Congress. Nonetheless, it is quite remarkable that just decades after the Revolutionary Era, and only years since the freedom of political expression had become enshrined in our Constitution, the federal government was willing to silence radical political views for fear of subversion. While this period in American history did not quite witness the sort of political witch hunt experienced in later American centuries, it undeniably presented a contradiction for a new nation recently birthed with the foundational premise that freedom of expression was a central element of its credo.

In summary, the Second Great Awakening, as a Counter-Enlightenment movement, rejected the Enlightenment basis for the American Revolution and infused it with a religious interpretation. Furthermore, the practice of rousing zeal via impassioned preaching revealed itself to be *a potent political force*. By tapping into the resurgence of religious piety, the Federalists were able to create and solidify a firmer bond with the citizens of the new nation by *appealing to their passions as opposed to their logic*. As a political technique for those in or seeking power, this would establish a powerful precedent that would shape the American political landscape of the future.

UNTANGLING POPULISM AND COUNTER-ENLIGHTENMENT BELIEFS

We have observed how, on both sides of the Atlantic, political leaders seeking power opportunistically leveraged the emotions and passions associated with religious fervor and the fear and anxiety associated with societal change for their own political ends. In both countries, in order to garner popular support and repudiate their rivals, shrewd political actors succeeded at co-opting populist movements that emerged from the ground up and reflected the authentic yearnings, fears, and sentiments of common people.

The fact that both of these Counter-Enlightenment movements were "populist" is somewhat ironic and illustrates how confusingly problematic the term "populism" has become in the evolution of our political discourse. As we will see repeatedly over the course of this book, Counter-Enlightenment religious views have frequently engendered or been associated with populist movements. But because the term "populist" can be quite misleading, let me clarify by distinguishing between two different uses of the term in our collective contemporary vernacular. The important distinction between these two common uses relates to the *agency* that invokes populist sentiment and the *motive and intent* behind its expression.

In its purest sense, "populism" refers to any political dynamic that strives to appeal to ordinary people who sense that their concerns are being disregarded or their needs marginalized by established political leaders. First and perhaps foremost, populism is the coalescing of antielite sentiments into a bottom-up people's movement, advocating inclusiveness of and support for ordinary nonelite citizens. Accordingly, any populist movement promoting the inclusion of broader egalitarian civic voices is fully consistent with Radical Enlightenment ideals. Such a movement can be considered "populist" based on its rejection of the concept that the elite should dictate or impose policy because they somehow know what is best for the ordinary people.

Given the tendency for elites to be in positions of political power, this form of populism, which gains momentum from the ground up and amalgamates critical mass by either rapidly or gradually accumulating followers, can be (and has been) a potent and effective force of democratic empowerment. One of the great examples of this type of populist movement was the late 19th-century emergence of the Farmers' Alliance that emerged bottom-up and progressively garnered support culminating in the creation of the People's Party (to be reviewed in Part II).

A priori, bottom-up populism does not necessarily denote a religious or nonrational Counter-Enlightenment orientation, although in practice it often has. In such circumstances, when populism is associated with religious viewpoints promoting a more egalitarian structure of society, this religiously inspired populism presents an apparent contradiction that merits exploration. Is religiously inspired populism a Counter-Enlightenment force since it relies on faith-based principles? Or is it a Radical Enlightenment force since its purpose is creating a more egalitarian society? The answer is *it can be both, depending on agency, motive, and intent.*

On one hand, religiously inspired populism can be characterized as Counter-Enlightenment since it appeals to faith instead of rational thought as its justifying motive. But at the same time, this form of populism reveals a Radical Enlightenment political impulse if its intent is the promotion of a more inclusive societal structure that apportions equal weight to all strata of the populace.

Here is an interesting illustration to elucidate the point: A religiously inspired populism that embraces the spirit of the biblical Sermon on the Mount in the Gospel of Matthew and uses it as a political justification for a more democratic society that apportions equal weight to all, expressly society's neediest (e.g., the meek shall inherit the earth), is wholly consistent with Radical Enlightenment principles. So is a rationally inspired populism that argues that a society must rely on the principle of equality for it to serve and authentically qualify as a government of, by, and for the people. Many social contract theorists have deduced such based on logic. The salient difference is one of motive: Radical Enlightenment thinkers use *reason and the rational structure* of the social contract to arrive at their policy, while the pious populist voices use *revelation* to arrive at theirs.[15]

Of course, in practical terms, bottom-up populism is often convoluted and multivocal, rarely surfacing due to one single unifying motive. Populist movements most commonly unite varied voices and draw upon an eclectic range of inspirations, including spiritual faith, rational thinking, popular culture, and empirical observation of developments in society that are perceived to be unfair or immoral. Regardless of motive, such populism has a shared intent. But to the degree that religious principles motivate a bottom-up populist struggle to achieve this egalitarianism (using the terminology of this discussion), we can characterize it as a political dynamic in which the justification or motive is based on Counter-Enlightenment (i.e., faith-based) impulses but the political intent is to realize Radical Enlightenment principles.

Importantly, I contend that bottom-up populist forms of political mobilization, defined as movements emerging from the sentiments of ordinary people (the agents) in order to achieve a more egalitarian society (the intent), have been and can be positive steps in progressively striving toward a democratic republic. Whether the underlying motive for the political mobilization is based on religious faith or rational principles does not nullify the desired intent. Undoubtedly, the Second Great Awakening in many aspects merits this classification, as it was an empowering mobilization of diverse authentic voices.

But what if the *agent* behind populist appeals is not representative of ordinary people but instead represents political actors? And what if the *intent* is not to promote an egalitarian society but to gain political support for their own benefit? The resulting populism evoked for political purposes has a strikingly different connotation. In this context, populism refers to a top-down political tactic used by those in or seeking power (the agent) by intentionally and deliberately rousing passions and often fears (the intent) to generate political support from the citizenry and bolster their own authority (the motive).

Typically, as a political tool, top-down populist appeals have been most effective when they stir passions by simultaneously evoking religious zealotry while demonizing the elite establishment. Furthermore, these appeals are opportunistic and frequently weaponized by those seeking power, mainly in periods of uncertainty or rapid and fear-provoking change. These were precisely the circumstances discussed previously during the 1790s when, in order to gain political support, the Federalists in certain respects hijacked the Second Great Awakening by deploying religious appeals to stir fears and anxiety among the citizenry.

There is a certain logic to why religion is frequently utilized as a theme in these types of appeals. Evoking the stability associated with religious institutions can be extremely comforting in the face of transformation and uncertainty. In addition, if these destabilizing changes are advocated or dictated by elite policymakers who seemingly imposed their policies on the people, these same elite leaders present a convenient political target. In these contexts, manipulating religious themes to further political ends has repeatedly, over the course of history, been quite effective. As discussed, for centuries, such was precisely the go-to tactic of the political power structures in the *ancien régime*.

Markedly, this latter type of top-down populist appeal as wielded by those seeking political power can often seem hypocritical because these same politicians are themselves elite. Of course, when a populist appeal is invoked by a political leader or candidate, the agent's true motive is often obscured; whether these political actors who rely on faith-based appeals are genuinely expressing their religious beliefs or are instead exploiting faith in a duplicitous manner is frequently a topic of heated debate.

Nonetheless, as all of these complexities illustrate, evaluating the forces driving populism in political discourse or antielitist crusades can be quite tricky; untangling motives and intents, specifically when shrewd seasoned politicians are involved, often requires wading through muddied waters. Some interesting questions arise: What are the genuine origins of the populist sentiment? Who initially introduces populist ideas into the political debate? And most importantly, what is their intent? As we will see in Part II, the answers to these questions have been quite inconsistent over the course of our history. At times, populist attitudes have initially bubbled up from the people via civic or religious groups and gradually built momentum over a certain period of time, such as the gradual emergence of the agrarian populist movement in the second half of the 19th century. This movement gained steam over decades as farmers throughout the South and West felt increasingly disenfranchised and ultimately forged a new political party, the People's Party (to be discussed in Part II).

But when these bottom-up movements emerge, political leaders will invariably detect these trends and embrace and champion these ideals. Whether these leaders are political opportunists whose intent is to garner support or genuine believers in faith-based egalitarian principles is sometimes difficult to discern. Nonetheless, quite frequently over the course of our history, political power seekers, sensing prevailing sentiments of economic anxiety and social fears of displacement, have relied on populist rhetoric as an effective tactic to get elected or remain in power.

In sum, I have no intent to vilify bottom-up populism, which can represent a genuine antielitist people's movement entirely consistent with the Radical Enlightenment spirit discussed throughout these pages. Nonetheless, the deployment of top-down populism as a political bludgeon by those seeking power is far too abundant throughout Western democratic societies today. Because evoking populist themes in disingenuous appeals to build political support has become such a mainstay in America, our use of the term populism has become imbued with an undeserved negative connotation. However, the anti-elite aspect of the term as it applies to political participation can be quite egalitarian, reflective of one of the Radical Enlightenment's principal tenets—a firm belief in the great potential of the individual and the conviction that all voices in a society matter.

THE ERRATIC EFFECTS OF COUNTER-ENLIGHTENMENT FORCES

The peculiarities and idiosyncrasies described previously suggest how perplexing it can be to analyze both faith-based Counter-Enlightenment forces and populist movements that have been superimposed upon the American political landscape over the course of our history. In different eras, the dramatic vicissitudes of these forces have resulted in disparate outcomes: at times, constructive and fruitful, at other times, quite detrimental to America's social fabric.

The Second Great Awakening, which we have explored here, is one such case. The period was extremely politically divisive for the American public and solidified the American Schism between the factions that sought to govern the young nation. The enduring result of this dynamic was to render the legacy of the Revolution more ambiguous than ever in the collective spirit of the citizenry at the dawn of the new century.

On the positive side, from the perspective of social and civic discourse, the Second Great Awakening provided an enduring democratizing influence on American society. The period marked the initial development and propagation of a significant voice for women in civic affairs. All through the Revolutionary Era, men dominated the debate about whether to adopt Moderate or Radical Enlightenment principles and governing structures, which invariably left little room for women in the political conversation. This trend was reversed during the Second Great Awakening, when women's voices became the driving force.

The preachers driving the Awakening at the turn of the century initially attracted women in great numbers; while many participants in the Awakening were searching for the stabilizing influence of the church in a sea of enormous change, many women also sought a forum for self-expression to give voice to their previously muffled opinions. In post-Revolutionary America, as working men focused on providing for their families, whether in the agrarian South or the industrializing North, preachers reached out to women who initially embraced these movements and subsequently brought their husbands and families under the stabilizing tent of the church. This church tradition also spawned the women-led temperance movement to combat the frequent abuse of alcohol that negatively impacted their families. Additionally, women became a driving force in the abolitionist movement, thanks in large part to religious principles that stressed the immorality of slavery.

Thus, in certain aspects, the Second Great Awakening set an important precedent by sanctioning a greater voice for women in American political discourse. The Protestant explosion at the dawn of the 19th century provided an expansive and influential platform upon which women could make their voices heard for the first time with respect to the most important issues of the era—the abolition of slavery and temperance.

By mobilizing women, the Second Great Awakening was a precursor to the fight for women's suffrage, which would gain momentum as the 19th century progressed. Mary Wollstonecraft, an important English Enlightenment thinker, published her groundbreaking book *A Vindication of the Rights of Woman* in 1792 after being inspired by the French Revolution. In this book, Wollstonecraft made a pointedly rational case for women's equality. But in America, it was the precedent of the Second Great Awakening that led to an explosion of many diverse women's voices making important contributions throughout the 19th century. For example, Sarah Grimké became an important contributor to the abolitionist movement. Grimké's activism was rooted in her religious beliefs as a Quaker. In contrast, Margaret Fuller, a journalist and women's rights activist, advanced her views in the Radical Enlightenment tradition. This broad set of women's voices entering the political discourse eventually led to pivotal events like the convention in Seneca Falls in 1848, which launched the national women's suffrage movement. Through the pioneering work of talented leaders like Susan B. Anthony, Elizabeth Cady Stanton, Lucy Stone, and countless others, and seven decades of persistence, women's suffrage became a reality in 1920 with the ratification of the 19th Amendment to the Constitution.

* * *

A second related and lasting impact of the Second Great Awakening was the establishment and elevation of the role of the church in the young nation's civic affairs. (A prior religious revival, the First Great Awakening, had occurred concurrently in Britain and the colonies in the 1730s and 1740s.) The rapid spread of religious institutions in the new country was indicative of their important role in bringing individuals together into community relationships and forming the bonds vital for the flourishing of civil society. In this sense, the Awakening was a harbinger of the central role the church would come to play in American society. Throughout our history, Americans would rely on many diverse structures and institutions to create a "public square," a communal forum in which to deliberate and act in unison with fellow citizens. In this regard, the Second Great Awakening established another important and enduring precedent in the young nation: that of the church occupying an indispensable and central place within the American public square.

With the benefit of hindsight, perhaps nowhere has the concept of a public square been more widely expressed through American history than in the hundreds of thousands of Christian, Muslim, and Jewish communities of worship that have propagated across the country. The role of the church in fostering tight-knit communities can hardly be overemphasized as a phenomenon linked intricately to the American experience.

While the Counter-Enlightenment episodes we have examined in the United States and France show how faith-based arguments have been manipulated, at times with damaging repercussions, once again, an important distinction is in order. The civic roles that local religious institutions have played as a critical part of the American social fabric must be distinguished from a very dissimilar Counter-Enlightenment force that often gets deployed in a political context: namely, the concept of imposing the strict dogma of *one centralized* religious institution on our governing structures. When one religion influences or commandeers our governing institutions, we encounter a very different type of Counter-Enlightenment force.

In terms of playing an important role in the public square, Counter-Enlightenment impulses clearly reflect their many wide-ranging positive aspects: empowering new and fresh voices within a community, providing fulfillment outside the secular realm, and endeavoring to create and sustain societal improvements. However, as described in some of the preceding episodes, aligning religious doctrine with governing powers or institutions can often represent an oppressive intrusion of religion into the civic structure of society.

Thus, in evaluating the Counter-Enlightenment impulses generated and nurtured in religious institutions, we need to carefully weigh their positive civic and social contributions against the negative propensities associated with those same institutions (e.g., frequent promulgation of intolerant thought and behavior, overabundance of cases of physical and sexual abuse, etc.). In any case, a debate about the pros and cons of American religious institutions is well beyond the scope of this book. A spiritual life transcending secular existence has always been and continues to be today a vibrant part of human experience across the globe. That religion and spiritual philosophies reject an *exclusive* focus on reason and secular knowledge and prescribe a greater importance to faith in the human experience is inarguably the modus operandi for the majority of Americans. It is the *balance between faith and reason* that is essential for assessing the political ramifications of Counter-Enlightenment thought on the American experience and which is central to our exploration here.

In any case, as discussed previously, Counter-Enlightenment strands of thought can have positive effects on society. At times in our history, they have contributed to the promotion of Radical Enlightenment principles such as expanded participation and representation. However, Counter-Enlightenment forces have also consistently produced the toxic effects of oppressive disenfranchisement throughout our history. When Counter-Enlightenment thinking is weaponized to enforce dogma and uphold discriminatory and oppressive hierarchies of power (which has happened all too frequently in America), its harmful effects on society and the impediments it presents to freedom and liberty must be condemned.

* * *

The schism between the Radical and Moderate Enlightenment ideals that emerged at the nation's founding resulted in two contrasting interpretations of the significance of the American Revolution and two conflicting visions of what the American republic could become. This schism would continue to influence debates about the country's governing structure and future outlook—omnipresent contending visions continually vying for predominance. At the same time, however, the rivalry was often muddled by other complicating factors. Counter-Enlightenment forces, as manifested in popular movements drawing inspiration from faith-based viewpoints and practices, would continue to be superimposed on the schism between Moderate and Radical Enlightenment principles in dynamic ways and with unpredictable consequences. Therefore, after the seminal period of the country's founding, the American landscape could no longer be accurately characterized solely as a struggle between Moderate and Radical Enlightenment ideals. Moving forward, this rivalry was also shaped by political movements and populist mobilizations echoing the powerful religious refrains of the Counter-Enlightenment.

Part II

HOW THE SCHISM
HAS DIVIDED AMERICA
ACROSS THE CENTURIES

One of the hallmarks of a pluralistic society characterized by freedom of expression is that a plethora of diverse thoughts and beliefs invariably contend for prominence in what manifests as a crowded sea of voices. At best, the resulting public discourse can be edifying, shedding new light on multifaceted problems and thereby enriching and advancing the debate to new and productive frontiers. However, during periods of great conflict or transformation, this clash of voices often gets escalated from a contentious yet still coherent discussion to higher levels of confrontation characterized by acrimonious division in society and, at times, unfortunately, horrific violence and tragic consequences. Such is the case with the American Schism.

In Part II, we will explore a few select eras in American history that are particularly illustrative of the more contentious episodes triggered by the American Schism, episodes that acutely reveal how the dramatic oscillations between the rival impulses reviewed in Part I left their mark on the country. However, in these eras, instead of a two-dimensional back-and-forth fluctuation between the Radical and Moderate Enlightenment views, which typified the earliest eras in our country's history, the superimposition of Counter-Enlightenment perspectives vastly complicated the picture. As we will see, as all of these forces intermingled in the crucible of the American landscape, the many vicissitudes resulted in unpredictable outcomes. As a result, the evolution of our republic has in no way, shape, or form moved in a straight line or in one direction.

As outlined in the first section of this book, the emerging and critical differences between two rival schools of Enlightenment thought crystallized into the first manifestation of the American Schism—a bifurcation of ideals contending for influence at the birth of the new nation that resulted in a stark contrast between two contending visions of the new republic. These opposing ideals and divergent visions spun into rival governing models that shaped our founding period. But as discussed in the last chapter, an important and consequential additional set of forces was superimposed in the decades following the revolutionary period.

As Newton's third law of physics states: for every force in nature there is an equal and opposite reaction or counterforce. While of course the physical world and the social and civic worlds operate in separate realms, with their own discrete laws, the Newtonian analogy is also illustrative of the socio-political forces acting on the American landscape. The overall thrust of the Enlightenment era, through all its vagaries, was a *secular focus on reason and human achievement.* Whether moderate or radical in nature, Enlightenment forces consistently stimulated, and at times coerced, societal change. Inexorably, such change is exhilarating for some, painful and threatening for others, and ambiguous and volatile for most.

Due to these erratic effects, significant societal transformation inevitably encounters Newtonian resistance in the form of a pull in the opposite direction, frequently toward the stabilizing nature of previous periods before such change occurred; the unfamiliar is often the enemy of the familiar. Intuitively this makes sense: the more volatile the current climate, the more uncertain the immediate future. In such environments, the stress associated with a precarious future breeds, among many, a yearning for the perceived greatness or stability of the past.

In the centuries following the Enlightenment, this Newtonian pull manifested as the magnetic allure of the steadiness and dependability of religious dogma and stratified societies of previous eras.

Just as Enlightenment principles led to unparalleled changes in society, along with great uncertainty about the future, Counter-Enlightenment beliefs intensified the thirst for the stability of religious doctrine and the familiarity of traditional societal roles. The order, structure, and comforting equanimity provided by the church were the core of its appeal during uncertain times.

However, the superimposition of this Counter-Enlightenment force was not a fleeting phenomenon; it would leave an indelible mark on American society for centuries to come. Ironically, the Revolutionary Era was unique in the respect that it was undoubtedly the most secular period in American history. Ever since, Counter-Enlightenment forces have pushed back with waxing or waning momentum. Just as Enlightenment principles themselves would endure and transform with various contours and new dimensions over the centuries up through contemporary times, opposing forces pulling toward nonsecular realms and new forms of spirituality would also acquire thrust. As the following "deep dives" illustrate, all of these influences (the differing Enlightenment views and opposing Counter-Enlightenment beliefs) are not only detectable but interact in consequential and often unexpected ways on the battleground that is the American experience.

Chapter 8

FROM THE 1776 RADICAL DECLARATION TO THE 1787 MODERATE CONSTITUTION

As examined previously, the revolutionary period itself was unique in that the Moderate and Radical Enlightenment schools contended for prominence in the absence of the strong Counter-Enlightenment forces that would superimpose themselves in subsequent periods. It is this period to which we now return for our first investigative dive into the back-and-forth pendulum swings between the opposing poles of the American Schism.

THE RADICAL THRUST LEADS TO A DECLARATION FOR A NEW AND MODERN WORLD

From today's perspective, one of the most interesting aspects of the Continental Congresses of the Revolutionary Era is that none of the delegates (including the Founders) were ever *elected* by the people. Yet these unelected leaders would be pushed by an intransigent Crown and pulled by the triumvirate of Franklin, Jefferson, and Paine to a more radical view of how best to resolve their grievances during the crucial two-year period from the meeting of the First Continental Congress (September 1774) up through the convening of the Second Continental Congress (June 1776). The push and pull dynamics during this period, sometimes referred to as "the Spirit of '76," swung the pendulum from a moderate set of solutions, specifically some form of settlement with the Crown, to the more radical posture of a total break with Britain and a fresh and independent new beginning.

The influence exerted by Franklin, Jefferson, and Paine was provided as much through their quilled pens as through intensive debates with their counterparts. And events on the ground during these years shifted in their favor. By the time the Second Continental Congress sat, the country was already at war following the opening set of armed conflicts at Lexington and Concord, Massachusetts, in April 1775. As a consequence of this dramatic escalation of tensions, British government mechanisms in the colonies were essentially on hiatus. Therefore, while the First Congress was predominantly a discussion about grievances, the Second Congress was forced to deal with the much more pressing problems of assuming the role of a functioning government and readying for combat.

The First Continental Congress had been convened in response to the blockade of Boston Harbor and Parliament's enactment of the punitive Intolerable Acts (itself a response to the Boston Tea Party). As a result of these earlier debates, "no one . . . favored separation from Britain, although delegates differed on the likelihood of reconciliation, on how best to seek it, and on what terms would be minimally acceptable."[1] Yet the dramatically intensified political context of the Second Continental Congress must have made the character of the first seem closer to a group venting session. The dire prospect of more sustained combat had caused a significant increase in unease among the colonists by the time of the Second Congress. It was against this backdrop that support for a radical-inspired approach shifted the balance, working against the resistance of the Moderates who themselves confronted the loyalists.

A vivid example of this shift in mood over this short period is provided by the contrast between the posture of the Olive Branch Petition (1775) and the tenor of the debate at the Second Congress. The tone of the Olive Branch Petition was akin to that of a misbehaving child asking for forgiveness and reconciliation from an angry parent; by the convening of the Second Continental Congress, with the war almost a year old, continued expression of allegiance to the king must have seemed almost absurd.

However, the securing of independence through the successful war effort against the Crown was, of course, far from the end of the story. Almost immediately following the conclusion of armed conflict, the pendulum swung back in a significant way to the Moderate Enlightenment flank. In some sense, this was bound to happen. It is one thing to declare independence, but it is quite another to build a working governmental structure complete with all its intricate details. In figuring out these particulars, competent solutions applicable in real-world contexts were sorely needed. And while it is relatively easy to critique existing circumstances, it is much harder to engineer viable alternatives. In this next phase of the Revolution, the Moderates turned out to have more concrete workable solutions to offer than did the Radicals.

At this point in history, the need for educated and experienced leaders was urgent, and the Moderate Enlightenment group's proficiency and familiarity with governing the colonies (gained from prior experience) proved invaluable. However, the governing intricacies of the new union were much more extensive than colonial governing. Transforming the colonies into a governing republic with a capable foreign affairs apparatus, the ability to regulate interstate commerce, and a mechanism to resolve domestic disputes (to name just a few) was a colossal undertaking.

In this respect, the Federalists (who became the political party of the Moderates) could hardly be faulted for their "aristocratic" bias since the knowledgeable and cultivated leaders who could capably implement such solutions were no doubt their educated and well-informed peers. As described previously, the consummate example of this "competence" model was epitomized by the leading Federalist, Alexander Hamilton.

For Hamilton, designing the complex mechanisms for a unified working nation necessitated a *prominent role for a central government*; leaving the individual states to resolve problems among themselves was no doubt a recipe for chaos. Furthermore, pressing problems could only be resolved by coordinating the differing responses of the states. Prime examples were financing the Revolution and setting up the Treasury, by no means trivial exercises.

By the time the Constitutional Convention convened in Philadelphia in May of 1787, when the Founders gathered to "amend" the existing Articles of Confederation, most of the delegates recognized that simple amendments to the Articles would not prove sufficient, and moreover, that developing a working framework to which the thirteen very diverse colonies could agree was surely no easy task. A federal Constitution was also required to reconcile the disparities among the individual state constitutions. These tenacious problems brought once again into sharp focus the many conflicts between the Radical and Moderate Enlightenment views of our Founders. It is precisely because the assignment presented such a formidable challenge, which was only quite imperfectly resolved, that the resulting federal Constitution that would eventually be ratified was so full of ambiguities.

From a philosophical perspective, the contrast between Jefferson and Hamilton is a case in point of the divergence between two sharply conflicting visions grounded in the two distinct Enlightenment traditions. For Alexander Hamilton's Federalist Party, the only adequate governing framework meeting the stringent requirements was to be found in a competent national government endowed with broad powers to coordinate the nation's activities. Further, for Hamilton, this central government could be led only by the educated elites well qualified for these highly demanding positions. Recall that, because they considered the capabilities of the masses inadequate, Hamilton and the Federalists did not have an expansive view of either inclusiveness in governing or broad suffrage. For the Federalists, both were reserved for the domain of the elite classes of society.

By contrast, the Jeffersonian republic was based on a much broader and more egalitarian vision in which the people themselves, through representatives, had access to firm controls on the executive and were afforded much broader overall participation in government. Furthermore, in this model, government was *decentralized*, firmly placing the locus of power closest to the people on the ground. Moreover, the role of the central power, in Jefferson's view, should be as limited as possible to avoid the inevitable abuses that strong central power engenders and from which America declared her independence. The Jeffersonian model stipulated that the preponderance of governing authority be held at the most local level possible. In addition, in many earlier writings, Jefferson, along with the other Radicals, abjured the concept of a chief executive unreservedly for fear of eventual abuse of power. Instead, they advocated that the executive branch comprise a "council of many," a governing concept from classic Greek and Roman philosophers.

It is evident that the Federalist and Republican camps drew on different Enlightenment legacies from Europe. Considering the similarities of the Federalist governing model with the British mixed-government model, the British Enlightenment (Locke, Newton, etc.) was likely a driving influence on their vision. In contrast, the French Enlightenment became the motivating inspiration for the egalitarian vision underpinning Jefferson's Radical Enlightenment camp, which formed the Democratic-Republican Party. The more aristocratic model with a strong, proficient federal government, represented best by Hamilton, quickly locked horns with the more radical Jeffersonian egalitarian model in a battle for the soul of the American Revolution. This would not be a passing trend. It would come to define the next formative period in the early history of the nation.

In addition to the divergent Enlightenment political philosophies of the Federalists and the Republicans, the orientation of the former was to forge practical solutions to exigent problems, whereas the emphasis for the latter was on remaining true to ideology. The Federalists were open to reaching pragmatic compromises and attributed the Republicans' reluctance to compromise their firmly held principles to inexperienced naïveté. As Ellis explains, Jeffersonian pure republicanism was "an intellectual tradition that Adams described as a 'school of folly' for its systematic confusion of what one could imagine with what was practical and possible . . . It was the classic criticism of an idealist by a realist."[2]

The contrast between these opposing views as well as the pendulum-like shifts back and forth between the two is illustrated in the evolution of James Madison's thinking, the actual drafter of the Constitution. Madison's fear of the potential for mob rule associated with broad suffrage pushed him closer to the Federalists' position on limited suffrage and the need for a strong central government. However, Madison had also become a close ally of Jefferson through their prior close collaboration in Virginia, and Jefferson unmistakably influenced his views. In many of the Federalist Papers he authored, Madison demonstrates his equivocation as he wrestles with the contradictions between the Moderate and Radical Enlightenment camps on a variety of issues.

Over time, Madison developed a special relationship with Jefferson that would become quite consequential for the new nation. Madison was influenced by Jefferson's pure republicanism and began questioning the role of a strong central government and advocating for more restraint in its powers. Based on their close collaboration, which continued for virtually their entire careers, Madison was one of the few trusted advisers capable of persuading Jefferson to reconsider a position and whose advice Jefferson would usually heed. These personal dynamics were consequential in shaping the first partisan opposition in the young nation. In the early 1790s, their coalition focused on opposing Alexander Hamilton's fiscal policies. It was at this point that Jefferson and Madison together formed the Democratic-Republican Party (in which Madison would later serve as Jefferson's vice president before himself winning the presidency). With this sequence of events in the 1790s, the Democratic-Republican Party and the Federalist Party would become the two primary parties in the early history of our country, each reflective of one of the two opposing Enlightenment schools of thought.

The symbiotic relationship between Jefferson and Madison was productive in another way. It allowed Jefferson to remain as the idealist above the fray since he could trust that Madison would continue "silently handling the messier specifics."[3] Thus, Madison, gifted with an astonishing ability to focus on the details, could forge the practical conciliations with the Federalists while also capturing the essence (to the degree possible) of Jeffersonian principles. To a great extent, Madison was the Founder who best straddled the two Enlightenment schools, firmly believing in the tenets of Jeffersonian republicanism and its commitment to personal liberty while also recognizing the need for a competent powerful and coordinated central government to develop and implement logical and pragmatic solutions. Based on Madison's abilities to act as a bridge, it is not surprising that he was assigned to draft the Constitution.

* * *

The texts of our nation's most important documents provide richly illustrative examples of the opposing Moderate and Radical Enlightenment philosophies, where they overlapped, and where they diverged. The evolution of these documents closely tracks the more radical character of the 1776 period, as embodied in the Declaration of Independence, and the shift back toward the Moderate Enlightenment path in the period prior to the convening of the Constitutional Convention in 1787.

THE DECLARATION OF INDEPENDENCE: AN ENLIGHTENMENT DOCUMENT

In comparing and contrasting America's foundational documents, we can immediately appreciate that the Declaration of Independence of 1776 represented a sweeping progression, affirming what was, at the time, the still very divisive principle of universal and equal human rights. This world-changing document stated that "all men are created equal, that they are endowed by their Creator with certain unalienable rights, that among these are Life, Liberty and the pursuit of Happiness."[4]

Jefferson was the primary drafter of the Declaration, but the document was also revised heavily during an intensive group effort in June 1776. Jefferson was appointed by Adams to run the drafting committee, which also included Benjamin Franklin, Roger Sherman from Connecticut, and New York's Robert Livingston. The final document was the product not only of significant input from all five but also included further revisions by the Continental Congress itself.

More has been written examining the impact of this document than perhaps any other official civic document since the Magna Carta of 1215. In more than the obvious ways, the Declaration of Independence is an Enlightenment document. First, the weighty ideals conveyed in the Declaration quite visibly have their roots in Enlightenment thinking generally and are especially consistent with the Radical Enlightenment camp. Teasing out the particular influences on Jefferson as he drafted is difficult precisely because Jefferson was so well-read. But in addition to the content itself, the form of logical reasoning in the Declaration is also a structural embodiment of the Enlightenment, a quintessential expression of the period's focus on rational argument as superordinate to divinely inspired dogma. Let's examine both the constituent ingredients and the structure of the Declaration.

Looking at its substantive elements, the document reveals abundant Enlightenment ideals throughout, and in some important areas, those ideals are rooted in the Radical Enlightenment philosophy. The notion that human beings are equally endowed with unalienable rights, both as free individuals and as part of civic communities, gives eloquent expression to the Enlightenment's emphasis on the capability and agency of the autonomous individual and the reciprocal bonds formed within self-governing social contracts.

The opening sentence alone, "When in the Course of human events, it becomes necessary"[5] seems scientific: "the Declaration's opening is Newtonian. It lays down the law."[6] Further, the depiction of the nature of "the Creator" referred to in the Declaration, who endows us with our unalienable rights, is quite consistent with Enlightenment concepts of divinity as an inextricable part of nature. After all, by not explicitly naming "God," the Christian God associated with divine revelation, the Declaration's Creator remains nebulous, more akin to the natural forces that exist in the universe, consistent with the writings of Spinoza.

Finally, the phrase "pursuit of Happiness" as the third in the list of unalienable rights stems from the Radical Enlightenment school of thought. In contrast, in Locke's social contract wording, this third position is occupied by "property rights." As discussed previously, Locke stressed the importance of property rights through much of his work and provided for their specific espousal within his social contract. By replacing Locke's "property rights" with the concept of "pursuit of Happiness," the Declaration of Independence emphatically crosses over a critical demarcation point from Moderate Enlightenment principles to the universal egalitarian tenets associated with the Radical Enlightenment. In society, only some, and in Locke's day, a select few, owned property. But in Jefferson's interpretation, everyone has the right to pursue happiness, whether a property holder or not. This elevation of the pursuit of happiness to the category of sacred rights to be protected is by no means a minor distinction.

Perhaps the most essential and indispensable of the substantive Enlightenment ideals expressed in the Declaration relates to the core question of just how expansive the phrase "all men are created equal" was meant to be. In recent centuries, many have lamented the notion that this phrase unequivocally applied only to White men with property. But, fortunately, this is not true. The intended meaning behind the phrase "all men are created equal" was much broader, and in fact encompassed enslaved people, women, and indeed all humanity (just as Lincoln promised it did, eighty years later). I offer a few pieces of historical evidence.

From a rational perspective, the assertion that "all men are created equal" was not required to declare independence from Britain; it served no practical purpose for the political goals of the time. So why was it put in the document? Clearly, the Framers recognized the blatant inequalities in the society of their day—in the American colonies of 1776, unequal treatment was quite unambiguous. Thus the phrase was deliberatively used as a foundational principle for perpetual reference, as an ideal to which the new nation must always aspire.

As indicated in many of their writings, most of the Founders, Jefferson included, believed that slavery was destined to be abolished. Evidence to support this comes from Jefferson's surviving historical drafts, which have extensive material that was deleted from the final edition. In one of the largest excised portions of Jefferson's original drafts, when listing the grievances against Britain, Jefferson accuses the Crown of being responsible for originating slavery and bringing it to the colonies, "instituting war against human nature itself, violating its most sacred rights of life and liberty in the persons of a distant people who never offended him, captivating and carrying them into slavery in another hemisphere."[7] In effect, Jefferson was blaming the imposition of slavery on King George himself, and referring to its horrors as one of the very pieces of evidence in the case supporting the Declaration.

The Continental Congress excised this material due to the delegates' firm conviction that the Southern colonies would strongly object, finding such offense in this material that they would not sign the Declaration. In the early days of our nation, the fear of alienating the South caused the Framers, whose goal was consensus, to avoid the question of slavery as much as possible. While an explicit denunciation of slavery would have likely been an unacceptable condition for the South, a general and forward-looking premise such as "all men are created equal" was likely an acceptable compromise.

We have yet more evidence of Jefferson's condemnation of slavery revealing his vision of extending unalienable rights to all people. As evidenced by the detailed investigations of dozens of Jeffersonian scholars, we have excellent analyses of Jefferson's own letters, correspondences, records, and formal writings. While in these materials Jefferson expressed doubts about the equality of the races, he expressly conveyed that the races were demonstrably equal in what he viewed as the most important quality—the moral sense, which Jefferson calls "the brightest gem with which the human character is studded."[8] Jefferson translates equality with respect to the moral sense into political equality, and by doing so he extends unalienable rights to all people. As mentioned earlier, though blatantly contradictory, while Jefferson enslaved people, he believed in the "basic integrity and equality for blacks themselves."[9]

In the social milieu of Jefferson's era, those holding a White supremacist view commonly supported their belief in African American "inferiority" by emphasizing evidence of theft and other "anti-societal" acts by enslaved people. Jefferson confidently refuted this common justification, finding the logic behind it altogether erroneous. Jefferson argued that respecting societal rules and mores is necessarily based on the *concept of reciprocity*: How can one possibly expect such of enslaved people when they are afforded none? For Jefferson, without reciprocal social bonds, societal expectations are meaningless.

In the years after the Declaration, Jefferson's writings seem to indicate his view that the demise of slavery as an institution was near. Between 1781 and 1784, Jefferson wrote *Notes on the State of Virginia*, first in response to a query posed by a French diplomat, and revised and expanded after. He writes:

> I think a change already perceptible, since the origin of the present revolution. The spirit of the master is abating, that of the slave rising from the dust, his condition mollifying, the way I hope preparing, under the auspices of heaven, for a total emancipation, and that this is disposed, in the order of events, to be with the consent of the masters, rather than by their extirpation.[10]

There is yet another important piece of historical evidence that lends further support to the notion that the intent of the phrase "all men are created equal" included enslaved people at the time it was written. In justifying their secession from the nation in the mid-19th century, the Confederate states explicitly declared that they could no longer adhere to the American Union precisely because it rested upon the assumption of the equality of the races. As Danielle Allen makes the case in her insightful 2014 analysis of the Declaration: "In other words, the slave owners who seceded from the United States and launched the Civil War thought that the words of the Declaration of Independence, and the phrase 'all men are created equal' did pertain to everyone,"[11] and consequently the seceding states could no longer remain in such a Union.

*   *   *

In addition to the substantive concepts in the Declaration, the structure of the document itself exemplifies an Enlightenment argument. As opposed to a reliance on any specific dogma or set of beliefs, the Declaration deploys two of the Enlightenment's most fundamental tools: Rationalism and Empiricism. The entire construction of the Declaration is based on empirical observations and deductive logic. Understanding the premises of the Declaration requires merely the powers of perception and reasoning. No knowledge of religious or spiritual doctrine is required to arrive at its cogent conclusions.

Consider the phrase "we hold these truths to be self-evident." Notice how the choice of words is deliberate. Jefferson did not write "we believe these truths." On the contrary, for something to be self-evident, it must be arrived at through the processes of observation and deduction. "To say that truths are self-evident is an epistemological claim . . . [meaning that] all the evidence you need to judge the proposition for yourself is in the proposition itself."[12] One need only deploy a deductive process to evaluate the evidence. Jefferson, like his Enlightenment colleagues, was above all beholden to the idea that reasoning and rational thought were not the exclusive purview of intellectuals but were attainable by the common citizen. Jefferson reported that his aim in writing the Declaration "was to place before mankind the common sense of the subject."[13]

When viewed in its entirety, the structure of the document is itself a rational and persuasive argument that independence was not just an option but a necessity. In 21st-century language, the argument goes something like this: We all possess a right to life, liberty, and the pursuit of happiness. Further, we recognize that we need an organizing and protective structure such as a government in order to secure these rights. And if the government we currently have is not adequately fulfilling that purpose based on our observations and reasonable deductions (and by the way, we have a long and detailed list of evidence to support this claim), then by definition, we are forced to alter or abolish that government and create a better one, one that is capable of securing our unalienable rights.

THE SPIRIT OF '76 DEVOLVES INTO THE MIRE OF 1787

The Spirit of '76 represented an era when Radical Enlightenment voices flourished. While it is true that the Declaration's drafting committee of five contained voices from both the Moderate and Radical Enlightenment camps, in that year the Radicals would prevail, pulling the pendulum with them. Within eleven short years, however, the pendulum would swing back under the influence of the strong countering force of the Moderates as they took hold of the reins of governance. The federal Constitution reflects this much more moderate view. This is most readily apparent when considering the Constitution without the addendum of the Bill of Rights, which was a concession to the Radical Enlightenment camp. During the tug-of-war leading up to ratification, the Radicals insisted on adding these individual and state protections. The back-and-forth nature of the drafting and ratifying debates is a quintessential illustration of the oscillation between the Moderate and Radical Enlightenment forces.

How exactly did the Moderate Enlightenment wing of the Founders come to dominate in such a short period of time following the Spirit of '76? The force behind these moderating winds can be explained, at least in part, by the inherent tension between elegant ideals and concepts, on the one hand, and the inevitable messiness of their implementation on the other. Lofty inspirational ideals might be both intellectually stimulating and emotionally uplifting, but unless they can be translated into meaningful and sustainable practices on the ground, they are essentially futile. At the same time, translating these ideals into pragmatic solutions invariably requires concessions; there is invariably and unavoidably messiness in the details.

The overarching focus in 1776 was to justify a break with the Crown and mobilize for armed conflict. However, by 1787, having gone through the painful ordeal of the Revolutionary War, the Founders had to shift their focus to the thorny problem of designing and implementing a comprehensive and workable model of self-government. To a large degree, the challenge within this eleven-year time frame was to create a new self-governing blueprint consistent with revolutionary ideals while forging pragmatic resolutions to the open issues of the day. Furthermore, in transforming the concept of self-government into a working reality, the Framers also had to overcome the myriad issues left open in the wake of the earlier Articles of Confederation. At the same time, the Framers had another important objective in mind. Since they recognized that they could not resolve all of the contentious issues of the day nor anticipate those of the future, they were intent on providing a flexible framework and supporting processes to allow adaptation and alteration over time.

The compelling issues of 1775–1776 were markedly different from those of 1787–1788. The former was about breaking bonds, justifying a split from a centrally powered governmental construction. The latter, however, was about building something new, the "creation, not the destruction of . . . a central national power that involved armed force, the aggressive management of international relations, and, potentially at least, the regulation of vital aspects of everyday life by a government dominant over all other, lesser governments."[14]

As they gathered at the Constitutional Convention to transform principles into actual governing structures and methods, the Framers undoubtedly recognized how monumental the task lying in front of them was, not only for the citizens of the new nation but as a model for people aspiring for freedom across the globe. As Bailyn points out, the Framers "looked ahead with anxiety rather than with confidence, for they knew, from the whole of their received tradition, of the desperate plight of liberty everywhere."[15]

Knowing how high the stakes were, the Founders aimed to create a promising new governing structure that could serve as a historical milestone but also dreaded the formidable difficulties that such a precedent would need to overcome. In any case, the Framers surely sensed that they were destined to play a special role in history. In their view, it was not only Europe that lacked well-constituted governments. They surely recognized that the principles used when forming the Constitution could later serve as a blueprint for liberal republics worldwide. Adams reflected on the entirety of the American revolutionary experience as "the opening of a grand scene and design in providence for the illumination of the ignorant and the emancipation of the slavish part of mankind all over the earth."[16] Anticipating pronounced disputes and intense debates as they sat down to work at the Convention, the Framers agreed to keep the deliberations secret, away from public view.

But in addition to the inherent strain between an elegant principle and its messy implementation, during the eleven-year period separating the signing of the Declaration and the Constitutional Convention, the political winds and on-the-ground mood shifted to the moderate side. The leaders of the time, White aristocratic men, were the very ones writing the rules; there is a natural human propensity for those in power to construct mechanisms that sustain their power. It may be the case that during the very process of framing the U.S. Constitution, the "great majority [of the Framers] had no wish to extend the reach of popular participation in political life; their main goal was to retain control within the hands of the existing political elites."[17]

Perhaps it was also consequential that Jefferson was not present at the Constitutional Convention to advocate for restricting the power of the federal government (he was serving as ambassador to France at that time). He was only able to contribute through the intermediary of his ally James Madison, who sent copious notes to Paris for Jefferson's feedback. Benjamin Franklin was the only radical voice present in the secret discussions. Franklin argued that "since poor men of no estate whatsoever had fought in the war, there could be no sound reason why they should not vote in the new government."[18] Franklin's call fell on deaf ears as voting requirements were ultimately left to the discretion of the individual states.

Irrespective of the underlying reasons, the end result was the mixed-government structure of the U.S. Constitution. "Combining elements of monarchy, aristocracy and democracy was in the eyes of Adams, Hamilton, and the other 'Moderates' the way to counter democracy's inherent instability and vulnerability to popular passion and tumult."[19] For the Federalists, republican democracies were best suited to small territories, whereas in larger territories they would inevitably lead to disorder, which eventually would require tyrannical authority to suppress and reign in the chaos engendered by the mob. "America is too unwieldy for the feeble, dilatory administration of democracy . . . the form of government in which the commons ruled—was generally associated with the threat of civil disorder and the early assumption of power by a dictator."[20]

However, during the long and unwieldy debates for ratification, anti-Federalists constantly pointed out that the entire revolution was fought *to oppose concentrated central power*, and thus renounced the concept of a strong central government in favor of more power distributed to the states. The Founders from the Radical Enlightenment school of thought held the view that liberty itself was threatened by the apparatus of a powerful national state. For them, the Federalist proposition endowing the central government with taxing power was eerily reminiscent of the British Parliament's seemingly limitless taxing power prior to the Revolution. Likewise, the proposed federal power to create armies was uncomfortably similar to the British use of standing armies to patrol the colonies. As Bailyn summarizes: "It was all a familiar story, with a predictable outcome to people who had been through it all before."[21]

The overarching goal of the Federalist Papers in the campaign to encourage ratification of the Constitution by the states was twofold. The first aim was to overcome these objections by convincing opponents that a centralized power system could be used to ensure people's liberties rather than to threaten them. The Federalists relied on Montesquieu's Moderate Enlightenment concepts of separation and balance of powers in making their case that abuses of power at the federal level could be effectively prevented. For example, they pointed to the concept of judicial review, which could check both the legislative and executive branches.

The second aim of the Federalist Papers was to underscore the critical need that could uniquely be provided by a central government in coordinating the disparate views of the states within the federation. In the pursuit of this objective, the authors meticulously delineated the practical and functional requirements that only a central government could fulfill for the budding new republic. Furthermore, they illustrated how the existing Articles of Confederation failed to fulfill such functions.

One of the fascinating aspects of the Federalist Papers as a political treatise is its animation of the pressing conflicts at this critical point in our early history between the different Enlightenment positions contesting in the background. The Federalist Papers have come to be considered among the most important political essays written in the modern world in part because of the vivid opposition they illustrate between Moderate and Radical Enlightenment forces in shaping our founding charter. In effect, they provide a more transparent window into the logic supporting both interpretations, lucidly illustrating the tensions between the democratic and more egalitarian principles advocating local sovereignty associated with the Radical Enlightenment camp and the more centralized and elite power structures associated with the Moderate Enlightenment view.

This is perhaps best illustrated in Madison's Federalist 39. In this pivotal paper, Madison was able to strike a balance between the two competing philosophies; he delineates in meticulous detail how each structural element specified in the Constitution has aspects he characterizes as "national"—implying that the jurisdiction of power is derived from individual citizens and vested in the central power of one national government—and "federal"—implying that the jurisdiction of power from citizens is vested in individual states that retain local sovereignty. The national aspects of the Constitution vest the central government with more power over all the citizens in a nation (consistent with the moderate view). In contrast, the federate aspects decentralize governance, leaving the states with more power and autonomy (consistent with the radical view). By depicting the Constitution as a *stable equilibrium* between these two models, and thus between two schools of Enlightenment thought, Madison anticipates the arguments on both sides, which he was sure would ensue in the ratification process.

Thus, the federal Constitution with all its imperfections, concessions, and seeming contradictions to the principles of 1776 would eventually be ratified by a sufficient number of states in June of 1788. Nonetheless, some of the resulting compromises, such as the one counting each enslaved person as three-fifths of a person in determining representation in Congress, starkly illustrate the extent of the departure from the "natural law and equal rights" wording of the Declaration only eleven years earlier.

In the final analysis, however, the effort at balancing the two clashing sets of Enlightenment principles left many aspects of American governance unresolved. As Ellis explains:

The distinguishing feature of the new Constitution was its purposeful ambiguity about the relationship between federal and state jurisdiction and about the overlapping authority of the respective branches of the federal government. The Constitution, in short, did not resolve the long-standing political disagreements that existed within the revolutionary generation so much as establish a fresh and more stable context within which they could be argued out.[22]

CONTRASTING THE INDIVIDUAL STATE CONSTITUTIONS

We can also observe this measured shift to the moderate point of view in the founding documents of the individual states, created from 1775 to 1776, and the constitutions they enacted eleven years later in the post-1787 period. Due to the specific sequence of events, many of the original state founding documents were drafted during the earlier and more radical Revolutionary War era. These first state constitutions were adopted in some haste and the existing British governmental structures quickly cast aside, as the case in New Hampshire vividly illustrates.

In 1775, the royal governor of New Hampshire, John Whitworth, fleeing a local squabble between the colonists and British troops, was trapped outside the colony, leaving the entire political and civil administration of the colony without a government. New Hampshire delegates sought advice from the Continental Congress, which was meeting at the time, led by John Adams, while British troops were already amassing in anticipation of further violent outbreaks from colonial rebels. Without a local functioning government, the Continental Congress recommended that the colony establish a new government, at the time regarded merely as a stopgap measure. Thus,

New Hampshire was the first state to build a new local government, which required founding documents.

The influence of Montesquieu on John Adams is evident in Adams's recommendations that new local governments for the individual colonies balance legislative, executive, and judicial powers. By early 1776, New Hampshire had adopted a new constitution, and Virginia and other states were in the process of doing so.

Many elements of the drafting of these state documents were straightforward, such as removing references to the Crown, which was considered imperative in the context of the early period of the Revolution. But at the same time, "each of the states was a laboratory, each new constitution another political experiment."[23] As Bailyn describes, during this period, colonial leaders:

> were forced to think through the fundamentals of their beliefs, and establish republican polities that expressed the principles they had earlier endorsed . . . they applied fresh ideas to existing structures and brought them as close as possible to their ideal . . . [they] worked through the problems of separating functioning powers of government to form balances . . . and probed the nature of representation, the operative meaning of sovereignty of the people, and individual rights. Few of their conclusions were applied uniformly or in absolute and complete form. But everywhere the institutional problems of republican government at the state level and the principles on which it was based were probed in this constructive phase of the ideological revolution.[24]

Because each of these new state constitutions specified an overall structure annotated with explicit executional details, we are left with historical evidence from two discrete historical periods. Consequently, the contrast between the Spirit of '76 and the later period of 1787 is richly illustrated through this documentation.

Two great examples illustrating the radical influence of the earlier period can be found in the early Virginia declaration of rights (June 1776) and Pennsylvania's early (1776) adoption of its state constitution. Not surprisingly, these examples come from two states in which leading radical voices were prominent (Jefferson and Franklin). The Virginia declaration broke entirely new ground and was the first among the world's declarations of human rights. According to the official state archives, the 1776 Pennsylvania constitution, authored primarily by and under the leadership of Benjamin Franklin, was "described as the most democratic in America, providing for universal all male suffrage."[25]

The Pennsylvania constitution of this era was the most radical ever written, providing for a sole unicameral legislative chamber elected by the people, without any aristocratic house. Furthermore, legislative elections were annual, and members held only limited terms. Finally, the constitution called for neither a governor nor other individual person with executive power. The French revolutionary Brissot called it a "plan of democracy as perfect as man can imagine,"[26] while John Adams expressed grave concerns lest the other states adopt Pennsylvania's "spirit of leveling." The new Pennsylvania constitution, published in October 1776, was a "landmark in the history of representative democracy, republicanism, and modernity. Abolishing all property and wealth qualifications for voting and officeholding."[27] All taxpayers could vote, including free Black people who paid taxes.

The debates during the drafting of these documents illustrate the conflict between the Radical Enlightenment spirit of the time and the opposing moderate viewpoint. This tension between competing visions of the American Revolution was developing and intensifying precisely during this time. George Mason, the primary author of the Virginia document, was a prominent Radical who "maintained, noticeably more energetically than his neighbor George Washington, that slavery was wholly unjust and incompatible with inherent natural rights."[28] Illustrating yet another contradiction, Mason, like Washington, was an enslaver but fervently believed in ending the trade of enslaved people. Thus, both men struggled with the very institution of slavery that they themselves engaged in. It was not until 1799 that Washington left instructions to emancipate the people he had enslaved, on the death of his wife Martha.[29]

The documents from this earlier era reflecting the Radical Enlightenment principles did manifest in the later period, first in the later 1789 French "Déclaration des droits de l'homme et du citoyen," and then again in Paine's *Rights of Man* (1791). However, when compared to the state constitutions from this later era, the movement to the more Moderate Enlightenment viewpoint becomes obvious. For example, South Carolina revised its earlier charter in 1790 after the U.S. Constitution was ratified. This latter document "retained its pre-1776 'aristocratic' systems largely unaltered."[30] Leadership of the colony was left to the elite group of landed aristocrats who had ruled it for decades prior, and suffrage was limited to landowners of large estates, usually enslavers. Furthermore, as the American Revolution passed from its radical phase into a moderate phase in the 1780s and 1790s, many of the earlier radical state constitutions were rescinded and recast in a more moderate framework.

SLAVERY: A FOUNDING CONTRADICTION

An important point related to all of the documents from the revolutionary period, irrespective of the schism they illustrate between Radical or Moderate Enlightenment ideals, is the failure of these founding documents to resolve the issue of slavery. "Black slavery was universally recognized as the prime contradiction of the American Revolution and defect of the new republic."[31] How could the same principles underlying the Declaration of Independence be proclaimed amid the active trading and enslavement of fellow human beings? As mentioned previously, the contradiction was "forcefully underlined . . . when Jefferson's draft clause denouncing the British Crown for introducing black slavery into America as a 'cruel war against human nature itself' was deleted from the final version of the Declaration of Independence."[32]

In the 1787 Constitutional Convention, many of the delegates recognized the contradiction. Maryland representative Luther Martin stated that slavery was inconsistent with the principles of the Revolution. Even Moderates like Gouverneur Morris from New York denounced slavery.[33] However, there was no possibility of forming a union with the Southern states without allowing slavery. In not explicitly addressing the issue in the Constitution, "Northern as well as Southern delegates colluded in burying the whole issue and excluding direct reference to 'slavery' in the Constitution's final wording . . . the result was that the United States Federal Constitution, utilizing respectable circumlocutions, condoned slavery indefinitely."[34] The Northern leaders seemingly thought that what many viewed as the scourge of slavery would somehow disappear over time. As W. E. B. Du Bois writes in his classic *Black Reconstruction in America: 1860–1880* (1935):

> The men who wrote the constitution sought by every evasion, and almost by subterfuge, to keep recognition of slavery out of the basic form of the new government. They founded their hopes on the prohibition of the slave trade, being sure that without continual additions from abroad, the tropical people would not long survive, and thus the problem of slavery would disappear . . . They miscalculated.[35]

Nonetheless, Radical Enlightenment principles were kept alive in the abolitionist movement that grew in the early United States and gained momentum in many strata of society. Perhaps unsurprisingly, the first enactment of the abolition of slavery was in Pennsylvania in 1780, led by Franklin's friend and Quaker colleague Anthony Benezet.[36] He and Franklin were to set up one of the first American antislavery societies. But tragically, many patriots, while recognizing the contradiction, enabled the prolonging and not the prohibition of slavery, especially as it became more lucrative with the invention of the cotton gin and the growth of textile mills in the North and in Europe.

The Radicals in France went further in their antislavery efforts, led by Condorcet, Brissot, Diderot, and others. Brissot worked tirelessly not just to promote the "abolition of slavery [in the French colonies] but to more comprehensively emancipate blacks through education and helping find appropriate work."[37] By 1793, the French Assembly banned slavery in all of its colonies, even if this was principally in reaction to the tenacious revolutionaries operating in Saint-Domingue (today's Haiti). Appallingly, slavery would be reestablished in the French colonies under Napoleon, only to be abolished once again in 1848. In the United States, abolition would take nearly a century from the signing of the Declaration in 1776 until Lincoln signed the Emancipation Proclamation.

MODERATES MEET THE "MOB": POPULAR DISCONTENT AND FEARS OF DEMOCRACY

As the Federalists asserted themselves both in formulizing the Constitution and assuming the practicalities of governing, one additional event helped solidify the shift in the balance of power in their favor, away from the Radicals, who had the upper hand in the early part of the Revolution up through the signing of the Declaration. Shays' Rebellion (1786–1787) and its aftermath confirmed for many new leaders the need to keep the democratic radical movement under a watchful eye.

Shays' Rebellion can be summarized against the following back-drop: The Massachusetts state constitution (as compared with that of Pennsylvania or Virginia) charted a much more aristocratic model, no doubt under the influences of Adams and the wealthy mercantile elite in Boston. These elites maintained firm control of the state, as the consti-tution provided for extremely restricted suffrage. Massachusetts chose to levy taxes on its citizens to help retire its portion of the state's war debt. Under threat of seizure of property for nonpayment, many of the farmers and nonwealthy residents were infuriated by the decision handed down from the wealthy ruling elites. Many were war veterans and had risked their lives fighting for independence and were now being forced to pay for the war itself. To add insult to injury, the wealthy financiers in Boston who held the debt were greatly enriched by the newly enacted scheme. Suddenly, the new United States had the same crushing financial inequal-ity as existed in Europe; this created new motivations for common people to mobilize around the populist themes as discussed previously.

Daniel Shay led hundreds of men in an armed conflict that forced the closing of state courthouses. The rebellion lasted from August of 1786 until February 1787. Ultimately, the state militia subdued the insurgents a few weeks after the conflict began. Nonetheless, there were two interrelated consequences from this episode. First, many distressed and now poor citizens became embittered as they realized that the prin-ciples for which they had fought in the recent Revolutionary War were in practice fully unrealized. The actual conditions on the ground fell far short of the dream represented by the new union.

Jefferson, in Paris at the time, viewed the whole affair as a shameful disgrace. Other radical leaders of the time, like William Whiting, a county justice, expressed the sentiment plainly. He felt, as Israel writes, that "the true principles of 'natural rights' and democratic republican-ism, the veritable basis of the Revolution, were now being subverted in the new United States." Whiting wrote that the "government is either defective in its original constitution or else the laws are unjustly and unequally administered."[38] The realization among many disenfranchised citizens of the new nation of the utter failure of the Revolution to improve the lives of many represented a precursor to the democratic protest movements of the 1790s discussed in the previous section.

At the same time, the need to quell the violent rebellion demonstrated to the Moderates just how dangerous a passionate democratic citizenry could be. Thus, the second consequence of the events was to staunchly crystalize in the eyes of the governing elite the very real danger that free democratic expression could generate a volatile powder keg that could potentially detonate, and a corresponding need for a more vigorous and forceful federal government. The timing of this recognition, immediately prior to the drafting of the U.S. Constitution to replace the Articles of Confederation, breathed new life into the Moderates' fears of egalitarian democracy and confirmed for many Moderates that democracy was a menacing form of government that could easily devolve into mob rule. This dynamic perpetuated the conflict between the democratic and aristocratic forces for decades and centuries to come.

Washington's farewell address famously warns about the dangers of disunion. Despite his own increasing tendency to side with the Federalists, at his departure Washington warned against the dangers of both political parties and agitators stirring the public's emotions in pursuit of power. Strikingly, Washington also reinforced a foundational element of the Radical Enlightenment by advising that for the country to survive, the citizens must be well-educated: "Promote, then, as an object of primary importance, institutions for the general diffusion of knowledge. . . In proportion as the structure of government gives force to public opinion, it is essential that public opinion should be enlightened."[39] Washington's warnings were prescient, accurately and precisely identifying three of the most difficult issues that would become great threats to our democracy in subsequent centuries: the peril of disunion, the danger of political parties, and the need for a well-educated populace for a democracy.

Chapter 9

A YOUNG NATION STRUGGLES WITH EXPANSION: AMERICA IN THE EARLY 19TH CENTURY

One of the dominant themes after the turn of the 19th century was the widespread belief in "manifest destiny," the impression that American settlers were destined to expand across the entire North American continent. While there was never a precise set of principles or formal government policy defining this concept, the overall thrust was that of an imperialist culture in the new nation that made expansionism inevitable.

This drive to expand had numerous justifications, including the belief that the American people were predominantly virtuous and endowed with a mission to develop and promulgate civilization westward. But support for the concept was not at all unanimous; both a large segment of the citizenry and some political leaders rejected this imperialist tendency. These opposing voices recognized that American expansion might bring greater prosperity but only at the expense of the well-being of Indigenous people of America. Nonetheless, expansion began almost immediately after the dawn of the century and would continue to be encouraged by many American leaders and big monied interests.

The push westward raised a myriad of issues related to the two grave and enduring stains on American egalitarianism. The duplicitous juxtaposition of the sweeping tenets of the new republic contrasted against the brutal institution of slavery, and continued persecution and displacement of Indigenous Americans was as jarring to many domestically as it was to observers of the American experiment from afar. Territory expansion exacerbated the grievous contradictions associated with both. First, since the power established between the North and the South had been carefully balanced, one of the most pressing questions associated with manifest destiny was the issue of slavery. Abolitionists at all levels of society were loath to see slavery extended to new territory, as were many leaders in government. However, the champions of abolition were opposed by powerful social and economic forces in the South that promoted its expansion. Second, the young nation's ruthless policies toward Indigenous Americans would complicate the country's expansion.

THE CONUNDRUM OF THE JEFFERSON PRESIDENCY

When Thomas Jefferson took over the presidency at the dawn of the 19th century, the new republic had already started to look much like the old world from which the Founders had fought so hard to break away. As reviewed in the previous chapter, the swing closer to the more moderate ideology of the Federalists was undeniably apparent in the recently adopted Constitution which, to a large extent, codified a governing prototype typified by the aristocratic elite rule with its roots in Moderate Enlightenment ideology that was already firmly established in both the

Northern and Southern states. However, the 3/5 clause, the infamous "compromise" of the 1787 Constitution, pleased neither the Moderates nor the Radicals.

In certain respects, Jefferson assuming the presidency in and of itself was quite paradoxical. Since the early days of Washington's presidency, Jefferson had resolutely moored himself in firm opposition to the Federalist agenda. Jefferson, the Founder *most* suspicious of the concept of consolidated central power, was now taking the reins to be in charge of it. As the adage indicates: There are a thousand critics for every playwright. How exactly would Jefferson leave his role as critic behind and adapt to his new role as the playwright? This prospect indeed worried the Federalists: "How could he take an oath to preserve, protect and defend the Constitution . . . if his primary goal as president was to dismantle the federal institutions created by the very document?"[1]

Jefferson reconciled this by avowing to use his tenure as president to restore the Spirit of '76 via a program of federal austerity. By shrinking the federal government and retiring the debt, Jefferson believed he could rein in its power. In fact, in Jefferson's eyes, the debt that prompted the federal government to tax its citizens was in itself an abuse of power. But at the same time, based on the fundamental belief in free speech associated with his pure republicanism, Jefferson famously embraced advocates of both political parties in a conciliatory gesture at his inauguration—"we are all republicans—we are all federalists."[2]

While Jefferson's early presidency signaled the end of the bitter partisan disputes of the 1790s, it was also a harbinger of how his tenure as president would require the very conciliations he had been so reluctant to strike earlier in his political career. As president, Jefferson was now burdened by the concomitant requirements of the office. As the messy and compromising details muddied the purity of his lofty ideals, Jefferson the 1801 president unquestionably contrasted with Jefferson the 1776 revolutionary.

More immediately problematic for President Jefferson, with

slavery established in the social and economic fabric of the South and with renewed religious fervor widespread and growing, the radical Spirit of '76 underlying the Declaration of Independence seemed demonstrably less manifest in the young country at the turn of the century. Nonetheless, given the strength of his convictions as the radical Democratic-Republican patriot of the earlier era, it remains perplexing as to why President Jefferson was not able to use his position at the helm to swing the pendulum back further toward his earlier and original egalitarian vision.

As president, Jefferson's greatest accomplishment in building the nation was, arguably, the Louisiana Purchase from Napoleon's France in 1803. Jefferson was both mystified and enthralled by the alluring pull of the West. The idea that the American republic could expand from sea to sea must have been quite seductive. From an economic perspective, the Louisiana Purchase was a great coup that in one fell swoop doubled the territory of the country, providing a vast new hinterland for expansion. However, the political bargaining made when incorporating the new territories into the union not only more deeply embedded the reprehensible institution of slavery as a "necessary engine" of prosperity, but also further disenfranchised Native Americans living in those territories.

How could this happen on Jefferson's watch? Did his revolutionary views as a younger man yield to the practical realities required to lead the nation? Did his enthrallment of manifest destiny overcome his earlier idealism? Did Jefferson lose the zest of his prior beliefs, or was he simply unable to implement his more egalitarian vision in the face of the gale-force political winds of the new century? While historians posit a wide variety of differing theories, there is some consensus that a few specific factors were at play.

One dynamic that inarguably influenced President Jefferson was the increasing estrangement from his fellow Radicals from 1776 and from his association with the now discredited French Revolution. Many of these Radicals (in addition to some of Jefferson's fellow Republicans) had now become "outsiders" and were vehement in their condemnation of the Moderates with whom President Jefferson was forced to run the government. For example, it was during these years of 1794 and 1795 that Thomas Paine's *The Age of Reason* appeared, containing strong critiques of Washington, who by that point had been lionized as the hero of the American Revolution. Jefferson viewed Paine as an authentic American hero, a central member of the revolutionary generation. At this juncture in 1794, as Jefferson was opposing the Federalists in power, he considered Paine's writing an attempt to reclaim the radical narrative of America's birth. However, the landscape had shifted significantly since the publication of *Common Sense*; the new predominance of religious piety in American life presented a significant obstacle to Jefferson's support for Paine's new treatise.

The Age of Reason presented a full-frontal attack on Christianity. Recall as discussed in Part I that at this same time in the mid-1790s, the Second Great Awakening began its ascendancy, and the climate in the country reflected the views of a more spiritually devoted citizenry. The antireligious zeal expressed in Paine's latest writings was widely rebuked in the popular press and forced Jefferson to distance himself from Paine. To a large extent, Paine's later writings greatly tarnished his reputation among the citizenry and made him a more controversial figure on this side of the Atlantic.

In addition, the image of America's partner in the age of revolutionary ideals, France, had deteriorated significantly as the repercussions of the disastrous Reign of Terror phase of its Revolution settled in the mind of the public. Unfortunately, and quite unfairly, U.S. citizens associated what they viewed as the blood-stained phase of the French Revolution with the Radicals whom they had perceived as the heroes of the prior era. This was understandable without the benefit of hindsight, since it was from the Radical Enlightenment group that Robespierre and his henchmen emerged.[3] Without the benefit of any historical perspective, there was still much widespread confusion regarding the way in which the French Revolution evolved, starting with radical egalitarian ideas, proceeding through a phase of terrible violence, and culminating with absolute power declared by a new Emperor Napoleon.

The general effect on the U.S. populace at the turn of the century was a terrible anxiety associated with the premonition that the anarchy that had been reported in France would reach American shores if the Radicals had their way. The result was that the radical wing of the Enlightenment was now tarnished with the blood and chaos in France. This anti-French fear not only penetrated the social mood but permeated actual government policy itself. The anti-British character of the Spirit of '76 had dissipated under the Federalists' reign partly because the South had become economically dependent on cotton exports to Britain. In addition, the Federalists were no longer able to rely on the French alliance, and as a young nation, solidifying other European support was an imperative. Moreover, ever since the "execution of Louis XVI and the onset of the Terror in 1793, the Federalists had shed any enthusiasm they once felt for the French Revolution."[4] These various factors shifted the balance from the previous era's alignment with French interests to alignment with those of Britain during the Adams administration (1797–1801), which "sought economic and diplomatic rapprochement with the one-time mother country."[5]

By the time of Jefferson's inauguration, the overall impact of the disastrous dénouement of the French Revolution undoubtedly reflected poorly on Jefferson himself and represented something of a public repudiation of his well-known prior political life. His position was not only weakened in the public eye but also in the eyes of the prevailing Moderates during the 1790s. Now that he was president, Jefferson surely had to be cautious of reopening that older wound by distancing himself from both the Radicals of the prior period as well as his prior association with the French Revolution.

The second development that started to emerge in the early 19th century was that slavery as an institution was becoming entrenched in and even inextricably linked to the economic success of the new nation. Between 1791 and 1822 the cotton crop went from nine thousand bales to half a million (and to two million by 1840). As the meteoric rise of the nascent U.S. economy relied on slavery, the South extended the slave trade (which was not finally abolished by Jefferson until 1807) and resorted to the abhorrent practice of the rape and forced impregnation of enslaved women, otherwise known as "commercial breeding."

The North was also complicit in the promulgation of slavery through its dependency on cotton to support the textile industry's rapid economic development. But whereas the Northern states, recognizing the inconsistency between slavery and the nation's founding principle, ended slavery in their territories in the first decades following the signing of the Declaration, slavery was too embedded in the South for the growing opposition to overcome its pervasive support.[6] In an ironic juxtaposition, just as the abolitionist movement intensified, more and more economic success resulted from this vile institution.

Of the various dynamic forces of the era described here, what perhaps constrained the Radical Enlightenment views associated with the younger Jefferson the most during his presidency were the powerful Counter-Enlightenment forces epitomized by the Second Great Awakening. The rapid growth of the Methodist and Baptist churches mobilized anti-Enlightenment sentiment extensively across the union. During this era, "American religion received a powerful boost at the grassroots level, arousing great numbers of individuals who had earlier shown less commitment," making "popular religiosity . . . the most powerful moral, social and educational force in the country."[7] Preachers routinely vilified Paine's *Age of Reason* ideology as a threat to the moral fabric of the nation, not unlike the threat of "communism" in the McCarthy era. A widespread fear of subversion, infiltration, and infidelity was promoted in the popular press.

In addition to Protestant leaders, many former Radicals shed their earlier ideology and became a voice for this anti-Enlightenment trend, embracing religion and calling on the American people to reject expanded suffrage, which was labeled as "corrupting." Noah Webster was a prime example. While he was a freethinker in his early life, Webster grew increasingly pious and authoritarian. Viewing language as an effective instrument to keep unruly thoughts and impulses at bay, Webster's *American Dictionary* emphasized the virtues of social control over human passions and individualism, submission to authority, and fear of God as all necessary for the preservation of the American social order. Webster famously said, "Education is useless without the Bible. The Bible was America's basic textbook in all fields. God's Word, contained in the Bible, has furnished all necessary rules to direct our conduct." The net result of the Awakening was that after 1800 the "entire radical Enlightenment tradition of thought . . . found itself under general public condemnation and attack."[8]

Taken together, these trends put Jefferson in an untenable position by the time of his inauguration in 1801. Yes, he won the presidency as a Republican, but the more moderate views of the Federalists, along with a new religious tenor, had taken hold of the nation. He was forced to distance himself from some of his former radical associates. Even with James Madison and James Monroe inside Jefferson's government still firmly associated with the convictions of the younger, more radical Jefferson, the more conservative social and political forces pushing against Jefferson's democratic views were considerable by the time he assumed the presidency.

A CRITICAL JUNCTURE: THE LOUISIANA PURCHASE

Indubitably, the marginalization of what Jefferson considered the American Revolution's true principles had a substantial effect on his presidency. However, President Jefferson was squeezed between forces on the right, represented by the Federalists, and on the left, by Jefferson's lingering attachments to the remaining hard-core Radicals who were increasingly antagonized by his new centrist position. He also had to navigate the powerful sway of populist opinion, composed of genuine antielitism and religious Counter-Enlightenment fervor.

Some of Jefferson's actions remained true to his radical instincts; he pardoned anyone who had been previously convicted under the Sedition Act, and by 1802, he let expire the elements of these acts that limited free speech and press. Ironically, reestablishing a free press ended up severely hurting Jefferson, as he himself often became the target of an increasingly populist and vicious press that was turning against him in the early 1800s. He had become the victim of the very freedom he had fought his whole life to safeguard.

All of these factors played a role in what was to become a critical juncture for policy during the Jefferson presidency: namely, the status of slavery in the new Louisiana territories. The fundamental question of whether the institution of slavery would be curtailed (as many of the original Founders had hoped) or extended loomed large. In practical terms, the details related to the integration of the Louisiana territory into the union presented an exhaustive array of immediate problems for Jefferson. And the local French and Spanish residents of the territory were themselves accustomed to the authoritarian governments of the old world and were not particularly enthusiastic about democracy or republicanism.

An additional complicating factor for Jefferson was the Haitian Revolution from 1791 to 1804, which created the second independent country in the Americas. For Jefferson, the Haitian Revolution presented something of a dilemma. He supported the revolutionary creed of the island's independence movement, but as a Virginia slaveholder he was keenly aware of the concurrent revolt of enslaved people that portended terrific violence (in Haiti, originally called Saint-Domingue, the majority of the population were enslaved people of African descent).

During Adams's presidency, Jefferson counseled limited assistance to the French to suppress the revolt. However, during Jefferson's presidency, the Haitian Revolution grew considerably more violent with the execution of many of the island's remaining White inhabitants. The specter of a vicious race war with bloodshed similar to the French Terror amplified Jefferson's hostility toward the Haitian Revolution and, ultimately, he refused to recognize Haitian independence.[9] (As an interesting and dismaying side note, although France recognized Haitian independence in 1825, Haitians would have to wait until 1862 for the United States to recognize Haiti's status as a sovereign, independent nation.)[10] Moreover, there was an influx into the United States of French planters fleeing the revolution. Many of these refugees were enslavers who brought enslaved people with them, which in itself raised concerns among Jefferson's cabinet about importing instability from the rebellious island into the United States.

It is important to remember that, as discussed previously, despite being an enslaver himself, the younger Jefferson had in fact devised and promoted the emancipation of enslaved people through his broad manumission and deportation plan. During the years he was living in France, Jefferson had aligned with the French Radicals and acknowledged that slavery was incompatible with the principles of the Enlightenment. But that was the younger, radical Thomas Jefferson, not the President Thomas Jefferson. At the time of incorporation of the Louisiana territory, Jefferson needed the political support of Virginia and the Southern states for his comprehensive plans to integrate the new lands. Further, by this point in his career, Jefferson's moderated position on slavery "emphasized the need to wait for public opinion to catch up with the moral imperative of emancipation. Instead of a crusading advocate, he became a cautious diplomat."[11]

Ultimately, Jefferson capitulated and allowed slavery to be expanded to the new territory. At first Jefferson resisted crossing this line. The issue was fiercely debated in Congress, but in the end the Southern senators allied with Jefferson's foes in the Northern Federalist coalition to defeat the bill that Jefferson supported, which would have banned a further extension of slavery to the new territories. "Avoiding responsibility for ending slavery certainly became, if it was not always, Jefferson's prime political and moral deficiency."[12]

Jefferson once again attempted to address the issue in 1806 with his promotion and successful passage of the Act Prohibiting Importation of Slaves (1807). The background here is interesting, as it indicates how the Founders during the Revolutionary Era seemed to hope that slavery would by some means dissolve with time.

During the American Revolution, all Thirteen Colonies agreed to ban the slave trade, recognizing that the institution of slavery was ultimately untenable with the principles of the Declaration. However, after the union was formed, three states subsequently passed legislation legalizing the slave trade once again. As a result, when the Constitution was drafted, a clause was included that protected a state's involvement in the Atlantic slave trade from federal prohibition for a limited duration of twenty years. Only starting on January 1, 1808, could a federal law be enacted to abolish the international slave trade in all states. Via this method, the Framers condoned slavery while effectively deferring its ultimate future to the next generation.

On December 2, 1806, in his annual message to Congress, President Jefferson firmly denounced the violations of human rights connected to the international slave trade and called for its criminalization on the first day that was possible (January 1, 1808). With passage of the act, the import and export of slaves was prohibited, although internal trade within and between the states continued (and the international slave trade to some degree continued illegally).

Ultimately, as neither Jefferson nor his successor Madison was able to definitively resolve the slavery question, they eventually realized that allowing slavery in the Louisiana territory and subsequently in the Florida territories had been a grave mistake. Further, the 1820 Missouri

Compromise reached during the Monroe administration, by which Missouri entered the union as a state that allowed the enslavement of people and Maine entered the union as a state where all people were free, failed to settle the core issue. The "ominous splitting of the United States into equally calibrated, politically competing, rival halves filled Jefferson and Madison with foreboding and presentiment of catastrophe. The question of how finally to resolve the slavery issue seemed . . . infinitely problematic."[13] These trends portended a dramatic conflict that would arrive just a few decades later. In the final analysis, "the real revolutionary legacy on the slavery question was not a belief in emancipation but rather a common commitment to delay and a common trust that northerners would not interfere with southern leadership in effecting a gradual policy of emancipation."[14]

*　*　*

The developments described in the preceding distinctly illustrate the shift from the Spirit of '76 to the more moderate stance of the Adams and Jefferson presidencies. However, during this period, there were limited advancements for the radical camp as well. First, not all religious expansion during this period was hostile to the Enlightenment. Jefferson and the remaining Radicals were optimistic about the growth during this period of Unitarianism, which promoted a much more tolerant approach to faith and was considerably less attached to rigid religious dogma. Second, and more importantly, as slavery continued to embed itself as an institution in the South in the first two decades of the 19th century, it prompted a concurrent reaction from a growing abolitionist movement that drew on both Enlightenment and faith-based Counter-Enlightenment motives to fervently condemn slavery. Nonetheless, in retrospect the strikingly ironic feature of the era was that despite Jefferson winning the presidency and the concurrent weakening of the opposing Federalists, the pendulum stubbornly resisted the radical pull of the prior revolutionary era.

THE RADICAL ENLIGHTENMENT RECEDES WORLDWIDE

By 1815, the Radical Enlightenment had taken a backseat in the United States and elsewhere. During these years, Europe was largely restructured by Napoleon. While Napoleon was unmistakably a tyrannical despot, his reign incorporated some Enlightenment principles (e.g., freedom of religion and emancipation of France's Jews). In addition, Napoleon enacted a new legal framework, the Napoleonic Code, which established a coherent system of justice and preserved family and individual rights. He also built a robust national education system that emphasized secular, Enlightenment-oriented curricula and built on the contributions of Condorcet and the other French Radicals from the Enlightenment era.

On the other hand, Napoleon held a quite retrograde view on the role of women in society. The Napoleonic Code, while reflecting a secular conception of society that moved beyond the religious limitations of the *ancien régime*, enshrined a patriarchal conception of the family in which women were expected to have a truly domestic role. Female participation in public life was largely rejected.

After Napoleon's defeat, the restoration of the monarchy in France in some ways followed the British government's mixed model, with the constitutions checking the power of the restored monarch. However, the Holy Alliance (Russia, Austria, and Prussia), which emerged from the Congress of Vienna, "sought to bury Napoleonism as well as the republican and democratizing principles of the American and French revolutions,"[15] restoring much of the *ancien régime* structure throughout

Europe. Accordingly, the Holy Alliance also reimposed the primacy of the authoritative dogma of the Catholic-Protestant-Orthodox churches.

Apart from Argentina and Chile, most of the Spanish American revolutions had been quashed, leaving the United States as the lone major republic. (However, by 1830 most of South America had achieved independence, and various types of republics had been formed.) The Spanish Revolution of the 1820s was crushed by Louis XVIII, and the Brazilian drive for independence was partially successful at best.

The waning of the Radical Enlightenment spirit was not confined to the United States. Across most of the Western world, with the exceptions of alienated radical thinkers and artists embracing the Romantic movement, the mass populations "showed little inclination to cease their passive acceptance of 'kings and priests.'"[16] Consequently, the world of Thomas Paine's *Common Sense* and *Rights of Man* (which had both been translated and distributed all over the world) seemed like an idyllic paradise quite far removed from the reality on the ground.

Despite this worldwide trend away from the radical camp, America prevented the reimposition of the *ancien régime* structure in the American hemisphere. As the restored European monarchies tried to reassert control over South America following the failed revolutions there, the decisive Monroe Doctrine of 1823 barred further European colonization of the Americas. This was a bold statement in support of the republican model, albeit perhaps for selfish and imperialistic reasons. The net effect was that the European powers could not expand the restored monarchical system in the New World. This audacious move convinced some Radicals in Europe that the United States could play an important role in the future in promoting egalitarian ideals in the Western hemisphere.

While many state constitutions were replaced in the 1780s with more narrowly defined suffrage laws (restricting voting to only landowners, taxpayers, etc.), by 1825 every state in the union except Rhode Island, Virginia, and Louisiana accepted the principle of universal White male suffrage without property restrictions. Thus, by this time, some leading Radicals were convinced that "American-style federal republicanism was proving a growing inspiration for the world."[17] However, many others also recognized that the lower classes of society in the New World remained just as miserable as those in the old world. This observation, combined with the continued scourge of Southern slavery, led many to be more skeptical.

Writers like James Fenimore Cooper, Ralph Waldo Emerson, and Alexis de Tocqueville embraced the democratic advances in America, but also severely condemned the elitist vestiges that remained. Cooper was particularly wary that an uneducated populace was vulnerable to the threat of "the dupes of demagogues and political schemers."[18] For many, America's capacity to survive depended on the common people's ability to discriminate and form sound judgments about what is true and what is false. Further, fostering the broad dissemination of these skills required a "sound commitment to an education grounded in the Enlightenment."[19]

In 1828, when Andrew Jackson defeated John Quincy Adams for the presidency, Jackson's new Democratic Party represented the first reign of populism in America. It symbolized the first real overthrow of the elites by the masses—yet here we must take care to recall our previous discussion and be circumspect when evaluating populist movements. Unarguably, bottom-up populist sentiment had been emerging among nonelite Americans since the early stages of the 19th century. But Jackson decidedly exploited the growing trend for political purposes, deploying top-down populist rhetoric to transform his party into a people's party ostensibly representing the common people against an out-of-touch elite.

As described in *A People's History of the United States* (1980) by Howard Zinn, "Jackson was the first President to master the liberal rhetoric—to speak for the common man."[20] The aging political elite feared this new trend, as it appeared to many that mob rule and the influence of demagogues would characterize the new political reality. But if Jackson shared Jefferson's belief in democratic principles, especially the importance of providing a voice in politics for the average person, Jacksonian democracy would present quite a different face from Jefferson's vision.

As reviewed previously, the Second Great Awakening was at its height at this time, propelling Counter-Enlightenment principles to the center of public debate. The religious revival caused Jacksonian democracy to become much less rational and enlightened compared to the system envisioned by the Founders who subscribed to the Radical Enlightenment school of thought. Jacksonian democracy was in fact much more spiritual and rooted in Protestant dogma. This result serves as a great example of how Counter-Enlightenment forces overlaid the split between the Moderate and Radical Enlightenment thinkers with unforeseeable consequences. Furthermore, this intermingling was enduring. Counter-Enlightenment themes, fusing religious refrains with calls to reject rule by an aristocratic elite, would repeatedly be deployed as a populist tactic used by political leaders seeking to build a broader base of public support.

In the Jacksonian era, the populist rhetoric translated into some important progressive policy achievements. For example, suffrage was expanded to all White men, making the United States at this time the largest democracy in the history of the world. Nonetheless, American democracy continued to exclude enslaved and free African Americans, Native Americans, and, of course, women. Furthermore, Jackson greatly intensified the assault on Native Americans. A firm believer in the manifest destiny described previously, Jackson aggressively pursued the land inhabited by Indigenous people. As Zinn describes, Jackson was "a land speculator, merchant, slave trader, and the most aggressive enemy of the Indians in early American history . . . [pursuing] land grabs which laid the basis for the cotton kingdom, the slave plantations."[21] To the degree that Jacksonian populism expanded democracy in certain regards, these gains must be evaluated against not only his assault on Indigenous people but on his further entrenchment of slavery. In any case, the period was characterized not by reasoned debate inspired by the Enlightenment, but by the strict religious and dogmatic tenor of the Counter-Enlightenment.

Chapter 10

THE HOPES OF RADICAL RECONSTRUCTION AND THE BRUTAL REALITY OF JIM CROW

It would be challenging to identify a sharper manifestation of the American Schism than the decades immediately before and after the Civil War, when the country was literally ripped asunder by two fundamentally opposing ideologies. As discussed in the last chapter, the Founders were intentionally ambiguous regarding slavery in the drafting of the Constitution. Because the delegates at the Constitutional Convention wanted to maintain the secrecy of their internal deliberations, they mandated that the notes detailing the proceedings and debates remained sealed for fifty years. Consequently, the release of these notes was greatly anticipated both by abolitionists and by advocates of slavery, both factions eagerly hoping for more detailed clues about where the Founders had stood on the issue of slavery. When the notes were finally printed in 1840, "far from settling the issue of whether the Constitution did or did not sanction slavery, publication gave partisans on all sides more ammunition for their arguments."[1] No suddenly revealed magic wisdom from the Founders would settle the fundamental division of the country.

While chattel slavery had always been a repugnant concept and a cause of monstrous suffering and death ever since the first slaves were brought to the Jamestown colony in 1619, specific economic forces in 19th-century America rendered its practice even more violent and barbaric. Specifically, plantation owners in the South were under increasing pressure from the mercantile forces in the North and in Europe to keep cotton prices low. As Du Bois writes, the enslaver was "continually forced to find his profit not in the high price of cotton and sugar, but in beating even further down the cost of his slave labor."[2]

This harsh reality had a devastating impact on the life of enslaved Southern Black people, who were forced to labor under deplorable conditions that circumscribed every aspect of their daily lives. Furthermore, many plantation owners perpetrated the rape of enslaved women and forced compulsory reproduction to increase their stock of free labor. Lower-class Whites were frequently employed by plantation owners as "enforcers" to keep the system of slavery intact. Moreover, a euphemistic "rational ethos" was spun to justify the construct of chattel slavery based on a fallacious assertion of the inferiority of enslaved people.[3] Thus, as the institution of slavery became more established and entrenched, the contradiction with the founding principles of the nation became more glaring, and the clash with rising abolitionist forces came to the front and center.

In the development of political and social theories during the 17th and 18th centuries, views on slavery had always been one of the clearest demarcation points between Moderate Enlightenment advocates, for whom protecting property rights was fundamental (and many considered enslaved people to be property), and the Radical Enlightenment advocates, who recognized that slavery was wholly contradictory to the notion of unalienable rights, despite the contradiction that some

were enslavers themselves. In this respect, slavery and racial subjugation were at the very heart of the American Schism. The fundamental
immorality of slavery steered abolitionists in both the North and South
into an alignment with the Radicals, even if the foundations of many
American abolitionist views were faith based and not overtly based on
Enlightenment principles.

The inherent horrors associated with the practice of slavery were
overwhelmingly recognized as the most flagrant and treacherous injustice in the new nation by both the educated classes of citizens in the
United States and by people all over the world. Consider the paradox:
America, a nation founded on the principle of equality, was extracting
tremendous wealth by brutally exploiting the labor of enslaved people.
This, along with industrialization, propelled the rise of capitalism not
only in the United States, but through trade worldwide.[4]

LINCOLN AT GETTYSBURG
FOUNDS A NEW NATION

In Garry Wills's illuminating book, *Lincoln at Gettysburg* (1992), the
author provides an insightful analysis of why the Gettysburg Address
has become one of the most consequential speeches in history. Wills
compares the impact of Lincoln's address to one given more than
2,000 years earlier by Pericles over the ashes of the fallen Athenians
during the Peloponnesian wars. But the genius of Wills's account is
how he illustrates Lincoln's incredible fortitude in refusing to allow
two key elements of his own American vision to remain unreconciled:
Lincoln believed the institution of slavery was repugnant *and* that the
Union had to be preserved. So, while for many, the only viable solution
seemed to be the severing of formal ties between the North and the
South, the tenacity of Lincoln's belief in the Union precluded such a

formal schism (even if, once the South seceded, Lincoln himself equiv-
ocated at times about whether the South was still part of the Union).

Lincoln had a brilliant legal mind and understood clearly that
the actions available to him as the nation's leader were carefully circumscribed by the powers vested in him by the Constitution. From a
legal point of view, the Southern states had no constitutional right to
secede. Therefore, Lincoln considered the conflict as an internal rebellion. Throughout the war years, he continued to regard himself as a
president of *all the people*, those residing in the North and the South.
But at the same time, Lincoln understood that he could not impose his
personal vision on the constitutionally protected rights of each state. In
the end, however, in his 272 words at Gettysburg, Lincoln triumphed
by using his oratory and not his constitutional powers to reconcile the
two conflicting elements of his vision. In fact, his words that day would
live on to transcend the limitations of the Constitution and single-
handedly give new life to the original promise of 1776.

In Lincoln's view, the whole purpose of the nation's founding was
predicated on the proclamation (in the Declaration of Independence)
that "all men are created equal." In his prior speeches and writings,
Lincoln referred frequently to the Declaration of Independence, as in
the Lincoln-Douglas debates: "There is no reason in the world why
the negro is not entitled to all the natural rights enumerated in the
Declaration of Independence, the right to life, liberty and the pursuit of happiness. I hold that he is as much entitled to these as the
white man . . . I think the authors of that notable instrument intended
to include *all* men."[5] By referring back to those sacred words of the
Declaration "that all men are created equal" and elevating them to
represent the apotheosis of the entire American experiment, Lincoln
explicitly recognized that the Constitution he had taken an oath to
protect was flawed, unable to fulfill the basic credo of the nation.

For Lincoln, the Declaration of Independence was the foundational
document of the nation; the Constitution was but our best effort up

to that point in time to achieve the premise (and the promise) of that original proclamation. Lincoln "distinguished between the Declaration as the statement of a permanent ideal and the Constitution as an early and provisional embodiment of that ideal to be tested against it."[6] It was precisely along these lines that Lincoln believed that our experiment in self-government as implemented through the Constitution remained deficient since the Radical Enlightenment ideal of the Declaration had demonstrably not been achieved. As a work in progress in 1863, much about our nation's aspirations was yet to be achieved (as remains the case today). Further, Lincoln's call to action compelled Americans to finish that work; "the great remaining task" at the end of the address was to modify the implementation vehicles of our government (in this case the Constitution) to fulfill that foundational promise.

As Wills argues, Lincoln at Gettysburg proclaims that merely preserving the Union is not enough; what is required is finishing the Founders' work, since "they did *not* accomplish the political equality they professed. They did not end slavery. They did not make self-government stable and enduring."[7] In Lincoln's own writings, the Founders had "no power to confer" equality on all people. "They meant simply to declare the *right*, so that the *enforcement* might follow as fast as circumstances should permit."[8] It is precisely in this manner (and not hyperbolic to state) that Lincoln undertook a new founding of the nation.

Many resented Lincoln's undertaking, to correct things he felt to be imperfect in the Framers' achievement. But over the course of the following decades, Lincoln's interpretation of and prominence of the Declaration took hold. Wills, writing in 1992, noted that "for most people now, the Declaration means what Lincoln told us it means, as a way of correcting the Constitution itself without overthrowing it."[9]

Lincoln had articulated a vision to fulfill the original promise that "all men are created equal"—thus bestowing an opportunity for meaningful changes to give rise to a more ethically just American republic. He summarized the entire war period as "an attempt to overthrow this government, which was built on a foundation of human rights, and to substitute one which should rest exclusively on the basis of human slavery."[10]

But if Lincoln's vision of the rebirth of the nation was dazzling, his strategy and tactics to achieve it were no less brilliant. In 1863, Lincoln achieved two huge victories in one stroke of a pen. "The Emancipation Proclamation itself, with its exemption of Union-held areas, reflected not only Lincoln's effort to make emancipation legally unassailable (as a wartime act), but also his determination to retain the support of the millions of Northerners who cared little about abolition but might support an act essential to military victory."[11] Thus, the Proclamation was both a moral triumph that would prove to be an inspiration to millions and the deployment of a brilliant political and military strategy.

*   *   *

The literature on the era of post–Civil War Reconstruction is voluminous, and to this day, a broad range of scholarly opinion exists on important issues regarding how Reconstruction might have more fruitfully achieved its intended twin goals of rebuilding economic prosperity in the South *and* achieving the enfranchisement and civil rights of African Americans. But there is no question that the period following the war reverberated back and forth between elements of an aspirational advancement toward an unfulfilled Radical Enlightenment vision and the bitterly discouraging and disappointing developments reflected in the reality on the ground. The era was yet another manifestation of the pendulum swinging between the two competing poles within the American Schism.

As the Civil War concluded, Lincoln strived to deliver on his promise in myriad ways up until his death. His short-term construct for bringing the Southern states back into the Union was conditional on the permanent emancipation of enslaved people and the abolition of slavery in the republic via the 13th Amendment, which passed in the Senate in 1863. While the amendment would not be ratified by the individual states until January of 1865, each state's consent represented the "table stakes" for readmission to the Union. Nonetheless, the question of how slavery was going to be actually abolished was not at all clear. Given the bitterness in the South, enforcing the emancipation required the presence of Union troops in the South for years following the war.

But beyond the important *de jure* achievement of emancipation, Lincoln galvanized support from various parts of the abolitionist movement to commence the political process that would ultimately lead to the first protection of civil rights for African Americans. Lincoln inarguably recognized what a momentous undertaking this would be for many reasons. He was surely cognizant of the fact that racist beliefs and culture were firmly inculcated throughout the entire nation, most intensely perhaps in the South but also reaching far beyond it. He also recognized that bringing both enslaved and free African Americans into the civil and political processes was a complex and multifaceted endeavor with no quick fixes.

Because the acrimony between former enslavers and formerly enslaved people made peaceful integration in the South seem arduous, perhaps even impossible, the concept of deporting the formerly enslaved people into a territory outside the country was once again discussed in the mainstream and garnered some support. Lincoln, along with most leading abolitionists, knew that this idea was not only impractical but failed to address the fundamental contradiction in the nation's fabric. Consequently, one of the pressing questions following emancipation was this: How could a largely illiterate population of formerly enslaved people achieve effective agency in the political process? This problem was acute in the South, of course, but it was also prevalent in the parts of the country where slavery had not been part of the economy or social order.

By war's end, few reconstruction efforts had been successful and, with the exception of West Virginia, not a single Confederate state had rejoined the Union. Nonetheless, in shaping his post-war vision, Lincoln absorbed two realities that had emerged by the time the South surrendered. First, African Americans both free and enslaved had played a decisive role in winning the war by serving in combat for the North. Columbia University Professor Eric Foner, in his epic work *Reconstruction: American's Unfinished Revolution 1863–1877* (1989), describes what a powerful model of transformation this represented: "Their service helped transform the nation's treatment of blacks and blacks' conception of them-selves . . . It was in the army that large numbers of former slaves first learned to read and write . . . For the first time in American his-tory, large numbers of blacks were treated as equal before the law."[12]

Second, some demonstrations of successful racial integration already existed at the time; well-educated articulate African Americans were frequently quite highly esteemed and already notably contributing to society, both in the North and in select places in the South. Lincoln not only met but was friends with Frederick Douglass (despite their disagreements), a leader of national stature and prominence. Moreover, Lincoln was keenly aware of the situation in Louisiana where African Americans, often educated in France, held diverse and quite reputable positions in society. Louisiana had already begun a reconstruction pro-gram before war's end, and New Orleans had the largest community of free Black people in the South. With this as a prototype, Lincoln devised and empowered government entities to lay the foundation for a new kind of society throughout the South.

In order to assist the transition of formerly enslaved people into adequate living conditions, the Freedmen's Bureau was created in early 1865, "the most extraordinary and far-reaching institution of social uplift that America had ever attempted."[13] The Freedmen's Bureau mandate was quite far reaching, with judicial powers to police the safety and security of formerly enslaved people and executive powers, including the creation of a system of schools all over the South to provide education. As Foner describes:

> [The Freedmen's Bureau] responsibilities can only be described as daunting; they included introducing a workable system of free labor . . . establishing schools for freedmen, providing aid to the destitute, aged, ill, and insane, adjudicating disputes among blacks and between the races, and attempting to secure for blacks . . . equal justice from the state and local governments established.[14]

In addition, many religious and benevolent organizations like the American Missionary Association played a mammoth role in Reconstruction. By early 1865, not only were schools being built, but public relief projects were incipient all over the South. With its creation, the bureau "symbolized the widespread belief among Republicans that the federal government must shoulder broad responsibility for the emancipated slaves."[15]

Another early win at this time was the establishment of all-Black churches, which would become central to many aspects of African American community life all over the South. As discussed in Part I, the civic role that these churches played assisted millions of recently emancipated individuals. "The rise of the independent black church provides only the most striking example of the thriving institutional structure blacks created in the aftermath of emancipation."[16] In church schools, the thirst for education among the communities of formerly enslaved people was profound and widespread, indicative of a tremendous desire for self-improvement. The extraordinary hope that these developments represented for formerly enslaved people must have been inspiring. Foner summarizes:

In the severing of ties that had bound black and white families and churches to one another under slavery, the coming together of blacks in an explosion of institution building, and the political and cultural fusion of former free blacks and former slaves, Reconstruction witnessed the birth of the modern black community. All in all, the months following the end of the Civil War were a period of remarkable accomplishment for Southern blacks.[17]

ANDREW JOHNSON VS. THE RADICAL REPUBLICANS

But despite these efforts and some concrete advances, by the time Andrew Johnson assumed the presidency upon Lincoln's death, the spirit on the ground in the South was not encouraging. Few formerly enslaved people could afford to purchase land or find secure and peaceful dwellings. In addition to very difficult living conditions for formerly enslaved people, the South remained occupied territory—"the presence of black troops among the occupying Union army . . . inspired constant complaint on the part of whites."[18] Yet even under the protection of these troops, violent acts perpetrated against formerly enslaved people were rampant. "Considering the extent of white violence against blacks, it is remarkable in how few instances blacks attacked whites."[19]

In order to reenter the Union, the confederate states needed to form new governments, prompting a series of individual state constitutional conventions. Initially, at these state conventions, Black delegates got little hearing, and any political agency for formerly enslaved people was minimal. Moreover, the labor contracts that plantation owners developed to employ formerly enslaved people were so onerous that the employment the latter desperately needed was in fact barely distinguishable from slavery.

President Johnson commissioned a study of the attitudes on the ground. Charles Schurz concluded in his report:

At last I was forced to the conclusion that, aside from a small number of honorable exceptions, the popular prejudice is almost as bitterly set against the Negro . . . I hear the people talk in such a way as to indicate that they are yet unable to conceive of the Negro as possessing any rights at all.[20]

While at first President Johnson indicated that he would continue building on Lincoln's legacy, it quickly became clear that he would advance the Reconstruction agenda only very begrudgingly, at best. Despite his promise to hold the former rebels accountable, by the summer of 1865 he was issuing frequent pardons that restored property to former Confederate plantation owners and soldiers. At heart, Johnson was in no way committed to political equality for African Americans, and furthermore, he believed in the sanctity of states' rights and constrained federal power.

One of Johnson's first acts as president was to dismantle the free state structure in Louisiana that Lincoln had overseen and fostered as a prospective prototype for other states. Then, in choosing provisional governors for other Confederate states, Johnson passed over unconditional Union loyalists and instead selected from among the prewar crop of Confederate leaders. These acts not only astonished many in Congress but served as warning flags to abolitionists nationwide. It became clear that Johnson was going to permit the rebel states to take affairs into their own hands via the adoption of the new locally developed state constitutions, which predictably lacked an expansionist view of the spirit of emancipation, much less of civic and political equality for formerly enslaved people.

The primary obstacle was that Andrew Johnson, a former enslaver himself, was in fact a veritable racist who could not possibly conceive of true African American enfranchisement. In addition to his overall approach of referring the problems of Reconstruction to the individual states themselves, astoundingly, he was blind to the most blatant needs of formerly enslaved people, such as ensuring their local protection. His statement in the first year after the war's end demonstrates his contemptuous attitude: "They are free. Let them go to work, earn wages and support their schools. Their civil rights and political rights must depend entirely upon their former masters, and the United States [federal government] has no constitutional authority to interfere to help them."[21] The *New York Herald* reported on the situation:

> If at the end of all the blood that has been shed . . . the unfortunate Negro is to be left in the hands of his infuriated and disappointed former owners to legislate and fix his status, God help him, for his cup of bitterness will overflow indeed.[22]

One of the most indicative portrayals of Andrew Johnson's true beliefs was revealed in his 1867 annual message to Congress, in which he "insisted that blacks possessed less 'capacity for government than any other race of people. No independent government of any form has ever been successful in their hands. On the contrary, wherever they have been left to their own devices they have shown a constant tendency to relapse into barbarism.'" Foner labels this "probably the most blatantly racist pronouncement ever to appear in an official state paper of an American President."[23]

While White Southerners were relieved that Johnson's Reconstruction plan endorsed local jurisdiction for the postwar transition, it became evident by 1866 that Congress was not going to remain silent. A group of Republicans in both the House and the Senate, usually referred to as the era's "Radical Republicans," had fought vociferously to abolish slavery and were plainly dismayed by Johnson's dithering, especially in the wake of the intrepid leadership of President Lincoln. (Use of the term "radical" to describe the Radical Republicans of the mid-19th century is distinct from use of the term to describe the Radical Enlightenment, although the thinking of these 19th-century legislators was unquestionably influenced by and in the spirit of their Radical Enlightenment predecessors.) Further, as the Southern states started passing new laws referred to as "Black Codes," it became apparent that Congress would intercede and play a larger role in Reconstruction overall.

These "Black Codes" were purportedly laws intended to delineate the freedmen's new rights and responsibilities, but in fact they imposed atrocious conditions that severely restricted the economic and civic possibilities and future outlook of formerly enslaved people. When Black leaders in the various Southern states raised their concerns, they did not find much local support. However, they did find a sympathetic ear in Congress. The blatant failure of Johnson's laissez-faire approach was conspicuously illustrated in that it not only galvanized the Radical Republicans in Congress but pushed their much more moderate colleagues (who were at first quite reluctant) to join in opposing Johnson. "The growing perception of white Southern intransigence and President Johnson's inability . . . would help propel the party's center of gravity to the left."[24] In addition, abolitionists in the North had been energetically drumming up popular support for a stronger stance against Southern state intransigence.

It was this confluence of events that led the Radical Republicans in Congress to seize the opportunity not only to move Reconstruction back onto a corrective trajectory capable of fulfilling the promise of emancipation, but also to spearhead the charting of a more sweeping and egalitarian mission to enfranchise formerly enslaved people. After Lincoln's death, this group of leaders in Congress breathed new life into the struggle and assumed the mantel of responsibility for the civic and political rights of all African Americans, be they in the North, South, or West.

For many of the Radical Republicans in Congress, abolition and obtaining racial civic equality represented a lifelong commitment. Unfortunately, their contributions are too often overlooked in today's historical narratives. But in confronting the pressing problems regarding emancipation enforcement as well as refining the criteria by which the rebel states would be readmitted to the Union, it was these leaders who pushed Reconstruction forward.

Massachusetts senator Charles Sumner and Pennsylvania representative Thaddeus Stevens led the cause, fully committed to the belief that African Americans were entitled to the same political and civil rights and opportunities as Whites. They were joined by many others, including Senator Benjamin Wade. But it was evident that Sumner and Stevens became the unrelenting bulls on a mission in Congress, as illustrated by their unyielding introduction and reintroduction of bills as long as necessary until they could garner adequate support from their colleagues.

What both Sumner and Stevens realized, perhaps more than most, was that the end of the Civil War represented a "'golden moment,' an opportunity for far-reaching change that, if allowed to pass, 'will have escaped for years, if not forever.'"[25] Furthermore, they both embraced an expansive view of wartime federal authority and advocated for a sweeping national program. In justifying this view, they pointed to the clause in the Constitution itself that guaranteed that each state would have a republican form of government.

Sumner himself created and then chaired the crucial Senate special committee on slavery and formerly enslaved people. He would recurrently speak on the Senate floor for hours and hours, at times with famous African Americans like Frederick Douglass in the gallery. "Sumner insisted that the black man's right to vote was 'the essence'— the great essential of guaranteeing his freedom. His speech laid down a Magna Carta of democracy in America."[26] "Yet the conversion of public opinion in the United States to Negro citizenship and suffrage would [prove to be] long and difficult."[27]

The argument that Sumner and Stevens deployed is best summarized by what each wrote at the end of 1865:

Thaddeus Stevens:

We have turned, or are about to turn, loose four million slaves without a hut to shelter them or a cent in their pockets. The infernal laws of slavery have prevented them from acquiring an education, understanding of the commonest of laws of contract, or of managing ordinary business life. The Congress is bound to provide for them until they can take care of themselves.[28]

And Charles Sumner at the same time:

That pledge [of emancipation] cannot be entrusted to another, least of all, can it be entrusted to the old slave-masters, embittered against their slaves. It must be performed by the National Government. The power that gave freedom must see that this freedom is maintained.[29]

Sumner and Stevens were also resolute about holding the former Confederate leaders accountable, as evidenced by their enforcement of appropriate punishments such as exclusion from all postwar government positions. This was in direct opposition to Johnson's approach of leniency vis-à-vis former Confederate leaders. Thaddeus Stevens struck the first blow in Congress at the end of 1865, when the former vice president of the Confederacy was elected as senator from Georgia. Insisting that he could not credibly take the oath of loyalty required to assume his seat, Stevens convened a joint committee of Congress to block not only this seating but to postpone the reseating of any further members from Southern states. This move strikingly demonstrated the congressional strength and determination to counter Johnson's indulgent approach.

Further, while Sumner and Stevens resorted to the stick, other legislators dangled a carrot; Senator Wade introduced the novel stance that only Confederate states that granted suffrage to Black people could adjust their population counts for the purposes of representation as they were readmitted to the Union. While at this particular time there was not broad discussion of or support for the concept of Black suffrage, Senator Wade put the notion on the table.

Between the strong convictions of these leaders and Johnson's intransigence, the congressional war with the president became increasingly vicious. Johnson's blocking of a whole series of legislative efforts raised the heat significantly. The Civil Rights Bill of 1866 was truly groundbreaking; it granted citizenship *to all people* born in the United States and guaranteed the same civil rights to everyone regardless of race. This bill interpreted equality before the law as an expansive principle embracing nearly all aspects of public life. "As the first statutory definition of the rights of American citizenship, the Civil Rights Bill embodied a profound change in federal-state relations and reflected how ideas once considered Radical had been adopted by the party's mainstream."[30]

In the same session, Congress passed a new bill extending the work of the Freedmen's Bureau. These two bills apparently indicated that Republican Moderates had been swayed by and joined forces with the Radicals, and as a group they had collective momentum to overcome resistance and counteract President's Johnson approach of affording the Southern states local jurisdiction of postwar matters.

Johnson flatly vetoed the extension of the Freedmen's Bureau, repudiated its mission, and reasserted his view that it was not a prerogative of Congress to provide on-the-ground assistance to formerly enslaved people. In his veto, Johnson articulated an argument that would echo for centuries; he "voiced themes that to this day have sustained opposition to federal intervention on behalf of blacks."[31] Johnson then went on to veto the Civil Rights Bill, which Republicans considered a declaration of war not only on Congress but on freedmen themselves. Johnson's Civil Rights Bill veto message

> repudiated not merely the specific terms of the Civil Rights Bill, but the entire principle behind it . . . what was most striking about the message was its blatant racism . . . Somehow, the President had convinced himself that clothing blacks with the privileges of citizenship discriminated against whites . . . He also presented the curious argument that immigrants from abroad were more deserving of citizenship than blacks, because they knew more about "the nature and character of our institutions."[32]

These actions by Johnson were a major miscalculation. Not only was he widely condemned in the press and in public circles, but his intransigence further emboldened the congressional opposition. Even moderate Republicans in Congress were appalled at Johnson's actions. Most now viewed working constructively with the president on Reconstruction as a hopeless endeavor. The Moderates joined with the Radicals to overturn Johnson's veto, the first override of a presidential veto of a major piece of legislation in the nation's history.

At this juncture, Congress clearly felt it had license to move forward on a more aggressive agenda but needed to do so outside the reach of changing political majorities or the presidential veto. Consequently, the key Radical Republican coalition on the Hill became determined to use a different vehicle *provided by the Framers* to fix the Constitution, and work on the 14th Amendment commenced.

It is hard to overemphasize the importance of the 14th Amendment in our subsequent history as a nation. Thoroughly in the spirit of the Radical Enlightenment, not only did this amendment define and extend the concept of citizenship to all native-born people of all races, but through the due process clause it enumerated and guaranteed a broad set of rights to all, acting in many ways as a complement to the original

Bill of Rights. The Amendment itself combined many of the most pressing issues related to Reconstruction into one proposition: granting citizenship, providing a federal government guarantee of equality, and prohibiting states or local governments from denying or abridging any of the full range of privileges underlying the concepts of life, liberty, and the pursuit of happiness without "due process of law."

With its eventual passage in 1866 and ratification in 1868, the 14th Amendment provided constitutional form to the values and ideals first defined by the Radical Enlightenment thinkers and subsequently embodied in the Declaration of Independence almost a century before. With the Black Codes instituted by the rebel states as the initial target, henceforth any "discriminatory state laws could be overturned by federal courts regardless of which party dominated Congress . . . a degree of federal intervention in state affairs scarcely conceivable before 1860."[33] Sumner, the ever-eloquent orator, summed up the situation after the passage of the 14th Amendment overcoming President Johnson's intransigence:

> The suffering at the South is great through the misconduct of the President. His course has kept the rebel spirit alive, and depressed the loyal, white and black. It makes me very sad to see this. Considering the difficulties of their position, the blacks have done wonderfully well. They should have had a Moses as a President; but they have found a Pharaoh.[34]

Not surprisingly, the Southern states at first repudiated the 14th Amendment. But Congress was ready to strike back, and it did so decisively. The Reconstruction Act of 1867 would in some sense rewind the clock back to the end of the war by imposing military rule anew in the South and delineating new conditions for Southern states to be readmitted. Importantly, among those conditions was the ratification of the 14th Amendment.

As Congress turned to the issue of universal suffrage, Black political mobilization in the South was promulgated via Union Leagues, a series of clubs and organizations that had been started during the war to promote loyalty to the Union. Formerly enslaved people in great numbers throughout the South joined these Leagues, which provided them with a foundation of political education and assisted with economic issues. A new generation of Black leaders arose from the Leagues and staked a claim to political equality. While the 15th Amendment (guaranteeing voting rights) had not yet passed, Black voters showed up in large numbers in places where they could vote. "In defiance of fatigue, hardship, hunger, and threats of employers, blacks had come en masse to the polls . . . Rarely has a community invested so many hopes in politics as did blacks during Radical Reconstruction."[35]

Also championing the Republican cause in the South were the many Northern Republicans who ventured to the South, called "carpetbaggers." These were usually well-educated members of the middle class, but many were professionals, like lawyers and doctors. Their motivation was primarily economic, but many were also eager to join what they viewed as an egalitarian democratic movement, inspired by what they hoped would be the dawning of a new society in the South. White Southerners who joined the Republicans in the fight for equality were viewed as traitors and chastised by many of their fellow Whites, who labeled them "scalawags." Thus, the new Republican Party in the South confronting the old regime Democrats, in the vernacular of the day, comprised formerly enslaved people, carpetbaggers, and scalawags.

Further adding to Republican strength, at least temporarily, was the fact that many former Confederates were disenfranchised; because they had been stripped of the vote, they could not lend their support to the Democratic Party. So, while the Republican Party in the South had barely existed in prior years, at this junction it began to build a more diversified base of support as each state convened to draft the new constitution required for reentry into the Union.

At these new state constitutional conventions, Black delegates played their first meaningful political roles in the South, sitting alongside White delegates. In Louisiana and South Carolina, free-born well-educated Black people also joined as delegates. Ultimately, it was at these conventions that all the states began establishing African Americans' civil and political rights in state law. However, the political results were mixed; myriad impediments related to schools, land reform, and access to public facilities remained in place, and many other intricate issues went unresolved. Nonetheless, the resulting state constitutions codified a radically changed South as compared to the antebellum era. While formerly enslaved people continued to face the specter of entrenched White supremacy, the pathways for a new life for African Americans in the South had been cleared. Further, Black leaders emerged who held authentic power in local governments as well as through representation in Washington.

While President Johnson was impeached in the House based on his record of intransigence and obstruction, he barely survived removal in the Senate trial by a margin of two votes. Although many historians widely lay the blame on Johnson for the ultimate failure of Reconstruction and believe that the outcome might have been far different had Lincoln lived, Reconstruction seemed to be on a very promising path by 1868–1869. While substantial challenges still lay ahead, much progress had been made. Not only was there significant turnout of Black people at recent elections, but the new Republican Party in the South had a firm grip on the agenda. Yet at the same time, it was far from clear whether these advancements would endure. As one Democratic newspaper wrote as the state conventions were ending: "These constitutions and governments will last just as long as the bayonets which ushered them into being, shall keep them in existence, and not one day longer."[36]

RECONSTRUCTION ENDS AS A NEW GILDED AGE DAWNS

The next period of the Reconstruction era would turn much gloomier, as Southern Democrats dug in their heels. In fact, the single most prominent platform issue for the Democrats in the 1868 presidential election was opposition to Reconstruction. Fortunately, Republican Ulysses S. Grant's victory ensured its continuation. At the same time as the Republican Party sought legitimacy in the South, it was pursuing an extensive plan to restructure society. The plan would affect not only the labor system, economic development, and education, but also fundamental race relations. In the years between 1868 and 1872, additional progress was made in achieving some of these goals, such as more economic prosperity in the South; in addition to plantation recovery, southern railroads were being rebuilt at an astounding pace. Further, huge gains were made in the establishment of Black educational institutions and churches.

Sharecropping emerged as a way in which formerly enslaved people could provide sustenance for their families and earn their own living without having to work directly for White plantation owners. While the sharecropping solution was a win-win for formerly enslaved people and owners who needed to make money from their land, race-based economic exploitation certainly continued. Nonetheless, "biracial democratic government, a thing unknown in American history, was functioning effectively in many parts of the old South. Men only recently released from bondage cast ballots and sat on juries."[37]

In the area of race relations, however, progress was minimal. Civil rights laws went largely unenforced, and in the public sphere, segregation became the *de facto* reality. The dour outlook for improving race relations was in large part due to the tremendous resentment felt by many Whites, who deeply regretted the loss of a legally sanctioned supremacist society of the antebellum era. Seemingly, the more gains formerly enslaved people attained in the political and economic areas, the more this antipathy grew. Undoubtedly, many Southern Whites felt on the losing end of the changes brought on by Reconstruction and were convinced that to ensure the destiny of the South, the entire experiment of Reconstruction had to be overturned. That their bitterness was to take such a horrid and violent turn was perhaps unexpected.

The emergence of the Ku Klux Klan and other sister organizations epitomized the horrific wrath of many White Southerners at the new reality they faced as a consequence of Reconstruction. It also exhibited, as it had through the Civil War ordeal itself, how the two opposing visions of the nation that defined the American Schism were not only at the root of contentious political debates but also instigated some of the most appalling episodes of barbaric viciousness with repercussions for large swaths of American society. These organizations brought down a veritable reign of terror on the South.

While violence had often been a part of elections in previous eras, the extent of the attacks and intimidation in the 1868 election was unprecedented. Some counties in Georgia, for example, recorded no votes for the Republican ticket. "It is a measure of how far change had progressed that the reaction against Reconstruction proved so extreme. In effect, the Klan was a military force serving the interests of the Democratic party . . . and all those who desired the restoration of white supremacy."[38]

Thousands of freedmen were murdered in these years, and hundreds of thousands more were intimidated. In the Colfax massacre of 1873, more than one hundred Black men were brutally murdered. Further, dread of violence made it virtually impossible for formerly enslaved people to vote in many parts of the South. It became clear that the progress of Reconstruction in the South depended not only on the Republican Party winning over more White voters to its cause, but also in doggedly confronting the horrific reality of the lawless and violent opposition that had taken root from the acrimonious racist seeds of the old South.

As the perpetrators of violence in the South increasingly terrorized formerly enslaved people and their families, seemingly with impunity, in 1871 Congress finally stepped in with the Ku Klux Klan Act. Whereas all previous federal legislation, including the Civil Rights Acts and the Amendments, had been designed to protect freedmen from hostile state actions, this act allowed federal authorities to prosecute private criminal acts for the first time, acts that would usually be under the purview of local law officials (however, lynching would not be outlawed until the 1940s).

Because of this reach into the area of state and local authority, the federal government would necessarily be limited in its abilities to administer the act. Also, many Democrats objected based on the principles of federalism—if the national government could punish crimes within the states, local self-government as a concept was rendered meaningless and would ultimately perish. Nonetheless, Republicans felt that suppression of the Klan required extraordinary means: "If the Federal Government cannot pass laws to protect the rights, liberty, and lives of citizens . . . why were guarantees of those fundamental rights put in the Constitution at all?"[39] Ultimately, the key question was just how far the federal government would go to enforce Reconstruction.

In 1871, the Grant Administration proclaimed a "condition of lawlessness" in nine counties of South Carolina, leading to the deployment of yet additional federal troops. The action led to hundreds of arrests and convictions, but most Klansmen successfully fled to other territories. The threat of federal power was marginally successful in producing a decline in violence for the time being. However, it remained unclear to what degree Reconstruction's enforcement could depend on federal intervention in the future. Thus, despite the progress of protecting Black suffrage through the 15th Amendment in 1869 and continued increases in political representation locally and in Congress (Hiram Revels became the first African American senator in 1870), the increasing uncertainty of Reconstruction's continued progress portended a worrisome future. While there was no question that a huge degree of positive change had occurred in a relatively short period of time, not only did further advances seem uncertain but the sustainability of gains achieved so far seemed tenuous.

*   *   *

The Gilded Age of the late 19th century in the United States saw rapid economic growth mostly in the northern and western states. Unfortunately, as industrial power grew, so did political favors and corruption in government. Thus, one drawback of increasing economic expansion was an increase in scandals involving government and the industrial barons of the era. Reform movements were spawned both to contain government corruption and to represent the condition of working-class voters. Still, patronage-based politics had become a key feature of the era by the time of Grant's reelection in 1872.

In his second term, President Grant's focus on the new politics of industrial expansion took priority over Reconstruction. While Republicans were able to hold power at many levels in the 1872 elections, the radicalism of the mid-1860s was in clear decline. Moreover, the economic depression that began in 1873 further complicated the progress of Reconstruction. The woes triggered by the depression produced a sizable shift in the 1874 midterm elections. The Democratic Party took the majority in the House, while Republicans retained control of the Senate.

At the state level, Republican power in the South also began to wane, and the reemergence of a climate of violence indubitably depressed vote counts. In Mississippi specifically, elections were compromised by fierce intimidation tactics that led to Democratic control of the state. Even though it was evident to all that the elections in Mississippi were in no way fair, the Grant Administration failed to intervene. With Northern Republicans' attention focused on economic recovery and the dramatic resurgence of the Democrats in the South, 1875 was a landmark in the retreat from Reconstruction.

The centennial election of 1876 proved to be the pivotal event that would definitively end Reconstruction. The presidential race between Rutherford B. Hayes and Samuel Tilden produced no clear winner. The Democrat candidate Tilden convincingly won the popular vote, but the election in the South was clearly compromised, as the Ku Klux Klan had ramped up their terrorizing tactics to encumber and impede Black voting. Because the existing constitutional regulations provided no clear path on how to end the election impasse, an independent Electoral Commission was created to resolve the issue. In a sinister grand bargain, the Democrats conceded the presidency to Republican Rutherford B. Hayes on the condition that the federal government would cease interfering in the affairs of the Southern states.

This principle of allowing home rule for the South marked the end of Reconstruction. The subsequent withdrawal of all troops from the South represented a decisive retreat from the overall construct "of a powerful national state protecting the fundamental rights of American citizens."[40] From the perspective of the former Confederate states, the end of the nightmare of federal intervention in the daily lives of White citizens signified a new era. The now-redeemed states together with the border states formed a united political front, referred to as the "Solid South," that could turn the page and close what many Southerners viewed as the dreadful chapter of Reconstruction.

The restoration of Democratic power in the South gradually allowed for the resumption of the old White supremacist order. Despite the legal protections provided by the 14th and 15th Amendments, local gerrymandering, poll taxes, and other nefarious tactics greatly restricted African American civic and political participation. This systematic disenfranchisement relied on many different tactics to achieve its goals: "The freedman was kept from voting by force, by economic intimidation, by propaganda destined to lead him to believe that there was no salvation for him in political lines but that he must depend entirely upon thrift and the goodwill of his white employers."[41]

One African American leader of this time, Booker T. Washington, advised African Americans to rely less on politics and more on education. Yet the systematic disenfranchisement at all levels was crippling. Moreover, the new government of the South continued its endless pursuit to reshape race relations to more closely resemble the antebellum South. In a reversal best expressed in the words of W. E. B. Du Bois, "The slave went free, stood a brief moment in the sun; and then moved back again toward slavery."[42]

In the end, despite the abolition of slavery and the extension of citizenship, Reconstruction must be judged as a failure. Historians in the last hundred years have vigorously debated the root causes of this tragic outcome. In hindsight, it is facile to point to the many missteps that could have perhaps been avoided by leaders with stronger resolve. Thousands of scholarly historical works have contemplated and conjectured how better outcomes might have been reached. However, it is unlikely that any of a myriad of other factors would have been decisive. In Foner's words, the failure of Reconstruction

> was a disaster whose magnitude cannot be obscured by the genuine accomplishments that did endure. For the nation as a whole, the collapse . . . was a tragedy that deeply affected the course of its future development. If racism contributed to the undoing of Reconstruction, by the same token Reconstruction's demise and the emergence of blacks as a disenfranchised class . . . greatly facilitated racism's further spread, until by the early 20th century, it had become more deeply embedded in the nation's culture and politics . . . Long into the 20th century, the South remained a one-party region under the control of a reactionary ruling elite who used the same violence and fraud that had helped defeat Reconstruction to stifle internal dissent. An enduring

consequence of Reconstruction's failure, the Solid South helped define the contours of American politics and weaken the prospects not simply of change in racial matters but of progressive legislation in many other realms.[43]

With Reconstruction abandoned, a new system of southern "slavery" would fossilize and remain intact for at least a century. While on paper the Confederacy was gone, the entrenched racism underpinning the antebellum South would continue to linger and disenfranchise African Americans, rescinding most political and economic gains made during Reconstruction. During the 1870s, this harsh reality was legally codified anew with the enactment of the Jim Crow Laws. Once again it became clear that a racially segregated society would cruelly and viciously continue to deny African Americans the ability to "pursue liberty and happiness." The entire structure created by these laws (and upheld by the U.S. Supreme Court in *Plessy v. Ferguson*) mandated segregation in all forms of public life. The Jim Crow South comprised "twin systems of oppression: segregation across public and private spheres that kept black people away from social and economic equality, and systematic political disenfranchisement that made sure black citizens weren't represented democratically."[44]

In conclusion, the Reconstruction era provides yet another great illustration of the pendulum swing between the two opposing poles of the American Schism. The struggle for a more egalitarian society in the aftermath of the Civil War was characterized by a continued oscillation in influence between conflicting visions of the country. The principles that drove the quest for racial equality as embodied in the positions advocated by the mid-19th-century Radical Republicans were unquestionably rooted in the Radical Enlightenment ideals of their predecessors. An opposing camp fiercely advocating that the fruits of the American vision be restricted, that progress toward modernity be the exclusive privilege of White society, has manifest strains of Moderate Enlightenment thought (albeit with exclusions based on race and not necessarily social class). The predictable reaction to the tidal wave of change that Radical Reconstruction represented was predominantly based on bigotry, beliefs in White supremacy, and racial intolerance. Here, as elsewhere in American history, we see the Newtonian law at play: As one force gathers momentum, as the Radical Republicans of the post–Civil War era did, countervailing forces push back, at times uncompromisingly, and often with equalizing force.

Chapter 11

THE "SOLID SOUTH" REDEEMED AND THE POPULIST MOVEMENT

In the discussion of Reconstruction in the previous chapter, the "South" referred to the former Confederacy—the thirteen states that attempted to secede from the Union. But terms such as "the South" and "southerners" indicate a region with many distinct kinds of people and geographies with porous borders. Columbia history professor Barbara J. Fields recounts an enchanting anecdote to illustrate her own struggles to accurately define the South:

> The South still seems to be a real place, notwithstanding the disputes the term elicits. These disputes turn on where to locate the boundaries rather than on whether "the South" is a meaningful entity. Are Maryland and Delaware part of the South? Is Missouri? If, as many people assume, Texas is both part of the South and part of the West, exactly where in Texas do you leave the one and enter the other? A distinguished past professor of this organization proposed a practical test. If two men arguing in a bar in Texas decide to "take it outside,"

you're in the South. If they proceed to brawl right there in the bar, you're in the West.[1]

In spite of the nebulous nature of the precise geographical boundaries, when southerners refer to the unique "southern way of life," they are often alluding to their distinctive brand of politeness and charm, hospitality, and charity. For decades, magazines like *Southern Living* (when magazines were still popular) showcased southern cooking, arts, entertainment, architecture and design, and many other rich and unique features of southern culture that are a proud part of our national heritage. But phrases like "southern way of life" and its many other incarnations also have served for hundreds of years in a more euphemistic capacity, one with an ominous undertone—inferring a society governed by the principle of White supremacy.

THE SOLID SOUTH WIELDS FEDERALISM AS ITS "HOME-RULE" FORTRESS

The concept of federalism in our Constitution, perpetually enshrined in the 10th Amendment, reserves all residual rights to the individual states. It also represents the fulfillment in our government structure of a Jeffersonian Radical Enlightenment principle. As discussed in the first section of this book, compared to the moderate Federalists, the more radical Democratic-Republicans of the young nation were quite suspicious of power centralized in the federal government. From their perspective, centralized power by definition inexorably leads to abuse. In Jefferson's idyllic republic, the locus of power was necessarily decentralized, allowing local agrarian communities the freedom to self-govern uninhibited by the will or imposition of a remote authority. Just as the centralized and concentrated power of the British Crown was abusive vis-à-vis the American colonies, centralizing power in the new nation's federal government was feared because of its potential to be abusive and even tyrannical vis-à-vis the individual states.

This component of Radical Enlightenment philosophy would have prevented the Constitution from being supported by the more radical Jeffersonians of the late 18th century without the inclusion of the Bill of Rights, which specifically safeguards rights and freedoms and protects individual states' autonomy. However, notwithstanding the *concept* of individual state autonomy, in what turned out to be quite a paradox, the *actual practice* of federalism provided the justification for sustaining the antithesis of an egalitarian society in the antebellum South: namely, the institution of slavery, from our nation's founding up through the conclusion of the Civil War, and a *de jure* system of racial segregation and oppression for a century thereafter.

How can we reconcile the fact that these Radical Enlightenment principles intended to promote local autonomy and freedom from a centralized power structure have been used to justify an oppressive regime and principles which are themselves antithetical to the American credo? The autonomy afforded the South to pursue the southern way of life, uninhibited by federal interference or curtailment, protracted this xenophobic status quo for generations and represented precisely this dilemma. As we will explore, this enigma would continue well into the 20th century.

Following the failure of Reconstruction and the reestablishment of home rule starting in 1877, political leaders reinstituted a White supremacist scaffold at the base of and encompassing all social, political, and economic facets of life throughout the Solid South. While many southerners did not condone these actions, a large enough majority of White southerners provided ample support for these political developments. From the perspective of the southern political leadership (and the supporting majority), the reinstatement of White supremacy symbolized a political and spiritual redemption that conclusively delivered the South from the traumatic experience of the Reconstruction experiment.

For many in the Southern White establishment, Reconstruction represented an era in which the federal government had not only usurped the political power that was constitutionally reserved to the states in accordance with the 10th Amendment, but also audaciously interfered in local affairs by attempting to dictate a new social order to replace the southern way of life.[2] Having been liberated from this failed experiment, the South once again was free to restore the ante-bellum social order. However, in the absence of the legal construct of slavery, such a reestablishment would require new and innovative legal constructs and social support mechanisms.

The official state and local governments throughout the South represented the most potent political forces of the White suprem-acist construct. These same forces, which had previously imposed "black codes" and other legal tactics to suppress the intent of the 14th and 15th Amendments, were intensified in the post-Recon-struction period. Limiting African American voter turnout was achieved through a myriad of nefarious tactics: affording local offi-cials the discretion for registering voters, gerrymandering, and poll tax qualifications.

But if local and state governments provided the legislative muscle to evade the reach of the Reconstruction Amendments, the unofficial enforcement mechanisms used in the South were much more ominous. Through their masked anonymity, an extensive set of clandestine orga-nizations such as the Ku Klux Klan mentioned previously continued to function as an extrapolitical force spreading terror via horrific vio-lence and intimidation. Since prosecuting criminal activity rested with the local and state authorities, these terrorist organizations acted most often with impunity.

It was thus through the "dual weapons of law and violence"[3] that the White South enforced its system of White supremacy. The results in terms of disenfranchisement of Black people were staggering: Three years after the end of the Civil War, Black voter registration was about eighty-five percent, "but by 1944, in the states of the Old Confederacy only 5% of age-eligible African Americans were registered to vote, which left millions of blacks politically voiceless."[4]

In addition to local legal structures and tacitly sanctioned domestic terrorist organizations, a third key pillar was necessary for the South to protect its renewed White supremacist order. Once they regained control of their party in Congress, White Southern Democrats, under the aegis of the concept of federalism, would erect a bastion of fortifications around the South to prevent outside forces from interfering or injecting foreign influences.

In their insightful book *Southern Nation* (2018), authors David Bateman, Ira Katznelson, and John Lapinski document in remarkable and astonishing detail the nature of these fortifications, which manifested not as an actual fortress around the Southern states but symbolically within the galleys of the U.S. Capitol. Southern legislators assembled a coalition in Washington, DC, designed specifically to keep the federal government out of the domain of southern home rule. "With the South believing itself to be under a 'continuous state of siege' [by the federal government], it deployed the Democratic Party" as an "army of resistance."[5]

This third pillar supporting White supremacy was the principle, subscribed to by the Southern Democratic leaders in both the House and Senate, that preventing federal government interference and defending the principle of home rule was paramount over any particular piece of legislation. By deploying a litmus test to screen every piece of proposed legislation, the Southern Democrats in Congress became the front lines in these fortifications, working under the principle that no federal program, no aid or support from Washington, could be so imperative as to risk compromising the sanctity of home rule. Consequently, for almost the next hundred years, the southern legislative coalition's policy interests necessarily took a subordinate position to this number one priority.[6]

BOTTOM-UP POPULISM AS A RADICAL ENLIGHTENMENT MOVEMENT

The explosive economic growth of the Gilded Age from the 1870s into the early 20th century was associated with the growing power and wealth of the Northeast and West. From railroads to mining, manufacturing to finance, American industry developed rapidly. One of the many consequences of this industrialization was the creation of large imbalances in the distribution of wealth along several dimensions. Soaring industry created affluence for certain strata of society, while others experienced intensified poverty. Furthermore, this imbalance in prosperity developed regionally.

The agricultural lifestyle in the South was rapidly being eclipsed by a much more prosperous Northeast and an expansive frontier of opportunity in the West. In the South, extreme poverty and illiteracy were widespread among both Black and White people. Further exacerbating the wealth imbalance was the significant problem of mounting corruption; the cozy alliance between northern business interests and government leaders became quite vexing in the nonelite world.

As the seeds of modern American capitalism took root during the Gilded Age, the political sorting that had evolved in the post–Civil War period left huge swaths of American society behind. As we reviewed previously, the failure of Reconstruction relegated the struggle for civil rights to the background. This fact alone was responsible for restricting millions of disenfranchised African Americans from accessing the promise of the nation's founding era. But as the country modernized and began industrializing, many additional segments of American society were also marginalized. Both political parties that had emerged from the Civil War era increasingly represented the interests of the upper strata of society, leaving millions of laborers, farmers, and other working people to fend for themselves.

The GOP that evolved after Reconstruction represented the interests of the "establishment"—business, corporations, and finance—centered in the Northeast. The Southern Democratic Party was largely controlled by the local monied class, the holders of large estates and agricultural plantations. In the north, the Democratic Party was increasingly commandeered by a class of political leaders who purportedly protected the interests of the working class, including millions of urban Irish, Catholic, and Jewish immigrants, but mostly consolidated their own power into corrupt local political machines that ruled cities with an iron fist.

As a consequence, millions of small farmers and agricultural laborers in the South and across the western frontier, as well as both skilled and unskilled workers in the industrial Northeast, were left voiceless. Although they were the invisible drivers of American prosperity, these groups of society were largely excluded from enjoying the fruits of rapidly growing American prosperity. "Everywhere—North and South, among Republicans and Democrats—business and financial entrepreneurs had achieved effective control of a restructured party system."[7]

In the last two decades of the 19th century, bottom-up movements advocating for the interests of those left-behind Americans began surfacing and gaining momentum. One of these was an agrarian movement in the South called the Farmers' Alliance, which began promoting collective economic action in the face of chronic agricultural hardships. The Alliance grew quite quickly, from approximately two hundred thousand members in 1887 to more than two million farm families by 1892.[8]

The Farmers' Alliance began as groups of farmers in west Texas who came together to assist each other in the face of their economic woes. At the time, small farmers were at the mercy of a crop-lien system in which they had to borrow most of the year until their crops went to market. Because they were so susceptible to the vagaries of commodity prices, farmers often operated at steep losses that would accumulate each year. Individually, without bargaining power, small farmers were wrung between their creditors on one hand, and powerful business interests that bought their crops on the other. They had no negotiating power in purchasing supplies nor in upholding fair prices at market as they sold their product.

Intent on forming local cooperatives to best defend their economic interests, these small farmer groups became progressively more organized. New leaders emerged such as Charles Macune, with a vision of social empowerment for farmers. Trained as a doctor, but immensely talented as an economic theorist and community organizer, Macune designed a groundbreaking concept for its time, called the sub-treasury plan, in 1889, which allowed farmers to gain scale and share risk through central purchasing, marketing, and storage.

In addition to commencing a crusade to form purchasing and marketing cooperatives, the Farmers' Alliance became a powerful engine of training and educational development for farmers. Macune designed a system of education based on technological advancements in agriculture and improved professionalism in business methods. As historian Charles Postel writes: "From its early stirring the Farmers' alliance defined itself as an educational movement. Believing in a progressive future, Farmers' alliance members looked upon education as their most effective implements to shape the contours of that future."[9]

A thirty-six-year-old former tenant farmer from Mississippi, S. O. Daws, became a leader in disseminating information on the latest agriculture technologies to thousands of small farmers across the country. The Alliance appointed him "Traveling Lecturer," and he quickly started educating farmers not only in modern farming techniques, but in best business practices for productively marketing their crops. This focus on education was supported by a centralized network of lecturers and newspapers and other publications focused on science and empirical findings that were broadly disseminated across the Alliance. These educational programs reached hundreds of thousands of rural men and women, fulfilling Macune's vision for the Alliance movement as an agency of intellectual progress and scientific farming.

William Lamb, one of Daws's converts, became a leading organizer and recruited hundreds of thousands of new farmers to join the Alliance as it spread through the South and the West. He helped transform the Alliance from a support and educational orientation into more of a political organization to advocate for farmers' interests at the local and federal levels of government, with varying degrees of success in different states.

The populist movement as represented through the Farmers' Alliance was instrumental in an important way beyond just educating and advocating for millions of farmers. It gave small farmers *a collective voice*. As historian Lawrence Goodwyn describes:

> In their alliance, they had found something new. That something may be described as individual self-respect and collective self-confidence, or what some would call "class consciousness" . . . a growing political sensibility, one free of deference and ridicule . . . it clearly represents a seminal kind of democratic instinct; it was this instinct that emerged in the alliance.[10]

By instilling hope in hundreds of thousands of people, the populism of the Farmers' Alliance was about empowerment, about millions of farmers gaining agency in the political process.

Because neither the Democratic nor Republican Parties were advancing their interests, the Farmers' Alliance leaders, in concert with an antimonopoly group called the Greenbacks, established a fully-fledged third political party called the People's Party or the Populist Party.

This new party vastly extended the reach of the bottom-up

populist movement. Its platform not only advocated for the interests of workers and farmers but called on the federal government to take a much more active role in reining in the abuses associated with the increasing concentration of power in the hands of industrial America and the wealthy elite. Specifically, the party platform included the advancement of collective bargaining, the creation of federally controlled warehouses to assist farmers, the federal regulation of railroad tariffs, and other leveling policies specifically designed to counter the influence of powerful corporate financial interests. At the party's Omaha convention in 1892, Populist leaders characterized their platform as a Second Declaration of Independence.

Despite its broad-based appeal, the Populist Party struggled to field viable national candidates. As a result, the party coalesced around the emerging national leader and Democratic presidential candidate William Jennings Bryan in the election of 1896, fusing with the Democratic Party. Bryan would run unsuccessfully for president three times, deploying his unique blend of powerful oratory espousing populist principles. But as a devoutly pious man, Bryan's message was firmly grounded in Counter-Enlightenment religious fervor. While some historical accounts often cast Bryan as a prominent leader of the populist movement, he in fact emerged as the movement was already losing steam. By the time of his involvement, many of the principles advocated by the Populist Party were already being co-opted by the mainstream parties.

From many perspectives, the populist movement of the late 19th century represented a reawakening of Enlightenment ideals. The Populist Party's vision of political mobilization was very much at the heart of the egalitarian Radical Enlightenment tradition of earlier centuries. In addition, the populists' embrace of education and empirical research to validate beliefs in science were grounded in the most fundamental tenets of the overall Enlightenment.

Interestingly, in 20th-century accounts of the populist movement, an assorted range of narratives presents conflicting views of what the populist movement signified. Some accounts depict populists as rural folk intimidated by modernity, or revolutionaries trying to overthrow capitalism. Others point to Bryan and conclude that the movement was motivated by religious zeal. Such accounts are in general gross misrepresentations. In actuality, this was a movement that fully embraced modernity, and one that endeavored to progressively reform American capitalist institutions, not overthrow or replace them.

Furthermore, emerging from the ground up, the movement was illustrative of the way populism can serve as a progressive means of reform in America as discussed in Part I. The entire populist revolt of the late 19th century demonstrated how powerful bottom-up movements can be. As historian Charles Postel describes:

> The power of the Populist movement lay in the efforts of common citizens to shape the national economy and governance . . . Few political or social movements brought so many men and women into lecture halls . . . The Populists themselves—a broad coalition of farmers, wage earners, and middle class activists—worked with self-confidence to challenge the status quo . . . The capitalist elite pursued a corporate power that left little room for the organized power of the men and women of the fields, mines, or factories . . . Populism was an expression of protest against impoverishment and against the power of the corporate elite. At stake was who should be included and who should wield what shares of power—a conflict that all concerned understood as vital to the future of a modern America.[11]

The Populist Party proved to be a harbinger of the overall Progressive Era that began at the turn of the century. During this period of widespread social activism and political reform, advocacy for new federal regulation to place controls and restraints on capitalism became widespread. The union movement in various manifestations also became quite prevalent at this time, advocating for the interests of working-class people. Populist historian Lawrence Goodwyn characterized the populist movement as the first multisectional democratic mass movement since the American Revolution and the most massive organizing drive of any citizen institution in the entire 19th century in America:

> Populism [can be seen as] a moment of democratic promise. It was a spirit of egalitarian hope, expressed in the actions of two million beings . . . It was a demonstration of how people of a society containing a number of democratic forms could labor in pursuit of freedom, of how people could generate their own democratic culture in order to challenge the received hierarchical culture . . . At root, American populism was a demonstration of what authentic political life can be in a functioning democracy.[12]

THE SEEDS OF POPULISM FLOWER DURING THE EARLY 20TH-CENTURY PROGRESSIVE ERA

Although the Populist Party itself did not endure, as the precursor to an age of true reform, it illustrated how new social forces had come into play on the American landscape. During the subsequent Progressive Era, social activism and advocacy ultimately led to successful implementation of meaningful political and economic reforms.

During the Progressive Era, additional bottom-up organizations emerged from various parts of the nation and coalesced into diverse reform movements. These were usually led by nongovernmental crusaders who targeted political corruption and the deleterious effects of industrialization and urbanization on working-class people. While objections to the status quo were distinct in each region, the grievances from the North, West, and South all shared a few common denominators, chiefly the advancement of the interests of the common citizenry against the big-moneyed industrial and political establishment, and the fight for women's suffrage.

Furthermore, realized Progressive Era reforms eventually addressed many of the goals that the Populist Party failed to achieve in the 1880s. A few examples are the 1913 Federal Reserve Act, which provided a more flexible currency; a constitutional amendment, which finally achieved the decades-long Populist demands for a federal income tax; and closer federal regulations of railroads and telecommunications. Overall, "the Populists wanted an active government to ensure fair access to the benefits of modernity . . . to reshape government as an agency of the majority rather than of the corporate and wealthy minority."[13] While their goals were not met during the life of the Populist Party, the seeds were certainly planted, and many would sprout in the early 20th century.

In terms of our overall thesis, the rise in populism in the 1880s and 1890s and the Progressive Era of the first decades of the 20th century were both richly demonstrative of a significant swing of the pendulum toward the Radical Enlightenment ideals discussed previously. The period marked concrete gains for the radical camp, restraining the economic and political power of the elite segments of society and their political leaders who represented the successors of the Moderate Enlightenment vision. The progressive movement overall was quite successful in achieving significant democratic reforms. Moreover, by targeting corrupt political machines, the movement forced the major political parties to be more sensitive to the political needs of ordinary citizens. This trend ultimately led to the government assuming a broader role in moderating the advantages of the most powerful in society.

One of the prime reasons that the Populist Party failed to survive is because the two major political parties successfully co-opted many of its ideas. National leaders of the early 20th century like Theodore

Roosevelt and Woodrow Wilson embraced progressive reforms originally inspired by the Populist Party. Although from different political
parties, both Roosevelt and Wilson believed that government could
address economic problems intrinsic to the incentive structure of
free-market capitalism. One important and concrete example was the
regulation of monopolies and corporations via antitrust legislation.

In addition to economic reforms, the Progressive Era led to dramatic social reforms. By further mobilizing support for the organized
women's suffrage movements that had gradually gathered momentum
for decades, the Progressive Era ultimately led to the ratification of the
19th Amendment in 1920, which finally granted women the right to
vote. In addition, the period was marked by a steady influx of immigration that grew significantly in the first twenty years of the century,
mostly from southern and eastern Europe.

Lamentably, one group in America's social fabric was notably
excluded from these gains. Not only were African Americans increasingly disenfranchised in the South, the Progressive Era represented yet
another nadir in American race relations. Despite the shared economic
interests of the working classes of both races, political leaders in the
South further advanced the Jim Crow system of racial segregation,
channeling any form of working-class relief to White working-class
southerners. Furthermore, a form of *de facto* segregation solidified
in the rest of the nation beyond the South. How exactly did this era
marked by such striking progress in some areas utterly ignore the civil
rights of African Americans? The obvious answer from the perspective
of social dynamics is that racist views not only persisted but deepened
among a plurality of Americans. But from the perspective of political
mechanisms, the answer lies in the dynamics that unfolded not only
locally in the states but also at the federal level in Congress.

THE SOUTHERN DEMOCRATIC COALITION
SETS THE CONGRESSIONAL AGENDA

In juxtaposition to the many gains made during the Progressive Era, the Southern Democratic coalition in Congress emerged as a formidable force that further entrenched a White supremacist society in their home territory. In both the House and the Senate, because the Southern Democrats held the chairpersonships of key committees, they thereby held enormous power to shape the legislative agenda for the nation.

Nonetheless, they were faced with a dilemma. They urgently wanted to support many aspects of the populist movement in order to raise the standard of living in the South and restrain the growing power of Northeastern industrial interests. But at the same time, the Southern Democrats were deeply fearful that any potential programs they might enact, while bringing federal aid to the South, might also threaten the local autonomy they had worked so hard to reestablish after Reconstruction. Thus, notwithstanding their desire for progressive economic reforms, Southern Democrats evaluated potential legislation in light of the degree to which it preserved the concept of home rule, to continue safeguarding the White supremacist racial order in the South.

Of course, as they proposed specific pieces of legislation, southern legislators in both the House and the Senate disguised their discriminatory intents. Eventually, they became quite skilled at drafting and passing laws that could accomplish both goals—bring economic benefits to the South while also sustaining the sanctity of home rule. Instead of explicitly codifying racial discrimination in any particular bill, which would have raised 14th Amendment alarms, their success formula involved insisting on provisions in bills that delegated discretion over the details of resource allocation and implementation to the individual state legislatures. As a result, the South was able to retain local control of how federal dollars ultimately were spent and who received the benefits of the associated programs.

At times, measures in areas such as education were sacrificed, forgoing significant benefits to the South, if they were perceived as a broader "package of reforms intended to renew the active involvement of the nation in southern racial affairs."[14] But in general, southern legislators successfully deployed this approach to balance the growing power in the North and West by maintaining their leadership on major initiatives related to economic regulation and federal spending and taxation. The goals of these programs were not only to reduce the burden of tariffs and taxation on the South but also to advance liberal ideals to counter the increasing power of big business. But all these legislative acts provided for local discretion and control in the funneling of benefits.

Ultimately, southern congressional leaders achieved both of their legislative goals of advancing progressive positions to benefit White southerners while constructing a firewall to block the passage of any meaningful civil rights legislation or enforcement of African American suffrage. Whenever the issue of "black civil or political rights was broached, southerners vividly communicated the intensity of their commitments, insisting that they would do whatever it took to 'protect ourselves.'"[15] Consequently, southern progressivism flourished while southern structural racism solidified. Moreover, the alliance of the various constituencies within the party allowed the Democrats to control Congress and the southerners to set the Democratic agenda. While northern progressives, usually middle-class urban reformers, were far from unanimous in their belief in racial equality, the reach of liberal policies in the North was much broader and deeper than in the South.

The height of southern progressive influence came when Woodrow Wilson, the first southern-born president since Andrew Johnson, was inaugurated president in 1913. A burst of reformist and broad-reaching legislation was passed that impacted areas like interstate commerce, financial and monetary systems, and antitrust and trade, finally addressing the demands of the bottom-up populist movement. The South also fruitfully led passage of agricultural bills that benefited its agrarian economy. However, while many of these programs were egalitarian in some respects, they uncontestably were not race-blind nor eroded the clout of White supremacy. "During the first presidential term of Woodrow Wilson, southern legislators helped frame much of the period's most important and far-reaching progressive legislation, and they did so while simultaneously ensuring that white supremacy was left not only undisturbed but strengthened."[16]

> The extent to which southerners dominated legislative committees was "the most complete proof that the South is in truth in charge of the nation's business" . . . Southern lawmakers used the influence these positions provided to fundamentally "shape the character of Wilsonian reform."[17]

Designed with southern influence, this legislative approach was applied throughout the nation. Accordingly, states outside the South would also locally control allocation of federal dollars, thus perpetuating race discrimination broadly, albeit perhaps less systematically than the South. White supremacy and liberal democracy were, to a large degree, fused together in the American experience on a national basis. The net result was that states' rights associated with federalism justified and perpetuated local race discrimination.

White Southern progressives succeeded at reinforcing many of Jim Crow's defining features by reframing the issue of racial inequality in political discourse as one of managing "race relations." This euphemism appeared benign to national leaders, and managing race relations locally seemed by far more appropriate than any kind of federal intervention. Furthermore, within the South, "with full-blown white supremacy encountering no resistance by other national political forces, the South could unleash efforts to advance black disenfranchisement, secure a control of black labor, and promote progressive policies to curb the excesses of the country's political-economic order."[18]

The approach of the Solid South also extended to new states entering the union. For example, in the new state of Oklahoma, the local authorities found a "creative" way of complying with the 15th Amendment intended to guarantee African American suffrage. Starting in 1916, the state maintained a voter roll of all previous voters before 1914, which were predominantly adult White men. For those who had not previously voted, the state established a twelve-day window for new voter registration in 1916. Oklahomans who missed this narrow deadline lost suffrage rights forever. By focusing on the dangers of centralization during the conversion of new territories into states, southern leaders helped "embed white supremacy into the structure of the new American state."[19]

All in all, the massive amount and sizable reach of southern coalition–led legislation that was enacted starting at the end of the Gilded Age and throughout most of the Progressive Era fundamentally shaped the new American economy and social order. Thus, ironically, but also tragically in many respects, despite its military defeat in the Civil War, the South ultimately dictated to a large degree how we remade the country in the late 19th and early 20th centuries.

Denying opportunities to African Americans was not unique to the South. The lack of federal oversight demanded by the southern legislative approach enabled the rest of the country to also maintain discriminatory practices in the local supervision of federal programs. While perhaps not as brutal as the Jim Crow South, the *de facto* segregation of housing and schooling in the North resulted in "ghettos" in many northern cities, often deprived of local services such as adequate sanitation and policing.

Thus, while Radical Enlightenment ideals, such as economic leveling consistent with a more egalitarian society, drove a considerable part of the Progressive Era's reforms, it was only part of the story of late 19th- and early 20th-century America. A much more ominous theme is illustrated by the fact that racism became even further embedded in

American society. With respect to the American racial divide, if the hopefulness and optimism of Reconstruction had reflected a dramatic pendulum swing toward a more egalitarian new nation, the reemergence of much of the antebellum social order in the South and the extension of racial prejudice in the North reflected the momentum of the pendulum crashing back.

*　*　*

The dominance of Southern Democrats in Congress continued all through the New Deal and World War II era. While Franklin Delano Roosevelt oversaw a comprehensive expansion of the government's role in safeguarding economic security for millions of Americans through his New Deal, the impact of this vast set of programs was greatly hampered in the South by systematic discrimination via the local administration.[20] Thus, millions of suffering White Americans were assisted by FDR's (Franklin Delano Roosevelt's) new and potent concept of a broader "economic Bill of Rights," including "the right to a useful and remunerative job," "the right of every family to a decent home," "the right to adequate medical care," and the "right to a good education," even if the full scope of FDR's vision remained unrealized.[21] And while the lives of many poor African Americans were ameliorated as well, principally in the North, federal assistance as applied by local governments was by no means colorblind.

After World War II, when President Truman integrated the military, infuriated Southern Democrats objected and broke off into what we usually refer to as the Dixiecrats. While the split-off party was officially short-lived, the Dixiecrats' policy-making alliance with the Democrats allowed it to retain its influence. Even though the northern and western Democrats might not have subscribed to the Dixiecrats' approach of a White supremacist social order, for the party as a whole to stay in power, the alliance with the Dixiecrats was essential for Democratic congressional control. It was the bargain Democrats made: "The Dixiecrats gave the national Democrats the votes they needed to control Congress, and the national Democrats let the Dixiecrats enforce segregation and one-party rule at home."[22] Based on their dominant position in Congress, Southern Democrats would continue to control the agenda of federal policy making for decades while forcefully maintaining home rule in the South. It would be more than half a century before any meaningful new pendulum swing occurred.

Chapter 12

A RENAISSANCE OF CIVIL RIGHTS AND THE RISE OF A NEW CONSERVATIVE COALITION

From the perspective of racial justice, the 1960s civil rights movement, which led to landmark legislation under the leadership of Lyndon Baines Johnson, was inarguably the greatest pendulum swing toward a more egalitarian vision of our nation since that led by the Radical Republicans in the years immediately following the Civil War and embodied in the Reconstruction Amendments. Johnson advanced both civil rights legislation and the "Great Society" program targeting poverty, and by doing so he oversaw the most overarching reawakening of Radical Enlightenment ideals since the pinnacle of the Reconstruction era. Johnson's programs endeavored not only to achieve the racial justice central to the phrase "all men are created equal," but to revitalize and extend the objectives of FDR's New Deal programs to provide economic opportunity to those whom the capitalist free-market system had left behind.

Johnson had grown up dirt poor in Texas; his father lost the family farm when Johnson was just a boy. He was a Texas schoolteacher before entering politics (he was first elected to Congress in 1937). In his formative years he was greatly inspired by FDR's New Deal and was emboldened by the overall notion that government has the potential to alleviate great suffering through effective problem-solving. His "Great Society" programs represented the most productive and consequential legislative agenda since FDR, despite the fact that his legacy has often been clouded and his great contributions overshadowed by the country's enmeshment in the Vietnam quagmire under his watch.

When we refer to the "civil rights movement of the 1960s," we use this label because in that decade the civil rights movement became mainstream. However, in reality, the fight for civil rights for African Americans in the United States has been omnipresent throughout our history, a process that began when slavery first came to the Americas in 1619 and continues to this day. In some respects, the label is unfortunate in that it implies that civil rights were not an important issue prior to the period in question. Of course, this is not at all the case; while ever present, at times the civil rights battle has been "swept under the rug," not because of some sudden resolution, but because many undoubtedly became exhausted by the unending struggle and because other more pressing and urgent issues arose (e.g., financial crises, World Wars).[1] Nonetheless, a renewed momentum began to build when President Truman first ended segregation in the military in 1948, followed by the *de jure* end to school segregation that came with the landmark Supreme Court case *Brown v. Board of Education* in 1954.

But it was in 1955 when the civil rights movement really gained steam, first as a reaction to the brutal killing of Emmett Till in Mississippi and then through a spark ignited by Rosa Parks's courageous refusal to give up her bus seat in Alabama. The Montgomery Improvement Association (MIA), led by Dr. Martin Luther King Jr. along with Ralph Abernathy and Edgar Nixon, was formed to assist the local community with the legendary bus boycott that followed. This series of events in Montgomery became the springboard for King's meteoric rise into national prominence.

Over the course of the next two years, King held pivotal organizing meetings with Black pastors and civil rights leaders. King and Abernathy were acutely focused on how the moral authority of the church could be used as a foundation for a broad movement of change. In 1957, they created the Southern Christian Leadership Conference (SCLC), an organization with the credentials to wield both religious and moral authority. Despite some early chafing with the NAACP (National Association for the Advancement of Colored People), King would lead the SCLC until his death. He propelled the organization's influence not only in the South, but throughout the entire nation, frequently through the use of dramatic standoffs with the segregationist authorities in the South.

David Garrow's seminal work, *Bearing the Cross* (1988), narrates this history in riveting detail while also depicting the brilliance, courage, and complexity of the journey of King himself, along with the many other advocates for change during those pivotal years. Interestingly, King initially resisted and even dreaded the world-changing role he was ultimately to play. Andrew Young later recalled that King was "thrust into a situation that he really didn't want to be in."[2] As Garrow notes in reference to demonstrations growing out of civil rights organizing efforts in Albany, Georgia, in 1961–1962, "It was not an involvement that Martin King had sought out, not a protest he had instigated or planned, not an event that he was eager to be involved in . . . [these were situations] King knew in good conscience he could not avoid; it was his responsibility because of the role into which he had been cast and from which he had found no escape . . . It was his to bear."[3]

When King met with Vice President Nixon at the White House in 1957, he emphasized six points: "that *neither* political party had done enough on civil rights; that problems in the South could be solved only with federal action; that most white southerners could cope with racial change, but needed prodding; that Eisenhower should speak out for civil rights; that Nixon should speak out for the pending civil rights bill, and do so in the South; and that the administration had to stop pondering and start acting."[4] By the time Eisenhower signed the first civil rights legislation protecting voters' rights in September 1957, King and the SCLC had launched a voter registration program on the ground in many parts of the South, labeled the "Crusade for Citizenship." But despite these signs of progress, the Eisenhower Administration fell short on all of King's other points.

From King's perspective, the tepid response from the Eisenhower Administration in the following months was surely disheartening, given the buildup to the White House meetings and the substantial momentum King himself had stimulated. Yet King remained undeterred even in the face of numerous acts of violence directed at him personally, including a near-death stabbing in New York.

King had already become familiar with the nonviolent approach to change practiced by the legendary crusader for freedom, Mahatma Gandhi, but King's visit to India and his meetings there with many of Gandhi's surviving disciples and government leaders convinced him that "India had had more success in eliminating caste discrimination . . . than had the United States in combating racial discrimination . . . The [visit to India] had given him a more sophisticated view of how social injustice and evil could be combated by the method of nonviolence."[5] On his return from India and with new resolve, King relocated to Atlanta and took the helm of the SCLC to mount a full-scale assault aimed at the heart of the system of segregation. At the time, King told his colleagues that they must "arouse the dozing consciences of the South" and reach what he called "the conscience of the great decent majority."[6]

Over the next years, through sit-ins and freedom rides, King attracted hundreds of thousands of students and other citizens in an incredible display of both fortitude and conviction. Via bus trips across the South, freedom riders protested racial segregation in all its forms even as they were met with mobs who often viciously attacked them, at times setting the buses on fire. The slow responses of local police infuriated the then Attorney General Robert Kennedy. But eventually, through the news media, the spectacle of these events began to paint a clearer picture for the entire nation of the violence condoned by the Southern authorities in confrontations with peaceful protesters.

As horrific as some of these events were, King and his entourage also realized that the news coverage of them could broaden support for the struggle, especially outside the South. In 1963, when Alabama Governor George Wallace blocked the doorway of the University of Alabama to prevent African American students from registering, President Kennedy was forced to deploy the National Guard to the campus. King was astute at using negotiations with local authorities, even against the threat of great violence, to demonstrate both the validity of the SCLC claims and the intransigence of local leaders. In one episode following a protest that turned violent in Albany, Georgia, in 1962, President Kennedy gave the following statement at the press conference:

> I find it wholly inexplicable why the city council of Albany will not sit down with the citizens of Albany, who may be Negroes, and attempt to secure them, in a peaceful way, their rights. The US government is involved in sitting down at Geneva with the Soviet Union. I can't understand why the government of Albany . . . cannot do the same for American citizens.[7]

After the protests in Birmingham, Alabama, King realized that the national impact of the protests could be leveraged not only for making local changes in the various communities, but for paving the way for new bold federal legislative initiatives on civil rights. As King's prominence skyrocketed, he pressed for a more aggressive agenda with the Kennedy brothers. In 1963, President Kennedy appeared on national television and for the first time "issued a clear moral call to the American people to banish segregation and racism from the land."[8]

Martin Luther King Jr. could never speak for the entirety of the civil rights movement, nor convey all the injustices perpetuated against millions of people of all colors that spanned many generations. Nonetheless, his voice rang out with more clarity and resonance than many other voices in the battle. King was the embodiment of our modern notion of classical liberalism, which assumed the mantle of the Radical Enlightenment tradition in the 20th century.

At the March on Washington in August 1963, in front of over 250,000 people and seen by millions around the world, in what has become known as his "I Have a Dream" speech, King irrevocably tied the civil rights movement back to the vision underlying the founding of the country and reaffirmed at the conclusion of the Civil War. Given how enduring his words have become, it seems remarkable that King dispensed with his prepared text and gave his remarks extemporaneously.

There is no question that King was working within the Radical Enlightenment civic tradition, even if his motivating inspiration was grounded in his deep spirituality as a minister and a devout Christian. As we described in previous chapters, while many Radical Enlightenment voices back in the 18th century condemned organized religion for its role in subduing the masses, in subsequent eras, Radical Enlightenment ideals have been frequently inspired and motivated by religious beliefs. This is far from surprising given that most leading religions are at their core based on analogous principles, despite such principles being faith based instead of derived from logic and observation.

As discussed in the first section, it is when religious authorities use faith-based beliefs as justification for discriminatory political interference in the affairs of state that we can accurately characterize them as a destructive Counter-Enlightenment force. If King's pious spirituality can be labeled as "Counter-Enlightenment," it was used in precisely the opposite manner. For King, America's sin was in neglecting to apply the principles of the Radical Enlightenment, the same ones in the Declaration of Independence, to all the disenfranchised groups in the United States, most predominantly African Americans.

To a large degree, King based his entire civil rights philosophy on the simplest of ideas: namely, *who is included* in the two key phrases in our founding documents: "all men are created equal" and "we the people." King was asking a modest question: To whom does "we the people" refer? And as simple as that question is, in the face of myriad intervening and confounding arguments, it nonetheless remains at the root of some of the most bitter divisions across the American Schism (a theme to which we will return in Part III).

King's analogy that the Declaration of Independence's words asserting that "all men are created equal" granted a "promissory note" to all those Americans who had not yet secured the "unalienable rights of life, liberty and the pursuit of happiness" was a triumphant rhetorical achievement. It would forevermore etch in our memories both the image of King in front of the Lincoln Memorial and the sound and inspiration of those potent and haunting words. But King's use of that simple analogy was no accident. On the contrary, its austerity reflects the elegance of its earnest truth and underlying premise. The rights that King was demanding for African Americans were the *same ones already being afforded* to millions of Americans. Such rights conspicuously existed, but were deliberately and blatantly not afforded to some. The analogy would not have worked if King did not feel that the money owed on the promissory note was in fact already in the bank waiting to be paid to those Americans who had not yet received their fair share.

As King finished with his last words, "free at last; thank God almighty, we are free at last," Garrow eloquently describes the scene: "Dripping with sweat, King stepped back as the audience gave him a thundering ovation. Although he did not know it, this speech had been the rhetorical achievement of a lifetime, the clarion call that conveyed the moral power of the movement's cause to the millions who had watched the live national network coverage . . . white America was confronted with the undeniable justice of blacks' demands."[9]

The protest in Selma, Alabama, in March 1965, leading up to the Voting Rights Act of 1965, was particularly vicious and riveted the nation's attention. It was here that John Lewis received a blow to the head as he and other protesters fled back across the Pettus bridge to seek refuge. President Johnson had already demonstrated his belief in the validity of the civil rights movement through his earlier emphatic condemnation of Governor George Wallace's intransigence. But his response to the events in Selma sincerely demonstrated his commitment to civil rights and the degree to which Johnson's vision of the country aligned with the Radical Enlightenment's vision from two centuries prior. Johnson addressed the nation:

> The blows that were received, the blood that was shed, the life of the good man that was lost, must strengthen the determination of each of us to bring full and equal and exact justice to all of our people.

> This is not just a policy of your government or your President. It is in the heart and the purpose and the meaning of America itself . . .

> It is wrong to do violence to peaceful citizens in the streets of their town. It is wrong to deny Americans the right to vote. It is wrong to deny any person full equality because of the color of his skin.[10]

Furthermore, a few weeks later, Johnson called Selma "a milestone in the nation's development comparable to Lexington, Concord, and Appomattox, one of those events where history and fate meet at a single time in a single place to shape a turning point in man's unending search for freedom."[11] He finished this speech with a declaration of what had become the motto of the movement itself: "We Shall Overcome."

As these images appeared throughout the 1960s, the true picture of the segregated Jim Crow South was laid out in its stark nakedness for all Americans to see. For many, perhaps for the first time, the obstacles preventing the "pursuit of happiness" for millions of American citizens became more openly visible through mass media. The frightening and graphic television images projected into the living rooms of millions of Americans would establish enduring images that would become engraved in the collective American conscience. Images of vicious policemen with clubs and dogs attacking peaceful protesters would serve as perhaps the most vivid and concrete visualization of the dreadful reality of African American life in the South. These images portrayed in riveting clarity how African Americans were systematically disenfranchised in all aspects of daily life, with their freedom, liberty, and political expression trampled upon with insolent disregard. But just as shockingly, these events also illustrated how many Southern Whites perpetrated horrific acts of violence in defense of this social structure.

These events generated significant support in both Washington and much of the nation for the movement to advance the rights of African Americans. But at the same time, these images proved to be a clear demonstration to the world of the contradictions in the American myth, challenging the country's ability to stake the moral high ground, and indelibly staining its claim to be a "free and just society." If Alexis de Tocqueville's *Democracy in America* (1835) portrayed to the world the great promise of America in the 19th century, Dr. Martin Luther King Jr. used these events to depict a much more horrifying reality in the 20th century. The entire global Cold War struggle, which was predicated on the sanctimonious position of America, seemed indeed to be resting on eggshells.

By the time Lyndon B. Johnson signed the Civil Rights Act of 1964, the whole world had a front-row seat to witness the struggle. For the next several years, horrific violent episodes like the brutal attack by police on the Selma to Montgomery March in 1965 were interspersed with concrete gains. This historic piece of legislation was the most significant codification of Radical Enlightenment egalitarian principles since the adoption of the Bill of Rights and the Reconstruction Amendments. The act prevented employment discrimination due to race, color, sex, religion, or national origin. Title VII of the act established the U.S. Equal Employment Opportunity Commission (EEOC) to help prevent workplace discrimination. In addition, the act prevented the use of literacy tests as a voting requirement and allowed federal examiners to review voter qualifications and federal observers to monitor polling places. Furthermore, the Immigration and Nationality Act of 1965 abolished the National Origins Formula which had, since the 1920s, restricted immigration to mostly northwestern Europeans. This new immigration act finally removed *de jure* discrimination against immigrants outside of northern and western Europe.[12]

President Johnson's Great Society program focused on the downtrodden in society with a far-reaching set of programs targeted at both poverty and racial injustice. Johnson was keenly aware that the legislation of previous decades failed to adequately reach African Americans due to discrimination in local implementation. The result was the perpetuation of economic and social inequality. It was against this backdrop that President Johnson was determined to specifically target racial injustice. But he was also committed to waging his "war on poverty" to correct economic injustices.

Johnson accomplished that objective through the establishment of Medicare and Medicaid as part of Title IX of the Social Security Act, and the Civil Rights Act of 1968, which provides equal housing opportunities. The latter bill was signed by President Johnson just seven days after the tragic assassination of King. Of course, in no way did these historic legislative achievements end *de facto* discrimination immediately, but to a large degree they codified the federal government's steadfast commitment to end constitutionally sanctioned racial discrimination.[13]

BACKLASH: NEOLIBERALISM AND THE CHRISTIAN ALLIANCE WITH THE CONSERVATIVE ESTABLISHMENT

While the 1960s was a decade full of horrifying violence—the Vietnam War, frequent assassinations, other racial killings and beatings—it was also a decade of measurable social progress toward achieving a more egalitarian nation. But in the following decade, the pendulum swung back as President Nixon's appeal as the "law and order" president brought a reassertion of White and elite privilege back as a mainstay of economic and social life.

The Nixon-era ideology marked the beginnings of an assault on the classical liberalism of the Radical Enlightenment tradition. What we now refer to as "neoliberalism" began its ascendancy by combining a resurgence of free-market capitalism with the political-economic policies of the pre–New Deal era. Overall, neoliberalism as a political and economic philosophy endorses the predominant role of the private sector in the economy, accompanied by a commensurate reduction in government spending. One of the principal roots of this new philosophy was a paradigm shift in economics away from the neoclassical Keynesian model (supporting activist fiscal and monetary government policies) in favor of the free-market laissez-faire and noninterventionist model associated with Milton Friedman and the Chicago school of economics.

If the policies of FDR and LBJ (Lyndon B. Johnson) represented the reemergence of the Radical Enlightenment tradition through the deployment of activist government programs and tools, the rise of neoliberalism and its laissez-faire political orientation represented a strong counterforce pushing the pendulum back toward the Moderate Enlightenment tradition. Neoliberalism's staunch opposition to the principles of using the power of the federal government to foster a more egalitarian society would have a huge effect on the American landscape for the remainder of the century through to the modern day. Neoliberal policies such as deregulation, privatization, and support for globalization and free trade have increasingly characterized successive administrations, and they continue to be dominant forces today.

In addition to the rise of neoliberalism, the 1970s also saw a revitalized overlay of Counter-Enlightenment influence, which further dampened the impact of the 1960s renaissance of Radical Enlightenment ideals. The Nixon era brought a renewed predominance of evangelical Christianity center stage, laced with a subtler and less overt form of racism.

The evangelical focus of this Counter-Enlightenment superimposition over the American political establishment actually commenced back in the 1950s, when the Reverend Billy Graham began preaching against the evils of communism. Graham's charisma carried a new evangelism to an increasing number of White Protestants by passionately articulating Counter-Enlightenment themes, and by contextualizing worldwide political dynamics in a familiar and long-established Christian narrative. For Graham, the Cold War was a religious battle in which communists, representing the new infidels, had declared war on God.[14]

In addition to his commanding sway throughout White Protestant America, Graham's enigmatic influence on the political leadership of the country was quite remarkable. Over the course of his long life, Graham would lead national prayer breakfasts with top political leaders and would frequently become a trusted adviser to many presidents. Throughout his career, Graham's ability to equate Christian evangelism with Americanism was indicative of the degree to which his Counter-Enlightenment focus penetrated deep into conservative America as well as into the mainstream of the Republican Party. This was also demonstrative of the degree to which partisan politics became shrouded in religious zeal. Furthermore, Graham effectually wrapped his preaching in a potent form of anti-intellectualism that targeted the progressive liberalism of the Democratic Party itself, further polarizing American society.[15]

Against the backdrop of the growth in the evangelical influence of Billy Graham, the counterculture movement of the 1960s in all its forms presented an unbridled shock to mainstream society. Civil rights, women's rights, and gay rights all directly and existentially challenged the conservative dogma to which many Americans were increasingly subscribing. In response, President Nixon evoked what he called the "moral majority" to reclaim the traditional position of White privilege atop the American social hierarchy. Numerous evangelical leaders and Protestant preachers, like the Reverend Jerry Falwell who in 1979 founded the Moral Majority, attracted large followings of American citizens in the following decades.

In addition to the ascent of the Christian evangelical movement, the yearning for a more peaceful era and a return to traditional American values manifested itself in reaction to the progressive women's movement of these decades. The National Federation of Republican Women, which originally mobilized to support Barry Goldwater, gained steam and led a moral crusade against the equal rights amendment (ERA) under the leadership of Phyllis Schlafly all through the 1970s.

All of these elements exemplified how the countervailing forces as commandeered by the conservative right were able to resist the leftward swing provided by the political movements of the 1960s and 1970s. These conservative forces were successfully able to seize the momentum and thereby reestablish conservatism as prominent once again in the political, economic, and social order of the nation. In Jill Lepore's 2018 comprehensive history of the United States, *These Truths*, the author describes this well:

> Conservatives have been trying since the 1930s to dismantle the New Deal coalition and to take over the Republican Party. In the 1970s and 1980s, by bringing Catholics, evangelical Christians, and white southern Democrats into their own coalition, they finally succeeded. No small number of conservative political strategists would take credit for this achievement. But it was Schlafly who built the road to the Reagan Revolution, paving it with stones labeled "END ABORTION NOW" and "STOP ERA."[16]

While the inauguration of Democratic President Jimmy Carter brought an evangelical to the White House, President Carter placed more emphasis on tolerance and human rights. Like King previously and as discussed, Carter demonstrated that Radical Enlightenment ideals can be motivated by faith and result in a religiously inspired progressive agenda. However, Carter failed to roll back the neoliberal economic policies described previously.

*   *   *

The inauguration of Ronald Reagan marked the beginning of the supremacy of the neoliberal agenda. During the Reagan revolution, this neoliberalism became more brazen as Reagan focused on attacking government itself. He was a master at recasting the federal government, which had over the course of the century lifted millions up by the bootstraps and assisted society's most needy and disenfranchised, not as a solution, but as the problem. For Reagan, the best government could do was to get out of the way of free enterprise. The energetic flame of enthusiasm that former President Kennedy had ignited in a new generation of Americans with his call to public service as enriching and vital to society was doused in the waters of deregulation and laissez-faire. With government cast as the enemy, the abuses of unchecked capitalism were free to reign unimpeded. Further, a new regressive tax system meant that government was also largely abandoning any meaningful role in redistributive economics, which negatively affected all poorer Americans, of all races.[17]

While this new conservative era perhaps seemed more serene and comforting to White Americans, it wreaked havoc on the lives of African American citizens, although with a new and insidious twist. The Reagan administration's "War on Drugs," with Nancy Reagan as cheerleader declaring "Just Say No," commenced a new era of reform in criminal justice, or more accurately criminal injustice. The war on drugs along with the war on crime would deploy a new strategy for African American subordination with terrible consequences.

In Ava DuVernay's brilliant 2016 documentary, *13th*, DuVernay and co-writer Spencer Averick chronologically narrate in chilling precision how this new approach to criminal justice led to the systematic mass criminalization of African Americans under the veil of the war on drugs and abetted by minimum sentence requirements.

In the 1980s and the 1990s, upper-class urban Whites partied in swanky clubs using cocaine with impunity; at the same time, the inner cities became a chase-and-capture game for local police forces to entrap and incarcerate crack cocaine users. These latter victims were prosecuted as hard criminals and not treated as drug addicts needing medical help. Moreover, this approach to criminal enforcement was sustained and even extended during the Clinton Administration.

Former President Clinton has since publicly called his propagation of this trend in criminal justice perhaps the greatest mistake of his presidency. The facts speak for themselves: In 1970 there were 196,441 sentenced prisoners in the federal and state prison systems; by 1990, this had grown to 771,242 and by 2000, to 1,3841,892. In all, forty-six percent of sentenced prisoners were African Americans (Hispanic inmates accounted for an additional sixteen percent). The United States has by far the highest incarceration rate anywhere in the world.[18]

As demonstrated in countless previous historical eras, once again the established American White political order proved quite innovative in conceiving of and implementing a new "solution" to exclude African Americans from the promise of the egalitarian vision of the Declaration of Independence. Throughout the 1960s, in spite of all the challenging, tempestuous, and frequently violent episodes, the decade had witnessed a sweeping renaissance of Radical Enlightenment ideals. However, as we have now seen repeatedly in prior eras of American history, the pendulum often swings back with as much or more momentum in the opposite direction.

During the last quarter of the 20th century, the twin forces of neoliberalism in the tradition of the Moderate Enlightenment and authoritarian evangelical Christianity in the spirit of the Counter-Enlightenment combined in a frontal assault on the egalitarianism of the Radical Enlightenment. As Martin Luther King Jr. simply but eloquently stated: "People fail to get along with each other because they fear each other. They fear each other because they don't know each other."[19] After a brief period of acquaintance, society's privileged and disadvantaged would each retreat to their own corner and remain there for decades.

Neoliberalism and evangelical Christianity would continue to keep Radical Enlightenment principles doggedly in check for the subsequent period of United States history through today. Over the last fifty years in America, the alliance forged between the evangelical religious movement and political conservatism in governmental leadership has been redoubtable and has had profound effects on the country.

The parallel between this current alliance and the alliance of the church with the *ancien régime* in earlier centuries is eerily familiar, with one important discrepancy. In prior eras and again in the late 18th century, the church colluded with the monarchy to reestablish the traditional societal structure of the *ancien régime*. In the last quarter of the 20th century, the Counter-Enlightenment impulse reflected in the power of the evangelical religious tradition in the United States has aligned, mostly but not exclusively, with the Moderate Enlightenment camp by way of the conservative movement. Just as the European monarchies of previous centuries sustained their power through an alliance with the Counter-Enlightenment beliefs of the clergy, so would the conservative wing of the Republican Party sustain its power through an alliance with a reemergent dogmatic religious temperament, as expressed principally through the American evangelical movement.

Chapter 13

THE EMERGENCE OF A NEW COUNTER-ENLIGHTENMENT: THE AGE OF TRUMPISM

The election of Barack Obama as president in November 2008 was an extraordinary milestone, not only in the United States but around the world. For disenfranchised people of all races across the globe, this moment in history ignited a striking and boundless "audacity of hope" and portended a future of soaring potential for humanity, of new possibilities perhaps finally unshackled from a history of oppression. For millions of Americans, it was a great symbol of the egalitarian vision of America founded on Radical Enlightenment ideals. For many, it confirmed their optimistic view of the American myth. Here was the coverage in *The New York Times*:

> Barack Hussein Obama was elected the 44th president of the United States on Tuesday, sweeping away the last racial barrier in American politics with ease as the country chose him as its first black chief executive.

Mr. Obama's election amounted to a national catharsis, a repudiation of a historically unpopular Republican president and his economic and foreign policies, and an embrace of Mr. Obama's call for a change in the direction and the tone of the country. But it was just as much a strikingly symbolic moment in the evolution of the nation's fraught racial history, a breakthrough that would have seemed unthinkable just two years ago.[1]

Twelve years later, given the reality of 2020 America, the assessment of 2008 seems incredibly jarring. If the election of the first African American as president signified an epic shift in society, a hefty swing in our proverbial pendulum to the left, the reactionary and thundering crash back to the right, that began less than a decade later, would be as severe. I remain remarkably struck by the phrase in the article "sweeping away the last racial barrier in American politics with ease." In retrospect, it is hard to know exactly what the reporter, Adam Nagourney, who wrote these words was intending to convey. Did we really believe that this "last racial barrier" could just be swept away with "ease" after 400 years of oppression and bloodshed? Would it suddenly just fade away like a mist?

Barack Obama was a Radical Enlightenment thinker at his core; central to Obama's ideology were the concepts of the primacy of representative democracy, an egalitarian society that provides equal access to opportunities, and clear boundaries and separations between civic society and religious observance. His economic, immigration, and foreign policies were arguably less egalitarian, but overall, the confidence that Obama inspired for the advancement of our civilization was robustly tangible.

However, in retrospect, perhaps the halo of hope represented by Obama's election and subsequent administrations fostered our naïveté; many of us remained largely unaware of the strength of the reactionary counterforces brewing underneath the surface. If so, the harsh reality of the subsequent years would provide a cruel reminder. One of the most frequent comments I hear from friends and professional colleagues is:

How did we devolve to where we are in just a few short years? But of course, we did not. In fact, the tracks of our current malaise had been laid long before 2020 and even long before the presidencies of both Trump and Obama.

TRUMP SUCCESSFULLY LINKS TWO CONCURRENT TRENDS

It is undeniable that Obama's election in 2008 seemed like a door opening on possibilities for so many, and the optimism in the air among millions of citizens was almost palpable. *But this was only part of the story.* For many Americans, Obama's election was symbolic of a new and threatening reality that seemed closer perhaps to a horrific dystopia in which they were losing control. In this other reality, the historical license associated with being White in America had become deeply eroded in a new modern pluralistic nation. Some Americans whose ancestors assumed a privileged and dominant position in society believed they came out on the losing side of 21st-century America. Thus, for many segments of our society, the breaking of racial barriers symbolized above all else an indication of their perceived forfeiture of power and status.

Even before Obama took office, the Republican machinery had already decided on a resistance strategy based on obstructionism—a declaration by Republicans on the Hill vowing to stop Obama at all costs. Blowing wind into the sails of this official Republican Party stance were the seeds of an incipient bottom-up populist momentum that did not materialize overnight but was gathering thrust by burning two grades of fuel: one based on socioeconomic trends and the other based on shifting racial dynamics. But neither of these fuels were new discoveries; they had been gradually refined for decades, which only augmented their combustibility.

The first of these, or as I like to say, "half the story" of this brewing populism, is the massive inequality gap in the United States that first emerged in the 1980s and has only accelerated in recent decades. In today's vernacular, we refer to those elite few who hold this vast concentration of wealth as the "one percent." In this context, the elite are not a traditional aristocratic elite, but the "affluent moneyed elite" of more recent generations—the ones who came out on top of the meritocratic race in which they competed. This is perhaps best described succinctly by Kurt Andersen's 2020 piece in *The Atlantic*:

> In 40 years, the share of wealth owned by our richest one percent has doubled, the collective net worth of the bottom half has dropped to almost zero, the median weekly pay for a full-time worker has increased by just 0.1 percent a year, *only* the incomes of the top 10 percent have grown in sync with the economy, and so on. Americans' boats stopped rising together; most of our boats stopped rising at all. Economic *inequality* has reverted to the levels of a century ago and earlier, and so has economic *insecurity*, while economic *immobility* is almost certainly worse than it's ever been.[2]

Andersen's analysis traces the original fissures underlying the inequality story back to the 1970s, when what he describes as the socially and politically left-leaning "yuppies" began pulling away from the traditional "proletariat" who formed the union base of the Democratic Party. But what is particularly insidious about the statistical realities Andersen accurately describes is that our current political system has become largely powerless to rectify, remedy, or even address the massive and still growing inequality gap. While the wealthy class had historically always wielded a strong influence on our political processes, the power and effective control by today's moneyed elite in a post–Citizens United world have become unrestrained.

One way to describe such a society is "plutocracy," a government or society ruled by the wealthy. The unfiltered truth is that the America of the 2020s is no longer operating as a democracy—America in 2021 is a plutocracy in which power and influence can be bought by those who can afford it. Moreover, we as citizens have been complicit in allowing the forces that are driving this inequality to remain unchecked by *our* government, a government purportedly of, by, and for the people. This inaction, in the face of continued economic squeezing of the working class, creates pent-up energy, representing the first grade of combustible fuel enabling the growth of bottom-up populist sentiment.

But documenting and analyzing the inequality gap alone does not tell the whole story of today's political landscape. In order to get a full picture, *we must consider how the evolution of this inequality in wealth has correlated with other socioeconomic and geographic trends*, specifically the concomitant significant increase in cultural diversity in the country.

Driven by rivalry in the global economy, the United States has increasingly demanded and relied on immigration both for access to technical innovation and a less-expensive working class. Furthermore, we have not only experienced faster organic growth among Hispanic Americans and other "non-White" Americans, we have afforded these populations unprecedented access to opportunity. As a result of these trends, American society and our economy have become more diverse and multiracial. For so many Americans, this diversity and broader access to opportunity is a welcome development. But for many others, these trends breed a mounting dread and lingering fears of a multiracial society that represent the other grade of combustible fuel.

In combination, the economic squeezing of the bottom fifty percent, along with rising ethnic and immigrant diversity, has incontrovertibly had a *disproportionate effect on working-class Whites*, leading them to frequently self-identify as the "losers" in this power shift. The truth is the working classes *of all races* have lost power as a result of escalating inequality. The data emphatically demonstrate that as the concentration of wealth rose in the top one percent, the *entire bottom half* (irrespective of race or country of origin) has experienced increasing stagnation of real income.

However, the economic pressure on the working classes has been acutely devastating in parts of the country largely populated by White working-class Americans, such as small towns and rural areas that have been ravaged by the effects of globalization on the modern American economy. These demographic factors highlight a starker *relative loss* of power and status impacting working-class Whites.

It is inarguable that the crippling devastation in rural America caused by economic and civic displacement has created real and deep suffering in thousands of communities across the country. This is not a new trend that suddenly emerged in the Obama era but has been developing for quite some time. In fact, the harmful effects of economic displacement due to globalization have been accumulating in rural areas over the past thirty-five years. However, the data clearly demonstrate an acceleration in more recent years, as these communities have been increasingly left behind by the new technology-based economy progressively concentrated in large cities and on the coasts. Moreover, the carryover or secondary effects of the loss of economic prosperity in these areas has broadly emaciated civic life in small-town America.

In the next section we will explore in more depth the origins of what has become an authentic crisis in thousands of towns and villages across the country. The overall point is that the genuine suffering of millions of the left-behind inhabitants of these places has caused an increasing disillusionment among working-class voters precisely because their woes have not only been *ignored* by successive administrations, but in fact been *caused* by these same administrations' explicit neoliberal and globalist policies that, whether explicitly or inexplicitly, dismiss working-class concerns as inconsequential.

In the run-up to the 2016 presidential election, Trump crafted a precise political formula to *dramatically exploit the correlation between these two trends.* By blending them, Trump simply took concurrent or *correlated* trends and intentionally implied *causality.* Each of these two fuels—the burning resentments associated with both growing inequality and the perceived losses in the face of racial and ethnic diversity—was abundantly volatile in isolation. Trump's mixing them together was as dangerously explosive as it was treacherously irresponsible. Well before he was elected, the rabbit that Trump managed to pull out of his "political hat" was creating persuasive rhetoric based on specious reasoning to suggest that it was specifically the trend toward a multiracial diverse society *that had directly caused* White working-class economic woes. As a consequence of Trump's rhetorical formula, he successfully channeled the angst of millions of disillusioned White Americans toward a new perceived villain—a dangerously and increasingly pluralistic society and its elite leaders who left millions of Americans behind.

Part of Trump's success with this formula is assuredly based on the fact that there is validity to the argument that diversity is related to working-class woes. Working-class Americans have been squeezed in between immigrant labor on the bottom and a talented skilled class on the top that includes many immigrants, African Americans, and Latinos. While the foundational origins of these same woes are multidimensional, most of the underlying causal factors are firmly rooted in the outcomes created by the brutal and relentless progression of global capitalism that has increasingly enriched society's most powerful while leaving an impoverished working class in its wake.

Trump's political feat was his ability to redirect White working-class fears and insecurities onto the concurrent social changes in America's fabric. Proof of its success is demonstrated in the 2016 election statistics. White working-class voters who reported feelings of cultural dislocation or favored deportation of undocumented immigrants were more than three times more likely to support Trump.[3] By election day 2016, thanks to Trump's rhetoric, the White working class had had enough of these developments.

Trump's narrative did not leave the moneyed elite blameless, but it firmly depicted racial and social diversity as the real threats to America. Trump wove a storyline that combined traditional economic populism with nativism in order to foster the feeling that White Americans born in this country (the majority of whose ancestors likely were as well) were being socially, politically, and economically displaced by people not born in America.[4] So, while Trump very expertly *exploited* working-class resentments, he is certainly *not responsible* for creating them. These divisive trends were getting more prominent even before Trump began his campaign.

ORIGINS OF WHITE WORKING-CLASS DISILLUSIONMENT AND RAGE

It should not be surprising that resentment among the White working class has taken root over the course of the last few decades since the ruling elite of *both* political parties have increasingly shown a disregard, and even a deep contempt, for the working classes. As Columbia University professor Jeffrey Sachs wrote in his review of a new book on the classical economist John Maynard Keynes, "Not only Republican presidents including Reagan and the Bushes, but also the Democratic presidents Clinton and Obama, abandoned the aims of social and economic justice in surrender to the demands of the rich and powerful, who championed the call for a new laissez-faire in order to enjoy tax cuts and deregulation while despoiling the environment."[5]

In the preceding chapter, we discussed the economic and political philosophy of neoliberalism that became predominant in the last quarter of the 20th century. In support of this new economic orthodoxy, the political establishment supported by both major political parties reached consensus on promoting laissez-faire economic policies.

Notably, neoliberalism became hypercharged during the Reagan Administration with an inexorable focus on deregulation across many sectors of the economy. As discussed previously, Reagan advocated not only that government had little role in solving the problems within regulated industries, but that government *was* the problem. Furthermore, Reagan's assault on government has been extended by subsequent presidents, both Democrat and Republican alike.

Our political system since the early 1980s has done the bidding of big business in the name of global free market capitalism; this can be most patently observed in the deregulatory policies of recent decades that have provided windfall benefits to business at the expense of consumer protections. While the policy intention of neoliberalism was allegedly to better prepare the U.S. economy for global competition, the overwhelming result was a dramatic upsurge in the inequality gap.

Over the last few decades, the Democratic Party increasingly began embracing the "knowledge workers" of the future, the educated white-collar jobs flourishing in a new technologically driven economy. But at the same time, the party began deserting traditional blue-collar union jobs. In doing so, the Democrats lost the mantle of being the "party of labor," a position it had held since the days of William Jennings Bryan in the late 19th and early 20th centuries. Since the Republican Party of recent decades has never genuinely advanced the interests of the working class, the result is that both major political parties presented a united political front promoting neoliberalism and favoring the wealthy at the expense of the working classes. The statistics are clear.

Critics of neoliberalism have therefore looked at the evidence that documents the results of this great experiment of the past 30 years, in which many markets have been set free. Looking at the evidence, we can see that the total amount of global trade has increased significantly, but that global poverty has increased, with more today living in abject poverty than before neoliberalism.[6]

In more recent years, in the wake of the Democratic Party's abandonment of the working class, the Republican Party, sensing the political opening, has moved to capitalize by courting the blue-collar White working class, primarily those who lost their manufacturing jobs. To further round out the political sorting, the Democrats embraced women and minorities. Such were the dynamics that led to the White working class coming into the fold of the Republican Party in the 1990s and at the turn of the 21st century.

But if the economic policies of the 1980s and 1990s demonstrated a disregard for the working class and the economically disadvantaged, this disregard has morphed into downright derision and disdain as conveyed by 21st-century government leaders. On both sides of the political spectrum in recent years, politicians have vividly illustrated this contempt: Hillary Clinton's "basket of deplorables," Mitt Romney's "half of Americans are dependent on government and oppose taking responsibility for their lives," Barack Obama's "bitter working-class conservatives clinging to guns, religion, and prejudice," and Paul Ryan's division of the world into "takers and makers." This bipartisan disdain for millions of Americans has created not only resentment but a pervasive sentiment of relentless marginalization. Regardless of political party, the condescending comments cited here are easily interpreted as reflective of what the moneyed and cultural elite think in private of much of the America between the coasts, which they label as "flyover country."

* * *

In addition to the economic realities and social divisions that have accumulated over the last decades, a concomitant trend has been a transformation in the very nature of the American political approach, which has become less about issues and more about identities. For generations, citizens viewed politics chiefly as a vehicle for desired policy, a demonstrably effective method for solving problems in the public arena. Accordingly, politics was viewed mostly as transactional. Voters asked questions like, "What will this policy do for me?" or "Will this candidate support the policies I favor?" However, in the last decades, the political discourse has increasingly become about identity. "When we participate in politics to solve a problem, we're participating transactionally. But when we participate in politics to express who we are, that's a signal that politics has become an identity."[7]

Part of this trend was stimulated long ago by the explosive growth of the polling industry, originally started by George Gallup in the middle of the last century. Over many decades, pollsters determined that inciting rage was an effective tool for voter mobilization, more effective than rational policy discussions, which are inevitably convoluted and do not fit neatly into 21st-century soundbites. Some of the most prominent manifestations of this phenomenon in recent decades are seen in the issues of abortion and guns. But this trend of using emotionally provoking triggers to mobilize voters has indisputably been supercharged in the last election cycles by social media and the internet.

This is not only an American phenomenon. In many Western democracies, politics is increasingly "dominated by issues of culture, identity and integration (such as national sovereignty, immigration, refugees and the role of Islam)."[8] While intensifying economic displacement and growing identity politics are perhaps global trends, in the United States, an additional factor has undeniably contributed to working-class resentment. By our collective failure to prosecute those responsible in the aftermath of the Great Recession, we unequivocally aggravated the problem.

In retrospect, perhaps one of the biggest shortcomings of the Obama Administration was its failure, following the 2008–2009 recession, to hold accountable the moneyed-elite masterminds of our financial system who knowingly cheated and robbed millions of American consumers and devastated many working-class families. Despite the tremendous scale of abuses that led to this economic meltdown, one of the bitter aftershocks was that it became increasingly clear to all those who suffered that the culpable Wall Street bankers, protected by their elite lawyers, would not be held responsible. Bending under pressure from the elite establishment itself, most of the industry got bailed out (since most banks were "too big to fail").[9] To add insult to injury, most of the privileged leaders of these same institutions walked away wholly unscathed, despite having meticulously overseen these abuses for years with impunity. At the same time, millions of Americans lost their homes and suffered greatly during the housing collapse.

The stark realization of this double standard stoked the embers of working-class wrath. Here was flagrant evidence that the working classes of American society were held to different rules than the elite American institutions. These same institutions, the engines of globalization, were eligible for a bailout, but the working classes in America were not. Unsurprisingly, this double standard has infuriated many economically suffering Americans since it blatantly confirms their assertions that the elite governing class systematically discriminates against the working class.

In the years following the Great Recession, the amalgamation of all of these factors incited working-class rage across large groups of Americans in places all over our country who were already suffering from the ongoing chronic economic displacement. As anger and resentment festered, many became increasingly cynical and disillusioned and withdrew from the political process entirely, finding both parties deaf to their concerns.

Ironically, many liberal elites seem to blame working-class Whites for their own rage. This is as misguided as it is counterproductive. It is vital to point out that people in the nonurban working class *are justified* in feeling enraged and must be vindicated. Their feelings are based on suffering that is as real as it has been ignored by the establishment. In order to appreciate the magnitude and validity of these sentiments, one needs a picture of the forsaken atmosphere that has too frequently enveloped small towns and rural America.

As far back as the 1980s, the effects of the loss of America's manufacturing industry to Asia had already been extensively documented; as factories were closing, small towns and rural America were suffering the consequences. The perpetuation of these stultifying economic trends has only intensified in recent decades. The children of those workers who were laid off as factories closed in the 1980s and 1990s were now experiencing all the secondary effects: The Rotary clubs, coffee shops, restaurants, and bars have closed, and the local church may have consolidated with another church in the next county. As Timothy P. Carney explains in *Alienated America* (2019): "Economic prosperity is concentrated in America's elite ZIP Codes but economic stability outside of those communities is rapidly deteriorating . . . the unequal geographic distribution opportunity helps explain the 2016 election so many ways."[10]

In short, the vibrant civic life that many nonurban working-class Americans today associate with their childhoods—the pulsating Fourth of July celebrations, the animated Memorial Day parade down Main Street—has vanished. In addition to economic suffering, the civic connectedness of a past era has evaporated, leaving many isolated and left only with fading memories of the animated public square and tight-knit community of their childhoods. And this is a loss not just of community but of opportunity: "Places with more civic activity, regardless of income, have more upward mobility."[11]

As successive American administrations continued to ignore the afflictions of rural working-class Americans while pursuing globalist policies that further devastated their local environments, these same disillusioned Americans became disaffected voters. In 2012, since neither Mitt Romney nor Barack Obama could relate to their troubles, they once again did not bother showing up at the polls.

However, in 2015, almost like the arrival of a white knight, Trump loudly and demonstrably recognized and acknowledged their pain. Moreover, he promised solutions, even if these were more symbolic than concrete. Interestingly, many early Trump supporters during the primaries self-identified as White evangelicals who did not go to church. And Trump portrayed himself as a savior to "persecuted" evangelical Christians. But the fact that the early Trump supporter did not attend church further accentuates the civic isolation felt by these previously disaffected voters described previously. A political system that has become increasingly blind to the real suffering of Americans heralds a coming storm.

A DEMAGOGUE IN THE WHITE HOUSE: TRUMP'S TACTICS TO GET ELECTED

The election and reelection of the first African American president in the nation's history provided a particularly incendiary spark for the not wholly unexpected conflagration. For many in the Republican base, Obama's presidency was the quintessential example of how racially diverse our society had become. And even before Obama's election, Trump's birther movement was sowing the seeds of a new narrative, one of both illegitimacy and resentment, in which traditional White America had come out on the losing side.

Throughout his 2016 campaign, Trump channeled this discontent by mixing the fuels discussed previously with oxygen in his quest to "Make America Great Again." In his 2017 inaugural address, Trump promised that "the forgotten men and women of our country will be forgotten no longer."[12] Working-class Whites felt rescued by Trump; here was their savior who could restore the America of better days. As coastal elites frequently debated the notion of "White privilege" when discussing race relations in America, Donald Trump spun a different narrative. As described by Daniel Markovits (in his 2019 book, to which we will return in a subsequent section):

> A white middle-class voter in Indiana, reflecting on Donald Trump's appeal, recently explained that the "whole idea" of white privilege irritates whites outside the elite "because they've never experienced it on a level that they understand. You hear privilege and you think money and opportunity and they don't have it." The meritocratic suggestion that a white man who cannot get ahead must be in some way deficient stokes this anger.[13]

Thus, Trump managed to become the savior of the working class by tapping into the festering rage among the growing population of the marginalized White Americans described previously. What tactics did he deploy in his quest for power?

One of the most effective ways Trump was able to mobilize the White working-class voting base was by evoking passions with his unique brand of top-down populism laced with Counter-Enlightenment themes. The trend of multiculturalism had already been perceived as threatening to Christian identity for some time. By continually emphasizing both the validity and enormity of this threat, and portraying the Christian community as representative of the sole "authentic America" at the exclusion of immigrants and people of color, Trump converted the seeds of this anxiety among the evangelical Christian community into a veritable petrified forest of distress.[14] Furthermore, by positioning himself as a reliable defender of Christianity, Trump was able to recast himself as a hero within the White evangelical community.

This seems counterintuitive. One might expect the Christian community to find Trump's behavior utterly deplorable, based on traditional Christian values. However, Trump was able to overcome this obstacle by first portraying evangelicals as more persecuted in this country than Muslims, and second by positioning himself as their most trustworthy champion. Consider the now infamous speech Trump gave on the campaign in January 2016 at Dordt University. This is the speech in which he said that he "could stand in the middle of Fifth Avenue and shoot somebody" and "wouldn't lose any voters." As reported by Elizabeth Dias in the August 9, 2020, *New York Times*, "The line that gained notoriety . . . overshadowed another message that morning." As per Dias's narration of the event, Trump said:

> "I will tell you, Christianity is under tremendous siege, whether we want to talk about it or we don't want to talk about it. Christians make up the overwhelming majority of the country," he said. And then he slowed slightly to stress each next word: "And yet we don't exert the power that we should have." If he were elected president, he promised, that would change. He raised a finger. "Christianity will have power," he said. "If I'm there, you're going to have plenty of power, you don't need anybody else. You're going to have somebody representing you very, very well. Remember that."[15]

There is no better illustration of Trump weaponizing a Counter-Enlightenment strain of thinking as a calculated political tool to garner support than this statement. For the evangelical community, this dynamic evidently outstrips the negative effect of his predatory sexual behavior toward women. Later in the same article, Dias writes:

> Evangelicals do not support Mr. Trump in spite of who he is. They support him because of who he is, and because of who they are. He is their protector, the bully who is on their side, the one who offered safety amid their fears that their country as they know it, and their place in it, is changing, and changing quickly. White straight married couples with children who go to church regularly are no longer the

American mainstream. An entire way of life, one in which their values were dominant, could be headed for extinction, and Mr. Trump offers to restore them to [their powerful position at the top of the American hierarchy].[16]

Revitalizing and fortifying the myth that "Christianity is under assault" is merely one of the many tactics in the Trumpian toolbox. He also deployed a distinctive type of antielite populism to amass working-class support. Trump's early attempts used distorted populist narratives to blame the coastal elite, an exceptionally convenient target. His ability to persuasively exploit antielite populist passions through crafty manipulation originally surfaced during Obama's presidency.

This is particularly ironic based on Trump's own in-group status. It is an important point to remember, however, that the term "elite" is often confounding. While Trump is part of the "moneyed elite" himself (or so he purports to be), he also recognizes that the term "elite" is essentially targeted clickbait for unleashing the rage and resentment of the working class. Consequently, Trump deploys the term to characterize the "cultural elite," the "academic elite," or the "bureaucratic elite." Indeed, his use of the term encompasses all those elites except the "moneyed elite," the group in which he, Mitch McConnell, and his cronies belong. Of course, Trump's efforts to channel working-class rage at the elite were particularly effective against the backdrop of the previously described condescending comments by Clinton, Obama, Romney, and Ryan.

Besides its irony given his in-group status, Trump's critique of the elite is interesting in another aspect. It provided a clear parallel to Bernie Sanders's populism on the left. Many of the supporters of both Trump and Sanders deplored the fact that the political elites who implement public policy are influenced by the lobbyists hired by the wealthy who finance their political campaigns. Ironically "drain the swamp" and "fight for the ninety-nine percent" are two sides of the same coin. However, there was one undeniable distinction between the Trump and the Sanders campaigns: The Trump campaign was ultimately embraced and actually funded by the power base that the Sanders campaign eschewed. Moreover, in contrast with the Sanders campaign, whose populist message was almost exclusively targeted at the billionaire class, Trumpian populism targeted the broader set of cultural, academic, and political elites who were deemed responsible for the loss of power and influence of the White working class. At rural campaign stops, Trump would emphasize the "coastal" or "urban elites."[17]

Trump's explicit evoking of populist Counter-Enlightenment themes also relied heavily on familiar nativist and racial tropes. Continually invoking the perceived dangers of immigrants, Trump aroused "fear of the outsider" to engender nativist resentment and retrograde racism. Trump was plugged into this way before the 2016 campaign; the aggressive pursuit of his birther campaign was emblematic of his desire to stir both nativist and racial resentment.[18] His "build the wall" campaign, which he had begun considerably before the 2016 campaign, accentuated Trump's targeting of Mexicans. His many other racist comments notoriously broadened the defining bounds of "the enemy" to anyone non-White.

In summary, Trump was fully tuned in to the fact that ample working-class rage was available and waiting to be exploited as a political mobilization tool; millions of working-class Americans had become completely disillusioned with the country during the Obama years. These working-class Americans were struggling and had categorically been marginalized by both major political parties over successive administrations. The fact that the first African American president coincided with the aftermath of the Great Recession only seemed to accentuate the suffering of working-class Whites and provided a perfect setting for Trump's particular strain of scapegoating. Trump's narrative portrayed a candidate who could understand and relate to the depth of that disillusionment. "Trump rode rather than raised the wave of anger that elected him."[19]

This worked especially well when Trump tailored his approach to various audiences: for Christians, he emphasized Counter-Enlightenment themes; for the working class, he emphasized populism and selective antielitism; and for the xenophobic, nativism and racism were the memes that did the trick. Tragically, Trump's trademark populism and nativism effectually manipulated the genuine pain and suffering of millions: "those trapped at the bottom end of rising meritocratic inequality and made . . . to feel rejected, in favor of strangers, by their own land. Nativism is, like every ressentiment, an 'anesthesia' or 'narcotic.' It deadens the internalized shame of nominally justified social and economic exclusion."[20]

COMMONALITIES OF DEMAGOGUES AND CULT-LIKE STATUS

Trump was far from history's first successful demagogue. He drew on a long-standing portfolio of stratagems used by previous demagogues to build a firm base of support and to suppress opposing points of view. The previous section provided an overview of how Trump, like most demagogues, fervidly exploited and weaponized passions and manipulated emotions to build his considerable base of support. But just as important were Trump's maneuvers for suppressing dissent and demonizing his opponents. In this area, Trump borrowed many of the political tactics pioneered in the 1990s by Newt Gingrich.

When Gingrich first arrived on the Hill, he deployed a "no holds barred" approach of partisan combat, replete with vicious name-calling, conspiracy theories, and obstructionism. Gingrich notoriously wrote a memo that he sent to all his Republican colleagues on the Hill in which he stipulated the use of a specific set of emotion-laden terms when describing Democrats. "Gingrich's list of recommended words

included betray, bizarre, decay, devour, greed, lie, pathetic, radical, selfish, shame, sick, steal and traitors."[21] Gingrich's tactics spurred a new
level of political dysfunction; in achieving his political goals, Gingrich
was more than happy to trash the political process and do lasting damage to our political institutions.[22]

Some political writers have blamed Gingrich for ushering in
an era of permanent dysfunction that allowed for Trump's rise. But
in fact, by using mob-like criminal language to demonize political
opponents, Gingrich himself was working from a well-established
script. History is rife with unexpected dramatic turns in which populist firebrands have tyrannically wielded this type of rhetoric to
unleash the wrath of the mob on their political rivals in a cult-like
way. The way Trump manipulated both Fox News and the Republican
establishment to play by his rules and begin parroting his refrains is
reminiscent of how Putin, following the breakup of the Soviet Union,
first tamed then controlled the powerful oligarchs around him. Or
how Joe McCarthy's use of red fear in the 1950s allowed his witch
hunts to go on as long as they did.

Trump's particular mix of provoking fears and twisting truths is
also reminiscent of Robespierre during the French Reign of Terror
(1792–1795). As illustrated in the first section of this book, Robespierre
waved the flag of Rousseau (one of the heroes of the revolution) even
while misinterpreting Rousseau's writings to harness the rage of the
sans-culottes and imprison or guillotine thousands of his rivals. These
same actions silenced a whole class of intellectuals and competent leaders, whom he successfully terrified. Perhaps Republican senators were
not quite terrified by the prospect of facing the guillotine, but Trump's
threat to wield the power of his electoral base against them decisively
silenced their critiques.

Another method by which Trump neutralized dissent is through
continual and relentless assaults on the free press, especially the news
media. In addition to incessant accusations of "fake news" in the face

of unflattering reporting, Trump vindictively and personally attacked specific journalists who dared to call him out. Trump also routinely suppressed public displays of opposition such as protests under the guise of maintaining "law and order," often through the use of force (or more often, the threat of such) by what Trump viewed as his "police state."

While some of these methods were adroitly deployed by President Nixon less than half a century ago, Trump's compulsive mendacity and habitual fearmongering went further than prior modern demagogues such as Nixon. With the goal of dismissing other points of view, Trump abandoned any semblance of dedication to truth. In fact, his consistent repetition of the same false narrative along with his pseudo-logic had the effect of causing his opponents to question their own sanity. Watching Trump give one of his press conferences was like watching an expert clinic on gaslighting; despite Trump spinning a storyline based entirely on deception and outright lies, skeptical viewers might have easily come away with the impression that Trump's narrative seemed reasonable. The spectacle was nauseating and perversely entertaining at the same time.

Perhaps most appallingly, an additional tactic that Trump deployed was his tacit support of violence and physical intimidation. This was exemplified by his raucous and disorderly campaign rallies where he encouraged both. His inciting of supremacist groups to violence was perhaps unprecedented for a United States president, and ultimately led to an insurrection, a storming of the U.S. Capitol by a furious mob directly provoked by Trump's incendiary comments. As the climax of Trump's six-week campaign intended to stop the validation of Joe Biden as the next president, finally ousting Trump from office, the violent insurgents seemed intent on hanging the vice president and assassinating the speaker of the house. The horrific spectacle followed Trump's exhaustive attempts to use the courts and other governmental tools at his disposal to overturn the election.

One seemingly paradoxical element of Trump's narrative was his attacks on and sabotage of the very government he led. But in fact it is very common for demagogues to attack democratic institutions and foster a deep and pervasive mistrust of expertise. As described by Masha Gessen:

> Contempt for the government and its work is a component of the disdain for elites, and a rhetorical trope shared by the current crop of the world's antipolitical leaders, from Vladimir Putin to Brazil's Jair Bolsonaro. They campaign on voters' resentment of elites for ruining their lives, and they continue to traffic in this resentment even after they take office—as though someone else, someone sinister and apparently all-powerful, were still in charge, as though they were still insurgents.[23]

As a candidate, Trump strategically honed his crusade against the governmental establishment through his "drain the swamp" message to fuel the populist mistrust of these elite academic and political institutions. Trump then doubled down on this tactic as president. His routine assaults on departments in his own administration, such as the FBI, were as startling to the public as they were humiliating to our proficient, hardworking career professionals who serve as nonpartisan public servants.

Trump's crusade at first alienated the political class. The Republican establishment initially rejected Trumpism in the early 2016 presidential campaign, but then watched in awe as he first won the nomination and then took aim at the "failed corrupt political establishment." Once he seized power, Republicans had a choice: As Trump overreaches started to pile up, a few stood by their principles and headed for the exits, but most made a deal to save their own skins. They would ignore, tolerate, or even condone Trump's sins in exchange for maintaining their select position in the ruling class. Not only had Trump tamed them into submission—he wielded the wrath of his populist base as an insurance policy to maintain their loyalty. The evolution of this broad part of the Republican Party, still in tatters in 2021, is one that few would have predicted in 2016.

*   *   *

Through his use of these tactics from the demagogues' playbook, Trump, over the course of his presidency, strengthened the bond between him and his base and achieved an almost cult-like status. Trump relied on a proven set of rhetorical tools that served as catalysts in the chemical bonding process. I label these tools Trump's "bond enablers." Interestingly, while none were originally created by Trump, all were reinforced and exploited by him. We'll explore how Trump used three of these bond enablers: tribalism, the creation of an alternative reality, and belief validation.[24]

Tribalism, in which loyalty to one's own group becomes paramount, served as Trump's base approach. As we discussed in the first section of this book, intergroup conflict elicits primitive fears and anger that easily transcend rational thought. Over the course of human evolution, tribalism has proven to be a very adaptable trait allowing groups to prepare for intergroup conflict. As we frequently observe today among sports fans, merging with a group can be extremely satisfying and empowering for individuals.

As described in a *New York Times* best seller, "In tribal mode, we seem to go blind to arguments and information that challenges our team's narrative. Merging with the group in this way is deeply pleasurable."[25] Furthermore, research has repeatedly shown that hostility toward perceived outsiders runs deep, even when zero-sum competition is not in play. The hormones released when participating in intergroup conflict are very powerful. In Lilliana Mason's research, she has shown how lashing out at partisan opponents is an effective way of soothing the damage associated with low or wounded self-esteem.[26] In this light, Trump campaign rallies provided the benefits of group therapy along with the endorphin rush of a sporting event.

One of the fascinating aspects of Trump's campaign was that, as a candidate, his policy positions were quite thin and flexible. In many ways, by ignoring substance and instead provoking the primitive fear and anger instinctively associated with natural human intergroup conflict, Trump was able to galvanize a tremendous amount of support with what was in the end very little real policy content.

It was this aspect of tribalism that Trump so vehemently exploited in his quest for the White House and continues to use today. By routinely framing the American political landscape in terms of intergroup antagonism, Trump effectively divided the electorate and promised those who felt left behind in recent decades that they were part of Trump's own in-group, which would start "winning." One of his most famous lines on the stump was: "We will have so much winning if I get elected that you may get bored with all the winning."

But Trump's reinforcement of tribalism was used not to *unite all Americans*, emphasizing our common heritage as most presidents have done historically, but on the contrary, to *divide Americans against each other*. By sowing division and discord, Trump bound his tribe together in shared hatred of a group, a unifying common enemy. What is particularly disturbing about Trump's use of tribalist tropes is that the enemy to which he steered such bitter conflict and resentment is not some foreign power. The *enemy is us*, the plurality of voters who did not and do not support him. Trump's objective was to mobilize his base by creating bitter conflict and resentment toward those U.S. citizens not in his base.

Political leaders routinely use these tactics when uniting the population against a foreign enemy, as American presidents did during the Cold War era. But Trump's use of tribalism to pit some Americans against others was not unprecedented. It is reminiscent of similar tactics deployed by President Nixon and his vice president, Spiro Agnew. (Like Trump, Nixon and Agnew also disdained the media.) Agnew once famously said: "If dividing the American people has been my main contribution to the national political scene. I not only plead guilty to this charge, but I am somewhat flattered by it."[27]

The second key bond enabler was Trump's willingness to discard any and all allegiance to empirical facts and the truth in general and fabricate an alternate reality. By complete abnegation of objective truth and its replacement with an alternative "truth," Trump was able to concoct his own narrative, which he then convinced his "new" media allies to corroborate.

The loss of objectivity in television news media has been a long trend since the 1990s when opinion-based news media proliferated as a result of Reagan's repeal in 1987 of the FCC (Federal Communications Commission) fairness doctrine. From the time of the fairness doctrine's introduction in 1949, it required holders of broadcast licenses to present balanced points of view. Since the doctrine's repeal, there has been a gradual but accelerating relinquishment of objectivity in television news. Furthermore, the explosion of Rush Limbaugh–style conservative talk radio since the 1990s facilitated the propagation of preposterous far-fetched theories, some bearing no semblance of truth whatsoever. Broadcast news media today has built "into its foundation a rejection of the idea that truth could come from weighing different points of view . . . The nation had lost its way in the politics of mutually assured epistemological destruction. There was no truth, only innuendo, rumor, and bias. There was no reasonable explanation; there was only conspiracy."[28]

Against this backdrop of a polarized media environment increasingly devoid of objective reporting, Trump uses social media to invent and foster his own reality in which his distressed constituents can seek soothing refuge. Outside of his blatant lies, Trump triggers his supporters' distress by carefully cherry-picking "factoids" that support his narrative. Once provoked, Trump presents himself as uniquely qualified to provide solace from their troubles by creating an imagined idyllic history to which he and only he can return his flock. His insistent repetition of catch phrases (such as "no collusion," "no quid pro quo," "I have tremendous respect for women," and "I am the least racist person you ever met") skillfully conditions his base to unconditionally accept his reality and instructs them on how to respond to any critique, all the while effectively ridiculing the rest of us.

The third key bond enabler underlying and solidifying this cult-like bond between Trump and his base has its roots in psychology: the concept of belief validation. All humans are brimming with preconceived biases, predispositions, and prejudices absorbed and amassed from our developmental environments—it is an established trait in humanity that has served us well over our evolutionary history. This cognitive power allows humans to efficiently process information in a complex world. The accompanying drawback is that it makes absorbing new data and new patterns that conflict with our established beliefs much more difficult.

Beyond the cognitive dimension, our beliefs and their contestation or validation come with an emotional world which is in itself quite multifaceted. Intuitively, we know that validation of our beliefs can feel good, while challenges to our beliefs can create tension and at times be extraordinarily painful. Further, beliefs can be associated with primal emotions like love, aggression, and fear. The expression of such beliefs in a public environment can induce feelings of shame or guilt. Thus, many of our core beliefs remain hidden within us, and if revealed beyond a close circle of loved ones, can be a source of embarrassment or even humiliation. During his reign, Trump's enormous gift to his cult-like followers was the *license he gave them* not only to unashamedly possess their beliefs but to express or act on them in public.

For core Trump supporters, the psychic relief that accompanied the expression of, and ultimately the justification of, previously concealed beliefs must have been both cathartic and liberating. Trump dared to say what his supporters were thinking but were afraid themselves to say. Because his offensive and despicable comments were so outside the norm for a political leader, they represented a form of validation that was enormously powerful in its ability to expunge guilt or shame. It was also at the core of why Trump's base identified so personally with him and went to great lengths to defend him.

Once united by these bond enablers, attacks on Trump became threatening to the individual members of his base on an individual psychological level. The physical aggression that exploded at Trump campaign rallies and in the assault on the U.S. Capitol on January 6, 2021, was also a clear manifestation of the power of this bond. By making it OK to say things that might have been difficult to express in today's politically correct environment, or even making it OK to rough up an adversary, Trump begat praise and loyalty and even adulation. (Lou Dobbs has routinely remarked that in his opinion Trump was the greatest president in the history of the United States.) Moreover, as part of a mutually beneficial symbiosis, the praise and adulation Trump received from his supporters in return substantiated his own belief system. His own power and greatness were, in turn, validated.

* * *

In summary, through the use of specific bond enablers, Trump passionately established a strong and profound connection between himself and his supporters. Ultimately, it was the strength of these bonds with his electoral base that afforded him sufficient political power to wield a successful coup of the Republican Party (and a nearly successful overturn of the results of the 2020 election). Few political leaders can establish such an intimate connection with their constituents. Trump started building this bond over the course of his campaign through his narrative (e.g., "build the wall," MAGA, "lock her up," etc.). Then he reinforced it with certain executive policies, but mostly through symbolic actions (e.g., holding a Bible in front of a church surrounded by police lines restraining protesters).

The bond was continually validated by Fox News and talk radio. He brandished his bond with the base as a threatening weapon to keep Republican leaders in line. Otherwise, why would so many in the Republican establishment form an alliance with Trump? He also ruthlessly controlled how the wrath of the base was wielded, be it on a disruptive "radical Democrat" at one of his rallies who got punched in the face or forced out of the crowd, or an incumbent RINO (Republican in name only) representative or senator who decided to disagree with or vote against the president. As assuredly as the establishment Republicans did not believe the lies he told, they feared his sway over the base upon which they depend to hold their power. So, supporting Trump allowed them to win their primaries and hold their seats in the next cycle, and thereby remain in power as part of the political elite.

In the final analysis, Trump is a formidable and gifted demagogue. However, his particular talents and expertise have nothing to do with any substantive or applicable policy issue. Moreover, the palliative relief he provided to struggling Americans is illusionary and ultimately offered no meaningful or constructive succor. On the contrary, his know-how is concentrated in the skillful deployment of an arsenal of tools used by demagogues, not for the amelioration of the United States of America, but for the inflation of his own ego and the enrichment of his family and friends.

THE CONSERVATIVE DILEMMA IN THE AGE OF TRUMP

As we explored in previous chapters, the top-down form of populism that politicians frequently deploy as a political tool to garner support feeds off of genuine bottom-up populist sentiment that builds over time. The last four decades of growing inequality and increasing multiculturalism have created a vast and fertile field in which populism can grow and flourish. And as reviewed, Trump supercharged his populist appeal by supplementing it with various techniques from the demagogue's toolkit.

It has been repeatedly demonstrated over the course of history that demagogues can create cult-like loyalty and powerful movements, but they cannot do so alone; they can only succeed with the help of others. They must carefully build a network of alliances and supporting architecture. Like the beams and joists supporting a house, these support structures are often invisible, hidden from outside view. Just as Hitler formed a powerful alliance with German industry away from the public eye, just as Putin privately disciplined the Russian oligarchs to gain their support, and just as Robespierre surreptitiously enticed the 18th-century French clergy, so Trump formed such alliances to consolidate his power. One of the most interesting elements of the Trump presidency was the multifaceted mesh of coalitions he built to attain and shore up his support.

The first step that allowed Trump to consolidate his power was his rapid takeover of the Republican Party. The leaders in power who constitute the formal part of the Republican Party aligned with Trump for reasons beyond just holding their seats or their positions of power. Trump delivered the goods in the form of achieving the desired policy positions that they had long been advocating. In fact, Trump preserved the economic interests of the elite moneyed class for whom most Republicans have advocated for their entire careers.

From an economic policy perspective, Trump and his allies continued the trend begun by Reagan of abandoning any government attempt at meaningful economic redistribution. They pursued an aggressive agenda of deregulation that eroded consumer protections and freed corporations to unabashedly pursue returns to shareholders, often at the expense of other stakeholders. Indeed, Reagan's crusade against almost all forms of government regulation was a religion, but Reagan's dubious trickle-down economic theories pale in comparison to Trump's obsession with lower taxes on corporations and the rich. The irony is that the biggest losers from these policies were the broad middle and working classes.

How is it that Trump gained the political support of voters who were undeniably hurt by his economic policies? Trumpism is often likened to a cult precisely because Trump convinced millions of his supporters to vote against their own economic interests in pursuit of some higher cause with which they identified. This mystifying and irra-tional occurrence is better understood by examining the nature of the complex web of alliances supporting Trumpism, which the next few sections of this chapter will attempt to do.

In the first part of this book, we saw that during the 18th cen-tury, Radical Enlightenment thinkers critically portrayed the coalition between the aristocrats and monarchs and the church as "the great collusion." The two estates of society (nobility and clergy) formed an alliance that kept the masses in check, controlled daily life, and kept society in order. Further, the Radical Enlightenment thinkers explained how the mutual symbiosis between these two classes had been going on for centuries, all through the Middle Ages. Throughout American history, we have also experienced similar collusions, often between the conservative political elite and American evangelicalism, which have been nearly as powerful (as discussed in the last chapter). The influ-ential religious leaders of megachurches have routinely sanctioned the power of the conservative wing of the Republican Party based on their common views on social issues.

To understand the blend of alliances that emerged in the early years of the 21st century and led to Trump, it is worth examining these dynamics in a bit more detail. The first most obvious alliance to note is that between the one-percent moneyed elite and the new Republican Party taken hostage by Donald Trump.

That conservatism and conservative parties have been linked to wealthy elites is not particularly novel. Such linkages have been demonstrated over many eras of our history. Today's technology one-percenters might have been steel or oil barons in prior generations, all with close linkages to conservative elements in the ruling parties. At the same time, however, this is precisely why over our history, we have been wary of extreme concentrations of wealth—we recognize the threat they present to our democratic institutions. The larger the gap between the interests of the elites and those of the masses, the bigger the potential threat.

This threat to democracy takes various forms. First, the moneyed elite wield unequal power in government, based on just how much policy their wealth can buy. As the one-percenters accrue more power, their interests diverge from those of the lower and middle classes, and maintaining their status quo becomes their number one goal. Based on the working-class's perception of the power and wealth imbalance, a simmering resentment develops among its members. But if the imbalance of interests gets dramatically out of proportion, *it can dangerously erode democracy.* As class interests diverge, the moneyed elite becomes less and less interested in true democracy since the policies that favor the rich tend to be unpopular with the masses. Consequently, members of the moneyed elite use their considerable influence to chip away at democracy itself, which inevitably emerges as a threat to their own position of power.

In Jacob Hacker and Paul Pierson's new book, *Let Them Eat Tweets: How the Right Rules in an Age of Extreme Inequality* (2020), the authors describe what they refer to as the "Conservative Dilemma"—the conundrum elected conservatives routinely face of pleasing their financial supporters when doing so conflicts with the more populist agenda that mass voters demand. While both political parties have historically faced this dilemma for as long as they have taken big money, the new Republican Party has gone all in. Hacker and Pierson's description is concise and accurate:

> American plutocracy has transformed both of America's two great political parties. The most profound effects, however, have been on the Republican Party . . . [which has] singularly focused on tax cuts for corporations and the superrich, whatever the effects on American inequality, or on the people who make up the Republican "base." When those cuts have conflicted with their traditional emphasis on fiscal restraint, they have run up huge deficits to finance them, abandoning the principle of budget balance . . . They have launched an intensifying assault on environmental, consumer, labor and financial protections. They have attempted to strip health insurance from millions of Americans. They have appointed the most consistently pro-business, anti-labor, anti-consumer judges in the modern history of the federal courts. And they have done all this despite the fact every one of these aims has strikingly little public support, even among Republican voters.[29]

So how exactly did Trump's Republican Party resolve the Conservative Dilemma? How is it possible that today's Republican Party can continue to amass electoral support while pursuing very unpopular policies? In the tax bill that Trump worked so hard to pass early in his administration (and is still in place as of this writing), eighty percent of the benefits go to the top one percent. How does a political party get away with that electorally? Other examples abound. As discussed previously, Trump aggressively pursued deregulation that benefits the top one-percent extreme wealthy class at the expense of the masses. The answer for Trump lies in the convoluted web of surrogates he constructed and deployed, each with a specific assignment, a precise piece to fit in the overall puzzle.

THE THREE-HEADED GIANT

Political parties have two objectives: to institute policies consistent with the interests of those they represent and to stay in power. But what if these two objectives are contradictory? How does the Republican Party of 2020 maintain sufficient electoral support to remain in power while implementing economic policies that mostly if not exclusively favor the very rich? In the era of transactional politics this was an enigma; however, in today's culture of identity politics, it has become somewhat easier to understand. "Inevitably, [they have] to offer something else to the voters. There is a set of noneconomic issues—many racially tinged, all involving strong identities and strong emotions—that draw a sharp line between 'us' and 'them'. . . In modern societies, the list of such 'cleavages' is short, and their history unpleasant."[30]

One additional factor that has played a role in facilitating a cleaner separation of social identity issues from "pocketbook" issues is the demise of unions. When unions were front and center in working-class American households, economic policies also took a center seat. Today, as the number of union households has shrunk enormously, seemingly so too has the prominence of economic issues in working-class voters' calculus.

Thus, the strategy of Trump's new Republican Party was to inflame *social divisions to elicit and mobilize broad popular support.* In order to implement the inherently unpopular economic policies that their donors support, Republicans must find a way to sustain power by building a base of voter support around other issues, or with other means. And identity politics provides an ideal framework for so doing.

As has been illustrated throughout this chapter, Trump, with his unique gifts of entertaining theatricality and brazen egotism, is remarkably talented at pushing the emotional buttons that trigger and mobilize these social forces. With these gifts, Trump possesses an enormous asset for the conservative ruling class—a unique ability to bring in the votes. The political engineering here works as follows: Trump's political class survives through mobilizing disenfranchised and resentful White working-class people—his base—by stirring their populist and nativist fears and passions, and promising to restore the security of a perhaps illusory prior societal order, to make America great again. The cruel irony is that the base is indirectly supporting economic policies that are contrary to the self-interests of its members and that will only deepen their economic hardships. Fortunately for Trump's political party, actual solutions to problems are not required. The use of powerful symbols suffices.

In practical terms, today's Republican Party has thus fashioned two distinct seemingly conflicting alliances to support its strategy—the deep and loyal bond described in the previous section between Trump and his voter base and a separate but just as vital bond between Trump's party and the moneyed elite. The fact that these two different alliances have distinct and often conflicting interests simply becomes a matter of balance. I dub this unique web of tied interests, but conflicting priorities, Trump's "three-headed giant"—Trump, his voter base, and his funding base—each needing to get fed.

The three-headed giant represents this collusion between Trump and his political cronies with, on one hand, the one-percenters whose lawyers actually write the economic policies that get implemented, and on the other, with the disenfranchised White working-class voters who are most hurt by these economic policies, but whose pain and fear are assuaged in another way. The irony is that the Republicans can pass an increasingly unpopular economic agenda through this arrangement: The moneyed elite funds the party in exchange for getting the *policy it wants*, and the party preaches a scary and divisive populism to motivate and mobilize the *voters it needs* to stay in power. This is why Trump speaks like the populist and nativist that he is but governed in the interest of the top one percent.

As Hacker and Pierson describe: "To advance an unpopular

plutocratic agenda, Republicans have escalated white backlash—and, increasingly, undermined democracy. In the United States, then, plutocracy and right-wing populism have not been opposing forces. Instead, they have been locked in a doom loop of escalating extremism that must be disrupted."[31]

OUTSOURCING OUTRAGE: USING SURROGATES TO SUSTAIN THE CONSERVATIVE COALITION

So how exactly did Trump's Republican Party manage these conflicting coalitions? By what methods are the tacit alliances underpinning the three-headed giant fashioned and supported? How does each head get fed? *The key enabling mechanism is outsourcing.* By engaging and managing effective surrogate groups, the Republican Party can create a smokescreen and maintain a healthy distance and hide from view the unsavory dealings upon which these alliances depend. By using proxies, as opposed to its own infrastructure, the Republican Party subcontracts both voter mobilization and fund-raising, each to a set of discretely focused and determined groups, and thereby keeps its hands clean through a veil of plausible separation.

The surrogate groups that do the work of mobilizing the voter base are the usual suspects: the Christian right, the National Rifle Association, Fox News, and right-wing talk radio. These groups have uniquely tailored abilities to reach deep down into communities and rile up voters by eliciting fear and rage. Many of these organizations have lengthy track records of exploiting racial conflict for political purposes.

The Christian right was an early specialist in fueling outrage during the growth of White resistance to desegregation by promoting and defending the growth of Christian schools. What is particularly interesting is that White evangelicals originally became a force in politics back in the 1970s when White southerners migrated from the Democratic Party to the Republican Party. Over the years, the Christian community has galvanized support for a wide range of social issues such as opposing the ERA, advocating for school prayer, and opposing abortion. But it was only when President Jimmy Carter failed to support Christian schools that the Christian leadership abandoned the Democrats and migrated to the Republican Party in droves.

It was at this time that Republican tactician Lee Atwater designed his brilliant and fruitful strategy of building a solid base of support for the Republican Party in the traditionally Democratic South. In many ways, Atwater astutely identified that southern conservatives, tradition-ally a key constituent base of the Democratic Party, could be poached with a blend of populist yet socially conservative messaging. Atwater was a pioneer in recognizing that *issues* are much less powerful than *identities* in successfully garnering electoral support. He recognized that identities, made up of passion-laden perceptions of shared alle-giances and shared threats, can mobilize voters much more efficiently.

Like the Christian right, the National Rifle Association histori-cally relied on racist tropes in making the case for gun deregulation by evoking White fear of the crime in integrated cities. Right-wing media has fanned the flames with a continual stream of "us versus them" appeals to rally and sustain broad voter support. Through all of these channels, today's Republican Party has become "reliant on . . . iden-tity claims to motivate voters, and on surrogate groups that [know] how to weaponize them."[32]

A separate set of surrogate groups are deployed to feed the second mouth of the three-headed giant, the funding base. The surrogates rep-resenting big money in politics have had a much easier go of it in recent years in a post–Citizens United world: the Koch brothers' network, a diverse group of assorted conservative PACs (political action commit-tees) and SUPERPACs, and the Chamber of Commerce. Charles and

David Koch, the heads of Koch Industries, emerged in the early 2000s as a fund-raising juggernaut espousing a hard-right philosophy. The magnitude of the money they raised and the power of the network they established would underwrite the conservative elements within the Republican Party for decades. While their influence focused on laissez-faire economic policies, including deregulation, the far-right viewpoints they advocated often encompassed social policy as well.

A whole host of other SUPERPACs complement the work. Unlike traditional PACs, SUPERPACs can raise funds from individuals, corporations, unions, and other groups without any legal limit on donation size. Furthermore, because much of this SUPERPAC money gets funneled through nonprofit organizations, now protected by the 2010 Citizens United Supreme Court decision, most is contributed under a veil of secrecy.

The Chamber of Commerce, which in decades past was bipartisan, has now become another juggernaut of financial support for the Republican Party. The scope of the Chamber's activities is impressive. In addition to massive campaign spending, the Chamber spends more money on lobbyists than any other Washington, DC, organization. "Indeed, it has effectively become a lobbyist-for-hire for industries . . . that want plausible deniability as they fight popular bills or try to pass unpopular ones."[33] The Chamber also plays an active role in the court system, both at the national and state levels, by placing pro-business judges on the court, advancing pro-business litigation, and selecting state attorneys general.

These powerful business and financial surrogates provide the money in exchange for desired policies, principally deregulation and lower taxes. The first group of mobilization surrogates described here focuses on rounding up the votes and keeping social issues front and center. Having outsourced these two vital components, the leadership of the Republican Party is left merely with the responsibility of coordinating the various surrogates' activities. In recent years, Trump and

Mitch McConnell acted like the conductors of an orchestra, bringing these different surrogate groups to work in concert with synchronized harmony. This allowed the Republican Party leaders to "reconcile their allegiance to wealth and power with the need to attract the electoral support of voters without much of either."[34]

No doubt, there are many tensions in this alliance. Both parties in the mix must tolerate elements they find distasteful. As the divisive rhetoric gets louder and more dominated by populist and nativist themes, the one-percenters supporting the financial surrogates must hold their noses. While members of the base support economic policies that may be contrary to their own self-interests, this is outweighed by the recompense they obtain knowing that we are building a wall to keep "illegal" immigrants out.

There is ample evidence that the Republican Party struggles to balance these competing forces at times. For example, it is in the money-eyed-elite's interest to get immigration reform passed, and they have tried numerous times, but this is antithetical to the populist base. One recent and startling example shows the tension in this balance plainly: In passing COVID-19 response legislation to provide needed popular aid in a time of a pandemic crisis, Mitch McConnell indicated that his top priority associated with the proposed legislation was to grant corporations immunity protection if they allowed personnel to come back to work. Even when supporting a piece of legislation to aid the struggling masses, Mitch McConnell's top priority is protecting the wealthy corporate shareholder class.

Thus, in the era of Trump, it was a novel mesh of collusions embodied in the three-headed giant that provided the essential support structure that allowed the elite one percent to effectively make the laws by which the remaining ninety-nine percent are forced to live. The trade here is amply clear: The rich and powerful supported Trump and his henchman financially, and in return the Republican Party allowed them (and their lobbyists) to write the laws that protect their wealth, power, and status. At the same time, through the savvy use of Trump's aforementioned bond enablers, the disenfranchised members of the nonurban lower-income White working class were convinced that they had a leader who, contrary to all evidence, was not an egotist out for himself, but was somebody who resembled them, shared their pain, and validated their prejudices and fears by promising a return to a time when America was "great."

ATTACKING DEMOCRACY TO PROTECT PLUTOCRACY

Another intriguing aspect of Trump's three-headed giant was that collectively it hardly represented a majority of the populace. Nevertheless, the three-headed giant demonstrated that even without a majority of the popular vote, a *new minority can dominate government policy*. Much of this is systemic; various features of our constitutional framework such as the Senate and the Electoral College tip the power balance significantly toward the rural, less-populated areas of the country. The fact that racial minorities and more cosmopolitan voices and thus liberal voters tend to concentrate in the relatively weakened urban areas exacerbates and accentuates this rural-urban imbalance.

But despite these structural advantages, when the intricate multipart alliances they construct do not provide enough popular voter support, today's Republican Party resorts to a more insidious method of sustaining its power: an attack on democracy itself. While "cheating" or vote rigging in the form of extreme gerrymandering and voter suppression are not new nor the exclusive purview of one political party, there is no question that these tactics have risen to the level of an obsession within the current Republican Party.

In pursuit of its goals, the Republican Party aggressively pursues antidemocratic tactics, thereby sacrificing democracy itself. In past generations, political operatives would conceal such tactics. Trump's party today openly displays its disdain for broadening the right to vote. In the aftermath of the 2020 election, the coordinated effort by Trump and the Republican Party to subvert the will of the voters and effectively overturn the results through farcical legal claims and concocted narratives and storms of the U.S. Capitol will certainly become beguiling fodder for the soon-to-be-written American historical chronicle.

For generations, American leadership, under the banner of our "exceptionalism," has been sanctimonious in its condemnation of these tactics when practiced in other less democratic countries. How today's leaders can so openly and blatantly deploy these same tactics in the United States seems at first glance to be quite a mystery. But it is not that hard to understand, given a broader than imagined willingness to eschew democracy within the Republican alliance. Due to their own particular fears of democracy, the plutocrats and right-wing populists conspire by sowing seeds of doubt about election results, joining frivolous lawsuits, and validating conspiracy theories of massive voter fraud. "Plutocrats fear democracy because they see it as imperiling their economic standing and narrowly defined priorities. Right-wing populists fear democracy because they see it as imperiling their electoral standing and [the interests of] their narrowly defined community."[35]

While many feared Trump's embrace of authoritarianism as he attempted to emulate his heroes Putin, Erdogan, and other ruthless leaders, perhaps the real threat is this creeping counter-majoritarianism, which allows a "more determined minority to not just resist the will of the majority, but increasingly to rule over it."[36] While the Framers were indisputably concerned about the "tyranny of the majority," and thus designed our system of government to make it difficult for majorities to rule without broad consensus, they also feared a "tyranny of the minority," in which a small cohesive group can wield its power over the majority. The most recent plutocratic populist in-chief, enabled by the three-headed giant, has dramatically served as an elucidatory example of the merit of their fears.

THE BILL OF DAMAGES

In the final analysis, the net result of all of these abuses of power is that Trump was personally further enriched and emboldened while the American people were further impoverished and democracy severely weakened. While Trump was not the first president to use his office to advance his own personal interests, he was indubitably the most blatant in so doing. His use of the office for self-enrichment, such as channeling official government affairs to his own business properties, seems mild compared to his other abuses of the office.

Trump essentially took our entire republic hostage in order to maintain his hold on power. He used diplomacy to support his bid for reelection, deployed the Justice Department to investigate his political opponents and defend his own crooked behavior, and hijacked coronavirus press conferences as televised campaign-style rallies to attack his opponents and fabricate his own achievements. More recently, he resorted to a seditious assault on the heart of our democracy by undermining our system of free and fair elections. It was unashamedly obvious early in his administration that "Trump has merged the institution of the presidency with his personal interests and has used the former to serve the latter like no previous occupant of the office."[37] In addition, the methods that the three-headed giant employed in underwriting Trumpism are themselves eroding our democracy and must be called out and condemned. Such methods have no place in the democratic republic as envisioned by our Founders.

Assessing the repercussions of the Trump era will be difficult and will require the benefit of time, healing, and perspective. One can only imagine the copious amounts of materials in the form of articles, books, and academic research that have yet to be written even though much has already started accumulating. Nonetheless, clues regarding the nature of the resulting "bill of damages" indicate just how extensive and multifaceted the impairment has already been and how much will likely endure.

Institutionalizing and thus prolonging the historical wealth imbalance in the United States is merely one starting point. Weaponizing the resentment created by this imbalance and recasting it as an ethnic identity or race war is as nauseating as it is immoral.

In the pursuit of its goals, the Trumpian alliance's willingness to wage an all-out assault on American institutions has had enormous consequences. In addition to leaving a huge gap in our present governing capacity, the assault on American institutions, which has been built over centuries, leaves immense and enduring collateral damage. In recent years, Trump's open disdain for government institutions has alienated an entire generation of hardworking, dedicated, and talented public servants. The bravest are those who have dared to speak out; they have been personally attacked and riddled by spiteful and rancorous character assassination. Countless others, disgusted with such shenanigans, have bitterly left government service. Moreover, a future generation of talented and needed public servants will now most likely be drawn to other careers. Will the next brilliant infectious disease specialist be so willing to fill the shoes of Dr. Anthony Fauci?

There's much more damage to account for on a global level. Much of the previously-described portfolio of activities has propagated a tremendous distrust of America among our allies and severely damaged our reputation throughout the world. Generations of Americans have lost their lives defending our country, and millions of others have dedicated their careers to building our prominent standing on the world stage (even with all its blemishes). At this point, we have no accurate sense of the cost of rebuilding our alliances or the time required to reestablish our global position of leadership.

Finally, this list of damages is an incomplete accounting since it represents the ramifications of policies that have been enacted and actions that have been committed by and in the name of Trump. What if we look at the opportunity cost side of the balance sheet? What are all the vital things that were *not* done during the Trump Administration? This list is perhaps even more damaging; not only have we forgone reinvestment in education for a future generation, but our severely threatened planet inches closer toward extinction. And of course, had the Trump administration taken the COVID-19 threat seriously from the start and then not grossly mismanaged the pandemic, how many American lives (almost 600,000 lost as of this writing) might have been saved?

*   *   *

While our current quandaries and difficulties have not materialized overnight and have surely been developing for many years, it is not accidental that the destructive forces that coalesced into the three-headed giant followed Obama's presidency. In many ways President Obama represented progression toward a multicultural society, one in which nativist culture might be delegitimized and dismantled for the benefit of all. In our familiar analogy, the Obama presidency represents a tremendous swing of the pendulum to a more egalitarian view of our country. However, the fact that today's Trumpism is in large part an opposing pendulum swing, a backlash reaction to the Obama era, does not by itself make it any less perilous, nor does it make the political tactics it deploys any less repulsive. Today's Robespierre is as much embodied in Mitch McConnell, Lindsey Graham, and William Barr as it is in the leader for whom they toed the line.

In another era, these enablers might have been called "all the President's men." The devastation they leave in their wake is the sacrifice of competence for cronyism and the reprehensible advancement of their own self-interests. Yet whatever may become of Trump's political fortunes in the future, Trumpism and the conservative coalition underpinning it will remain a corrosive threat not only to America's public health but to our country's democracy and civic life as well. It is incumbent on us to stop the putrefaction and rebuild a more durable foundation for an America that lives up to the Radical Enlightenment principles that were its birthright.

Part III

THE FUTURE IS ON THE LINE

"A Republic if You Can Keep It"
—Benjamin Franklin

In the preceding chapters, I have argued that the divisions that have torn our nation apart over the course of our history are rooted in conflicting ideals that first surfaced and began contending for prominence during the era of our nation's founding. The disparities between these philosophies have their origins in distinct schools of Enlightenment thought that emerged in the 18th century and greatly shaped our nation's birth.

Today, we are inundated daily from all sides with unremitting displays of the polarization of American politics, the "us versus them" partitions that divide us based on race, socioeconomic status, geography, gender, and sexual orientation. We frequently attribute our "culture wars" to profound differences across our various identities, and we seek comfort by associating with our self-affirming in-groups, those who share our view of the world, validate our beliefs, and protect us from overtaxing challenges to our convictions.

While this description of our contemporary American society (and of other liberal democratic societies as well) rings true, I nevertheless find this level of analysis of our present dilemmas to be wearying and counterproductive. Yes, we can focus on our superficial differences more than our commonalities, and undoubtedly, at times doing so is necessary to confront and address important issues of justice. But such an approach can also be overly facile. In order to make real progress, we need to more assiduously progress to a deeper level of understanding and to investigate the beliefs underlying and motivating these differences.

Identities matter, of course, but so do the ideals, aspirations, hopes, and dreams that inspire and inform them. The more we focus on shallow differences among our group identities, the more we trigger the primitive emotions associated with intergroup competition, and most importantly, the more we *crowd out rational thinking*. As part of our collective debate, we need to consciously and deliberately resist the pressure of the business as usual *modus operandi* exerted by our own self-identified in-groups. By continuing to display knee-jerk reactions or Pavlovian responses in this polarizing context, we further cement divisions based *less on substantive issues and more on the perceived political standing of our chosen mobs.*

Of course, we cannot eliminate group and individual differences; they will always be present. However, we must collectively, within our in-groups and individually, strive to deemphasize them and restore rational conversation to our political discourse. We can surrender to the endorphin rush associated with defending our in-group and bashing the out-group, or we can choose an alternate path. Specifically, we can endeavor to inject logical concepts, thoughtful and cogent ideas, and more sympathetic and considered reflection into our civic discussion. Like so many facets of life in a democratic society, these changes cannot be mandated by law; they must bubble up from the desires of its citizens. We must individually and collectively choose to *fight unreason with reason.*

Historical accounts of a nation or civilization are largely subjective, shaped by the storytellers' biases and perspectives. American history is no exception. Are we telling the story of great and flawed leaders who changed America? Or are we telling the story of how American people from all different classes, races, and geographies formed and shaped a nation from the bottom up? Are we consciously striving to adjust for the inherent bias in historical accounts that are written by "the winners"? How do we more objectively incorporate the stories of those who lost, often tragically?

In reflecting on the multilayered issue of how we might achieve an actualization of our republic more closely following in the Radical Enlightenment tradition, the historical chapters that come to mind are episodes that forged a convergence between bottom-up movements and intrepid top-down leadership. Our historical periods of greatest progress have most often been characterized by great leaders inspired by the plight of less-fortunate Americans. But these pioneers themselves were stirred by the bottom-up mobilizations of brave and gutsy citizens. On such occasions, inspired leaders recognized the suffering and injustices demonstrated by these bottom-up movements and boldly proclaimed that we have work to do to redress these harms and create a brighter future for all. These audacious leaders often commenced bold endeavors to release the pent-up energy of bottom-up movements and thereby drive change, often in the face of great uncertainty. Lincoln at Gettysburg, King's promissory note, FDR's New Deal, and LBJ's Great Society all represented clarion calls to action to fulfill the creed expressed in the Declaration. Millions of lesser-known but equally brave leaders have also fought for comparable ideals with varying degrees of success—some unsung heroes, others thwarted patriots.

This concluding section represents my humble attempt to consider how we might better fulfill the credo of our Radical Enlightenment tradition. Here, I discuss my view of the core issues that have defined the American Schism throughout our history and that have been omnipresent in the episodes discussed previously. My perspective is of course biased, founded in my conviction that the Radical Enlightenment vision of truly representative democracy with equality of voice, access, and opportunity, accompanied by a strong separation between civic affairs and spiritual life, is the vision most consistent with the promise laid out in the Declaration of Independence. While the Declaration's promises have been frequently overlooked, too seldomly codified through explicit laws and guaranteed through enforcement, and recurrently and unambiguously withheld from many throughout our history, this founding document's Radical Enlightenment credo must endure as the central core of our democratic republic—our "American experiment."

In the chapters that follow, I seek to answer some fundamental questions: Putting aside our distinctions based on group identities, what are the substantive differences in how we view society and the role of public policy within it? How do we differ on the role of government in society and why? Are our different views reconcilable? Do we differ on who should have a seat at the table for these discussions? And finally, can we establish a more level playing field with access to opportunities open to all, akin to the one envisioned by Radical Enlightenment thinkers?

Chapter 14

GOVERNMENT TOP-DOWN
OR BOTTOM-UP

In Mattathias Schwartz's profile of William Barr in the June 1, 2020, *New York Times Magazine*, our former attorney general reflects on the evolution of our republic. One section in particular stood out to me:

> He [Barr] is committed to the "hierarchical" and "authoritarian" premise that a "top-down ordering of society will produce a more moral society" . . . In Barr's view, piety lay at the heart of the founders' model of self-government, which depended on religious values to restrain human passions. "The founding generation were Christians," Barr said. Goodness flows from "a transcendent Supreme Being" through "individual morality" to form "the social order." Reason and experience merely serve to confirm the infallible divine law. That law, he said, is under threat from "militant secularists," including "so-called progressives," who call on the state "to mitigate the social costs of personal misconduct and irresponsibility." At their feet, Barr places mental illness, drug overdoses, violence and suicide. All these things, he said, are getting worse. All are "the bitter results of the new secular age."[1]

Barr may indeed have a law degree, but he needs to brush up on his history. His view is as fallacious as it is ignominious. The picture he paints of the founding of our country is entirely off the mark—a concocted fantasy. Yes, many of the colonists possessed faith and some practiced according to specific denominations, but Founders subscribing to both the Moderate and Radical Enlightenment schools of thought would take great issue with Barr's interpretation of their philosophy. The Radicals would view religion as unconditionally outside the purview of the governing process. Whether mainstream Christian, "deists," or atheists, they would have fiercely repudiated Barr's view. Even the Moderates eschewed an authoritarian or dogmatic religious influence in the political arena. As Israel writes:

> Americans often remained (and remain) unaware that their Founding Fathers were predominantly irreligious deists and atheists privately repudiating religion. Freeing the individual as far as possible from clerical tutelage and widening toleration, as well as disestablishing churches, and separating church and state, represented an indispensable goal for the American Revolution's leading figures since most were Unitarians, deists, or nonbelievers . . . Jefferson's explicit goal with respect to religious authority and church government was to secure freedom *from* religion, as much as freedom of religion.[2]

In addition to being factually incorrect, the premise that Barr expresses reflects Counter-Enlightenment impulses directed in a way our Founders most feared, namely, justifying governmental authority based on one particular religious doctrine. The commonalities between Barr's view and the revisionist interpretation of our nation's founding diffused during the Second Great Awakening could not be more pointed. Underpinning the philosophy of both is that the license to govern is miraculously ordained by God. The influential Awakening movement apocryphally wrapped the events of the American Revolution in a cloak of piety. This revisionist story line is particularly ironic, given the documented intent of most of the Founders; whether Moderate or Radical, the Founders clearly wanted to *free the governing framework from religion*, not *justify it because of religion*.[3] That Barr's faith is a core part of his identity, intrinsic to his being, is not at all at issue. However, what Barr advocates is precisely what our Founders warned us against.

TWO IRRECONCILABLE VISIONS OF GOVERNMENT

Barr's particular revisionist view of American history, one grounded in divinely inspired beliefs, is not uncommon. Counter-Enlightenment forces have been present throughout our history and often increase in prominence during particular periods of religious fervor in the United States.[4] The growth of the size and influence of the White Christian evangelical mainstream in America over the last fifty years has given considerable validation to this Counter-Enlightenment view of our history. Yet in addition to offering a rival (and false) narrative of the nation's founding, Counter-Enlightenment thought often reveals an interpretation of the origins and theory of government that itself is diametrically opposed to that of the Enlightenment.

The Enlightenment point of view can be expressed as follows:

> Government derives its authority as a form of Social Contract created by, subscribed to, and for the benefit of the people. By agreeing to form a self-governing society, citizens abide by a system of law and order supported by a framework comprising a balance of powers in order to maximize the well-being of all, the common good.

Radical Enlightenment thinkers might add:

> The optimal governing structure is a democracy representative of, and with participation from, all citizens. This necessarily relies on an educated public capable of conducting informed debate and choosing leaders to represent their common interests.

We can think of this framework as bottom-up.

The Counter-Enlightenment point of view could be expressed this way:

> Government is divinely ordained by God and pursued through a sacred endeavor to create a system of law and order that is consistent with religious doctrine and which facilitates the spiritual observance (and therefore well-being) of the masses.

We can think of this framework as top-down.

As discussed in the first section of this book, both Enlightenment schools and the founding documents of the United States precisely infer the bottom-up approach. The Moderate Enlightenment's espousal of religion as a legitimate governing element does not conflict with or obscure the fact that the Moderates wholeheartedly endorsed the concept of citizens *voluntarily* entering into a social contract to secure their rights (not because they were so ordained by a divinity). Consider the following text from the Declaration of Independence (italics are added):

> We hold these truths to be self-evident, that all men are created equal, that they are endowed by their Creator with certain unalienable Rights, that among these are Life, Liberty and the pursuit of

Happiness. *That to secure these rights, Governments are instituted among Men, deriving their just powers from the consent of the governed.* That whenever any Form of Government becomes destructive to these ends, it is the Right of the People to alter or to abolish it, and to institute new Government, laying its foundation on such principles and organizing its powers in such form, as to them shall seem most likely to effect their Safety and Happiness.[5]

An important demarcation bridges the first two sentences. God is referenced as being responsible for creation of humanity and for our endowments, and people are created by God with certain unalienable rights. However, the act of forming a government is expressly *initiated by people* to secure and protect these rights. As the social contract theorists frequently describe, humanity can remain in its state of nature or it can make a choice to self-govern cooperatively with others. But self-government can only be achieved with the consent of the governed. That government derives its power and authority through the consent of the people is by definition a bottom-up concept.

Even as the pendulum had shifted to a more Moderate Enlightenment philosophy by the time of the framing of the Constitution, the Framers reaffirmed the bottom-up social contract nature of our founding charter with the opening words: "We the people of the United States." Furthermore, as the Founders absorbed and applied the diverse Enlightenment theories regarding the balance of powers, the idea of representation of the people expanded from being a check on government to being the government itself. As Bailyn describes this important nuance:

In effect the people were present through their representatives, and were themselves, step-by-step and point by point, acting in the conduct of public affairs. No longer merely an ultimate check on government, they *were* in some sense that government. Government had no separate existence apart from them; it was by the people as well as for the people; it gained its authority from their continuous consent.[6]

This is further supported by the understanding that when government fails to meet its needs, the people have the right to alter or abolish it or institute a new government. If governments were divinely created, how could they ever be cast aside for an alternative? The capacity of self-organization among humans is perhaps divinely endowed, but its *actualization* requires human desire and abilities and entails demanding and often grueling endeavor. This is what we mean by a bottom-up approach to self-government.

In first articulating this approach to government, the great social contract philosophers explicitly rejected the "divine right" thesis, thereby profoundly challenging and reimagining the society of their era.[7] From our perspective today, it is perhaps hard to imagine how groundbreaking this departure was. The political doctrine of the divine right of kings had shaped European history for centuries as a justification for monarchical absolute power. According to this theory, the monarch was divinely bestowed with absolute power over both church and state. The concept of monarchy as divined by God took root during the Middle Ages and became firmly established. It was however challenged at various points in time by more progressive members of the nobility or aristocracy who wanted to curtail the power of the monarch. But critical debate over the concept of government for the benefit of the common good did not begin (for the first time since the Greek and Roman classical era) *until the Enlightenment.*

Ever since the Magna Carta in the 13th century, limits to absolute monarchy were considered and at times effectively imposed, but it would take many more centuries before Enlightenment philosophers would create the social contract framework in which humans willfully enter a society, relinquishing certain rights in exchange for the guarantee of other rights (as discussed in Part I). At this juncture in history, the idea of government *for*, if not always *by*, the people came into prominence. The social contract itself implied a grant of power from the people to those who governed and was thus, by definition, an inherently bottom-up concept.

Interestingly, before the American and French Revolutions discussed throughout this book, the writings of John Locke in the early Enlightenment were quite influential in challenging the notion of top-down government during the English Glorious Revolution in 1688. That Revolution involved a bloodless coup at the invitation of Parliament and was followed the next year by the adoption of the English Bill of Rights. This landmark bill not only secured a broad set of rights for the British people (similar to our Bill of Rights), but also constrained certain powers of the monarch and stipulated constitutional requirements for the Crown to seek the consent of the people on specific issues, as represented by Parliament. This sequence of events, a harbinger both of future revolutions and the modern republic, provides a vivid illustration of the will of the people to establish a bottom-up form of government to replace a top-down one, once again influenced by Locke and the other British Enlightenment thinkers.

MODERATE, RADICAL, AND COUNTER-ENLIGHTENMENT TODAY

Given this essential discrepancy between a top-down and a bottom-up approach to the political authority of governance, how exactly can we classify our contemporary political landscape in terms of the framework described throughout this book? Can we map the patterns associated with the frameworks discussed within these pages onto our current political environment? The concepts and categories we use to make sense of the past are complicated and evolve over time. But an exploration of these historical forces provides valuable insights into the current political and cultural state of our nation.

Today's *Counter-Enlightenment* impulse can readily be observed in the many Americans who subordinate the role of government to the doctrine of their church. As discussed, over the last fifty years this has become quite prominent within the Christian evangelical movement in America. This Counter-Enlightenment thinking is precisely reflected in Trumpian populism and its reliance on top-down rule complemented by a near-total subordination of reason to passion. In fact, top-down authority in the form of concentrated power unconstrained by the traditional checks and balances was perhaps the most salient characteristic of Trump's presidency and of the powerful autocrats he most esteemed and attempted to emulate. Even with Trump no longer in the White House, since Trump's coup of the Party, Republicans have (with some notable exceptions) fully assimilated this Counter-Enlightenment impulse in their political philosophy.

The implicit rejection of Enlightenment ideals in the Trumpian ideological approach represents a *profound* shift toward Counter-Enlightenment thinking in 21st-century America. Like many Counter-Enlightenment movements historically, Trumpism eschews reason and objective truth and instead indulges raw emotions and fervent passions. As one revealing indication, the *New England Journal of Medicine*, arguably the world's most prestigious medical journal, for the first time in its 200-year history of remaining nonpartisan repudiated Trump for his denial of scientific truth in responding to the coronavirus pandemic.[8] Trump's denial of global warming provides another example, as does his entire approach to the COVID-19 pandemic, such as ignoring the advice of scientists and advocating his own scientifically unproven treatments.

As discussed in the previous chapter, Trump's particular approach to authoritarian top-down rule was facilitated through the standard fare on the demagogue's menu: a cult of personality trumping established governmental institutions and norms, and facilitating powerful affective bonds with his followers; vicious attacks on political opponents, the media, and anyone considered outside of his in-group; and divisive scapegoating instead of collective deliberation, shared responsibility, and mutual respect.

Furthermore, Trump, perhaps more than any other president in our history, expressly used the office of the presidency for the enrichment of himself and his entourage at the expense of the interests of the people. Of course these latter characteristics of Trumpism are more explicitly tyrannical and authoritarian than Counter-Enlightenment. But as central to Trumpism is an assault on objective truth itself and its subordination to passion that so lucidly reflects Trump's Counter-Enlightenment impulse.

Moreover, the imposition of this top-down governing authority is abetted by the direct or tacit approval of the church through its influential leadership, best represented by the White Christian evangelical mainstream in America today. As described earlier, Counter-Enlightenment forces can superimpose themselves on the American landscape with both positive and negative effects. However, the tenor of Counter-Enlightenment thought in today's Trumpian populism is characterized not by promoting humane spirituality or tolerance through Christian acts, but on the contrary by subordinating science, objective truth, and fact-based reasoning to fears and passions. These emotions are then opportunistically roused in order to reinforce church dogma, sow division among the populace, and reestablish an inegalitarian and oppressive political hierarchy.

Prior to Trump's Republican Party coup, the philosophical influence of the *Moderate Enlightenment* was most accurately observed in the centrist politics of the status quo, be it center-left liberals or center-right conservatives, at times referred to as the "political establishment." However, even within this broad political spectrum, the most prevalent manifestation of Moderate Enlightenment philosophy is found in the Republican Party establishment's contradictory rhetorical commitment to *the theory of* bottom-up democratic government and its *top-down practice of* "aristocratic" rule by the elite.

In prior eras, the Republican Party camouflaged its disdain for broad democratic participation. Today, its voter suppression tactics are practiced in the open, brazenly and without shame. The result is that the Republican Party is not only sanctioning but actively participating in the corrosion of democracy in order to further inequalities of wealth and imbalanced political access. For example, while both major party establishments have commonly resorted to gerrymandering as a tool to maintain political control when redistricting, the conservative Republicans have been far more audacious in their efforts to gerrymander districts. Further, Republicans have adopted a complete gamut of maneuvers to undermine the democratic process itself through routine voter suppression by deploying such tactics as stringent voter ID laws, the purging of voter rolls, and more recently, limiting methods of casting ballots (as seen once again in Georgia's new 2021 voter law).

In contrast, the Democratic establishment has largely sanctified the centrality of universal suffrage and fair and open elections as a fundamental requisite of our democracy. Furthermore, while the Democratic establishment has been hesitant to make bold structural changes in the policies it advocates, some of its most prominent leaders have been willing to occasionally compromise with the advocates of a more Radical Enlightenment ideology.

Finally, a more *Radical Enlightenment* philosophy is readily apparent among those who recognize that our bottom-up democracy is deeply broken and advocate a comprehensive program to fix it. Despite the formidable difficulties inherent in a democratic form of government, this third group encourages a renewed commitment to "small d" democracy and does not shy away from embracing the bold structural reforms required to attain it.

* * *

In the age of Trump, some members of the Republican Party have been emboldened to articulate a view that has long been in vogue on the American right but which Republican politicians were generally hesitant to openly express. The premise is that the values of equality and democracy are somehow subordinate to liberty. In early October 2020, Utah Senator Mike Lee tweeted the following: "Democracy isn't the objective; liberty, peace, and prospefity [sic] are. We want the human condition to flourish. Rank democracy can thwart that." Senator Lee, along with many of his colleagues in Trump's Republican Party, are at least candid about their desire to restrict the voting franchise to those whom they deem as the most worthy citizens. Recall that this view was quite prominent among the Moderate Enlightenment Founders discussed in the first part of this book.

My knee-jerk reaction when I first saw this tweet was a vindictive desire to "out" Senator Lee for revealing what I and many others had already come to believe are the genuine but often concealed and tacit beliefs of the conservative wing of the Republican Party. However, after some reflection, I now sincerely applaud the senator. While I do not agree with his position, his forthrightness enables a more authentic debate about democratic principles. By owning up to his Moderate Enlightenment views, Senator Lee has demonstrated that a discussion based on ideas is once again feasible, and I would welcome such a discussion with him.

However painful and divisive our current political environment, we must return to these types of debates *about ideas* in order to move forward. If the "American experiment" is to survive, those who subscribe to the Radical Enlightenment philosophy behind the American vision must not resort to indignation but instead advance reasoned explanations of why Counter-Enlightenment attacks on democracy are inconsistent with our founding principles. In addition, we must illuminate how advocates of solutions consistent with Moderate Enlightenment philosophy, despite their frequent rhetoric of inclusion and democracy, are contradicting the established evolution of our Constitution toward inclusion. They are negating this persistent march through the Constitution's amendment process toward broader participation and causing our democracy to degenerate. Simply put, we must make a convincing and rational case that achieving material realization of Radical Enlightenment values can only be accomplished through major reforms.

THE IMPERATIVE TO REVITALIZE OUR DEMOCRACY

Even if we endorse the concept of a bottom-up form of government, a plethora of looming questions remains regarding how to adopt or achieve such a government. Today, we frequently hear comments about our democratic form of government being "broken." Myriad political scientists, historians, and others have described how and why democratic government is difficult to establish and uphold, relative to other forms of government. However, if we firmly believe in the ideal of democracy, a bottom-up government of, by, and for the people, we have no choice but to remedy ours to the best of our abilities.

Danielle Allen, a professor at Harvard University and director of its Edmond J. Safra Center for Ethics, is a big champion of the need to repair our democracy and has outlined a concrete program on just how to do so (we will return to discuss elements of this plan in more detail in the last chapter).[9] For Allen the notion of political equality—the idea that every American should play an active role in the workings of our democracy—is fundamental. Allen insists that for democracy, a government of the people, to work, the populace *must fully embrace and even cherish* democracy. This love of democracy must be strong enough to overcome the pain and conflict that its practice entails.

In Allen's words, "One must sign up for the whole package, recognizing that you will have to share decision-making, you won't win all the time, and you will have to sacrifice but you have to stay in the game."[10] Furthermore, Allen advocates that unless we make fixing our democracy the top priority, of higher importance than any other substantive goal, specific policy "wins" will not be durable or sustainable and thus will be ultimately fruitless.

A recent political anecdote helps illustrate the predicament of our withering commitment to democracy even among our highest ranking leaders. In the aftermath of the Trump presidential victory in early 2017, Mitch McConnell gave a speech in which he claimed: "Winners make policy, losers go home." According to Allen's theory, this is exactly the flipside of what a democracy is supposed to be. The Trump/McConnell philosophy of dividing and excluding the losers from the conversation is antithetical to democracy's most fundamental ethic: *Everyone belongs in the conversation.*[11] In any particular argument or policy vote, even the losing side needs to be welcomed back into the conversation. Allen argues that "winning" in the context of a democracy simply identifies who gets the authority to lead the conversation, to chair the committee responsible for crafting the policy. But the conversation must still include both the winners *and* the losers. Furthermore, it is the responsibility of the winners to bring the losers back into the conversation.

In declaring victory in the modern era, every newly elected president of the United States (with the exception of Trump) routinely embraces the other side, those who voted for the losing candidate, and further, makes an explicit effort to pull those nonsupporters back into the conversation, back into the tent, as president of *all the people.* As Doris Kearns Goodwin illustrates so vividly in *Team of Rivals*, Lincoln, perhaps the epitome of this quality of democracy, pulled all his losing presidential competitors into his cabinet, knowing this was the best practice for instituting a scrupulous and thorough problem-solving process. For Allen, belonging in the conversation also means listening to and understanding dissimilar and often divergent perspectives before judging and dismissing them. She states that people need to "bring their authentic selves" into the conversation and to do so they need charitable space with basic rights protection.[12]

One of the benefits of this approach to democracy is that it has the potential to lead to *robust and durable* change. When a decision by an autocrat is handed down to the people, the autocrat's tool for change is not changing minds, but heavy-handed enforcement. Many countries, including China, Russia, and Turkey, to name a few, are run precisely in this way. But the democratic process of explicitly incorporating disparate views into the development of solutions has greater potential to shift underlying beliefs and opinions, provided it allows honest and nuanced debate in the public square (as opposed to in social media). Furthermore, once such debate does shift underlying beliefs and opinions, any resulting justice gains tend to be more resilient.

A great example of this phenomenon was illustrated in the recent debate in the United States on the question of same-sex marriage. The many forums of genuine debate on this topic, from the early discussions around the Defense of Marriage Act through the many state ballot proposals banning same-sex marriage, afforded the populace a period of sustained and deep exploration of the topic. The LGBT community stayed in the conversation while enduring many losses. Arguably, the 2015 Supreme Court decision was not so much a "verdict handed on down from up high" but merely a recognition of a significant shift in thinking that had already occurred within the broader population.

RESTORING FAITH IN OBJECTIVE TRUTH

Epistemology is a fancy and sophisticated term that philosophers and other academics use for the study of knowledge; it is the analysis of how humans acquire knowledge through perception, reason, memory, etc., and how they develop and justify their beliefs. Based on the characteristics of democracy that Allen so eloquently describes, in spite of all its difficulties and many drawbacks, democracy is *epistemologically superior* to other forms of government. Democracy is a rigorous process of bringing diverse data sources into the epistemological process. With a more diverse set of underlying data and different perspectives a wider solution space is created within which more competing ideas can be identified and evaluated.

But as a corollary, democracy is extremely vulnerable, fully contingent on the legitimacy of its underlying epistemological process. The more that objective truth is elusive, the greater the threat to democracy. While traditional forms of political persuasion are as old as time, modern-day honed techniques of sophisticated marketing such as targeting capabilities and data analytics render misrepresentation and falsification of facts and data relatively trouble-free. In other words, public opinion today can be more easily swayed by anyone who wishes to distort or bend the truth.

Ubiquitous access to state-of-the-art analytical tools and social media digital platforms serve to evade the objective sieve of credible and independent news authorities as well as corroborating experts. As a consequence, filtering truth from falsehoods becomes nearly impossible. While demagogues have never lacked the willingness to shape popular opinion for personal gain and questionable or even nefarious purposes, today they undeniably have access to more refined instruments for doing so.[13] Given the formidable challenges that the political mechanisms of democracy face, as Professor Allen advocates, we need to be all in, committed as a nation to making it work by overcoming these impediments.

Based on the data alone, it is undeniable that democracy is in crisis today. Public approval rates for Congress and our other governmental institutions are at all-time lows. Most alarming is the large degree of indifference expressed by younger generations of Americans regarding the importance of the concept of democracy itself. In the United States, merely thirty percent of millennials consider it essential to live in a democracy, and the majority have lost faith in democracy as a form of governance.[14]

The reasons for this are complex and multifaceted. Some millennials have categorically given up on the political establishment; for them, government has demonstrated an unwillingness to address injustices and an inability to tackle looming problems such as global warming. Others might take democracy for granted or are unconvinced of the severity of the threats it faces. There are interesting hints in voting patterns among college students. College graduates with majors in the hard sciences are less likely to vote than those who study humanities.[15] In many ways this makes intuitive sense: People attracted to engineering, mathematics, and other such fields are conditioned to find the right answer, to maximize or optimize their identified objective function. Perhaps for such mindsets, politics, and the realm of public policy, with its erratic and unreliable value sets, are too messy and unpredictable and therefore excessively frustrating. But for democracy to work, it must be deemed essential and demanded by the populace. Viewed in this light, the urgency of Allen's case of making democracy the number one priority is not only convincing, but quite compelling.

Finally, the greatest threat to democracy today may be a more common acquiescence among citizens to the apparent disappearance of objective truth itself. As described previously, 21st-century digital tools and communication platforms present a miasma in which sifting and assessing information to distill truth is quite difficult and requires ample time and dogged persistence. It appears that many Americans are giving up the undertaking.

As we discussed at the beginning of this book, one of the most fundamental ideals from the Enlightenment is that objective truth is attainable through the innately human tools of empirical observation and rational thinking. Our greatest thinkers over the course of the last centuries built our modern technologically advanced world based on this principle. Despite the perspective of postmodern academics who argue that objective truth does not exist, the formation of effective public policy requires data analysis and meticulous compilation and study of factual truth. *A democracy cannot function without objective truth.* (Consequently, while beyond the scope of this book, it would be interesting to understand what type of government postmodern academics would advocate.) While objective truth is arguably more elusive within the social sciences, established facts and data within the hard sciences must be held to this standard. So how exactly do we determine what is objective truth and accepted knowledge and what is not?

Jonathan Rauch, a fellow at the Brookings Institute, has written eloquently about our contemporary epistemological crisis. He describes our commonly agreed upon base of objective truth as a "constitution of knowledge" having a set of checks and balances like peer review and a form of separation of powers via field of study specialization. The governing body of this constitution consists of an ecosystem of credible academics in recognized professional associations, clergy members, teachers, journalists, and others who *disagree* about many substantive issues, but *agree* on a shared system of rules for weighing evidence and building knowledge. In other words, they have an agreed-upon system to manage their disagreements. This system operates like a funnel allowing consideration of a large volume of ideas from which only a narrow group of ideas survives collective scrutiny.[16] In Rauch's words:

> We let alt-truth talk but we don't let it write textbooks, receive tenure, bypass peer review, set the research agenda, dominate the front pages, give expert testimony or dictate the flow of public dollars. A

hypothesis can join reality only insofar as it persuades people after withstanding vigorous questioning and criticism . . . Only those propositions that are broadly agreed to have withstood testing over time qualify as knowledge, and even they stand only unless and until debunked.[17]

Rauch goes on to describe how this "crowd sourcing" decentralized model of knowledge acquisition has achieved spectacular results.

First, by organizing millions of minds to tackle billions of problems, the epistemic constitution disseminates knowledge at a staggering rate. Every day . . . it adds more to the canon of knowledge than was accumulated in the 200,000 years of human history prior to Galileo's time. Second, by insisting on validating truths through a decentralized, non-coercive process that forces us to convince each other with evidence and argument . . . the marketplace of ideas would be more accurately described as a marketplace of *persuasion* . . . Third, by placing reality under the control of no one in particular, it dethrones intellectual authoritarianism and commits liberal society foundationally to intellectual pluralism and freedom of thought.[18]

The core problem with today's social media platforms is that they are based on a business model that encourages disinformation—a clickbait economy where anyone can make money by "putting stuff out there" as long as it gets clicks and shares. Within this business model, the incentives are not grounded in criteria based on the ascertainment of truth. *What makes money is not what is true, but what gets attention.* "Tribal outrage works as a business model for social media, cable television and talk radio."[19] At the same time, this business model is terribly weakening our democracy.

In the political arena, citizens can never be wholly informed on all the issues; it would be impossible for each of us to individually discover or ascertain the objective truth on all controversial or thorny issues. Instead, citizens of democracies use shortcuts, such as supporting political parties whose values they share and electing politicians they deem to have good judgment and a commitment to seek the facts even when difficult and to consult specific experts when needed. Our democracy is based on us choosing representative leaders who are committed to these principles. Nevertheless, facts and truth represent the very oxygen that allows a democracy to survive.

Incredibly, in our country, the use of contemporary media to spread disinformation and conspiracy theories is not solely the purview of unruly or disruptive citizens. It became the primary propaganda tool of the former president himself, through which he and his Republican Party became detached from reality. "America has faced many challenges to its political culture, but this is the first time we have seen a national-level *epistemic* attack: a systematic attack, emanating from the very highest reaches of power, on our collective ability to distinguish truth from falsehood."[20] Furthermore, in the years leading up to 2020, our governing regime not only abandoned reality, but its leaders also encouraged a disdain for expertise, and for truth itself.

In the last century alone, numerous examples illustrate the tragic consequences of authoritarian leaders inventing and disseminating their own truth through propaganda to ordain top-down and usually tyrannical and oppressive regimes. When the president of the world's oldest surviving democracy is the one leading a vicious assault on truth, the one tearing down our public and private institutions (such as the free press) that are most devoted to the pursuit of truth, the one most committed to robbing democracy of its very oxygen, we are left with only our tribal identities and their associated fears and passions.

Denying objective truth may be the most explicit example of Trump's Counter-Enlightenment orientation. Without objective truth, democracy is unachievable. In this sense, it is perhaps no wonder that so many young people are giving up on the concept of democracy.

Trump made that much easier. Hopefully, the new Biden administration will elevate the pursuit of truth to the high priority it has assumed in recent centuries and should merit in this one.

*   *   *

The case for democracy has been made in many different ways throughout our history. The legendary Supreme Court Justice Hugo Black made a constitutional case for it in a 1964 opinion:

> No right is more precious in a free country than that of having a voice in the election of those who make the laws under which, as good citizens, we must live. Other rights, even the most basic, are illusory if the right to vote is undermined. Our Constitution leaves no room for classification of people in a way that unnecessarily abridges this right.[21]

More recently, the writer Marilynne Robinson made a moral and spiritual case in *The New York Times* (October 9, 2020) for the values that underlie democracy:

> Human beings are sacred, therefore equal . . . The ethic in these words should be the standard by which we judge ourselves, our social arrangements, our dealings with the vast family of humankind. It will always find us wanting. The idea is a progressive force, constantly and necessarily exposing our failures and showing us new paths forward . . . There is much to be done, more than inevitably limited people can see at a given moment. But the other side of our limitation is the fact that it carries with it a promise that we still might see a new birth of freedom, and another one beyond that. Democracy is the great instrument of human advancement. We have no right to fail it.[22]

The Radical Enlightenment case for democracy is a synthesis of Black's and Robinson's views, drawing on both constitutional and moral imperatives. It urges us to revitalize our democracy because it is the highest form of government, despite how difficult it may be to achieve. In addition to being epistemologically superior, democracy's insistence on fundamental equality is consistent with most major spiritual movements and faiths. The alternatives to democracy are invariably unjust, often totalitarian, and usually repressive of the human spirit. A democracy in which all are equal in voice and respect, and equal before the law, is the only form of government that is truly supportive and expansive of human potential.

Chapter 15

WE THE PEOPLE—WHO IS US?

As discussed in the previous chapter, one of the hallmarks of an effective democracy is that it brings many points of view into the problem-solving debate and accordingly leads to a richer and more innovative solution set. Nonetheless, at the heart of the many persistent conflicts over 250 years of our nation's history is a remarkably simple question: Who gets to be included in the debate? *Who is "us"?* Much of the unrest and divisiveness across American history (inclusive of many of the episodes reviewed throughout the course of this book) has turned on the widely conflicting answers given to this question.

As Ta-Nehisi Coates writes in his award-winning book, *Between the World and Me* (2015): "The question is not whether Lincoln truly meant 'government of the people' but what our country has, throughout its history, taken the political term 'people' to actually mean . . . America's problem is not its betrayal of 'government of the people,' but the means by which 'the people' acquired their names."[1] In many eras of our history, the problems we have faced as a nation have been formidable, sometimes daunting. Moreover, some of our most brilliant minds, political leaders and citizens alike, have been baffled in their attempts to craft effective and practical solutions that were often deficient and at times utterly misguided. But at the core of many of these heated issues lies some form or variant of this basic question. Although rarely posed directly or in a straightforward manner, the spirit of the question underlies many of our most vehement political disagreements.

A PERSISTENTLY OPEN QUESTION

As discussed in Part I, the Founders realized that the Articles of Confederation were grossly inadequate for effectively and pragmatically implementing the ideals laid out in the Declaration of Independence. This original attempt at an American governance structure lacked any enforcement power for the federal government, rendering its ability to conduct most affairs (e.g., printing money, regulating commerce, conducting foreign policy) quite restricted. Consequently, the Framers gathered at the Constitutional Convention in the summer of 1787, by which time the pendulum had oscillated to the Moderate Enlightenment side, to develop a more effective alternative, one that kept true to the ideals in the Declaration but created a more workable framework for governance. One of the Framers' key goals was to imbue this new structure with a balance of power to inhibit abuse or tyrannical influence by any one individual element.

In a geographically diverse nation, the Framers recognized that a balance of power was required both among the different branches of government at the federal level and between the central government and the states. But a basic premise left unclear is the definition of the reference in the first words penned by our Framers:

We the People of the United States, in Order to form a more perfect Union . . .

However prosaic it may seem, the basic question this document has forever left ambiguous in its wake is: To whom does "we the people" refer? Whom did it include at the nation's founding in 1776? To whom did it refer in 1787? Did the Framers of the Constitution agree with the signers of the Declaration? How has the definition of "we the people" evolved over the history of our republic? Furthermore, is the social definition of "we the people" distinct from the political definition, and has this changed over time?

This fundamental question was undoubtedly a point of disagreement among the Founders. Franklin's and Paine's egalitarian vision was much more inclusive than that of the Moderates like Adams and Hamilton. Regardless of their philosophical differences, when the Framers codified the Constitution, they concurred that for the purposes of representation, enslaved people were considered "three-fifths" of a person and evidently excluded from "we the people." Moreover, since Indigenous people in America were recognized as sovereign within their own territories, these Native American sovereign territories also fell outside of "we the people" as defined in the Constitution.[2]

With the exception of White males with property, Americans of every race, creed, class, and gender owe a tremendous debt to their predecessors who persevered over the last two hundred plus years, often through grueling torments, to gain inclusion in the collective "we the people." We have reviewed select examples throughout this book. But even more inconsolably tragic, as we have repeatedly seen in these episodes across our history, is that a *de jure* seat at the table rarely translated to *de facto* inclusion without persistent and ongoing struggle that continues today.

How and on what basis the definition of "we the people" could and should be expanded is, in many respects, the underlying theme of our country's conflict-ridden history. In the nation's first decades, the answer to this question disqualified many based on race, gender, and social class. But even within the privileged group that originally comprised "we the people," landholding was an additional criterion for inclusion that was commonly stipulated at the state level. Over the next century, struggles over including people of various races, countries of origin, and genders would emerge and, at times, explode. In the 21st century, other dimensions of "we the people" would emerge as different groups fought for full access to equality for those who did not fit traditional norms of gender and sexuality. In many ways, the historical progress toward universal suffrage provides a moving image of how our answer to this question has evolved over time.

THE EXAMPLE OF IMMIGRATION

Throughout our history, one of the clearest manifestations of the tension inherent in the question of defining and expanding "who is us?" is seen in deliberations over legal immigration. Immigration policy requires delineating paths to citizenship and thus brings this question into sharp focus. The centrality of this issue—this need to define citizenship and the path to citizenship—has made the immigration policy debate incredibly divisive over the course of our history, and, since we are a nation of immigrants, at the same time quite distressing for many.

The question boils down to this: How does an individual or a group of individuals join the club and become one of "us"? Do we have an agreed-upon process for expanding who we bring under the tent? Immigration policy has always been a burning issue because it has never definitively settled the answers to these questions. The rules have varied enormously over the eras, as has the degree of enforcement of those rules.

As embodied by the iconic symbol of the Statue of Liberty and its inscription of lines from Emma Lazarus's sonnet "The New Colossus," "Give me your tired, your poor, your huddled masses yearning to be free," a central element of our founding myth is that America is a nation of immigrants. But there is a potent tension at the root of this myth. As Masha Gessen describes, this aspirational narrative of a vision of America as a nation of immigrants conflicts with the natural human tendency to resist relinquishing self-privilege. Through much of our history, immigration policy has reflected

> the dueling demands of our moral ambition and fear of the other. On the one hand, the country proclaimed itself a nation of immigrants ... On the other hand, the country enforced racist immigration policies, created quotas, and harshly punished those who sought to make their home on its shores without submitting to onerous and arbitrary procedures.[3]

Immigration has indeed been a contentious fault line throughout much of our country's history. It has been explored from many angles and is often linked to wider social and economic anxieties, like blue-collar workers fearing displacement, white-collar workers fearing competition, concerns regarding labor devaluation and labor relations, and worries about crime, terrorism, and foreign cultural and political influence. As a consequence, U.S. immigration policy has followed its own pendulum-like trajectory.

Until LBJ's immigration bill in 1968, immigration had virtually ceased since the 1920s. However, at times in our history when immigration proved advantageous for economic advancement and expansion, a broader consensus of support for increasing immigration and relaxing quotas emerged. For example, during the Progressive Era, a steady influx of unskilled workers arriving from southern and eastern Europe filled a needed gap for labor in steel mills, the fishing industry, and other rapidly growing industries. At that time, explosive growth of industry required a larger pool of labor that could not be supplied domestically, and accordingly corporate America opposed immigration restrictions. However, nativist fears, predominantly with respect to non–Western European immigrants, always existed and, by the 1920s, the pendulum swung toward a much more restricted immigration policy that persisted through the end of World War II.

In periods when immigration is perceived as a zero-sum issue, the debate often becomes acrimonious. Anti-immigrant sentiment has manifested differently at various times in our nation's history. In the early 20th century, people of Protestant faiths (who mostly lived in rural areas) distrusted people of the Catholic and Jewish faiths (who mostly settled in urban areas and came from southern and eastern Europe). In a parallel fashion, restrictions on immigration from Asia started in the late 19th century and have been intermittently tightened and loosened over the subsequent decades.

In recent years, fears of immigration have been rekindled among large portions of the American populace, especially as the amount and visibility of *illegal* immigration has ebbed and flowed. During periods when nativist sentiment increases, so does support for restrictions on immigration. As a consequence, in the minds of many, sentiments regarding the problem of *illegal* immigration get conjoined or conflated with those concerning *legal* immigration. This is understandable since debates regarding status or a path to citizenship for people who have arrived in the country illegally is a related and easily confounded issue.

Unquestionably, Trump raised the stakes in the immigration debate from the start of his campaign. As president, Trump revised the mission of the U.S. Citizenship and Immigration Services agency, dropping the phrase "nation of immigrants." Moreover, he floated the idea of revoking birthright citizenship. Trump consistently advocated for a "radical narrowing of the definition of 'us,' . . . of closing the community of 'us' to those not already included in it . . . Trump's policies have created a moat around the shrunken circle of 'us.'"[4]

By recasting the debate in incendiary terms, Trump effectively made pragmatic solutions more unlikely; provocative symbols evoking fear and anger replaced rational approaches to problem-solving. Unfortunately, and even paradoxically, Trump's deployment of extreme rhetoric in today's immigration debate recast what should be a coherent discussion of complex issues into a polemic in which the two fervently opposing sides were, for all intents and purposes, utterly irreconcilable. We are living through a strange phenomenon as it relates to this issue (along with many others), in which each camp in the debate advances its argument by creating a disparaging caricature of the opposing point of view. This is a self-perpetuating cycle that Trump frequently provoked; each side, more and more outraged by the rival point of view, gets pushed to an extreme position in its own defense, as if screaming at each other about walls and open borders is going to engender solutions to authentic problems that meaningfully impede the lives of millions. A dose of logical perspective can help us to see the absurdity at play here.

It is hard to disagree with the statement that we need a fair process that society at large sanctions to regulate immigration. Most would agree that if we have no framework nor process of regulation, mass immigration would generate destabilizing conditions for any country. Where would the line between mass immigration and incursion or invasion be drawn? Empirically, excessive immigration has usually been disruptive and, at times, chaos-producing. The extensive (perhaps even massive) immigration to Europe in recent years is wreaking havoc on many of the liberal democracies in the EU and was clearly a prominent factor leading to Brexit. The notion that the UK should be able to decide for itself how to regulate immigration (instead of having it dictated by the EU) received a plurality of votes.

But the opposing extreme of closing borders is an equally untenable position. The benefits of legal immigration for a liberal society in terms of economic growth are well documented. Greater diversity of perspective is one of the catalytic forces of innovation. The United States itself provides an illustrative example through our history of great contributions made by immigrants in all areas of society. While anecdotal, the number of immigrants among prominent Americans is astounding. And while there will always be disagreements regarding the degree to which cultural diversity is enriching or desirable, the argument in support of immigration on humanitarian grounds alone is quite compelling. Further, if there is no legal process for immigration, it will happen illegally, to the detriment of the entire society.

But despite the merit of and need for rational arguments informing a sensible approach to immigration, we as a people have chosen to let fear-inducing simplistic slogans dominate the conversation. Trump's symbolic chant of "build the wall" transcended any meaningful policy debate and assumed a life of its own as an unstoppable force within the ranks of his supporters. This is yet another example of how unreason has crowded out reason in our public debate. As a result of Trump's rousing rhetoric, those who opposed his policies were portrayed as "demanding open borders," which in itself confirms how Trump parodied his opponents to make them appear ridiculous.

The tragedy here, which demonstrates the degree to which our political discourse has become dysfunctional, is that there are unambiguously non-zero-sum solutions to the immigration crisis in this country. In fact, the Gang of Eight (legislators on the Hill from both sides of the aisle) had achieved meaningful progress toward a compromise solution in 2013 that would have addressed many of the pressing issues while also reestablishing a legitimate process for a fair and balanced immigration policy approach going forward. Republican and Democratic leaders were coalescing around this solution that seemed attainable just a few years ago, one that would have likely garnered majority support.

Trump's strategy of using immigration as a wedge issue to provoke nativist fears was remarkably successful at both garnering him a tremendous amount of support among his base, and at the same time, pushing opposing points of view into an indefensible absolutist corner. Moreover, the divisiveness created by this spectacle and the distance we have traveled from the previously developed solution space are immeasurable. Because Trump replaced a meaningful discussion of issues or actual policy differences with inflaming and agitating images and symbols, the disruptiveness he sowed will likely be enduring. Practical solutions in the immigration space are not only forgone today, but they will likely be lost for decades, perhaps even for a generation. As opposed to concrete solutions, the political debate will continue to spin around walls and open borders, once again exposing how potent emotion-laden symbols have crowded out logical solutions.

OTHER EXPRESSIONS OF "WHO IS US?"

The immigration issue is not the only relevant "who is us?" debate. It is important to remember that African Americans have for the most part been born in this country, with many tracing their American lineages back for centuries, and are nonetheless excluded in so many respects to this day. The pervasive White supremacy we previously discussed need not rely on immigration structures to wage its war on inclusiveness. It is disheartening that recent "birther" conspiracies have become a proxy for racism by hiding underneath the immigration mantle.[5]

In addition, the "who is us?" question can be germane to other rights and privileges afforded to most Americans but denied to some. In this vein, in recent years an interesting debate was the same-sex marriage movement discussed in the previous chapter. This episode provides a vivid illustration of the fact that the *expansion* of the definition of "who is us?" tends to acquire greater support in situations where the results of such expansion are not perceived as zero sum.

Much of the fervor around the opposition to same-sex marriage, and the related support for passing a "Defense of [traditional] Marriage Act," developed from the early perception that this issue was in fact zero sum. Because gay and lesbian people wanted to take part, the institution of marriage seemed somehow threatened in the eyes of its traditional proponents. Was same-sex marriage going to diminish the sanctity of a traditional marriage? Would it somehow weaken the institution of marriage as a whole or invalidate the bonds of matrimony avowed by millions over the course of centuries? In its earlier incantations, the debate circled around these questions.

The shift in popular sentiment seemed to occur swiftly once proponents of gay marriage were able to shift the conversation and convincingly and successfully persuade many that the case of marriage is not a zero-sum proposition. The argument was a crisp and concise example of expanding the definition of marriage. As Andrew Sullivan describes it: "We want to be part of the family of our society, we want to take responsibility for our relationships through marriage."[6] This pivot toward inclusiveness allowed the same-sex marriage debate to be recast in a non-zero-sum light. In economic terms, love and commitment are not bound by supply constraints; these are not scarce commodities. Once the zero-sum argument fell apart, the Western world seemed ready to accept the notion of expanding inclusion in terms of marriage. Not only did this expansion not diminish the concept of marriage, but on the contrary, in many ways the same-sex marriage movement itself reaffirmed the power of an existing and hallowed institution.

COMPARING THE CHALLENGES OF MULTICULTURALISM IN THE UNITED STATES AND FRANCE

Additional perspectives on the "who is us?" question can be gained by exploring how other open societies address the challenge of multiculturalism. How do other liberal democracies expand the definition of "who is us"? There is no doubt that creating a pluralistic multicultural society is difficult; the people who consider themselves "real citizens" greedily reserve self-privilege, withholding it from new arrivals who, in turn, often bind together in tight-knit communities. Within the human psyche, there is a natural predilection for forming bonds based on common characteristics; familiarity brings comfort while differences create unease. For example, groups of immigrants derive both social comfort and economic benefits by living together in communities. To a certain degree, Chinatowns, Italian communities, and other insular groups arose as enclaves to provide immigrants with a better chance of surviving in a harsh new world.[7]

A comparison between France and the United States can provide useful insights since, as we have seen, both French and American modern societies were inspired by ideals that germinated in the same intellectual movements of the late 18th century. While there are unequivocally significant differences between the American and French experiences, interestingly, both the United States and France are societies that have been often sullied by many racist elements and social tensions between those protecting the interests of native-born or established inhabitants, sometimes referred to as "nativists" (or in France, *Français de souche*), and immigrant citizens who have arrived more recently.

In France, the concept of identity has been rendered quite multifaceted by a long history of colonization. Just as American immigrants who become citizens often face a cultural divide when integrating into American cultural society, immigrants from former French colonies *who are often already French citizens* frequently encounter similar hurdles. The degree to which various communities in both France and the United States assimilate or retain their original cultural customs and mores frequently depends on how warmly or harshly they are welcomed. And in both countries, beliefs and feelings about race among nativists are ultimately the most consequential in determining whether the resulting society is more pluralistic or xenophobic.

For all of these reasons, in both the United States and France, despite many differences, the evolution of a more expansive definition of "who is us" has been marked by some parallels. While a detailed comparison of how the U.S. and France have confronted these challenges is outside the scope of this book, a few striking analogies and dissimilarities can be pointed out. Both societies have struggled to achieve the aspirations of Enlightenment egalitarianism over the course of their recent histories.

As Norimitsu Onishi explains in a *New York Times* article (July 15, 2020): "Rooted in the Enlightenment and the Revolution, France's universalism has long held that each human being enjoys fundamental rights like equality and liberty. In keeping with the belief that no group should be given preference, it remains illegal to collect data on race for the census and almost all other official purposes." Ironically, as Onishi states, "France's reluctance to discuss or even acknowledge race has served as an obstacle to integration of change."[8]

Unlike the United States, France does not explicitly use government resources to differentiate policy based on race or country of origin. Without data, the scale of the problem of discrimination on racial or ethnic grounds cannot easily be measured, making demonstrable progress difficult to gauge. Inarguably, France, like the United States, has quite imperfectly achieved its own Enlightenment ideals in terms of the secular and egalitarian aspects of French civil society.

In many aspects, French society has remained quite socially and culturally elitist. Despite almost a century of tumultuous back-and-forth undulations related to her many revolutions and restorations (1780s–1870s), France's broadly encompassing democratic norms to this day have scarcely eroded the privileges accompanying corporate and political power that still largely accrue to the traditional White French upper class.

But at the same time, even without official data or explicit policy edicts, *by enforcing and administering the existing egalitarian legal structures* for all citizens, the French state has arguably done more to correct historical racial injustices in comparison to the magnitude of America's historical mistreatment of African Americans, Indigenous people, and other disenfranchised groups. So while in both countries, *de facto* discriminatory prejudice exists, in certain respects France has more evenly enforced the *de jure* concept of equality. For example, in France, bigotry has rarely been legally codified or sanctioned by the government as it has in the United States through black codes or Jim Crow laws. Further, from a de facto perspective, racism in France has not been as brutal or systematic as the White supremacist society that was characteristic of the South for more than a century in the United States, even after abolition. Furthermore, there was never systemic slavery in mainland France, although slavery had been practiced in some French colonies in earlier centuries.

In France, since the post–Revolutionary Era, being legally blind to race or religion has not just been an empty promise: Since the early 19th century, the Napoleonic Code established a base level of secular and egalitarian principles by providing access to health care and schooling for all French citizens *of all races, religions, and origins*. Secularism (or in French, the concept of *laïcité*) has been a genuine constitutional principle since the end of the 19th century and denotes the freedom of public institutions from the influence of the Roman Catholic Church. Other structural elements of the French Republic's constitutions over the last hundred years have reinforced this egalitarianism with additional race-blind mechanisms. A 1905 law dictates that *"the Republic neither recognizes nor employs nor subsidizes cults,"* and guarantees the freedom of each cult, as long as they do not violate public order.[9]

Undeniably, France's deployment of these legal mechanisms has brought more equality of access to important services like education and health. Nevertheless, most minorities in France do have direct or indirect experience with structural racism in many spheres, notably policing and access to employment. Further, advancement prospects and mobility opportunities continue to be largely limited for non-White French citizens. Moreover, France has implicitly arrogated the cultural superiority of its traditional mores relative to the rich civilizations of its former colonies, even as it has tried to explicitly evince the opposite. As a result, consensus on the meaning of "French identity" has remained elusive.

The brutal French-Algerian conflict in Algeria's struggle for independence from France was in part a struggle over the concept of French identity as well as a demonstration of France's tenacious domination of its overseas territories and former colonies. With respect to her former colonies, France's stance reveals clear parallels to America's stance vis-à-vis African Americans and Indigenous Americans, even if the French colonial practice of slavery was nowhere near as brutal and systemically institutionalized as it had been in the United States. Here is one perspective by an academic who has extensively studied French colonial history:

> In seeming contradiction to the doctrines of assimilation and *Mission Civilisatrice* (civilizing mission) that came increasingly to guide and shape French policy in and for Algeria, France steadfastly refused to grant the Muslim populace the same political and civil rights enjoyed by its own citizens. The marginalization and abuse of the Muslim population this gave rise to was encouraged and, on many occasions, demanded by the European settler community that developed during the course of the nineteenth and twentieth centuries.[10]

In addition to its colonial history, France has struggled with this same question of French identity even in metropolitan France, albeit on a smaller scale. The infamous Dreyfus Affair at the turn of the 20th century epitomized the French struggle with the concept of French identity and anti-Semitism. Can a French Jew, even a war-honored patriot, be considered and trusted as a "Frenchman"? In addition, while deportation of French Jews under the Nazi regime was of quite small scale relative to other European countries, memories of the harsh realities of the period such as the Drancy internment camp and the *Vel' d'Hiv* round-up (*Rafle du Vélodrome d'Hiver*) linger as recent stains on the collective conscience of French society.[11]

In the last half of the 20th century, as post–World War II France began coming to terms with its colonial past, French society was characterized by seemingly contradicting tensions: French administrations since François Mitterrand have implemented generous social policies for immigrants and their children from former colonies. The generosity of these more recent economic and social policies may be inspired by a healthy collective "guilt" meant to redress past injustices.

At the same time, these programs have led to accusations from some segments of society that French political leadership coddles new arrivals on French soil. These same policies that are more generous to French immigrants raise significant resentment among working-class French, who feel alienated by what they view as preferential government policies imposed by the ruling elite. In fact, the same working-class White rage emerging from an antielite sentiment that has been starkly observed in the United States of late was quite evident in the *gilets jaunes* or "yellow vest" movement over the last few years in France. In reaction to tax and benefit reforms imposed by a perceived elitist President Emmanuel Macron, yellow vest protests, which were originally concentrated in rural areas, eventually brought the entire country to its knees. The demonstrations over many months, infiltrated by reckless anarchists, turned quite violent and resulted in smashed windows and looted private property.

Thus, as in the United States, resentment among White French citizens has fueled support for racist sentiments and populist and nativist movements. The National Front movement created by Jean-Marie Le Pen in the 1970s and 1980s used to be perceived among the French as an extremist political party. Today, the National Front is very much in the mainstream and is in fact one of the most supported political parties.[12] Whether the National Front has moderated its extreme positions, or whether the French have gravitated to the right, remains an open point of debate.

The overall lesson from both the United States' and France's struggles to create a pluralistic society is that the principle of egalitarianism proves challenging to establish in practice. Like in the United States, determining "who is us" has been an issue of continual struggle in France. In both societies, Moderate Enlightenment impulses that have tended to reserve the realm of "self"-governance to a group of "selves" who are in fact privileged elites actively contend with a more radical egalitarianism rooted in the Radical Enlightenment. The point is not whether France or the United States as a society is more or less xenophobic, or more or less egalitarian, than the other. The salient issue is what we can learn from a comparison of how each country has struggled with these issues over its history. Are there parallels in each country's struggle that can provide opportunities for reflection and learning? Can we draw ideas or inspiration from successes and draw sobering and constructive lessons from failures?

It is not coincidental that modern France and the United States were both born out of tenets stemming from the same philosophical movements. In both countries, the 18th-century Radical and Moderate Enlightenment visions contended for prominence during transformative revolutionary eras. In both countries, the clash between these opposing visions persisted throughout subsequent historical periods and is still operative today. One persistent manifestation of this struggle has been in how wide or narrow to define "who is us?" over time. And both countries have witnessed the superimposition of Counter-Enlightenment forces with varied results. Consequently, both countries have provided strikingly vivid illustrations of how large and small discrepancies manifest in most liberal democracies at three discrete layers: the comprehensiveness of legally codified *de jure* equality, its realized *de facto* enforcement, and the remaining and persistent injustices resulting from the deep-seated feelings of cultural superiority and privilege that can be so resistant to change.

$$* \quad * \quad *$$

As discussed throughout this book, the fundamental political construct of the Enlightenment (and arguably one of its most consequential constructs overall) is that of the social contract, which lies at the root of most modern liberal societies. Intrinsic to the social contract is the question of "who is us?" Any type of social contract necessarily requires a clear definition of who is included. Who exactly did the social contract refer to when it was initially created? What is the process for admitting new entrants following the social contract's initial establishment? How can this process be amended and by what methods? Just as the social contract is an essential element of the Enlightenment, so the question of "who is us?" is an essential element of the social contract itself.

As we have seen, this question has always been a contentious one and has presented various challenges and tribulations in different contexts throughout American history, down to the present day. Undoubtedly, it will be asked in the future too. Yet while a definitive answer to the question may elude our grasp in any given historical moment, history plainly shows us how essential it is to ask and endeavor to answer: "who is us?"

Chapter 16

A NEW VISION FOR AMERICA: CAN WE BUILD A "JUST" MERITOCRACY?

Over the past two hundred and fifty years, key aspects of the vision that the Radical Enlightenment thinkers posited in the 18th century have been not only underappreciated, but also misconstrued and misinterpreted. The most conspicuous misunderstanding surrounds the core notion of egalitarianism itself (a term I have employed frequently throughout this book).

The particular concept that the Radical Enlightenment thinkers envisioned was quite distinct from that of their Moderate Enlightenment counterparts. Furthermore, the Radicals' view diverged markedly from the subsequent schools of egalitarianism that surfaced in the late 19th and 20th centuries against the backdrop of the ascendancy of Marxist ideology. The discrepancies between these alternative visions of egalitarianism are not small nuances; on the contrary, they have fostered profoundly disparate societies based on incongruent socioeconomic frameworks. Consequently, a meticulous examination of these discrete forms of egalitarianism is merited.

The common definition of egalitarianism is "the doctrine that all people are equal and deserve equal rights and opportunities," or according to Webster:

Egalitarianism
1: a belief in human equality especially with respect to social, political, and economic affairs
2: a social philosophy advocating the removal of inequalities among people

However, as far as the most prominent advocates of the French Radical Enlightenment understood it, this definition is misleading. At the core of the contrasting notions of egalitarianism is the very definition of the term "equality" itself, and its many vicissitudes. *Equality before the law is not the same thing as complete equality of individuals.* As Danielle Allen crisply explains: "These days too many of us think that to say two things are 'equal' is to say that they are 'the same' . . . but 'equal' and 'same' are not synonyms. To be 'the same' is to be 'identical.' But to be 'equal' is to have an equivalent degree of some specific quality or attribute."[1]

What did the Radical Enlightenment thinkers mean when they used the term "equality"—what qualities did they intend to convey? What about the Moderates? In what ways did their visions of equality differ? How did subsequent schools of thought differ in their conception of "equality" underlying the various forms of egalitarianism they advocated?

EQUALITY BEFORE THE LAW AND EQUALITY OF VOICE

With careful study of the foundational Enlightenment texts, one realizes that the general intent of Enlightenment thinkers overall was to make reference to *the legal and political standing of the individual.* The term "equality" was meant to describe the characteristic of "equality before and subject to the law." Enlightenment thinkers postulated that all citizens should be subject to the same law and rules of order as an inherent part of the ideal of the social contract. But once we go beyond affirmations of this particular aspect of equality, there were important distinctions between the Moderates and Radicals related to *other aspects* of equality, such as *equality of voice* and *equality of opportunity.*

Recall that the Moderates were circumspect in their consideration of the concept of democracy. In fact, the Moderates behind the American Revolution, such as Adams and Hamilton, while affirming the concept of "equality before and subject to the law," strongly advocated for *inequality* in government participation. For them, the importance of the elite construct of the Senate, the specification that presidents were *not* to be elected by popular vote, and their conviction that governing was, in fact, exclusively the domain of a new modern "aristocracy" illustrate their belief in *inequality of voice and participation.*

Contrarily, the Radicals had a more expansive definition of "equality." In addition to "equality before the law," they added the important attribute of "equality of voice," or equal access to *participate* in the democracy, *to have equal representation.* This difference in views is by no means trivial. As described in previous chapters, the Radicals' vision of a representative democracy as the preferred form of government highlights this salient discrepancy of equality of voice in their political philosophy as compared with that of the Moderate Enlightenment thinkers. For the Radicals, equality before the law, while an essential component of a just and fair society, meant little if it was not accompanied by equal rights to be involved in the *developing and reshaping* of that law through democratic participation.

Importantly, with respect to equality of voice, the breadth of the definition is far from a settled matter even today. The same discrepancies that divided the Moderates and the Radicals are still very much alive. This is conspicuously manifested in the many "back-door" forms of voter suppression that are only increasing today; such efforts obviously undermine the concept of equality of voice. But so do our campaign finance rules. The ability to buy votes with both individual and corporate wealth has dramatically increased in recent decades.

Moreover, systemic sources of inequality of voice are also codified in our Constitution. Inarguably, as a New Yorker, I do not have an equal participatory voice in government as compared to my counterparts in Montana or Wyoming. "In 2020, the 26 states with the smallest populations control the majority of votes in the Senate while representing only 18 percent of the U.S. population."[2] Inequality in participatory voice is propagated in our nation through vehicles like the Senate and the Electoral College, clear vestiges of the Moderate Enlightenment, which advocated strong guardrails on democracy, usually through more elite control of government.

Why do we as citizens tolerate the glaring incongruity of this inequality? Why are North Dakota and South Dakota together, with a combined population of 1.5 million people, and a combined GDP (gross domestic product) of $100 billion, represented by four senators, while California, with a population of 40 million (28 times that of the Dakotas), and GDP of $3.2 trillion (32 times that of the Dakotas), is represented by only two? Should we not, at the least, have a separate North and South California (which would provide the two states collectively with four senators)? Mind you, I have nothing against people from North or South Dakota, or those from Montana or Wyoming, for that matter. But if I were stuck on a desert island with one person from each of these four states, and we used the implied mathematical formula above for allocating our scarce island resources, I might be a tad bit upset.

In conclusion, I consider (and hope to have convinced the reader) that these differing definitions of equality of voice are by no means trivial. The gap between them is large enough to drive through not only the proverbial truck, but the entire fleet currently hurtling along on our nation's interstate highway system.

AN EGALITARIAN SOCIETY CELEBRATES DIFFERENCE

Another argument supporting the sense that to be "equal" does not mean to be "identical" can be found in the often frustrating discussion, so common today, regarding the root causes of the variance in achievements or success across individuals in a society. How can we still be equal despite huge inequalities in certain aspects such as wealth and status? How much of the disparity in human achievement is due to differences in our natural endowments versus those in our developmental environments? This is sometimes referred to as the classic nature versus nurture debate.

One of the beautiful aspects of the natural world is the variation of traits found within a species. Biologists have studied this for centuries, and evolutionary biologists since Charles Darwin have been particularly interested in how these variations lead to adaptations conducive for survival in the natural world. Yet, while we recognize as inarguable that differences in traits *across individuals* exist (e.g., some people are short, some tall, some blue-eyed, some green-eyed), we get uncomfortable when discussing variations in traits *across groups* of individuals, outside the most visually obvious physical differences such as height, skin color, hair color, etc. Somehow, we conflate equality in political and social life with equality in personal attributes or abilities. In fact, *inequality* in terms of talents, abilities, and other attributes is a phenomenon of nature.

Over the course of history, questioning, doubting, and denying political and social equality based on differences in traits, attributes, and abilities across groups has been consistently concomitant with insidious themes—a primary source of prejudice, discrimination, racial violence and oppression, and even genocide. The unjustified fear of and abhorrence of a particular group of people based on genetic variation has inevitably led to virulent racism and persecution in most eras of history and continues to this day. It is against this backdrop that there is a valid basis for our discomfort in broaching this topic.

However, it is these very differences across individuals that create the richness of a society. Skills and interests are as often collectively complementary as they are collectively competitive. These differences should be celebrated, not exploited. Most importantly, the variation in traits, attributes, and abilities across individuals does not negate the fact that people are still equal before and subject to the law as described previously.

ENSURING EQUALITY OF OPPORTUNITY

Irrespective of our individual natural endowments, our environment is a critical determinant of our success. And here again, Enlightenment views on the concept of egalitarianism are frequently misunderstood since there are important distinctions between the Moderates and the Radicals.

Based on the centrality of nurture in human development, theories and discussions of the social contract appropriately address the *educational and developmental environments* we create for our citizens, and for the collective good of our society. Recognizing that individuals are born into and inhabit different environments through no fault of their own, we debate the degree to which it is the onus of the social contract to balance or adjust for the unfairness of the birth lottery and to redress historical inequalities.

The Radical Enlightenment thinkers, with their more expansive view of equality, made a monumental, though often overlooked, contribution precisely in this sphere. Stated simply, the Radical Enlightenment view is that *the government has a responsibility to create equal access to an optimal development environment for all.* By vesting government with the responsibility of creating a level playing field to equally nurture all of its citizens, the critical notion of *equality of opportunity* is added to the portfolio of attributes stipulated in the Radical Enlightenment definition of equality. Moreover, this concept is notably missing from the Moderate Enlightenment definition.

It is important to clarify here that Radical Enlightenment thinkers sought to ensure equality of opportunity while explicitly recognizing and without attempting to erase or eliminate human differences. D'Holbach, for example, wrote extensively about how the variances in traits among individuals of the human species was one of the glories of nature. He noted that some people are more clever than others intellectually, some are more athletic and stronger, some are better at certain specific skills and worse at others, and some are more resilient in certain situations but less so in others. Accordingly, Diderot, d'Holbach, and Condorcet, recognizing that human beings *were far from equal* in all aspects, advocated that the role for government should be vested with the power to provide and secure a base level of equality of opportunity.

In other words, Radical Enlightenment thinkers welcomed and celebrated innately biological as well as environmentally developed differences among individuals. At the same time, they were well aware that in the societies in which they lived, most people were deprived of any meaningful chances to develop their own talents and abilities. To Radical Enlightenment thinkers, this was a great injustice, and one that the modern republic was obligated to address. Specifically, they believed that the government had a duty to intervene in order to create the conditions in which there could be true equality of opportunity among free individuals.

Radical Enlightenment thinkers, in addition to vesting government with this formidable obligation, *specified the methods* by which government could fulfill this responsibility. A society that could expand access to opportunity and incentivize human achievement was not merely theoretical to them, but attainable through concrete solutions. This is evident in their intense interest in and emphasis on the importance of a broad secular education and placing it within reach of the entire populace, not just the elite. It was based precisely on the concept of equality of opportunity that Condorcet invested so much effort in designing and advocating for broad public education. In Condorcet's extensive writings on this subject, he stressed the study of reason and the empirical sciences, as well as morality and civic responsibilities. One of his favorite maxims was "Inequality of education is one of the main sources of tyranny."[3]

Foundational to their Enlightenment heritage, the Radicals firmly believed in the vast capacity of human potential. As contrasted with their Moderate Enlightenment counterparts, who undervalued the potential for common people, the Radicals concentrated so heavily on the need for mass education because they understood that human potential needed to be nurtured and fostered in order to be realized. Only through equal access to a quality education could all members of society develop their different talents in an optimal manner.[4] Without this access, there was no possibility of giving all members of society a fair chance to succeed.

For most Radical Enlightenment philosophers, without an ample investment in education, a democratic representative republic was simply not possible. This alone mandated that government provide a base level of education to all citizens. However, the Radicals went further; in addition to education as requisite for a functioning democratic republic, they also believed that education held the key to unleashing human capacity for the greater benefit of the collective society. Beyond just empowering democracy, the provision of a broad secular education was at the crux of achieving a more egalitarian society in which all citizens had equal access to opportunities to develop and flourish. The Radical

Enlightenment thinkers viewed education as the first step in transcending the limits of the birth lottery, providing a path to social mobility based on achievement.

Finally, while recognizing that variations in individual achievement were inevitable, the Radicals were concerned that excessive economic inequality in society would threaten justice and overall well-being and greatly curtail equality of opportunity. Consequently, for the Radical Enlightenment thinkers, the government had an obligation to ensure that extreme economic inequalities in society were remedied. They believed that the duty of "properly constituted government . . . is to combat the three prime causes and factors of inequality."[5] In other words, the government should address first, inequality of status or hereditary or caste distinction by enabling equality of voice and access to government; second, great inequalities of wealth through progressive and estate taxation; and third, inequality in education and access to skills by providing these uniformly to all citizens.[6]

SUMMARIZING THE RADICAL ENLIGHTENMENT'S EGALITARIANISM

The Radical Enlightenment thinkers' comprehensive view of equality underlying their model of egalitarianism was essentially articulated in d'Holbach's philosophical position, which was based on two fundamental principles:

1. *In spite of their natural differences*, all humans possess the same unalienable rights, should be equal before the law, should be provided with the same legal protections and the same access to education and opportunity, and should be held to the same responsibilities; and

2. *Precisely because some humans are weaker than others in specific areas*, and to the degree that such weakness might result in an inability to thrive, one of the roles of the social contract in a civilized society must be to protect those members, ensuring that they can still (despite their weakness) enjoy their unalienable rights and have a meaningful sustained existence.[7]

Here, simply and concisely stated, is the real essence of Radical Enlightenment egalitarianism, what Radical Enlightenment thinkers might have described as "human equality with respect to social, political and economic affairs."

In summation, encompassing all of the components delineated in the preceding, the extensiveness of the Radicals' definition of equality considerably surpasses that of their Moderate counterparts. First is the idea that each individual has the right to be free from the domination of someone else, be it a tyrant like King George or a fellow citizen; in a just society, one human being cannot dominate another. Second, equality also connotes equality before and with respect to the law of the land, indicating that the laws in society apply equally to everyone, not just to some. Third, a fundamental aspect of equality is participation. All individuals should have equal access to the tools of government as well as equal participation, or said another way, equal voice through representation. Furthermore, the recurrent ravaging effects of free-market capitalism do not excuse the government from its obligation to protect the individuals' unalienable rights. Accordingly, great disparities in economic equality must be tempered through fiscal and taxation policy. And finally, true equality means equal access to opportunity; everyone should have the benefit of an education and be given an even playing field on which to develop their talents and build their qualifications. This Radical Enlightenment concept—this expansive definition of equality—evolved into our modern understanding of a liberal democratic and meritocratic society.

RADICAL ENLIGHTENMENT EQUALITY AS DISTINCT FROM EQUALITY OF OUTCOMES

The misinterpretation of the Radical Enlightenment view of egalitarianism has been consequential beyond merely conflating it with that of the Moderate Enlightenment thinkers. Many schools of thought birthed after the Enlightenment have arrogated the Radical Enlightenment egalitarian vision and confused it with the idea of the *equality of outcomes*, which has become a prominent, if not preeminent concept influencing the development of political thought since the 19th century. Yet the Radical Enlightenment principle that all participants should have *equal access to participate and equal access to opportunity* in a political economy is quite a distinct notion than socialistic or communistic philosophies that strive to *equalize results and expectations* within the political economy.

Radical Enlightenment thinkers by no means envisaged that all citizens would end up with equality in status or wealth, for example. The idea behind their vision was to correct for inequalities of such at birth, to level the playing field early on to give everyone a fair shake. In the end, the Radical Enlightenment thinkers viewed the social contract as a civilizing vehicle fundamental to ensuring the protection of unalienable rights and equality before the law in the face of human differences. They further argued that a just society should endeavor to provide uniform opportunities for development for all its citizenry.

This idea of broadening the concept of equality of opportunity to incorporate equality of outcomes is the *prime* difference between Enlightenment schools of thought and their 19th-century successors. The Radical Enlightenment movement of the 18th and early 19th centuries has largely disappeared, even if its intellectual traditions have endured. To a large degree, many of its underlying ideas have been appropriated, subsumed, and overshadowed by the explosion of Marxist ideology that began in the late 19th century. This is unfortunate, as it muddles the benefits and criticisms of both the Radical Enlightenment and Marxist schools of thought.

The writings of Marx and Engels, along with the official literature from the 20th-century International Communist Party, have been interpreted in myriad ways and have formed the basis of many different subsequent political philosophies (and influenced countless others). Variants of modern socialism have, to a large degree, tempered Marx's original characterization of society as based on the concept of "class warfare."[8] Without detracting from the validity and contributions of these schools of thought, there are significant dissimilarities, which must not be conflated, between Radical Enlightenment philosophy and the socialist trend that would follow it. These differences are not trivial; on the contrary, they are quite substantial. So, what are those differences and why are they so important?

It is imperative here to distinguish between conventional Marxist ideology and the contemporary concepts of democratic socialism. The former, in its most basic form, stipulated an end to the exploitation of labor by capital via a shift of control of the means of production, ultimately liberating the proletariat. In essence, traditional Marxist theory calls into question the very property rights held so dear by the Moderate Enlightenment thinkers.[9] Yet in today's democratic socialist societies, ownership of the means of production is more complex, with both public and private actors owning stakes in various industries and sectors of the economy. Even many newly industrialized capitalist countries have deployed formulas for state sponsorship of industry, but these mixed economies generally maintain the sanctity of property rights in non-state-sponsored activities.

Democratic socialism in the 21st century is also characterized by the pursuit of redistributive justice and stronger safety nets, while still retaining the concept of property rights as well as many elements of a free-market economy. Because of these moderations, aspects of these modern currents of democratic socialism can be consonant with the Radical Enlightenment view that government must play a role in ensuring a level playing field for all citizens and redressing injustices caused by failures within the free market system.

For purposes of clarity, the contrast to which I refer to here is the one between the Radical Enlightenment view and the traditional socialist doctrine of eliminating or curtailing private ownership of the means of production. The salient point for our discussion here is that this latter approach has in practical terms rarely proven to be an effective solution leading to a more egalitarian society. The act of prohibiting or discouraging ownership in assets is usually accompanied by a loss of agency or motivational drive to improve the value or return of the assets in question. This is often best observed in mixed economies where the large state-owned companies rarely outperform and uncontestably do not out-innovate smaller, privately owned ventures.

Furthermore, the implementation of traditional Marxist doctrine in almost every case has been an economic misfortune, if not disaster, as the government-planned allocation of resources is inevitably much less efficient than allocation by the free market. Further, single-minded pursuits of a more equal distribution of resources and equalization of outcomes has often led to a totalitarian state relying on a planned economy as a means of "equalization." Ironically, the very equality such a totalitarian state purports to strive for is indisputably compromised by the power and its associated abuses accruing to the state bureaucrats who oversee the means of production and thereby control the allocation of resources.

For precisely these reasons, it is important to differentiate and distinguish between the traditional Marxist ideology of equality of outcomes and the Radical Enlightenment perspective of treating humans equally before the law and with respect to the other attributes of equality discussed previously. In practice, the former eschews reliance on a market economy while the latter can definitively embrace a market economy. All members of society being at the same level in a Marxist utopia is *quite a different concept* from the Radical Enlightenment ideal of creating a more level playing field for the pursuit of human endeavors. *Equality of opportunities and equality of outcomes are markedly dissimilar concepts.*

In the Radical Enlightenment framework, achievement in human endeavors that are valued by society *earn rewards,* which are commensurate with the degree of effort, courage, or skill underlying the specific achievement; those who accomplish more, earn more rewards. This system not only provides a natural mechanism encouraging people to pursue success, to develop their talents, and to make valuable societal contributions, but it creates a competition for novel ideas, products, and services that businesses and end-consumers value. Thus, while "all men are created equal," they do not remain so over the course of their lives; some, based on a combination of natural talents and often lifelong labors and struggles, achieve much more than others. In short, such a system merits and rewards *achievement.*

There are always robust disputes about whether the status or financial rewards accruing to some for their achievements are commensurate or perhaps disproportionate to the true value of their contribution in the eyes of others. Put another way, are the rewards earned for achievement "just" rewards? This is a healthy debate to have, and one that has often been initiated by democratic socialists and left-wing populists demanding economic justice from the bottom up. Such movements thus deserve credit for raising the alarm when the market system seems to be perpetuating unfairness beyond the standard mechanisms of incentivizing achievement. In any case, such criticisms can and should be made of all systems where rewards accrue solely to those connected to power or born into good circumstances, systems in which arguably two-thirds of the world's population live today. In addition to the associated infringements of most liberties, such as free speech, the method of allocating or distributing rewards in these systems can hardly be characterized as more "just."

IN DEFENSE OF MERITOCRACY

In modern parlance, we have a word for the type of society that the Radical Enlightenment thinkers envisioned and that is described in the previous sections—a *meritocracy*. Ideally, the role of government is to get all members of society as close as possible to the same starting line, to provide equal access in life's formative years to educational development irrespective of ancestral differences in resources.[10] In such a world, based on both natural talents and opportunities for educational and qualification development, members of society earn rewards based on their *achievements*. The competition is fair because everyone begins at the same starting line and everyone has equal access to opportunities to acquire qualifications.

In addition to aspiring toward fairness, meritocracy is efficient at developing and channeling the best and the brightest toward opportunities where they can contribute the most to the collective societal good. Thus, while in such a society people focus on maximizing their personal gain, because the accomplishments they produce are valued as measured by society, people concurrently contribute to the society overall. As political commentator Chris Hayes has written: "By conferring the most power on those best equipped to wield it, the meritocracy produces a better society for us all. In rewarding efforts and smarts we incentivize both."[11] At the same time, for those who are less successful within any specific period, the republic's role is to ensure a "safety net" so that these members can still pursue a dignified life. Sounds pretty simple.

Nonetheless, in recent years, many political writers have disparaged the concept of meritocracy. Some complain that meritocracy in America is nothing but a myth; they argue that because access to opportunity, especially educational opportunities, is so skewed toward the wealthy, in touting meritocracy we are in fact romanticizing a model that in reality has never been achieved. There certainly is validity to this argument; the data convincingly demonstrate that the social mobility associated with earlier eras in American history has stagnated over recent decades. Since the 1980s, entrenched mechanisms within the political economy have permitted and legitimized the upper one percent of the wealthy to guarantee that their elite inheritance is transferred to their children, seemingly ossifying our existing social structure.

Other critiques of meritocracy are more frontal, arguing that the entire mechanistic structure of meritocracy is systemically flawed, that by design it is a rigged system that affords the elite a handy justification that their rewards are earned through their own efforts and marked by their own achievements, instead of bestowed upon them by their wealthy ancestors. We will explore some of these critiques in more detail in the following. However, as evidenced by its demonstrable successes, the concept of meritocracy withstands these critiques.

There are a few wonderful examples of a meritocratic vision being put into practice with manifestly impressive results. The United States in the mid-20th century following World War II may be one of the best examples. This era was characterized by the lowest levels of inequality in the 20th century and possibly in the nation's history. It is also worth noting that during this era, unions were strong, marginal tax rates were high, and financial markets were tightly controlled—none of which is true today.

Based on the stratospheric level of inequality in the United States today, arguably the post–World War II meritocracies in Western Europe have had more success. Those economies have generated lower levels of inequality and more endurably sustained leveling mechanisms over time. Whereas the neoliberal wave associated with Reagan and Thatcher abjured redistributive economic policies, collective bargaining through unions, and societal safety nets, all under the rhetorical umbrella of freedom and the inherent evils of government, the European continent sustained, and in many cases extended, all three.

A meritocratic society ideally has the best of both worlds: *liberal economic principles* to ensure that a free market can efficiently allocate the resources for production *and strong incentives for achievement* based on its commensurate rewards. The demonstrable evidence that late 20th-century policies of neoliberalism have bastardized these concepts is crystal clear in the near abandonment of the critical roles of government in a market-based economy. The liberal economic principles to which I refer *stipulate* unequivocally that government must assume an essential portfolio of activities for the proper functioning of a free-market economy. In simple terms, the government's role is threefold: (1) to correct for market failures of a capitalistic free-market economy (of which there are many, such as externalities, monopolistic power, unequal access to infrastructure and information, etc.); (2) to invest, build, and ensure uniform access to valuable public goods like public education and job training, which together provide equal access to opportunity;[12] and (3) to achieve better equity across the strata of society through redistribution so that all can have access to liberty and freedom and enjoy a basic ability to pursue happiness, that is, to provide a safety net for those who cannot do so on their own.

A fundamental problem that needs to be resolved to establish a true meritocracy is *how to define* equality of opportunity. Equal access to education is one aspect, but there are many others such as access to infrastructure and public goods, job opportunities and job training, and social benefits, to name but a few. A more all-inclusive concept of equality of opportunity must include *equal access to acquire qualifications in all settings.*

John Rawls, in his landmark 1971 work *A Theory of Justice*, distinguishes between various conceptions of equality of opportunity. For Rawls, the hurdle is quite high; he argues that justice requires that equality of opportunity be as near complete as possible—the concept of "careers open to talents" where qualified applicants have equal access to particular positions is not sufficient. For Rawls, a just society must also provide equal access for all to *acquire* those talents, that is, necessary qualifications for those positions, quite a demanding concept and difficult to achieve in practice. One of the most important principles introduced by Rawls is the "veil of ignorance," a simple yet brilliant construct which elucidates that in postulating how to set up any system of justice, the postulator must have no *a priori* knowledge of where she would end up *a posteriori*, that is, once the system of justice in question is implemented.[13] (It turns out that once the condition of the veil of ignorance is scrupulously imposed, the one who gets to write the rules suddenly has quite a different perspective.)

Another recent concept of justice is provided by Greg Lukianoff and Jonathan Haidt, in their 2018 book, *The Coddling of the American Mind*. The authors introduce the concept of *intuitive justice*, "the combination of *distributive justice* (the perception that people are getting what is deserved) and *procedural justice* (the perception that the process by which things are distributed and rules are enforced is fair and trustworthy)."[14] While most Americans might subscribe to a belief in this type of intuitive justice in theory, what divides Americans greatly is to what degree government should be responsible for equalizing access to opportunity, redressing past injustices, and redistributing rewards more equitably. In a functioning meritocracy, these debates are welcomed and essential.

In many ways, the concept of the American dream that I referred to in the opening of this book, where anyone can succeed regardless of societal class, origin, race, or religion, is precisely this type of meritocratic model. I am loath to forsake this part of the American myth, despite the fact that I know that meritocracy, as an ideal, is one we have only imperfectly achieved. For certain segments of society, such as African Americans and Indigenous Americans, our track record of creating a level playing field with equal access to opportunity has been nothing less than atrocious. For some immigrant groups, it has been quite successful. For most Americans, however, in the last fifty years social mobility has been largely unattainable.

But the harsh reality that we have achieved quite unequal success and at times appalling failures in our quest to attain a true meritocracy does not in any way compromise the validity of the principle nor obviate the imperative to strive for its greater realization. The model of a meritocracy can still be a sacrosanct model, a goal to which all societies might strive. I cling to the ideal of a true meritocracy, *not* because it is the societal model most closely consistent with the French Radical Enlightenment thinkers (which it happens to be), but because I believe it is the only model that aspires to simultaneously establish a just society and preserve the American spirit of innovation and entrepreneurship. It is also the model I would design if given the authority to do so while under Rawls's compulsory "veil of ignorance."

DEBATING THE MERITOCRATIC IDEAL IN THEORY AND PRACTICE

Recently, quite a different line of thinking has diverged from this line of thought. In *The Meritocracy Trap* (2019), Daniel Markovits outlines how he believes meritocracy itself is at the core of the ills of modern-day American society. His thesis is that our very system of meritocracy causes tremendous discontent by polarizing society into an elite aristocracy (the one percent we discussed previously) and a majority of the lower working class, crowding out the middle class that served as the broad center of American society at midcentury.

Markovits's observations and arguments are valid in many respects. His reflections are astute, and the data analysis supporting his logic is sound and at times quite rigorous. He argues, at times convincingly, that meritocracy achieves the precise opposite of its intended goals. He claims that because the competition is rigged in favor of the affluent at every level of education and training, the outcome of a meritocracy is inevitably a caste system where the modern elite pass down the benefits of their status to their children in an analogous manner to how, in centuries past, the aristocratic elite passed down land and capital. Markovits explains that, perhaps counterintuitively, the result of our meritocracy is much more dramatic inequality caused by a deeply skewed distribution of wealth and the disappearance of the social mobility witnessed earlier in the 20th century.

> The present American elite, unlike in the past, and more so than in virtually every other nation, possesses exceptional skills and derives these skills from extraordinary training . . . But meritocracy's narrow economic successes have turned out to undermine its broader democratic ambitions . . . The new elite . . . knows better than anything how to turn competition to its children's advantage. The very same mechanisms that once destroyed aristocratic hierarchies and dynasties now erect meritocratic hierarchies and dynasties in their stead.[15]

Christopher Hayes advanced a similar critique of meritocracy in his earlier book *Twilight of the Elites: America after Meritocracy* (2012). In his insightful analysis, Hayes points to what he calls the "Iron Law of Meritocracy": "The inequality produced by a meritocratic system will grow large enough to subvert the mechanisms of mobility. Those who are able to climb up the ladder will find ways to pull it up after them, or to selectively lower it down to allow their friends, allies, and kin to scramble up."[16] Hayes argues that this law lies at the root of the decreasing social mobility we have observed since the 1970s. Those who advance in a meritocracy "create a means of preserving and defending their privilege and find ways to pass it on across generations."[17]

Markovits has documented that the data undeniably show these trends. As one example, a poor child in a poor state receives approximately $8K of schooling a year and a middle-class child receives between $12K and $25K depending on the state. However, a rich child in an elite private school receives approximately $75K of schooling per year. And the differences in educational investment compound cumulatively year after year. Furthermore, the same trends of unequal access to education, increasing gaps between the very rich and the rest, and diminishing social mobility have all been documented extensively by others.[18]

The hollowing out of the tier of midlevel managers, as elite workers subsume their supervisory functions through their own sponsored technological innovations, is also well documented. Consider the thousands of Amazon warehouses across the country that are fully controlled by state-of-the-art software, negating the need for supervisors and managers. This software dictates when and how lower-level pickers (and eventually robots) assemble customers' orders. As Markovits writes, as midlevel jobs disappear, middle-class workers are deprived "of the status and income that their managerial responsibilities once sustained."[19]

The core question posed by Markovits is: Who or what is the culprit behind this phenomenon? There are myriad theories. A few years ago, Thomas Piketty's compelling model and accompanying analysis in *Capital in the Twenty-First Century* (2014) provided a rich root-cause analysis of the disparity of income and wealth distribution across many developed market economies. Others have documented how the U.S. federal tax system has become so regressive that almost any form of government redistribution is practically nonexistent. The affluent find ways to avoid most income and capital gains taxes, while their skilled financial planners create structures to avoid most estate taxes.

The uniqueness of Markovits's thesis is that he impugns the very notion of meritocracy itself. For Markovits, merit is only "a pretense, constructed to rationalize an unjust distribution of advantage" and "a mechanism for the concentration and dynastic transmission of wealth and privilege and caste across generations."[20] In my analysis, however, Markovits's core thesis and Hayes's prognostication are both off the mark in two essential ways. First, the ills that both writers so accurately describe and vividly support in their books have less to do with meritocracy as a concept and more to do with our failed attempts, most notably in recent decades, to achieve it. Their portrayals of meritocracy instead illustrate how our *currently existing* version of meritocracy fails to live up to its very definition.

Markovits describes how our current society fails to provide a level playing field since we allow the wealthy to endow their children with a huge head start, ensuring that they outcompete the nonwealthy at every stage. Whether in private preschool, prep school, or the Ivy League, the system is rigged since the affluent can ensure that their offspring have unfair advantages in accessing the best resources at every level in the developmental ladder. In addition, since educational resources are quite scarce (in addition to being inequitably distributed), every extra dollar invested by a rich parent in their child's education is a dollar that is not invested in the education of a kid from a lower socioeconomic group. And because these advantages accumulate at each level, Markovits estimates that the "meritocratic inheritance" the affluent give to their children amounts to a tax-free donation of approximately $10 million per child by the time she gets through college.

This "immense excess investment that rich parents make in their children's human capital, over and above what middle-class children receive"[21] is a driving factor in stagnating social mobility. In any society, meritocracy or not, if one child receives a foundational education investment that is hundreds of times greater than another child, the resulting achievement and mobility gaps are hardly surprising.

Further, as Markovits describes, once members of the wealthy class enter the job market, they become superordinate workers who, based on their exceptional training, get enormous returns from their very valuable labor. To add insult to injury, these superordinate workers continue to design technological innovations and structures to ensure that the value of their own impeccably developed skills is sustained, usually at the expense of the semiskilled midlevel workers whose tasks are subsumed or made unnecessary by the working elites' "improvements." As the technologies and innovations implemented by these elites create redundancy for midlevel skills, midlevel workers are terminated. Only select elite superordinate workers on top and lower-class gofers on the bottom remain. For Markovits, the American labor market is "epitomized by Walmart greeters and Goldman Sachs bankers."[22]

These illustrations pointing to a disconcerting disparity in access to opportunities to develop qualifications early in life, and opportunities to catch up along the way, are indicative of our failure to create a true meritocracy. But Hayes concedes as much in his discussion of meritocracy. He specifies that the failure may lie not in the concept itself but in our current manifestation: "In reality our meritocracy has failed not because it's too meritocratic, but because in practice, it isn't very meritocratic at all."[23]

In his recommendations for a course of action, Markovits reinforces the idea that the market failures that allow meritocracy, as it currently exists, to be so unequitable can be corrected by enabling and ensuring more equal access to educational resources for youth and industry-based training for midskilled labor. The fact that our meritocracy can have a much more level set of points for entry and development, with more equitable access to training along the way, indicates that a *better implementation of meritocracy is the goal, not its entire replacement.*

Further, the notion that merit is only a pretense to justify a gamed and unfair system ignores the fact that merit is based on achievements that are usually *quite valuable* to society, as measured by the free-market system. Whether discoveries to heal the sick, fresh forms of entertainment, or innovative goods and services that people enjoy, the achievements resulting from meritocratic competition have tremendous value in the eyes of consumers. In many cases, the economic value of these achievements is reflected via pricing in the free market; in other cases, the social value of these achievements is reflected through fame, though not always economic reward.

In addition, Markovits's argument that the meritocratic race is a zero-sum game is a flawed one. He asserts that "when elites buy extravagant education, they directly diminish the educations that everyone else has . . . Meritocratic education inexorably engenders a wasteful and destructive educational arms race, which ultimately benefits no one, not even the victors."[24] But as a society we can *choose* to make higher absolute levels of investment in education. And we can spread these investments more evenly. We can even choose as a matter of public policy to invest more heavily in education for the less advantaged (as in programs like Head Start), since often the incremental investments in education for less well-off children have the greatest returns. Moreover, investments at all income levels in education and training should result in a higher and more widely spread level of achievement (provided these investments have a good return—that the programs created are successful and attain good results).

Meritocracy does not have to be a zero-sum game as Markovits describes. In fact, he explains how Germany, unlike the United States, has spread education more broadly and provides intensive vocational training to those outside the university. Further, whereas American firms allocate new investments "in plants and machinery disproportionately to complement high-skilled workers . . . German firms, by contrast, channel new capital toward sectors in which unskilled or mid-skilled labor dominates production . . . capital deepening in the United States is associated with increased wage dispersion . . . while in Germany it is associated with wage compression."[25]

These very examples illustrate that *public policy* is what facilitates or impedes the development of a meritocracy. Meritocracy does not just materialize out of thin air but is molded by the choices a society makes. As an example, it has been well documented that countries rich in primary resources and commodities tend to invest more in resource extraction industries and less in mass education. These investment choices have consequential and profound impacts on society as a whole. Contrast Japan, a country with few natural resources and a broad and vastly educated middle class, with Brazil, a country with tremendous investment in resource extraction industries benefiting an elite while leaving widespread poverty and illiteracy unaddressed. The observation that a country's natural endowment of resources dramatically influences where its government makes investments, which in turn results in a more or less educated society, is itself indicative of the power of public policy in determining how narrow or broad the access to opportunity is within its borders.

This brings me to my second overall objection to Markovits's and Hayes's characterization of meritocracy as the problem itself. Much like free-market capitalism or a representative democratic republic, meritocracy is an *ideal*. As such, it provides a model or a target, a *perfect form in the Platonic sense*, toward which one must strive. Any given execution of that ideal necessarily has flaws and needs to be constantly enhanced and corrected. Achieving fair and equal access to opportunity as Rawls conceived it is never perfect nor complete; it is an evolution, a progression that needs to be continually assessed and improved upon. Once such an implementation no longer becomes dynamic, no longer strives to correct its faults, it becomes, much like an untended garden, rife with weeds that grow over and kill many other valuable forms of life.

The real question that Markovits would need to answer if meritocracy *itself* were the cause of the ills he describes is this: What is the alternative? Since the only suggestions he provides are more equitable access to preparation mechanisms for the meritocratic system, in essence, more leveling, his argument of meritocracy *itself* being the source of the problem collapses.

The closest analogy to the very grave problems that Markovits so excellently identifies in his work seems (to me) to be the argument related to free-market capitalism. Economists of many generations since Adam Smith have lauded the free market as the optimal way to allocate scarce resources. But free-market capitalism is also an ideal, much like meritocracy. For the free market to function optimally, one must believe myriad assumptions that, in practice, are rarely true. But the value of the study of economics is that it provides specific solutions to correct the problems that arise when certain assumptions fail. In fact, many of the socialist models in today's European social democracies, and to some extent the policies advocated by Elizabeth Warren and Bernie Sanders, endeavor to fix the problems that result from the imperfect free market system with prescriptions to achieve a more pervasive equality of opportunity in society, to better level the playing field.[26] Advocating for such fixes does not imply that we wish to abandon market capitalism, or that we have to deploy a better system to make societal resource allocations, or that we no longer value and reward achievement. Proverbially, *we don't throw out the baby with the bath water.*

One could follow the same line of argument regarding our experiment in self-government. As Lincoln stated, our imperfect union is striving to reach a higher ideal, the vision laid out by our Founders in the Declaration of Independence. Richard Beeman, in his insightful article, "Perspectives on the Constitution: A Republic, If You Can Keep It" (1998), illustrates the powerful concept of the republic as an ideal. Any particular governmental framework and implementation needs constant vigilance and improvement. Beeman points out that upon the presentation of the U.S. Constitution, Benjamin Franklin,

> ever the optimist even at the age of 81, gave what was for him a remarkably restrained assessment in his final speech before the Constitutional Convention: " . . . when you assemble a number of men to have the advantage of their joint wisdom, you inevitably assemble with those men, all their prejudices, their passions, their errors of opinion, their local interests, and their selfish views." He thought it impossible to expect a "perfect production" from such a gathering, but he believed that the Constitution they had just drafted, "with all its faults," was better than any alternative that was likely to

emerge . . . our Constitution is neither a self-actuating nor a self-correcting document. It requires the constant attention and devotion of all citizens.[27]

There is a story, often told, that upon exiting the Constitutional Convention Benjamin Franklin was approached by a group of citizens asking what sort of government the delegates had created. His answer was: "*A republic, if you can keep it.*" The brevity of that response should not cause us to undervalue its essential meaning: Democratic republics are not merely founded upon the consent of the people; they are also absolutely dependent upon the active and informed involvement of the people for their continued good health.[28]

Franklin's quote could not be more relevant today in the United States. One of the most dangerous aspects of our current dilemma is that it seems we have lost our ability to do the vital housework to which the eighty-one-year-old Franklin was referring. Today, the Senate appears to have become a kangaroo court, the House rarely gets much done, and an unconstrained supply of "dark" money has corrupted many of our elected leaders. Further, many Americans have lost faith in the institutions of governance we have built over the centuries. Today, a majority of Americans seem reluctant to undertake the indispensable work required to fix our broken system. Further, they appear resigned toward fatalistically accepting a different one, which at present seems to be autocratic leadership by the powerful ideologues Trump so admires and emulates.

But for purposes of our evaluation of the concept of meritocracy, we need to view it as an aspirational ideal with the understanding that its perfect realization will be elusive, analogous to how Benjamin Franklin and Abraham Lincoln understood the potential of our democratic republic. Indeed, the philosophical roots of the meritocracy that I am describing are grounded in the Radical Enlightenment ideas of Diderot, d'Holbach, Paine, and Franklin.

By contrast, Moderate Enlightenment thinkers in many ways sold the common people short. They failed to believe that ordinary citizens warrant significant levels of investment in the development of their human capacities. While not advocating for the *control* of the masses as had their *ancien régime* predecessors, they relegated the masses to a set of contributory but nonetheless predetermined roles in society. By not envisioning a world in which broad investments in modern education would enable the masses to flourish and make contributions to society commensurate with those of the aristocratic enlightened like themselves, they failed to evince the high level of faith in human potential that so distinguished their radical contemporaries. Accordingly, they failed to live up to the spirit of the Enlightenment itself.

As Christopher Hayes concedes: "The logic of the meritocracy is ironclad: putting the most qualified, best equipped people into the positions of greatest responsibility and import. It would be foolhardy to toss the principle out in its entirety. You certainly wouldn't want surgeons' licenses to be handed out via lottery, or have major cabinet members selected through reality TV-style voting."[29] Instead of abandoning meritocracy, we need to develop better strategies for its effective and measurable 21st-century implementation. It is to this topic that we now turn in the concluding section of the book.

Chapter 17

HEALING THE AMERICAN SCHISM: CRUCIAL FIRST STEPS

No single program or initiative, no matter how brilliantly designed or far-reaching, can bridge the gap across the American Schism. Reconciling its disparities and resolving its core conflicts will not be quickly achieved, nor will the spirit of our political discourse improve overnight. But at the same time, unless we nurture a mutual understanding of the nature of the divide and begin to rationally discuss and debate its constituent elements, our efforts to address our contemporary predicaments will remain frustrated and our efforts to attain a more civil society, thwarted. If we continue to center our political discourse around our inveterate identities and our polarizing but shallow differences, if we continue to brandish passion-laden symbols and slogans designed to accentuate these differences and deride the points of view of our rivals, if we continue to sanctimoniously indulge the analgesic effects of the endorphins released by the affirmation of our in-groups and the vilification of our out-groups, we are playing a losing game. We are merely spinning in circles, desensitized to what are ultimately futile attempts to resolve merely derivative issues.

Nonetheless, there is reason for hope. Political polls that seemingly verify that we are a "50:50 society, divided into two opposing political tribes and trapped in a spiral of conflict and division"[1] are in certain respects counting the trees but missing the forest. This binary split is misleading, as our political landscape is propitiously more complex and nuanced.

A 2018 study by More in Common, a civically minded research organization, indicates that while the two poles in the political spectrum are *the loudest, they are not representative of the majority*. In their research-based segmentation study, More in Common characterizes many slices of the American electorate as part of an "exhausted majority," quite distinct from the extreme poles, and who do not subscribe to the views of either. A methodical analysis of the data indicates that the polarization so characteristic of both traditional and social media creates a misperception that the entirety of America falls neatly into two rival groups.

> In talking to everyday Americans, we have found a large segment of the population whose voices are rarely heard above the shouts of the partisan tribes. These are the people who believe that Americans have more in common than that which divides them. While they differ on important issues, they feel exhausted by the division in the United States. They believe that compromise is necessary in politics, as in other parts of life, and want to see the country come together to solve its problems.[2]

As revealed in the details of this study, a great plurality of Americans, if not blinded by the toxicity of today's identity politics, could successfully come to consensus on some of the core issues that perpetuate and reinforce the American Schism. But we cannot do so by continuing down our current truculent and confrontational path. Simply viewing our problems through the lens of our physical or cultural differences will hardly suffice to beget mutual understanding. On the contrary, if we remain transfixed by the frame of reference prescribed by our modern media platforms, we will only exacerbate the divisions between us. Today "our conflicts are largely over who we think we are rather than over reasoned differences of opinion . . . [our conflicts have become] less about governing and more about the conflict itself."[3]

The obstacle encumbering us is that collectively we have completely lost sight of the goal. So many care more about their party winning than about achieving specific public policy objectives. As a consequence, we behave like we disagree more than we actually do. As Lilliana Mason reminds us, due to intergroup conflict, our rational thinking has been displaced:

> All citizens want to believe that their political values are solid and well-reasoned. More often, though, policy attitudes grow out of group-based defense . . . Policy preferences, over time, take a backseat to the team loyalty that is bound to grow out of these increasingly homogenous and isolated partisan collections.[4]

So then, how do we move beyond the frustratingly obtuse nature of our current political discourse, and forward to a more productive one? The first step is to unshackle ourselves from our in-groups, liberating sufficient space for individual reflection on the core issues and principles underlying the American Schism. We must confront the harsh reality that our in-groups are uncompromisingly reinforcing our unproductive behavior. While remaining in our bubbles may grant us the benefits of emotional affirmation, we need to break free of their restraining boundaries and think for ourselves, in the redemptive spirit of the Enlightenment.

What is required is not a *collective* acceptance or rejection of specific points of view nor a consensus of principles by our tribal groups, but instead individual reflection on and meaningful consideration of *our own personal views* on the substantive principles themselves, divorced from the pressures of our self-created mobs. The second step is to be open to listening and more munificently understanding, considering, and pondering on the perspective of others, especially those not in our in-groups, without resorting to ad hominem attacks. *Personal introspection and empathetic listening to rival points of view are the essential prerequisites for a fruitful discussion and constructive debate.* Unfortunately, today's public forums do not provide space for either. Trying to do so over Twitter is only a recipe for perpetuating our current morass.

* * *

The fundamental rifts separating the rival visions of our nation are as deep rooted as they are long established. They are complex because, as we have seen throughout this journey, they are multidimensional and stimulated by distinct and competing influences.

First, still conflicting are the rival strains of Moderate and Radical Enlightenment thought that originally vied for prominence at our nation's birth and trace their history back to the 18th century. Second, these contending strains of thought have been intermingled with Counter-Enlightenment impulses that have occasioned indeterminate and, at times, seemingly paradoxical political outcomes. And third, in any given era, all of these influences get intermingled with the exigent issues of the day in the American political and social crucible. While the resulting amalgamation at times leads to productive problem solving and progressive strides forward, just as frequently the combination triggers a volatile chemical reaction, resulting in a violent explosion with tragic consequences.

In the first section of this book, I delineated the disparities between the contending Enlightenment forces. In the second section, I analyzed how these dynamics played out on our civic battlegrounds during discrete periods in our history. As with all analyses of social systems, the numerous variables and the many complications sometimes result in what seems closer to a perplexing adumbration rather than the intended useful elucidation. Despite these limitations, I trust the reader can draw some clear if not conclusive connections and more profoundly appreciate the many textures and nuances of our common American heritage.

In this third section, I attempt to connect the dots. At their core, the particular fissures between the Moderate, Radical, and Counter-Enlightenment boil down to several key questions that manifest as much today as they have throughout our history: First, do we embrace a representative democracy where all citizens get a voice, or do we want to perpetuate government by the few? If we settle for government *by* the few, we must then also accept government *for* the few, which will most likely perpetuate wealth and opportunity for these same few and their descendants.

Second, do we want to maintain and strengthen the separation of church and state in our civic landscape? Can we recognize the fact that spiritual impulses can play an enormously positive role in civic life, while concurrently accepting boundaries that prevent religious forces from intruding in the governmental sphere, dominating civic society, or restricting the basic tolerance required in a liberal democracy? The empirical evidence demonstrating that individual churches are vital parts of tight-knit communities and further, that they foster constructive local civic affairs, is compelling. Can we welcome these as vibrant elements in the public square within our local communities while resisting a centralized dogmatic top-down church power that is sanctioned and ascribed to by our governing structures, whether local or federal? Or contrarily, are we comfortable living in a theocracy where a single faith is closely aligned with or dictates government authority?

And finally, by what yardstick do we measure and reward success in our society? Can we incentivize the achievement so foundational to the American entrepreneurial spirit while giving all Americans a fair chance to succeed? How do we ensure that those who accrue economic success and political power due to their expert qualifications or unique accomplishments continue to advocate for the general will of all the people?

THE URGENCY OF THE PROBLEM: OUR DETERIORATING DEMOCRACY

The first order of business must be addressing the state of our democracy, which is inarguably in crisis. Some pundits point to the ultimate triumph of our democratic traditions in the 2020 presidential elections as indicative of their vigor. While true that our democracy withstood an unprecedented barrage of assaults instigated by a sore loser in the aftermath, the view that our elections are safe is illusory.

As a result of the cumulative damage of recent years, the January 2021 transfer of presidential power was anything but peaceful, and as of this writing, the U.S. Capitol remains a war zone characterized by fencing, barbed wire, and barricades, and policed by National Guard troops around the clock. Moreover, millions of Americans falsely believe that the 2020 presidential election was stolen. Thus, with persistent threats both foreign and domestic, the notion that our democracy is healthy is apocryphal.

While I concede that if we queried 100 random people today to identify what they believed were the *three most basic shared values* foundational to the American ideal, we might venture to guess that "democracy" would be one of the most cited responses, in addition to freedom, liberty, and equality. For many Americans, the notion that democracy is a core American value has been profoundly wired into our consciousness since we were born, so much so, that the statement itself sounds hackneyed, almost worn out. And we repeat it by rote, as if we are reciting the ABCs of the American credo. However, recall as indicated in an earlier chapter that in previous eras, the word "democracy" had a negative connotation, implying the kind of mob rule associated with malevolent demagogues; indeed, many of our most esteemed Founders including John Adams, James Madison, Alexander Hamilton, and many others were quite trepidatious of the concept of democracy.

In 21st-century America, democracy's foes are stronger than ever, though often more subtle in their opposition. Though many citizens rest assured, buoyed in their belief that it is democracy's defenders that are in the majority, a preponderance of qualitative and quantitative evidence indicates otherwise.

Recent surveys indicate that only thirty percent of millennials assert that living in a democracy is essential, and even fewer rate it as a top priority.[5] Given how difficult it can be in practice to achieve a highly participatory democracy, the fact that younger generations either take democracy for granted or underappreciate it seems to be a predictable omen of its demise.

Furthermore, it is undeniable that democracy's adversaries have become more emboldened as of late. The voter suppression efforts that manifested throughout much of our history have made a remarkable comeback after an all-too-short period of respite. This is undoubtedly contributing to a loss of faith in our democracy. The fact that voting, the most fundamental democratic norm, is so difficult today—one can routinely wait up to three hours, if not more, to cast a ballot—indicates that perhaps our spoken commitment to democracy reveals itself as hollow. We are all talk and no action; maybe our inaction indicates that democracy is not the priority we are inclined to say it is.

Another indication of democracy's peril is just how willing so many are today to allow "alternative facts" to replace the objective truth that is its oxygen supply. As a result of this frontal assault on the truth, balanced and rational discourse is no longer prevalent in our daily lives, and democracy is further eroded.

Research data also indicate that public trust in our country has severely declined in recent years. Americans' confidence in both the federal government and our public institutions are at historically low levels, with the exception of the military (which is the one public institution that Americans still trust). Americans also put less faith in business and the news media, and perhaps most importantly, Americans' trust in each other has "begun to show signs of decline."[6] What ails the public today cannot be blamed on one institution, or one branch of government, or one autocratic president; our entire self-governing structure is rotting due to a systemic loss of trust and confidence.

A significant part of this loss has resulted from the fact that public service expertise has been compromised by its increasing politicization. The consequences of this trend are multilayered; most immediately we get biased analyses and misguided policy prescriptions. But the secondary effects are perhaps just as damaging: an increasing willingness on the part of the public to denigrate our public servants. For many of these public servants, the fact that dispassionate expertise in the civic sphere has now become vilified is as disturbing as it is brazenly disrespectful to their lifelong careers.

All of these indications of erosion in our democratic life—popular skepticism about democracy, increased voter suppression, tribal information bubbles, declining trust in our institutions and in expertise, popular insurrections to arrest our sacred tradition of the peaceful transfer of power—have precedents in our past. They are by no means new phenomena. Yet at the same time it is clear that our democracy faces challenges today that are unparalleled in our nation's recent history. The beacon that we have offered much of the world over the past century has been reduced to a frail flickering.

What explains our complacency in the face of these abundant signs that our democracy is deteriorating? Some of our most distinguished leaders who so habitually and facilely claim that democracy remains America's saving grace, are perhaps instead revealing "thou doth protest too much." Conceivably, many of the upper echelons, those who have a lot to lose, are in fact quite fearful that a more robust democracy, a more thorough enfranchisement within the lower socioeconomic strata, might be threatening to their achievements (I do not exclude myself from this group). Our history has been quite illustrative of the frequent inclination of the elite echelons, often wealthy conservatives, to tolerate, fail to condemn, or worse, perpetrate specific actions to disrupt or subvert broader democratic participation.

Furthermore, all voices are demonstrably not equal when money can buy votes and influence as easily as it does today. Perhaps we underestimate the degree to which the most powerful in our society pay "lip service" to the importance of democracy while covertly dreading it and, in some cases, taking active steps to undermine it. Can we be genuine in our support for democracy? How willing are we to sacrifice in order to defend it? And what kinds of structural reforms would we be willing to entertain in order to do so?

As individuals, we all have our own idiosyncratic hierarchy of values. In addition, the groups to which we belong adhere to their own, which no doubt intersect with our own to a large extent. However, as discussed previously, a democracy is necessarily based on a set of *shared values*. Despite all of our differences and our extremely polarized environment, can we arrive at an agreed-upon set of common values? The only way our democracy can survive is if within this set of shared values a clear and unambiguous imperative for democracy falls consistently at or near the zenith, the top of the pyramid that represents our collective hierarchy of values.

While often harrowing, as with any problem, identifying it and recognizing its magnitude are the first steps. Only then might we begin to consider viable solutions together. As the reader is surely aware of by now, if you have made it this far in the book, my choices are clear: I vote for a renewed and vigorous democracy that guarantees a voice for all citizens; a clear separation between church and state in all civic arenas; a restoration of meaningful public discussion anchored in objective facts; and an openness to collectively enact much-needed reforms to our civic culture, governing structures, and social policies. If we can agree on those premises as a starting point (which I believe most Americans can, as corroborated by the *Hidden Tribes* report, especially the exhausted majority), then I offer in the following my thoughts on how the seventy-seven percent of Americans—those who believe our differences are not so great that we cannot come together—can move forward.[7]

Recommitting to Our Democratic Form of Government

One of the first steps for restoring our democracy must be to develop and foster a newfound appreciation for public service and reinforce mechanisms to shield our public institutions from the political interference that they have been at the mercy of in recent years. Durable and resilient American institutions that hold the accumulation of our historical knowledge and expertise are hallmarks of our democracy, and it is only through the robustness of these institutions that we can survive the corrosive effects of incompetent or corrupt politicians.

Over the course of his presidency, Trump recurrently demonstrated his solipsistic willingness to tear down these institutions and foster cynicism about public service. Some of our public institutions, notably parts of the Justice Department, succumbed. Fortunately, many others, such as the Postal Service, seem to have survived the onslaught with minimal damage (perhaps due to the sanctity of the memory of our first postmaster general). Nonetheless, our public institutions need to be fortified so trust in them can be earned anew.

It is for these reasons that Danielle Allen believes that creating a more inclusive and tolerant version of our *democracy* must be the number one priority (as discussed in a previous chapter). The committee that she has chaired for the American Academy of Arts and Sciences, The Commission on the Practice of Democratic Citizenship, has made an enormous contribution through its comprehensive study, *Our Common Purpose: Reinventing American Democracy for the 21st Century.* This pivotal work is foundational and far-reaching, comprising clear and concrete reparative prescriptions on what needs to be done, delineating the essential requirements to revitalize our democracy.

What was surprising for me as I read through this report was just how many practical solutions do in fact exist. The only salient question is whether we as a nation will muster the collective political resolve to embark on their pursuit. Based on the views of our Founders illustrated in Part I of this book, I believe the recommendations in this recent study fall wholeheartedly within the tradition of the civic principles to which they devoted most of their lives—that is, after all, precisely why they made the Constitution malleable. As discussed previously, our Founders did not view our nation's charter as rigid dogma.

But in our current political climate, marshaling the broad public support required to implement these meaningful changes will be challenging. And even if we were all to embrace the thrust of the ideas and programs described, achieving measurable improvement will be a long-term endeavor.

Commencing on this path is necessary but not sufficient. We also need to repair our civic culture. As stated in the commission's report:

> Healthy constitutional democracy depends on a virtuous cycle in which responsive political institutions foster a healthy civic culture of participation and responsibility, while a healthy civic culture—a combination of values, norms, and narratives—keeps our political institutions responsive and inclusive. Institutions and culture intersect in the realm of civil society.[8]

Thus, alongside structural and institutional changes, a renewed emphasis on instilling civic responsibility is a prerequisite for ensuring the sustainability of any gains realized. Only by rejuvenating an authentic enthusiasm for democratic ideals among a new generation of Americans can we nourish and sustain the principles for which so many in previous generations have lost their lives. A key jumping-off point for this endeavor is to reinject civic education into curricula at all levels of education (more details on this later).

In addition to building and repairing, we also need to remove some of the formidable obstacles that impede our democratic norms today. We need to better curate and moderate our political discourse and resist the insidious provocations of cable news, talk radio, and social media. Furthermore, we should no longer tolerate the creation and propagation of evil caricatures of those with opposing points of view; a democracy prescribes a responsibility to empathetically understand and appreciate opposing points of view. We must honor that prescription.

Moreover, if the private sector cannot provide the required infrastructure for healthy debate, if it insists on a business model that is reliant on shock value and clickbait at the expense and neglect of truth and accuracy, then the public sector must intervene. From an economic perspective, healthy and constructive debate in the public sphere is a public good. As such, it provides tangible and accruing benefits beyond the investment capacity or purview of any individual firm. Therefore, a new interstate digital highway system with fair and equal access to a broad range of views on the political spectrum warrants public investment.

Finally, threats to democracy such as extremist views on both the left and right must be exposed for what they are: doctrines where beliefs are absolute and go unquestioned, where stances become nonnegotiable. Why do we allow the extreme ends of the partisan spectrum to dominate our political debate when they are the least interested in finding common ground? Our country already accommodates innumerable settings where zealous proponents can express their shared views comfortably surrounded by their fellow believers, ranging from organized religions to smaller groups and cults, which taken together already occupy a hefty space in American society. Let us leave questions involving dogmatic faith to those domains. The public civic domain should have no use for them and should not tolerate such unbending doctrine. Just as individuals have the right to express their beliefs, however existential and constituent of their identity, other citizens have the right to be free from such beliefs and pursue their own unique brands of happiness, so long as they do not infringe on the freedom and liberty of fellow citizens. As always within a social contract, multiple and distinct rights must be balanced, as in Jefferson's famous example: "In America, there must not only be freedom *of* religion, but freedom *from* religion."[9]

Another aspect at the heart of the crisis in our democracy today is a notable lack of consensus on how we define equality in theory and apply it in practice. As we saw previously, one aspect of the Radical Enlightenment view of equality is the principle that all are equal *under* the law and equally *subject* to the law. Fortunately, this has become one of our most basic and prized national creeds. However, as demonstrated throughout this book, this basic tenet has been violated repeatedly throughout our history. If we selectively permit different laws to apply to different classes and races of people, we can never hope to achieve a democratic society in the Radical Enlightenment tradition.

In addition to fairness before the law, the Radical Enlightenment concept of equality also pertains to equal voice in civic affairs. Once again, in addition to the enforcement of voting rights, providing broader access to participation in public affairs at federal, state, and local levels needs to become a higher priority. In Danielle Allen's work, she expounds on the definition of equality with great clarity and detail. Her definition of equality includes "egalitarian approaches to the development of collective intelligence, egalitarian practices of reciprocity, and equality entailed in sharing ownership of public life and in co-creating our common world."[10] Unless and until we build broad consensus on exactly what equality implies, we are unlikely to surmount our impasse. In addition, Allen contends that those who claim that freedom and equality are contraindicated, that they are virtues in mutual competition, are relying on specious arguments.

> Political philosophers have generated the view that equality and freedom are necessarily in tension with each other. As a public, we have swallowed this argument whole. We think we are required to choose between freedom and equality. Our choice in recent years has tipped toward freedom. [But in fact], equality has precedence over freedom; only on the basis of equality can freedom be securely achieved.[11]

Whether we embrace Allen's notion of equality as a prerequisite for freedom or not, we should not be forced to choose between the two. Our republic was founded precisely on the ability to guarantee its citizens both equality and freedom.

Who Gets a Seat at the Table

A key second order of business is agreeing on a commonly accepted definition of "who is us?" and a consensus regarding transparent rules and processes for expanding the group. One would think that the starting point for demarcating who is included would be all citizens, but as evidenced by the increasing deployment of voter suppression techniques, we cannot take this for granted—it must be continually reaffirmed that all citizens are entitled to a seat.

The more intractable issue is the status of the millions of undocumented Americans. Somehow, because this issue is so contentious, our elected leaders abdicate and let the problem grow. But inaction is also a decision, and one with horrible consequences. Lost tax revenue and magnified incentives for illicit activities are minimal compared to the strife propagated on millions of people forced to live in the shadows. By returning to the 2013 Gang of Eight agreement (that reached agreement in the Senate but expired before being taken up by the House), we can effectively establish a jumping-off point for negotiations as President Biden has recently begun to do.

From a long-term perspective, if global birth trends continue, we will undoubtedly encounter pressure for a higher level of immigration from the south. In order to develop coherent and balanced immigration policies, we must accept that open borders would not only be unmanageable and promote chaos, but might decimate American culture, itself a unique blend of or an umbrella encompassing many cultures. Unlimited or forced migration from South and Central America to the United States, just as from Africa and the Middle East to Europe, would be destabilizing and provoke racist views and nativist fears.

The empirical evidence demonstrates that when demographic change happens too rapidly, it becomes perceived more and more as a zero-sum proposition, with undue pressure foisted upon local communities. It is in fact when excessively rapid change or excessive demographic change is imposed upon a society that the seeds of prejudicial beliefs are sown and ultimately allow racism to flourish most rapidly. Abundant evidence supports this claim such as the study cited here:

> Past research has emphasized two critical economic concerns that appear to generate anti-immigrant sentiment among native citizens: concerns about labor market competition and concerns about the fiscal burden on public services.[12]

Clearly, concerns such as these lend support to a more measured approach to immigration accompanied by the fostering of a culture of respect and appreciation of individual identities. Whether efforts at immigrant assimilation result in the proverbial "melting pot," or more closely resemble a "salad bowl," the combined characteristics of many diverse and individual cultures make our country unique.[13] While few truly multicultural societies exist, the American experiment has achieved some manifold successes, alongside, of course, its disappointing and abject failures.

Outside of the immigration arena, many citizens born or naturalized in the United States continue to be denied a voice in so many aspects of our public dialogue and civic affairs. Populations subject to select disenfranchisement remain relegated to lesser political standing—African Americans and Indigenous people are the most obvious examples. It should not be surprising that the most egregious oversights in the protection of unalienable rights will require the most attention to redress and the deepest wounds the most time to heal.

Once we decide who gets to sit at the table, we have to guarantee voting rights as a fundamental right of all citizenry. After all, elections are democracy's cornerstone. The more recent trend of tolerating and even inviting foreign interference in our elections presents an existential threat and needs to be unequivocally and unwaveringly rooted out. In addition, sowing doubt about the validity of our free and fair elections with the political goal of overturning the will of the people is reprehensible. The precedents set by Trump on both of these accounts are as destructive and disgraceful as they are seditious. The fact that so many Republicans on the Hill let him act with impunity and fail to hold him accountable for inciting an insurrection against our democracy is indicative of the degree to which the current Republican leadership is complicit in his reprobate activities.[14]

However, putting aside these existential threats to our democracy, securing voting rights *within* the United States should be eminently achievable (provided that the will is there). Unfortunately, today, as in many prior eras in our country, voter suppression seems to be the new normal. We need to stop such deplorable practices. But in addition, the petty tactics of election cheating must be rooted out.

Gerrymandering, the practice of engineering voting districts by the party in power to perpetuate their control via irregular district structures, should be prohibited. Instead, districts should be delimited based on measuring population in concentric circles from the county seat or largest town. Cleansing voter rolls or purging voters off rolls should be prohibited in every state, as should voter ID laws. Voter intimidation is also unacceptable and needs to be ruthlessly eradicated. As Vann Newkirk wrote in *The Atlantic*, "From the days of Jim Crow election rigging on, the specter of voter fraud has always been cover for disenfranchisement. American history is brimming with examples of strong-arm tactics used during elections."[15]

Finally, voting should be a requirement of citizenship (like jury duty), and exercising the vote must be less onerous. A country that can send humans to the moon can certainly implement safe, secure, and trouble-free methods for all to cast a ballot. Solutions are already quite evident, for example, enacting a federally mandated election week (not day), within which every citizen should be entitled to choose a one-day holiday to go vote.

Campaign Advertising Reform

Advertising in the private sector is quite heavily regulated, as it should be based on the principle that if information is not evenly available in the marketplace, consumers cannot make educated choices. In many areas, such as prescription drugs and financial products, since consumers cannot possibly have all the required information, they rely on government protections, lest advertisers make misleading or false claims.

In one of my recent business roles, I served as CEO of a leading brand of acne products that advertises extensively in all forms of media, including television (you have most likely seen these ads). Every single advertisement for this product must go through a rigorous review process to ensure that all claims are substantiated (under the regulatory purview of the FDA [Food and Drug Administration]) and to ensure consumer fairness and transparency in marketing offers (under the regulatory purview of the FTC [Federal Trade Commission]). Consumers can rest assured that deceptive advertising is policed by the appropriate federal agencies.

Yet, in the marketplace of ideas, the consumer is offered no such protection. Campaign advertisements are permitted to deceive consumers, and in fact this seems to be their express purpose today. Political campaign ads not only stretch the truth to excessive degrees, but they routinely present distorted facts and devious lies and regularly malign and attack the character of opposing candidates. These political advertisements are allowed to make claims that would never be permitted in the private sector, all based on one overriding justification—namely, that according to our constitutional heritage, political speech is the most protected type of free speech and is thereby associated with an extremely high hurdle safeguarding against its infringement.

Since we essentially cannot regulate the content of political advertising without sacrificing this most hallowed protection, all political advertising on television and social media platforms should be prohibited entirely. Candidates should be permitted to advertise as much as they desire but obliged to make their case with the written word, using long-form media like print, mail, or email that voters can read at their discretion (of course with consumer opt-out rights).

The recent Supreme Court decision in Citizens United, which extends the protection of free speech to corporate speech, is not only perpetuating the uncontrolled power of the one-percent elite, but is flawed in its logic.[16] That legal jurisprudence in the United States has granted express liberties to corporations based on their inclusion in the definition of "person" defies reason. Corporations are legal structures, societal fabrications for the specific tax and liability benefits they convey; that they should be guaranteed an unalienable right such as freedom of speech takes absurdity to new levels. Corporate speech is not protected by the Constitution since corporations are not people, and thus cannot be citizens.

If these straightforward changes cannot be adopted, the only other alternative is to prohibit all political advertising altogether and extend the public funding of elections.

Structural Changes

In an earlier chapter of this book, we explored how during the period of the Second Great Awakening, Americans adopted a revisionist view of the nation's founding. The image that captured the imagination of many Americans at this time was one of Moses (in the form of George Washington) handing down the tablets of the Constitution from God to the newly established American citizenry.

But cloaking the Constitution under a veil of religious zeal is fully antagonistic to the Founders' explicit intentions precisely because it conveys the sense that the Constitution is sacred and unassailable. This is perfectly antithetical to the goal of the Framers, who were prescient in understanding that its design could not possibly envision all future scenarios and thus expressly designed our nation's charter to be pliable and malleable. Over the course of our history, we have successfully amended the Constitution twenty-seven times, along with a few failed attempts (most notably, the ERA in 1979 and 1982). However, in recent decades, the idea that our Constitution is literally "set in stone" has fossilized. This trend is quite dangerous—structures that are not pliable or flexible usually break completely under pressure.

Whether through constitutional amendments or acts of Congress, structural changes are needed if our American experiment is to endure. In today's political gridlock with our do-nothing Congress, many believe meaningful structural change is simply not possible.

Nonetheless, I am optimistic about the potential for major democratic reform. We have accomplished this in the not-so-distant-past: The Progressive Era, FDR's New Deal, and LBJ's domestic agenda are three examples.

Numerous proposals have been advanced regarding specific structural changes that are most pressing. The Commission on the Practice of Democratic Citizenship from the American Academy of Arts and Sciences has put forth over twenty-five concrete recommendations that include the use of ranked-choice voting, enlarging the House of Representatives and the Electoral College to make them more representative of the nation's population, and regulating campaign finance, along with many other proposals.[17]

In Lee Drutman's recent book *Breaking the Two-Party Doom Loop* (2020), the author makes a compelling case for the concrete changes he recommends. Some prime examples are enabling a multiple-party system and adopting ranked-choice voting and proportional elections, as many advanced democracies around the world have done.[18] The United States has relied on the two-party system for most of its history; third-party candidates have almost always been subjugated to the role of spoilers. Drutman's recommendations would allow multiple parties to compete and thereby inject a much more expansive set of viewpoints into the marketplace of ideas. Further, with the benefit of ranked-choice voting and proportional elections, these third-party candidates would make valuable contributions to this dialogue without serving as spoiler candidates. Both the Commission's and Drutman's (and many other) recent proposals merit serious consideration. To this list I will add a few of my own.

The Electoral College is a vestige of another era and must be eliminated. Presidents should be elected by popular vote. The justification for this has been made so frequently that I will not repeat it here. Instead, I refer the reader to John Dingell's suggestions, since before his recent death, he had served in Congress longer than any other living human being.[19]

Incidentally, one of Mr. Dingell's other recommendations is to abolish the Senate. For quite some time now, the Senate has failed to live up to its claim of being the greatest deliberative body in the world. Before the leadership of Mitch McConnell, I had personally thought that the Senate might once again be able to reclaim this mantle. Unfortunately, I fear the senator from Kentucky has done such extensive damage to the institution that this will no longer be possible. Nonetheless, I would not advocate giving up on the institution altogether, although the disgracefully abused filibuster must be eliminated.

One of the most important structural changes that we can adopt for congressional representatives and Supreme Court justices is *term limits*. Having had the fortune of leading large organizations, I have a good understanding of and appreciation for the domain of human capital development, at least in the private sector. I have been intricately involved not only in hiring and promoting (and less commonly but unfortunately, firing and laying off) many hundreds of people, but also in designing career paths for professionals across many diverse areas of expertise. This latter activity has fortunately allowed me to observe the skill-based training and leadership development of some extraordinary people.

As a result of these experiences, I can share one common practice in private sector professional development which assuredly translates into the realm of public service. Achieving competency in any given position usually requires surmounting a steep learning curve—sometimes this can take a few years. But on the other end of the spectrum, remaining too long in any one role is a recipe for complacency and stagnation. In the private sector we often abide by the following guideline: As soon as one feels comfortable or achieves excellence in one's current position, it is most likely time for a new challenge, a chance to do something else. In many such cases, a promotion is in order with increasing responsibility. But just as often, pursuing endeavors in a different area altogether can be equally career rejuvenating.

I believe the same applies in the legislative and judicial arenas. One common argument against term limits for elected officials is that they would curb the accumulation of longer-term expertise in legislators. Along these lines, detractors of term limits point out that some of the best legislation has emerged from several of the longest-serving representatives and senators. No doubt, there is some truth to this. The learning curve to become an effective legislator probably takes a few years.

But at the same time, too many legislators have a firm lock on their voting districts and become exceedingly comfortable, smug, and overwhelmingly complacent. Many have simply stayed too long. A senator should be limited to two six-year terms and a House representative to six two-year terms, thus giving both a cumulative limit of twelve years of service. With these term limits (which are just one suggestion; other lengths may prove more optimal), legislators in both houses will have up to twelve years to get really good at their jobs. If any given legislator cannot learn the tricks of the trade to become extremely effective based on that time frame, he or she is probably the wrong person for the job.

To some degree, Congress is dominated by self-dealing incumbents due to gerrymandering. But even if gerrymandering were remedied, excessively long periods of service in Congress are associated with stifling political entrenchment and a tendency toward increased corruption. Thus, while there are indeed benefits in having more experienced legislators, such benefits are far outweighed by the attendant costs. Furthermore, the amount of time and money elected leaders on the Hill spend on their own reelection campaigns (instead of doing productive legislative work) is, by itself, a good enough argument for adopting term limits.

Given the nearly unrestricted power of the Supreme Court, lifetime court appointments are as unjust to future generations as hereditary rule would be in the executive branch. Supreme Court justices should have term limits of twenty years of service on the bench, after which time they can either retire or return to a lower court.

New American Meritocracy Must Start with Equality of Opportunity

One of the additional aspects of equality that the Radical Enlightenment thinkers advanced, contrary to their Moderate Enlightenment counterparts, was the idea of equality of access to opportunity. This concept is the foundation of our framework of meritocracy explored in the previous chapter.

American individualism and entrepreneurial spirit can be sustained and even strengthened via the meritocratic model, but we must recognize that our current meritocracy is largely broken. Conversely, pursuing a more drastic equality-of-outcomes-based agenda is, I believe, antithetical to American society. The same uniquely American ethos of entrepreneurship and individual achievement that fueled our drive for economic expansion and innovation in the nation's first centuries is still present today. Yet at the same time, it is inarguable that there are excessive structural inequalities of opportunity in our system that have in recent decades grown overpowering and are beyond restraint. Over time, a genuine meritocracy needs to progressively reduce structural inequalities. Instead, over the last forty to fifty years, we have allowed them to balloon enormously and become cumulatively entrenched.

Often, a measure of the progressiveness of a society is represented by the height at which it sets the bar for providing equality of access to opportunity. In recent decades in America, this bar has fallen to new depths, which is regrettable but also reversible through public policy. Addressing these inequalities of opportunity will require both predistributive endeavors, such as more even access to quality education from the earliest levels, and redistributive programs, including a more progressive taxation system and other methods of leveling the playing field. The fact that complete equality of opportunity is never achievable does not obviate the need or the societal responsibility to mark concrete progress toward chipping away at the effects of the immutable consequences of the "birth lottery."

The task of fixing our meritocracy seems Herculean, and expertise is required in so many domains in order to succeed that it is indeed a huge undertaking. I would argue that two important places to begin, the areas that need the most focus and require renewed commitments, are education, specifically civic education, and redistributive justice through a return to progressive taxation.

A constitutional democracy requires its citizens to develop the "knowledge, skills and habits that allow them to participate fully in the democratic process."[20] Indubitably, access to education has become so dramatically unequal in the United States that no conceivable sense of Rawlsian "equality of opportunity" is close to being achieved. There are concrete methods of addressing this, and the supporting literature is abundant. Initial steps including the progressive taxation and redistribution of the massive amount of "excess" educational inheritance of the moneyed elite are certainly viable. Raising the quality of all levels of education and subsidizing access for the bottom half, for example, is eminently feasible, provided society has the will to do it.

The availability of free education, or lack thereof, at all levels from pre-K through university is in no way predestined in any society. The Radical Enlightenment's argument that access to quality education is a "right" in a democratic society that depends on participation from an educated citizenry is compelling. It is the fundamental means by which we create the conditions for genuine equality. As discussed in the first part of this book, one of the greatest champions of the criticality of education in the modern republic was Condorcet. One of his greatest contributions to the Radical Enlightenment was his design of a comprehensive education agenda, which he stipulated be afforded equally to all citizens (even the poorest). Condorcet's prescience in this regard also makes him the embodiment of the very notion of meritocracy itself.

But the problem in education is not only one of access; as Condorcet also instructed us, the constituent substance of education needs to be based on Enlightenment principles of empirical science and rationalism and provide the average citizens with the tools they need to be effective participants in a democracy. Based on Condorcet's criteria, our contemporary goals of education need to be reassessed. We need to build a broader consensus around the identification of educational objectives, encompassing both multidisciplinary expert (i.e. pedagogic) and parental points of view. Inarguably, there are multiple and often conflicting goals within any proposed or adopted hierarchy of educational needs. Nonetheless, a society that aspires to a democratic form of government requires a civically oriented approach to education. This is not about just adding one civics class to the curriculum. It would most likely require a more thorough reorientation of the educational agenda, including the development of analytical tools in the soft sciences; a rejuvenation of the study of language arts, both written and oral communications; and more in-depth exploration of what we used to call "social studies."

In short, our educational framework must more systematically foster the skills of conducting discriminating analysis of multifaceted issues and constructing logical and persuasive arguments based on impartial data. Our current focus on STEM (science, technology, engineering, and math) education, vocational training and skill development, and preparation for individual economic success may have crowded out these other critical parts of the education agenda that a democracy demands.

Professor Danielle Allen, drawing on the work of the philosopher Hannah Arendt, provides a useful framework for thinking about this hierarchy of goals in the educational arena. Her framework includes:

1. Prepare ourselves for breadwinning work

2. Prepare ourselves for civic and political engagement

3. Prepare ourselves for creative self-expression and world-making

4. Prepare ourselves for rewarding relationships in spaces of intimacy and leisure[21]

Within this framework, one which is manifestly in the Radical Enlightenment tradition of Condorcet, the first two goals have strong social justification, while the latter two pertain more (although not entirely) to rewards for the individual. The intense focus in recent decades on the STEM educational approach indicates that we currently place priority on the first of these. Perhaps this is wise. But arguably, in a well-functioning democracy, the second is just as vital. Without a ubiquitous participatory readiness, power will unavoidably accrue to a narrow slice of the wealthy and/or able. Defining both the substance and the methods for achieving the second goal will undoubtedly require a significant commitment. A renewed dedication to critical analysis, language empowerment, and the humanities in general will likely offer a starting point.

The complexity of addressing both the access and substance sides of our educational crisis lies *less* in identifying and engaging the required expertise, and *more* with our lack of meaningful political determination to demand action. Why as a society do we so appreciably undervalue this undertaking relative to other pursuits? This is particularly damaging to those children and young adults for whom the educational inheritance of the wealthy elite remains inaccessible.

The French economist Thomas Piketty's book *Capital in the Twenty-First Century* (2014) is often quoted on this topic: "Historical experience suggests that the principal mechanism for convergence [of incomes] at the international as well as domestic level is the diffusion of knowledge."[22] Further, the "political competitiveness that has historically flowed from education is itself a force for big egalitarian reforms in other domains, most importantly the economic and the social."[23] Education and equality are inextricably linked; if we truly value the latter (as we say we do), we had better invest in the former.

There is broad existing consensus that investments in education yield superb returns. Arguably, one of the greatest investment returns of any government program in the history of our country, which led to decades of prosperity, was the post–World War II G.I. Bill that provided educational benefits to millions of veterans. For many veterans, this program facilitated postwar integration back into society at large and then assisted many in pursuing the education requisites for a purposeful and meaningful life, allowing these veterans to support their families for a generation. Yet somehow, less than a century removed from this astonishing validation, as a society we continually abdicate our responsibility for judiciously managing educational investments and maximizing their returns at a societal level.

On examination, this presents a quite perplexing conundrum: How is it that the financial planning industry, a colossal part of our overall economy (approximately $58 billion managing some $89 trillion in assets in the United States alone) attracts the highest level of talent and status? Of course, it does so based on an ever-soaring level of consumer demand. Consumers, especially wealthy consumers, expend a magnificent amount of energy, time, and money maximizing the return on their own individual financial assets. Further, as individuals, the amount of time, energy, and money we spend on such activities most likely correlates closely with how much wealth we have.

In contrast, the development of the *collective human talent* of our society merits much less attention. Yes, many consumers carefully oversee the education of the members of their own household, but most pay less attention to our educational capacities or performance at a more aggregate community or societal level.

Further, the entire educational structure, at every level, from teachers and administrators to academic experts in pedagogy and human development, do not accrue anywhere near the level of status and economic reward in contemporary society as matched to those who manage financial capital. Assuredly, our collective human capital represents a much greater and more endurable asset than our financial wealth. But individually, we meticulously manage our financial wealth—we plant, we sow, we reap. Yet in contrast, we seem to value our collective human capital far less dearly, and consequently, too often and tragically allow its field to lay fallow.

Once again, in a classical economic sense, the development of our *collective* human capital is a public good, meaning returns on its investment not only accrue to the individual but spill over to society as a whole. Like all public goods, left alone, this economic dynamic results in structural underinvestment. As our Radical Enlightenment ancestors understood, it is precisely in this context that the government initiated through our social contract needs to step up to the plate.

In addition to education, another potential path to provide better equality of opportunity may be found in programs of government-sponsored asset ownership. Recently, reformist economic think tanks have been exploring the idea of "baby bonds."[24]

The concept involves giving every child a progressively scaled investment account with a return guaranteed by the government. The funds associated with these programs are locked up until adulthood when they can be voluntarily withdrawn and used for a "clearly defined asset enhancing activity, like financing a debt-free education, purchasing a business, or buying a home."[25]

Lynn Parramore from the Institute for New Economic Thinking suggests that a program providing an average $20,000 baby bond to every eligible child might cost the government around $80–100 billion a year. (The bonds would be progressively scaled so that a child born to a wealthy family might not be eligible, while a child born to an upper-class family might receive a $5,000 baby bond, a working-class family a $35,000 bond, and a poor child upward of $50,000.) If $80–100 billion sounds like an enormous annual investment, by way of comparison, each year the federal government spends approximately $720 billion on defense and $400 billion on interest on the national debt.

This type of baby bond program might provide a politically achievable means to break down structural inequalities and close the racial wealth gap, in combination with other reforms. Generally, ideas for increasing asset ownership receive support from both sides of the aisle since they fit well with conservatives' stated goals of increasing individuals' personal ownership and autonomy. Furthermore, the concept is thoroughly consistent with the Rawlsian ideal of giving everybody an equal leg up from the start of their lives, and it is justified within a Radical Enlightenment framework. (Incidentally, in 1797, Paine wrote a pamphlet, *Agrarian Justice*, which essentially called for universal capital grants to all citizens that they could use when they came of age, a precursor to proposals of asset-based egalitarianism that have proliferated since.)[26] Moreover, other proposals for widening asset ownership within the economy (which can entice broader democratic participation) include employee stock ownership plans and other visions of cooperative ownership in firms.

By abandoning the progressive tax structure of prior generations, we Americans are undermining our own meritocracy. Political leaders of both parties have tolerated tremendous estate tax and income tax loopholes for the affluent. By rendering calls to increase taxes akin to political suicide in the Grover Norquist era of the Republican Party, the federal government has over the last forty years dramatically abandoned the principle of progressiveness in our tax system.

But loopholes in estate taxes and low marginal tax rates for the wealthy and corporations are unjust from two distinct perspectives. First, proportionately, the wealthy are paying nowhere near their fair share for all of the public goods and services that have provided the foundational pillars upon which they built their success. In essence, the wealthy are depending upon (and mooching off) the less wealthy taxpayers to subsidize their own springboards for achievement. Second, beyond more equitably sharing the burden for public goods and services, there is a moral responsibility for redistribution when inequalities of well-being across different strata of society have become as extreme as they are today. The well-being of society requires such lest we abandon the social contract and return to Hobbes's "war of all against all—*bellum omnium contra omnes*."

In the final analysis, fixing our meritocracy will likely require efforts in three main areas: predistributive structural changes such as a larger and more egalitarian investment in education, new innovative programs promoting broader access to asset ownership, and redistributive policies such as a more progressive taxation system.

*   *   *

Over the course of this book, we have seen how philosophies associated with distinct and divergent Enlightenment schools have vied for prominence in the American political, economic, and social landscape over the course of our 250-year history. But even as they vigorously competed, both Moderate and Radical Enlightenment schools of thought have made prominent contributions to American society and must share credit for America's greatest successes.

Looking back over this history, we have seen how Moderate Enlightenment principles played an important role in building the proficiencies required to shape our republic. The enduring influence of these ideals is manifest in our proclivity to rely on elite meritocratic institutions and competition for authoritative power, usually justified by the need for expertise and proficiency in the civic sphere. The formulation and implementation of public policy in a pluralistic liberal democracy can be quite complicated, and public leadership requires a broad mix of well-refined analytic and communication skills. Hamilton was well advised in tapping *the most talented* to build from scratch the institutions needed in a blossoming nation. In light of the intial COVID-19 response fiasco, perhaps as a society, we will appreciate anew how vital competency in government truly is.

At the same time, however, the Radical Enlightenment's principles of democratic egalitarianism, which assert that equal access and participation are fundamental to democracy, have been continually present in the American spirit. Its rejection of elitism and aspiration to broaden participation in government has put the Radical Enlightenment tradition into recurring conflict with Moderate Enlightenment ideas.

But we must appreciate that both Moderate and Radical Enlightenment impulses can and do contribute to the contemporary social contract. As Chris Hayes has written, "So while the history of enfranchisement moves steadily—if slowly—in the direction of inclusion, the social contract must also accommodate the fact that management of affairs of state and market grow evermore complex and specialized. The result is a cycle of populism, antielite revolt, and oligarchic retrenchment, with each new ruling elite displacing its predecessor."[27] It is precisely the competition between Radical and Moderate Enlightenment ideals that is at the root of this oscillation.

As we have seen, further obfuscating the competing ideals of the Radical and Moderate Enlightenment are Counter-Enlightenment forces that have injected religious belief and spiritual instincts into debates about the relationship between government and citizens and the responsibilities of each. Piety, faith, and spirituality in their various forms are indispensable parts of the lives of most Americans. But at the same time, if any single religious or spiritual authority intrudes, dictates, or overly influences our governing practices or structures, we risk compromising the very freedom and liberty upon which our republic is based.

A 21st-century democracy needs to balance the Moderate and Radical Enlightenment impulses, reconciling both the need for the broad participatory voices of the heterogeneous many *and* the required expertise of the most capable. My wish for the future of our democracy is that it attains a more effective formula that can productively incorporate both of these impulses, while maintaining civic autonomy from Counter-Enlightenment forces.

*   *   *

Since our journey began with the Enlightenment, and since the thrust of my argument throughout this book has been that only by embracing Enlightenment principles can we build a civilized, progressive, and tolerant society, it seems fitting that we should end by returning to the Enlightenment.

In the Declaration of Independence, Jefferson wrote: "Let facts be submitted to a candid world." For Jefferson and the enlightened thinkers of his age, discovering truth was dependent on empirical observation, rational argument, and thoughtful reflection. Based on these principles, political discourse spanned an enormous variety of opposing points of view. As assuredly as we can have objective facts, as a pluralistic society we can have different opinions. We can respectfully disagree, for instance, on the policy ideas and structural reforms I have proposed in this chapter. Like Enlightenment thinkers of the 18th century, we can all fall on disparate points in the Radical–Moderate Enlightenment spectrum (or in today's political vernacular the liberal–conservative spectrum). A healthy liberal democracy can encompass a moderate Alexander Hamilton alongside a radical Thomas Paine.

As reviewed previously, in the post–Revolutionary Era, the Federalists, inspired by Moderate Enlightenment ideas, and the Jeffersonian Republicans, inspired by those of the Radical Enlightenment, conducted vicious debates over their respective interpretations of the American Revolution. All through the late 1780s and the entire decade of the 1790s, both sides scornfully admonished their rivals, with the heat rising to levels perhaps similar to those of today. The animosity between Hamilton and Jefferson was exceptionally rancorous. Jefferson remained ever faithful to his vision of diffuse governing power and was convinced that Hamilton was embroiled in Machiavellian conspiracies, plotting to increase the nation's debt to justify expanding federal power over the entire country. As the Federalists consolidated power, the Republicans remained suspicious of their every move. Further, when Jefferson prevailed for the presidency over Adams in 1800, Jefferson was committed to restoring the Spirit of '76 that he was convinced the Federalists had utterly betrayed.

For Jefferson, the central achievement of the Revolutionary Era was the Declaration of Independence and the vitality of the liberty, freedom, and equality it had released. For the realist Adams, social equality was never the goal of the Revolution; for Adams, Jefferson's idealist vision was but a naïve illusion. For Adams, the "outstanding achievement of the revolutionary generation had been the realistic recognition of the need for limits as well as liberation."[28] Adams believed the genius of the American movement for independence was to harness its energy for the creation of an enduring republic founded on reasonable compromises on the part of the populace with political power. As Ellis describes, "The Jeffersonian formulation rendered all political history into a moral clash between benevolent popular majorities and despotic elites . . . [while] the core of the Adams position was that elites had always been and always would be a permanent fixture in society."[29]

But much later in their lives, with the benefit of time and perspective, Adams and Jefferson developed a cordial and earnest correspondence that reveals how much respect each had developed for his former rival. Beginning in 1812 up through their deaths, they revisited some of their earlier views and motivations and seemingly came to better appreciate the opposing point of view. Was the fact that they both died on the same day, our nation's birthday, July 4, 1826, not a mere coincidence but some providential sign that both perspectives were fittingly interwoven in the American experiment?

We know definitively that Adams and Jefferson agreed upon one thing: A republic cannot exist without the Enlightenment principles of empirical observation and rational debate. If we cannot have objective fact, if we deny the existence of unbiased scientific truth, the American experiment is doomed. As discussed previously, forging a set of common values among a diverse citizenry is an arduous enough endeavor in itself, requiring broad and deep commitment. If we add to this task the demand to reconcile our values with sets of "alternative facts," the impediments to democracy reach a breaking point and inexorably become too much to overcome.

In facing our most pressing problems, the power of free expression infuses the marketplace with a broad set of ideas, which invariably leads to superior solutions. And not only is society made stronger by grappling with rival ideas, but liberty of expression alone should be cherished in a world where so many do not have it. However, unless we as a society freshly embrace anew the pursuit of truth founded in inquiry and curiosity, data and science, our only hope for the future will surely lie exclusively in the divine and eternal salvation of a different realm. I sincerely hope that future generations commit to a revitalization of reason and truth consistent with our Enlightenment heritage and do not relinquish hopes for our secular world quite yet.

In the early 21st century , this question looms over us: How can we navigate our way out of America's current crisis? Throughout the course of history, societal change has occurred in complex ways, at various paces, and with different methods. For those of us seeking to improve our civic environment, it is challenging to determine what methods to adopt and what rate of change to hope for. Radical change sometimes requires razing and rebuilding structures and institutions from the ground up. However, much more often it would behoove us to acknowledge the astonishing amount of generational experience built into the institutions we currently have. Tearing them down indiscriminately is reckless and destructive. Activism has its place, principally when certain aspects of society seem rigid or resistant to change, or when the rules of the game become calcified over long periods of time. A prime example here is the repugnant institution of slavery, followed by the long and painful struggle that African Americans continue to endure in their justified quest for genuine equality.

Nonetheless, in today's discourse regarding the pace and method of change, both the extreme-left and extreme-right approaches are unacceptable and must be flatly rejected. The destruction propagated during the Trump Administration included the radicalization of many through the spread of lies, myths, and conspiracy theories. The effects of this catastrophe linger stubbornly in today's political discourse, even after Trump has vacated the White House, and may continue to do so for a generation. In four years of Trump's administration we have also witnessed an irresponsible assault that has caused permanent damage to a broad range of American institutions.

But those on the extreme left are also doing injury when they too hastily advocate tearing down some of those same institutions. The obsessive focus on political correctness on the left also needs to be recognized for the damage that it does to free and open discourse. I should be clear that the two extremes are not analogous, and in that respect it is a false equivalency to compare them. The extreme right has recklessly abandoned the pursuit of any semblance of truth in advancing its goals. Instead, it specializes in propagating preposterous conspiracies and frequently resorts to violent means to advance its goals. The extreme left has not done this, despite duplicitous attempts by the alt-right to project its own vicious behavior onto its opponents.

Yet the extreme left has been too quick to suppress or stifle opposing points of view by insisting on the safety afforded by political correctness. American political discourse needs to tolerate a broad range of views, but these views must be grounded in heuristic reality.

Unfortunately, "cancel culture" on both extremes abjures this formula. As Andrew Sullivan writes in *New York Magazine*:

> The left will increasingly tolerate nothing that gets in the way of what it calls "social justice," which far too often reduces individuals to their racial or class or gender identities rather than their merits, or character, or talents. The conservative approach to a multicultural and multiracial society is to keep our focus on the individual and do what's best to help every individual, regardless of their race, gender, or whatever, to be part of our shared liberal democratic inheritance. Conservatism is about enfolding the new into the old, sustaining a society's coherence and cohesion, while being extremely tough on particular injustices against particular individuals, vigilant about corruption, and anguished when the criminal justice system loses legitimacy, because of embedded racism.[30]

The accusation that Sullivan directs against the extreme left could just as easily be made against the far right. Nonetheless, the definition of conservatism that Sullivan describes seems overly generous today. It more closely resembles the conservatism of the Republican Party's exiles who now wander in the wilderness. It is undeniably not the conservatism propagated by the Republican Party in the age of Trump, which vigorously and sanctimoniously sustains the old against any incursion by the new.

But focusing on the extremes is itself part of the problem. Doing so creates the false impression that they are representative of the majority. As the research indicates, "Millions of Americans are going about their lives with absurdly inaccurate perceptions of each other."[31] As the *Hidden Tribes* report shows: "Widespread agreement [exists] on matters of principle, such as rejecting racism and discrimination . . . taking responsibility for vulnerable children and those fleeing conflict."[32] Most members of the exhausted majority support compromise. One of the most reliable remedies to heal our political discourse is person-to-person contact.

> People have this experience consistently when they meet others with different views in an environment that fosters listening and respectful engagement. Differences in core beliefs do not disappear, but these differences, which are constantly magnified on our screens, are placed into an entirely different perspective by person-to-person contact . . . [The participants in the study] finished those interviews with a sense of hope that our differences are much smaller than what we have in common.[33]

As individuals, we all have our own idiosyncratic hierarchy of values. Our in-groups have their own. Yet democracy itself requires a set of *shared values*. Despite all of our differences and our extremely polarized environment, can we arrive at an agreed-upon set of common values? Is there enough of an intersection in the collective Venn diagram of our individual hierarchies of values? The only way our democracy can survive is if democracy as a virtue consistently falls within the intersection of this collective set.

Our contemporary political debate is not lacking in passion. What is sorely lacking today is rational argument. Today, all sides seem to vent their fury incessantly. But we must remember that "the compromise and cooperation required by democracy grow less obtainable as partisan isolation and conflict increase . . . the more parts of our identities that we link with our parties, the more the success of our parties becomes more important than any other real policy outcomes."[34]

Our collective call to action is this: Resist adding to vehement provocations *in kind*; instead, *battle unreason with reason*.

ACKNOWLEDGMENTS

The idea for this book surfaced during the first year of the Trump presidency. At that time, because I was still occupied with leading a consumer products business, the early concept development was intermittent and greatly facilitated by friends, family, and professional colleagues with whom I was able to have engaging, if often distressing, discussions.

As I observed the administration's increasingly brazen assault on what I had assumed to be inviolable principles of balance of powers and well-established norms of presidential conduct, I was most distraught by two concurrent trends. First, the brashness and insolence of the president's statements and actions were escalating considerably faster than the proportionate rage in most Americans. On the contrary, citizens appeared to become progressively more inured to just how menacing and recurrent the barrage of presidential violations had become. Second, the obsequious and treacherous posture of many Republicans (outside of those who headed for the exit) portended a level of political enabling that was soon to become unprecedented.

I am indebted to Professor Jonathan Israel from the Institute for Advanced Study, Princeton, who encouraged me in my early drafts to continue this journey. In addition, Andrew Downey Orrick Professor of Philosophy at Yale, Stephen Darwell, served as an invaluable sounding board and provided constructive review of the inchoate premise and structure of what became *American Schism*. I am also grateful to

Sanford Goldberg—Chester D. Tripp Professor in the Humanities and professor of philosophy at Northwestern University, and professorial fellow at Arché Research Center, University of St. Andrews—who provided feedback on an early draft.

I owe my sincere thanks to several PhD candidates who were enormously helpful in uncovering promising avenues of investigation and providing research material and sources. Jonathan Nunez, a graduate student in history at Columbia University and London School of Economics, and David Lehrer were particularly supportive and provided countless valuable and constructive suggestions. Grant Klesier, also a PhD candidate at Columbia, provided additional suggestions. Additional early readers who provided valuable feedback on both structure and content include Stephen Power, Bill Strachan, and David Groff. I thank you all.

In addition, I am exceptionally indebted to my wonderful team at Greenleaf Books—they performed like a veritable dream team for a first-time author. Heather Stettler's meticulous copyediting and many suggestions refined *American Schism* enormously. The list of invaluable contributions includes Sheila Parr's design creativity, Erin Brown's editorial guidance, Emily Maulding's marketing savvy, Kristine Peyre-Ferry's distribution support, Justin Branch's encouragement, and Jen Glynn's capable project management. It certainly took a village to get to the finish line.

Finally, the support and encouragement from my family and friends ultimately empowered me to write *American Schism*. I am so blessed to have them in my life.

PERMISSIONS

Grateful acknowledgment is made to the following sources for permission to reproduce copyrighted material.

NOTES

Prologue
1. Packer, "The President Is Winning His War."
2. Two excellent and recent sources that discuss these trends are: Hawkins et al., *Hidden Tribes: A Study of America's Polarized Landscape* and Mason, *Uncivil Agreement: How Politics Became Our Identity.*
3. Mason, *Uncivil Agreement*, pp. 86–87.
4. Hawkins et al., *Hidden Tribes*, p. 4
5. Mason, *Uncivil Agreement*, p.101.

Chapter 1
1. Houston, *Literacy in Early Modern Europe*, pp. 1–8.
2. For a good example, see Beik, *Louis XIV and Absolutism.*

Chapter 2
1. Israel, *Revolutionary Ideas*, p. 696.
2. Burke, *Reflections on the Revolution in France*, p. 34.
3. Duignan, "Postmodernism | Definition, Doctrines, & Facts."
4. Drake, "Notes from English 258."
5. Gessen, *Surviving Autocracy*, p. 95.
6. See Bourke, *The History of Ethics*, for an overview.
7. The Greek Orthodox Church had its own dogma, as did the leading Protestant churches following the Reformation. Nonetheless, it was primarily the authority of the Roman Catholic Church that was questioned here.
8. Psillos and Curd, *The Routledge Companion*, pp. 129–138.

9. Spinoza, *Theological-Political Treatise*, Cambridge Texts series, p. 76.
10. Himmelfarb, *The Road to Modernity*.

Chapter 3
1. Israel, *The Enlightenment That Failed*, pp. 178–214.
2. Hobbes, *Leviathan*, Chapter 18, Part II.
3. Hobbes, Leviathan, Chapter 18, Part II.
4. Hobbes, Leviathan, p. 112.
5. See, for example, Apperley, "Hobbes on Democracy."

Chapter 4
1. Israel, *Revolutionary Ideas*, p. 621.
2. Israel, *Radical Enlightenment*, p. 259.
3. Israel, Radical Enlightenment, p. 260.
4. Israel, Radical Enlightenment, p. 267.
5. Israel, Radical Enlightenment, p. 10.
6. Israel, *The Enlightenment That Failed*, p. 59.
7. Israel, The Enlightenment That Failed, p. 125.
8. Israel, The Enlightenment That Failed, p. 96.
9. Israel, *Revolutionary Ideas*, p. 708.

Chapter 5
1. Bailyn, *The Ideological Origins*, pp. 17–51.
2. Israel, *The Enlightenment That Failed*, p. 195.
3. Montesquieu et al., *The Spirit of Laws*, p. 152.
4. Israel, *The Enlightenment That Failed*, p. 166.
5. Israel, The Enlightenment That Failed, p. 471.
6. Rousseau, *The Social Contract*, p. 70.
7. Rousseau, *Discourse on Political Economy*, pp. 76–78.
8. Israel, *Revolutionary Ideas*, p. 20.
9. Diderot (attributed), "Intolerance."
10. Israel, *The Enlightenment That Failed*, p. 160.
11. Israel, *Revolutionary Ideas*, pp. 656–657.
12. Israel, *Radical Enlightenment*, p. 78.
13. Israel, Radical Enlightenment, p. 78.
14. Israel, Radical Enlightenment, p. 178.
15. Israel, *The Enlightenment That Failed*, p. 179.

16. Hume from Essays and Treatises on Several Subjects (1758) as quoted in Bailyn, *The Ideological Origins*, p. 98.

17. From d'Holbach, *Système Social and Politique Naturelle*. Quoted in Israel, *The Enlightenment That Failed*, p. 186.

18. From d'Holbach, *Système Social and Politique Naturelle*. Quoted in Israel, *The Enlightenment That Failed* p. 181.

19. Israel, *The Enlightenment That Failed*, p. 197.

20. Israel, The Enlightenment That Failed, p. 180.

21. Israel, The Enlightenment That Failed, p. 187.

22. Israel, The Enlightenment That Failed, p. 189.

23. Lauren, *The Evolution of International Human Rights*, pp. 18–20.

24. Israel, *Revolutionary Ideas*, pp. 379–381. For a spectacular summary of the importance the Radical Enlightenment placed on education, please refer to Israel, *Revolutionary Ideas*, chapter 14.

25. Israel, Revolutionary Ideas, p. 620.

26. Israel, Revolutionary Ideas, p. 347.

27. Israel, Revolutionary Ideas, p. 349.

28. Israel, *The Enlightenment That Failed*, p. 265.

29. Israel, *Revolutionary Ideas*, p. 54.

30. Israel, Revolutionary Ideas, p. 478.

31. Helvétius, *De l'esprit*, p. 21.

32. Israel, *The Enlightenment That Failed*, p.195.

33. Israel, The Enlightenment That Failed, pp. 200–201.

34. Israel, The Enlightenment That Failed, p. 210. I am grateful to Jonathan Nunez from Columbia for pointing out that Thomas Moore, in *Utopia* (1516), made similar claims, quite earlier than d'Holbach.

35. Israel, *The Expanding Blaze*, p. 267.

Chapter 6

1. Israel, *The Expanding Blaze*, p. 4.

2. Bailyn, *The Ideological Origins*, p. 113.

3. Bailyn, The Ideological Origins, p. 136.

4. Israel, *The Expanding Blaze*, p. 28.

5. Wills, *Inventing America*, p. xvii.

6. Israel, *The Expanding Blaze*, p. 2.

7. Adams, John Quincy, "Letter to John Adams," in *Writings of John Quincy Adams*, vol. 1, pp. 40–43.

8. Bailyn, *The Ideological Origins*, p. 36.
9. Zinn, *A People's History*, pp. 64–69.
10. Adams, John Quincy, "Letters of Publicola," published in the Columbian Centinel 1791 in *Writings of John Quincy Adams*, specifically pp. 80–81 where Adams condemns Paine's idea of a new government.
11. From Becker, *The History of Political Parties in the Province of New York, 1760–1776*. Quoted in Gould, "The Question of Home Rule," p. 255.
12. Israel, *The Expanding Blaze*, p. 34.
13. Israel, The Expanding Blaze, p. 11.
14. John Jay's and John Dickinson's moderate stance is evidenced in these two sources: John Jay, "Federalist No. 64: The Powers of the Senate" in Drexler, *Research Guides: Federalist Papers*, and the "'Olive Branch' Petition" of the 1775 United States Continental Congress.
15. Israel, *The Expanding Blaze*, p. 212.
16. Bailyn, *The Ideological Origins*, p. 70.
17. From Wilentz, *Rise of American Democracy*. Quoted in Israel, *The Expanding Blaze*, p. 213.
18. McCullough, *John Adams*, p. 97.
19. Adams, "Thoughts on Government," vol. VI, p. 195.
20. The Gilder Lehrman Institute of American History, "John Adams on the abolition of slavery, 1801."
21. For an excellent overview of Madison's many contributions, see Steward, *Madison's Gift*.
22. Chernow, *Alexander Hamilton*, pp. 310–330.
23. Israel, *The Expanding Blaze*, 246.
24. Jefferson, *Notes on the State of Virginia*, pp. 209–214.
25. Jefferson, Notes on the State of Virginia, pp. 159–161.
26. Jefferson, Notes on the State of Virginia, pp. 117–118.
27. Ellis, *American Sphinx*, p. 151.
28. Israel, *The Expanding Blaze*, p. 246.
29. From Jefferson's writings in Kloppenberg, *Toward Democracy*, pp. 488–489.
30. Ellis, *American Sphinx*, p. 156.
31. Ellis, American Sphinx, p. 171.
32. Ellis, American Sphinx, p. 63.
33. Ellis, American Sphinx, p. 171.
34. Ellis, American Sphinx, p. 176.

35. The classic biography of Thomas Jefferson is *Jefferson and His Time*, by Dumas Malone, in six volumes, published over thirty-three years. Merrill D. Peterson is another very well-respected scholar on Jefferson. His *The Jefferson Image in the American Mind* (1960) won many awards and accolades. *American Sphinx* (1996) by Joseph J. Ellis is exceptional and gives a nuanced and textured view in a relatively concise tome. *Inventing America: Jefferson's Declaration of Independence* (1978) by Gary Wills is an outstanding book on Jefferson's writing of the Declaration. Other reputable sources include *Twilight at Monticello* (2008) by Alan Pell Crawford, Julian P. Boyd's *The Papers of Thomas Jefferson* (multiple volumes), and *The Hemingses of Monticello* (2008) by Annette Gordon-Reed.

36. Ellis, *American Sphinx*, p. xvi.

37. Israel, *The Expanding Blaze*, pp. 47–48.

38. Lepore, *These Truths*, p. 95.

39. Maier, *American Scripture*, p. 31.

40. Israel, *The Expanding Blaze*, p. 49.

41. Maier, *American Scripture*, p. 33.

42. Israel, *The Expanding Blaze*, p. 4.

43. Israel, The Expanding Blaze, p. 2.

44. Israel, The Expanding Blaze, p. 50.

45. Bailyn, *The Ideological Origins*, pp. 288–289.

46. Israel, *The Expanding Blaze*, p. 53.

47. Israel, The Expanding Blaze, p. 399.

48. Israel, The Expanding Blaze, p. 415.

49. Israel, The Expanding Blaze, p. 113.

50. Israel, The Expanding Blaze, p. 133.

51. Israel, The Expanding Blaze, p. 131.

52. Israel, The Expanding Blaze, p. 131.

53. Israel, The Expanding Blaze, p. 12.

Chapter 7

1. Israel, *The Expanding Blaze*, p. 281.

2. Israel, *Revolutionary Ideas*, p. 164.

3. Israel, *The Expanding Blaze*, p. 281.

4. Israel, *Revolutionary Ideas*, p. 624.

5. Israel, *The Expanding Blaze*, p. 328.

6. Ellis, *American Sphinx*, p. 155.

7. Ellis, *American Sphinx*, pp. 188–189.
8. Israel, *The Expanding Blaze*, p. 346.
9. Israel, The Expanding Blaze, p. 348.
10. Lambert, *The Founding Fathers*, pp. 240–241.
11. Israel, *The Expanding Blaze*, p. 358.
12. Israel, The Expanding Blaze, p. 420.
13. Israel, The Expanding Blaze, p. 349.
14. Israel, The Expanding Blaze, p. 350.
15. One of the most compelling philosophical documents that explores in parallel a faith-based path and a rational argument to justify political principles is Benedict de Spinoza's *Theological-Political Treatise*.

Chapter 8

1. Maier, *American Scripture*, p. 18.
2. Ellis, *American Sphinx*, p. 294.
3. Ellis, American Sphinx, p. 145.
4. National Archives, "Declaration of Independence."
5. National Archives, "Declaration of Independence."
6. Wills, *Inventing America*, p. 93.
7. Wills, Inventing America, p. 187.
8. Wills, Inventing America, p. 211.
9. Wills, Inventing America, p. 211.
10. Jefferson, *Notes on the State of Virginia*, p. 169.
11. Allen, *Our Declaration*, p. 241.
12. Allen, Our Declaration, p. 137.
13. Wills, *Inventing America*, p. 190.
14. Bailyn, *The Ideological Origins*, p. 325.
15. Bailyn, The Ideological Origins, p. 79.
16. Bailyn, The Ideological Origins, p. 140.
17. Israel, *The Expanding Blaze*, p. 79.
18. Lepore, *These Truths*, p. 122.
19. Israel, *The Expanding Blaze*, p. 81.
20. Bailyn, *The Ideological Origins,* p. 282.
21. Bailyn, The Ideological Origins, p. 343.
22. Ellis, *American Sphinx*, p. 143.
23. Lepore, *These Truths*, p. 112.
24. Bailyn, *The Ideological Origins*, p. 324.

25. Pennsylvania Historical & Museum Commission, "Pennsylvania Constitution of 1776."
26. Israel, *The Expanding Blaze*, p. 59.
27. Israel, The Expanding Blaze, p. 61.
28. Israel, The *Enlightenment That Failed*, p. 306.
29. George Washington's Mount Vernon, "10 Facts."
30. Israel, *The Enlightenment That Failed*, p. 311.
31. Israel, The *Expanding Blaze*, p. 140.
32. Israel, The Expanding Blaze, p. 141.
33. Israel, The Expanding Blaze, p. 156.
34. Israel, The Expanding Blaze, p. 156.
35. Du Bois, *Black Reconstruction in America*, p. 4.
36. Israel, *The Expanding Blaze*, p. 144.
37. Israel, The Expanding Blaze, p. 147.
38. Israel, The Expanding Blaze, p. 186.
39. Lepore, *These Truths*, p. 146.

Chapter 9

1. Ellis, *American Sphinx*, p. 212.
2. Ellis, American Sphinx, p. 215.
3. Miller, *The Federalist Era*, pp. 8–21.
4. Maier, *American Scripture*, p. 170.
5. Maier, American Scripture, p. 170.
6. Genovese, *The Political Economy of Slavery*, pp. xxi–xxv.
7. Israel, *The Expanding Blaze*, p. 390.
8. Israel, The Expanding Blaze, p. 417.
9. Matthewson, "Jefferson and the Nonrecognition of Haiti," pp. 22–25.
10. U.S. Department of State, Office of the Historian, "The United States and the Haitian Revolution."
11. Ellis, *American Sphinx*, p. 103.
12. Israel, *The Expanding Blaze*, p. 409.
13. Israel, The Expanding Blaze, p. 414.
14. Ellis, *American Sphinx*, p. 319.
15. Israel, *The Expanding Blaze*, p. 457.
16. Israel, The Expanding Blaze, p. 469.
17. Israel, The Expanding Blaze, p. 490.
18. Cooper, *The American Democrat*.

19. Israel, *The Expanding Blaze*, p. 494.
20. Zinn, *A People's History*, p. 217.
21. Zinn, A People's History, pp. 127–129.

Chapter 10

1. Lepore, *These Truths*, p. 241.
2. Du Bois, *Black Reconstruction*, p. 11.
3. Du Bois, Black Reconstruction, p. 39.
4. Beckert, *Empire of Cotton*, Introduction.
5. Wills, *Lincoln at Gettysburg*, p. 100.
6. Wills, Lincoln at Gettysburg, p. 101.
7. Wills, Lincoln at *Gettysburg* p. 87, emphasis in the original.
8. Fehrenbacher (ed.), *Abraham Lincoln, Speeches and Writings*, p. 1398, emphasis added.
9. Wills, *Lincoln at Gettysburg* p. 147.
10. Du Bois, *Black Reconstruction*, p. 91.
11. Foner, *Reconstruction*, p. 7.
12. Foner, Reconstruction, p. 8.
13. Du Bois, *Black Reconstruction*, p. 219.
14. Foner, *Reconstruction*, p. 142.
15. Foner, Reconstruction, p. 68.
16. Foner, Reconstruction, p. 95.
17. Foner, Reconstruction, p. 102.
18. Foner, Reconstruction, p. 80.
19. Foner, Reconstruction, p. 121.
20. Du Bois, *Black Reconstruction*, pp. 135–136.
21. Du Bois, Black Reconstruction, p. 277.
22. Du Bois, Black Reconstruction, p. 140.
23. Foner, *Reconstruction*, p. 180.
24. Foner, Reconstruction, p. 238.
25. Foner, Reconstruction, p. 230.
26. Du Bois, *Black Reconstruction*, pp. 193, 249.
27. Du Bois, Black Reconstruction, p. 257.
28. Du Bois, Black Reconstruction, p. 265.
29. Du Bois, Black Reconstruction, p. 272.
30. Foner, *Reconstruction*, p. 244.
31. Foner, Reconstruction, p. 248.

32. Foner, *Reconstruction*, p. 250.

33. Foner, Reconstruction, pp. 258–259.

34. Du Bois, *Black Reconstruction*, p. 314.

35. Foner, *Reconstruction*, p. 291.

36. Foner, Reconstruction, p. 333.

37. Foner, Reconstruction, p. 410.

38. Foner, Reconstruction, p. 425.

39. Foner, Reconstruction, p. 455.

40. Foner, Reconstruction, p. 582.

41. Du Bois, *Black Reconstruction*, p. 694.

42. Du Bois, Black *Reconstruction*.

43. Foner, *Reconstruction*, pp. 603–604.

44. Hayes, *A Colony*, p. 34.

Chapter 11

1. Fields, "Dysplacement and Southern History."

2. Woodward, *Origins of the New South*, pp. 461–463.

3. Klein, *Why We're Polarized,* p. 22.

4. Klein, Why We're Polarized, p. 25.

5. Bateman, Katznelson, and Lapinski, *Southern Nation*, p. 6.

6. Woodward, *Origins of the New South*, pp. 460–469.

7. Goodwyn, *The Populist Movement*, p. 7.

8. Zinn, *A People's History*, p. 286.

9. Postel, Charles. *The Populist Vision*, p. 49.

10. Goodwyn, *The Populist Moment*, p. 33.

11. Postel, Charles. *The Populist Vision*, pp. 4–5.

12. Goodwyn, *The Populist Moment*, pp. 295–296.

13. Postel, Charles. *The Populist Vision*, pp. 279–288.

14. Bateman, Katznelson, and Lapinski, *Southern Nation*, p. 153.

15. Bateman, Katznelson, and Lapinski, Southern Nation, p. 227.

16. Bateman, Katznelson, and Lapinski, Southern Nation, p. 15.

17. Bateman, Katznelson, and Lapinski, Southern Nation, p. 292.

18. Bateman, Katznelson, and Lapinski, Southern Nation, p. 16.

19. Bateman, Katznelson, and Lapinski, Southern Nation, p. 306.

20. Rothstein, *The Color of Law*, Introduction.

21. Lepore, *These Truths*, p. 503.

22. Klein, *Why We're Polarized*, p. 23.

Chapter 12

1. Horne, *The Counter-Revolution of 1776*, chapter 7.
2. Garrow, *Bearing the Cross*, p. 219.
3. Garrow, Bearing the Cross, p. 219.
4. Garrow, Bearing the Cross, p. 95.
5. Garrow, Bearing the Cross, p. 114.
6. Garrow, Bearing the Cross, p. 124.
7. Garrow, Bearing the Cross, p. 212.
8. Garrow, Bearing the Cross, p. 269.
9. Garrow, Bearing the Cross, p. 284.
10. Garrow, Bearing the Cross, p. 407.
11. Garrow, Bearing the Cross, p. 408.
12. Berlin, *The Making of African America*, pp. 3–6, 202, 230.
13. Rothstein, *The Color of Law*, Chapter 11.
14. How To Combat Communism – Billy Graham.
15. Graham, "Do I Need To Go To Church."
16. Lepore, *These Truths*, p. 656.
17. Prasad, "The Popular Origins of Neoliberalism."
18. Data are from the following sources: Sentencing Project, "Trends in U.S. Corrections"; Langan, Fundis, and Greenfeld, "Historical Statistics on Prisoners"; Cohen, "Prisoners in 1990"; Beck and Harrison, "Prisoners in 2000." "Sentenced prisoners" refers to prisoners with sentences of more than one year.
19. Garrow, *Bearing the Cross*, p. 105.

Chapter 13

1. Nagourney, "Obama Wins Election."
2. Andersen, "College-Educated Professionals."
3. Cox, Lienesch, and Jones, "Beyond Economics."
4. Cox, Lienesch, and Jones, "Beyond Economics."
5. Sachs, "Keynes and the Good Life."
6. Jones, Parker, and Ten Bos, *For Business Ethics,* p. 101.
7. Klein, *Why We're Polarized,* p. 48.
8. Hawkins et al., *Hidden Tribes,* p. 19.
9. Wall Street Journal Editorial Board, "Opinion | Limiting Too Big to Fail."
10. Carney, *Alienated America*, pp. 59–60.
11. Carney, Alienated America, p. 84.
12. White House, "The Inaugural Address."

13. Markovits, *The Meritocracy Trap*, p. 63.
14. Graham, "Jeff Sessions Explains Why Christians Support Trump."
15. Dias, "'Christianity Will Have Power.'"
16. Dias, "'Christianity Will Have Power.'"
17. Kazin, "Trump and American Populism."
18. Elving, "With Latest Nativist Rhetoric."
19. Markovits, *The Meritocracy Trap*, p. 68.
20. Markovits, The Meritocracy Trap, p. 63.
21. Mason, *Uncivil Agreement*, p. 132.
22. Packer, *The Unwinding*, pp. 18–25.
23. Gessen, *Surviving Autocracy*, p. 18.
24. Dean, "Trump's Base."
25. Lukianoff, Greg, and Haidt, Jonathan. *The Coddling of the American Mind*, p. 58.
26. See Mason, *Uncivil Agreement*.
27. Lepore, *These Truths*, p. 639.
28. Lepore, These Truths, p. 711.
29. Hacker and Pierson, *Let Them Eat Tweets*, pp. 2–3.
30. Hacker and Pierson, Let Them Eat Tweets, p. 22.
31. Hacker and Pierson, Let Them Eat Tweets, p. 1.
32. Hacker and Pierson, Let Them Eat Tweets, p. 117.
33. Hacker and Pierson, Let Them Eat Tweets, p. 71.
34. Hacker and Pierson, Let Them Eat Tweets, p. 77.
35. Hacker and Pierson, Let Them Eat Tweets, p. 12.
36. Hacker and Pierson, Let Them Eat Tweets, p. 217.
37. Bauer and Goldsmith, *After Trump*, p. 2.

Chapter 14
1. Schwartz, "William Barr's State of Emergency," emphasis in the original.
2. Israel, *The Expanding Blaze*, p. 86.
3. Samuelson, "Jefferson and Religion," p. 143.
4. Walker, "Nuclear Enlightenment," pp. 431–433.
5. National Archives, "Declaration of Independence."
6. Bailyn, *The Ideological Origins,* p. 173.
7. Encyclopedia Britannica, "John Locke."
8. Kolata, "The New England Journal of Medicine."
9. Commission on the Practice of Democratic Citizenship, *Our Common Purpose.*

10. Allen, podcast with Ezra Klein, September 30, 2019.
11. See Allen, *Education and Equality*.
12. Allen, *Our Declaration*, Chapter 1.
13. Lepore, *These Truths*, p. xiv.
14. Howe, "Are Millennials Giving Up"; Guilford, "Harvard Research"; Breene, "Millennials Are Rapidly Losing Interest."
15. Ro and Bergom, "Why Don't STEM Majors Vote."
16. Brooks, "The Rotting of the Republican Mind."
17. Rauch, "The Constitution of Knowledge."
18. Rauch, "The Constitution of Knowledge."
19. Hawkins et al., *Hidden Tribes*, p. 136.
20. Rauch, "The Constitution of Knowledge."
21. *Wesberry et al. v. Sanders et al.*
22. Robinson, "Don't Give Up on America."

Chapter 15

1. Coates, *Between the World and Me*, p. 6.
2. Online Library of Liberty, *The Writings of James Madison*; Avalon Project, "Madison Debates: July 12."
3. Gessen, *Surviving Autocracy*, p. 175.
4. Gessen, Surviving Autocracy, pp. 173, 218.
5. See Glazer, *Beyond the Melting Pot*; Schlesinger, *The Disuniting of America*.
6. Sullivan, podcast with Ezra Klein, February 19, 2019.
7. Wallace, *Greater Gotham*.
8. Onishi, "A Racial Awakening in France." This lack of government-held data on race or religion in fact saved many Jews from being identified and deported during the Nazi occupation. Onishi, "George Floyd Protests Stir a Difficult Debate on Race in France."
9. Colosimo, "Laïcité."
10. Hill, *Identity in Algerian Politics*, p. 2.
11. Griffioen and Zeller, "The Netherlands."
12. Baker, "Far-Right Wins French Vote."

Chapter 16

1. Allen, *Our Declaration*, p. 107.
2. American Academy of Arts and Sciences, *Our Common Purpose*, p. 15.
3. Israel, *Revolutionary Ideas*, p. 380.

4. Israel, *The Enlightenment That Failed*, Chapter 7.

5. Israel, *Revolutionary Ideas*, p. 625.

6. Israel, Revolutionary Ideas, pp. 625–626.

7. Israel, *The Enlightenment That Failed*, Chapter 7.

8. Marx and Engels, *The Communist Manifesto*.

9. For a good discussion of modern forms of socialism, see Roemer, "What Is Socialism Today?"

10. Locke, *Two Treatises of Government*, pp. 188–199.

11. Hayes, *Twilight of the Elites*, p. 53.

12. Of course, there are many categories and classes of public goods like law enforcement, infrastructure, clean air and water, and national defense. For a discussion of knowledge and access to information as a public good, see Verschraegen and Schiltz, *Knowledge as a Global Public Good*.

13. See Rawls, *A Theory of Justice*, pp. 136–142.

14. Lukianoff and Haidt, *The Coddling of the American Mind*, p. 217, emphasis added.

15. Markovits, *The Meritocracy Trap*, p. 115.

16. Hayes, *Twilight of the Elites*, p. 57.

17. Hayes, Twilight of the Elites, p. 59.

18. Meatto, "Still Separate, Still Unequal."

19. Markovits, *The Meritocracy Trap*, p. 173.

20. Markovits, The Meritocracy Trap, p. 111.

21. Markovits, The Meritocracy Trap, p. 147.

22. Markovits, The Meritocracy Trap, p. 183.

23. Hayes, *Twilight of the Elites*, p. 53.

24. Markovits, *The Meritocracy Trap*, p. 153.

25. Markovits, The Meritocracy Trap, pp. 253–254.

26. Birnbaum, "Bernie Sanders and Elizabeth Warren."

27. Beeman, "Perspectives on the Constitution."

28. Beeman, "Perspectives on the Constitution."

29. Hayes, *Twilight of the Elites*, p. 217.

Chapter 17

1. Hawkins et al., *Hidden Tribes*, p. 4.

2. Hawkins et al., Hidden Tribes, p. 4.

3. Mason, *Uncivil Agreement*, pp. 4, 129.

4. Mason, Uncivil Agreement, pp. 20–21.

5. Hartsoe, "Why So Many Young People Don't Vote."

6. American Academy of Arts and Sciences, *Our Common Purpose*, p. 11.

7. Hawkins et al., *Hidden Tribes*, p. 5.

8. American Academy of Arts and Sciences, *Our Common Purpose*, p. 3.

9. Jefferson, *Notes on the State of Virginia*.

10. Allen, *Our Declaration*, p. 109.

11. Allen, Our Declaration, p. 275.

12. Hainmueller and Hiscox, "Attitudes toward Highly Skilled," pp. 61–68.

13. Vitiello and Sugrue (eds.), *Immigration and Metropolitan Revitalization*.

14. Swanson, "Trump Says Mail Ballots."

15. Newkirk, "Voter Suppression."

16. Winkler, "'Corporations Are People.'"

17. American Academy of Arts and Sciences, *Our Common Purpose*.

18. Drutman, *Breaking the Two-Party Doom Loop*.

19. Dingell, "I Served in Congress."

20. American Academy of Arts and Sciences, *Our Common Purpose*, p. 63.

21. Allen, *Education and Equality*, p. 17.

22. Piketty, *Capital in the Twenty-First Century*, p. 91.

23. Allen, *Education and Equality*, p. 99.

24. Parramore, "Baby Bonds."

25. Parramore, "Baby Bonds."

26. Social Security Administration, "Thomas Paine."

27. Hayes, *Twilight of the Elites*, p. 45.

28. Ellis, *American Sphinx*, p. 333.

29. Ellis, American Sphinx, pp. 296–297.

30. Sullivan, "America Desperately Needs."

31. Hawkins et al., *Hidden Tribes*, p. 137.

32. Hawkins et al., Hidden Tribes, p. 70.

33. Hawkins et al., Hidden Tribes, p. 137.

34. Mason, *Uncivil Agreement*, pp. 4, 74.

BIBLIOGRAPHY

Adams, John. *Thoughts on Government*. Amazon Kindle edition, 2011. First published 1776.

Adams, John Quincy. *Writings of John Quincy Adams*, New York, 1913. http://hdl. handle.net/2027/uc2.ark:/13960/t0wp9t60s.

Allen, Danielle. *An Inspiring Conversation About Democracy*. Podcast with Ezra Klein, September 30, 2019.

Allen, Danielle. *Education and Equality*. Chicago: The University of Chicago Press, 2016.

Allen, Danielle. *Our Declaration: A Reading of the Declaration of Independence in Defense of Equality*. New York: W.W. Norton and Company, 2014.

American Academy of Arts and Sciences. Commission on the Practice of Democratic Citizenship. *Our Common Purpose: Reinventing American Democracy for the 21st Century*. Cambridge, Massachusetts, 2020.

Andersen, Kurt. "College-Educated Professionals Are Capitalism's Useful Idiots: How I got co-opted into helping the rich prevail at the expense of everybody else." *The Atlantic*, August 7, 2020. https://www.theatlantic.com/ideas/archive/2020/08/i-was-useful-idiot-capitalism/615031.

Apperley, Alan. "Hobbes on Democracy." *Politics* 19, no. 3 (September 1, 1999): 165–171. https://doi.org/10.1111/1467-9256.00101.

Arendt, Hannah. *Men in Dark Times*. Harcourt Brace & Company, 1968.

Avalon Project. "Madison Debates: July 12." https://avalon.law.yale.edu/18th_century/debates_712.asp, accessed September 22, 2020.

Bailyn, Bernard. *The Ideological Origins of the American Revolution*. Cambridge, Massachusetts: Harvard University Press, 1967.

Baker, Luke. "Far-Right Wins French Vote in EU Election, but Macron Limits Damage." *Reuters*, May 26, 2019. https://www.reuters.com/article/us-eu-election-france-lepen-idUSKCN1SW0SF.

Bateman, David A., Ira Katznelson, and John S. Lapinski. *Southern Nation: Congress and White Supremacy after Reconstruction.* Princeton, New Jersey: Princeton University Press, 2018.

Bauer, Bob, and Jack Goldsmith. *After Trump: Reconstructing the Presidency.* Washington, DC: Lawfare Press, 2020.

Beck, Allen J., and Paige M. Harrison. "Prisoners in 2000." *Bureau of Justice Statistics Bulletin,* August 2001, pp. 1–16. https://www.bjs.gov/content/pub/pdf/p00.pdf.

Beckert, Sven. *Empire of Cotton: A Global History.* New York: Alfred A. Knopf, 2014.

Beeman, Richard R. "Perspectives on the Constitution: A Republic, If You Can Keep It." National Constitution Center. https://constitutioncenter.org/learn/educational-resources/historical-documents/perspectives-on-the-constitution-a-republic-if-you-can-keep-it.

Beik, William. *Louis XIV and Absolutism: A Brief Study with Documents.* Boston, Massachusetts: Bedford, 2000.

Berkhofer, Robert F. *The Experience of Power in Medieval Europe: 950–1350.* Burlington, Vermont: Ashgate, 2005.

Berlin, Ira. *The Making of African America: The Four Great Migrations.* New York: Viking, 2010.

Billy Graham on the Communist Threat, 2012. https://www.youtube.com/watch?v=-SpyppSVrmA&pbjreload=101&ab_channel=ChristopherD.Cantwell.

Birchfield, Vicki L. *Income Inequality in Capitalist Democracies: The Interplay of Values and Institutions.* University Park: Pennsylvania State University Press, 2008.

Birnbaum, Michael. "Bernie Sanders and Elizabeth Warren Want a Wealth Tax. Wealthy Swiss Say Their Model Could Work for America." *Washington Post.* https://www.washingtonpost.com/world/europe/swiss-wealth-tax-inspired-bernie-sanders-and-elizabeth-warren/2020/03/02/6b786e76-540b-11ea-80ce-37a8d4266c09_story.html, accessed September 23, 2020.

Bourke, Vernon J. *The History of Ethics.* Cluny Media Edition, 2020.

Boyd, Julian P. *The Papers of Thomas Jefferson.* Princeton, New Jersey: Princeton University Press, multiple volumes, 1950–2019.

Breene, Keith. "Millennials are rapidly losing interest in democracy." World Economic Forum, June 8, 2017. https://www.weforum.org/agenda/2017/06/millennials-are-rapidly-losing-interest-in-democracy/.

Brooks, David. "The Rotting of the Republican Mind." *The New York Times,* November 26, 2020.

Brucker, Gene A. *Renaissance Florence.* Electronic Resource. Berkeley: University of California Press, 1983.

Burckhardt, Jacob. *The Civilization of the Renaissance in Italy*. New York: Harper & Row, 1975.

Burke, Edmund. *Reflections on the Revolution in France*. Electronic Resource. New Haven: Yale University Press, c. 2003.

Carney, Timothy P. *Alienated America: Why Some Places Thrive While Others Collapse*. New York: Harper Collins, 2019.

Carroll, Stuart. *Blood and Violence in Early Modern France*. Electronic Resource. New York: Oxford University Press, 2006.

Chernow, Ron. *Alexander Hamilton*. New York: Penguin Press, 2004.

Coates, Ta-Nehisi. *Between the World and Me*. New York: Spiegel & Grau, 2015.

Cohen, Robyn L. "Prisoners in 1990." *Bureau of Justice Statistics Bulletin*, May 1991, pp. 1–12. https://www.bjs.gov/content/pub/pdf/p90.pdf.

Colosimo, Anastasia. "Laïcité: Why French Secularism Is So Hard to Grasp." Institut Montaigne blog, December 11, 2017. https://www.institutmontaigne. org/en/blog/laicite-why-french-secularism-so-hard-grasp.

Cooper, James Fenimore. *The American Democrat, or Hints on the Social and Civic Relations of the United States of America*. Amazon Kindle edition, 2007 (1838).

Cox, Daniel, Rachel Lienesch, and Robert P. Jones. "Beyond Economics: Fears of Cultural Displacement Pushed the White Working Class to Trump." *PRRI/The Atlantic Report*, PRRI (blog), 05.09.2017. https://www.prri.org/research/white-working-class-attitudes-economy-trade-immigration-election-donald-trump, accessed September 26, 2020.

Crawford, Alan Pell. *Twilight at Monticello: The Final Years of Thomas Jefferson*. New York: Random House, 2008.

Dean, John. "Trump's Base: Broadly Speaking, Who Are They?" https://verdict. justia.com/2018/02/16/trumps-base-broadly-speaking. Accessed September 26, 2020.

Dias, Elizabeth. "'Christianity Will Have Power.'" *The New York Times*, August 9, 2020 (corrected version August 10, 2020). https://www.nytimes. com/2020/08/09/us/evangelicals-trump-christianity.html?action=click& module=Top%20Stories&pgtype=Homepage.

Diderot, Denis (attributed). "Intolerance." *The Encyclopedia of Diderot & d'Alembert Collaborative Translation Project*. Translated by Philip Whalen. Ann Arbor: Michigan Publishing, University of Michigan Library, 2002.

Dingell, John D. "I Served in Congress Longer Than Anyone. Here's How to Fix It: Abolish the Senate and publicly fund elections." *The Atlantic*, December 4, 2018. https://www.theatlantic.com/ideas/archive/2018/12/john-dingell-how -restore-faith-government/577222/.

Drake, Tom. Notes from English 258: *Literature of Western Civilization. Masterpieces reflecting development of Western thought and culture, 17th Century to Present*. 2019. https://www.webpages.uidaho.edu/engl_258/Lecture%20Notes/modernism_vs_postmodernism.htm#:~:text=%20%20%20Modernism%20%28or%20Enlightenment%20Empiricism%20a,concept%20%20...%20%206%20more%20rows%20.

Drexler, Ken. *Research Guides: Federalist Papers: Primary Documents in American History: Federalist Nos. 61–70*. Research guide. Accessed September 26, 2020.

Drutman, Lee. *Breaking the Two-Party Doom Loop: The Case for Multiparty Democracy in America*. New York: Oxford University Press, 2020.

Du Bois, W.E.B. *Black Reconstruction in America: 1860–1880*. New York: The Free Press, 1935.

Duignan, Brian. "Postmodernism: philosophy." *Encyclopedia Britannica*. https://www.britannica.com/topic/postmodernism-philosophy, accessed September 24, 2020.

Ellis, Joseph J. *American Sphinx*. New York: First Vintage Edition, 1998.

Elving, Ron. "With Latest Nativist Rhetoric, Trump Takes America Back To Where It Came From." NPR, All Things Considered. July 16, 2019. https://www.npr.org/2019/07/16/742000247/with-latest-nativist-rhetoric-trump-takes-america-back-to-where-it-came-from, accessed September 26, 2020.

The Encyclopedia of Diderot and d'Alembert: Collaborative Translation Project. Electronic resource. Michigan: DLXS, 2002.

Fehrenbacher, Don E., ed. *Abraham Lincoln, Speeches and Writings*. New York: Library of America, 1989.

Fields, Barbara J. "Dysplacement and Southern History." *The Journal of Southern History*, Volume LXXXII, No.1, February 2016.

Foner, Eric. *Reconstruction. America's Unfinished Revolution: 1863–1877*. New York: Free Perennial Library (Harper Collins), 1989.

Garrow, David J. *Bearing the Cross: Martin Luther King, JR, and the Southern Christian Leadership Conference*. New York: Vintage Books, 1988.

Genovese, Eugene D. *The Political Economy of Slavery*. Electronic Resource. *Studies in the Economy and Society of the Slave South*. Middletown, Connecticut: Wesleyan University Press, 1989.

George Washington's Mount Vernon. "10 Facts About Washington & Slavery." https://www.mountvernon.org/george-washington/slavery/ten-facts-about-washington-slavery/.

Gessen, Masha. *Surviving Autocracy*. New York: Riverhead Books, 2020.

Gilder Lehrman Institute of American History, The. "John Adams on the abolition of slavery, 1801." https://www.gilderlehrman.org/history-resources/spotlight-primary-source/john-adams-abolition-slavery-1801.

Glazer, Nathan. *Beyond the Melting Pot: The Negroes, Puerto Ricans, Jews, Italians, and Irish of New York City*. Cambridge, Massachusetts: MIT Press, c. 1963.

Goodwin, Doris Kearns. *Team of Rivals*. New York: Simon & Schuster, 2005.

Goodwyn, Lawrence. *The Populist Movement: A Short History of the Agrarian Revolt in America*. New York: Oxford University Press, 1978.

Gordon-Reed, Annette. *The Hemingses of Monticello: An American Family*. New York: W.W. Norton, 2008.

Gould, Eliga H. "The Question of Home Rule." *The William and Mary Quarterly* 64, no. 2 (2007): 255–258.

Graham, Billy. *Do I Need To Go To Church (Billy Graham 1957 in Madison Square Garden)*, 2016. Electronic resource. https://www.youtube.com/watch?time_continue=247&v=Eo9KLcMm-ek&feature=emb_logo&ab_channel=Jesus Doctrine.

Graham, David A. "Jeff Sessions Explains Why Christians Support Trump." *The Atlantic*, June 30, 2020. https://www.theatlantic.com/ideas/archive/2020/06/why-christians-support-trump/613669/.

Griffioen, Pim, and Ron Zeller. "The Netherlands: the greatest number of Jewish victims
in Western Europe." Anne Frank House. https://www.annefrank.org/en/anne-frank/go-in-depth/netherlands-greatest-number-jewish-victims-western-europe.

Guilford, Gwynn. "Harvard research suggests that an entire global generation has lost faith in democracy." *Quartz*, November 30, 2016. https://qz.com/848031/harvard-research-suggests-that-an-entire-global-generation-has-lost-faith-in-democracy/.

Hacker, Jacob S. and Pierson, Paul. *Let Them Eat Tweets: How the Right Rules in an Age of Extreme Inequality*. London: W.W. Norton, 2020.

Haidt, Jonathan. *The Righteous Mind: Why Good People are Divided by Politics and Religion*. New York: Pantheon Books, 2012.

Hainmueller, Jens, and Michael J. Hiscox. "Attitudes toward Highly Skilled and Low-Skilled Immigration: Evidence from a Survey Experiment." *The American Political Science Review* 104, no. 1 (2010): 61–84. https://doi.org/10.2307/27798540.

Hartsoe, Steve. "Why so many young people don't vote." Duke Today, Academics, October 29, 2018. https://today.duke.edu/2018/10/why-so-many-young-people-don%E2%80%99t-vote, accessed September 23, 2020.

Hawkins, Stephen, Daniel Yudkin, Miriam Juan-Torres, and Tim Dixon. *Hidden Tribes: A Study of America's Polarized Landscape*. New York: More in Common, 2018. https://hiddentribes.us/pdf/hidden_tribes_report.pdf.

Hayes, Christopher. *A Colony in a Nation*. New York: W.W. Norton, 2017.

Hayes, Christopher. *Twilight of the Elites: America After Meritocracy*. New York: Broadway Paperbacks, 2012.

Hill, J.N.C. *Identity in Algerian Politics: The Legacy of Colonial Rule*. Boulder, Colorado: Lynne Rienner Publishers, 2009.

Himmelfarb, Gertrude. *The Roads to Modernity: The British, French, and American Enlightenments*. New York: Vintage Books, 2004.

Hobbes, Thomas. *Leviathan*. New York: Penguin Books, 1968. First published 1651.

Horne, Gerald Horne. *The Counter-Revolution of 1776: Slave Resistance and the Origins of the United States of America*. New York: New York University Press, 2014.

Houston, R. A. (Robert Allan). *Literacy in Early Modern Europe: Culture and Education, 1500–1800*. Electronic Resource. New York: Longman, 1988.

How To Combat Communism – Billy Graham, 2012. https://www.youtube.com/watch?v=eub7tc-hT58&ab_channel=WorldwideIndexofSermons.

Howe, Neil. "Are Millennials Giving Up On Democracy?" *Forbes*, October 31, 2017. https://www.forbes.com/sites/neilhowe/2017/10/31/are-millennials-giving-up-on-democracy/#7da252132be1.

Humboldt, Wilhelm von. *The Limits of State Action*. Electronic Resource. London: Cambridge University Press, 1969.

Hume, David. *Collected Writings*. Oxford: Benediction Classics, 2013.

Institut Montaigne. *Why French Secularism Is So Hard to Grasp*. Digital Blog, December 2017.

Isaacson, Walter. *Benjamin Franklin: An American Life*. New York: Simon & Schuster, 2003.

Israel, Jonathan. *Radical Enlightenment*. New York: Oxford University Press, 2001.

Israel, Jonathan. *Revolutionary Ideas: An Intellectual History of the French Revolution from The Rights of Man to Robespierre*. Princeton, New Jersey: Princeton University Press, 2014.

Israel, Jonathan. *The Enlightenment That Failed*. New York: Oxford University Press, 2019.

Israel, Jonathan. *The Expanding Blaze: How the American Revolution Ignited the World, 1775–1848*. New York: Oxford University Press, 2017.

Jefferson, Thomas. *Notes on the State of Virginia*. New York: Penguin Books, 1999.

"John Locke," *Encyclopedia Britannica*. https://www.britannica.com/biography/John-Locke, accessed September 22, 2020.

Jones, Campbell, Martin Parker, and Rene Ten Bos. *For Business Ethics*. New York: Routledge, 2005.

Kazin, Michael. "Trump and American Populism," August 19, 2019. https://www.foreignaffairs.com/articles/united-states/2016-10-06/trump-and-american-populism.

Klein, Ezra. *Why We're Polarized*. New York: Avid Reader Press, 2020.

Kloppenberg, James T. *Towards Democracy: The Struggle for Self-Rule in European and American Thought*. New York: Oxford University Press, 2016.

Kolata, Gina. "The New England Journal of Medicine has remained nonpartisan for more than 200 years—until now." *Daily Press*, October 8, 2020. https://www.dailypress.com/nation-world/ct-nw-nyt-new-england-journal-of-medicine-trump-biden-20201008-igwtug7zxvatldxcfx5bfayb24-story.html.

Lambert, Frank. *The Founding Fathers and the Place of Religion in America*. Princeton, New Jersey: Princeton University Press, 2006.

Langan, Patrick A., John V. Fundis, and Lawrence A. Greenfeld. "Historical Statistics on Prisoners in State and Federal Institutions, Yearend 1925–86." U.S. Department of Justice, Bureau of Justice Statistics. https://www.ncjrs.gov/pdffiles1/digitization/111098ncjrs.pdf.

Lauren, Paul Gordon. *The Evolution of International Human Rights*. Philadelphia: University of Pennsylvania Press, 2003.

Lepore, Jill. *These Truths: A History of the United States*. New York: W.W. Norton & Company, 2018.

Locke, John. *Second Treatise of Government*. Los Angeles: Enhanced Media Publishing, 2016. First published 1690.

Locke, John. *Two Treatises of Government*. New Haven: Yale University Press, n.d.

Lukes, Steven, and Nadia Urbinati, eds. *Condorcet: Political Writings*. Cambridge Texts in the History of Political Thought. Cambridge: Cambridge University Press, 2012.

Lukianoff, Greg, and Jonathan Haidt. *The Coddling of the American Mind: How Good Intentions and Bad Ideas Are Setting Up a Generation for Failure*. New York: Penguin Books, 2019.

Maier, Pauline. *American Scripture: Making the Declaration of Independence*. New York, Vintage Books, 1998.

Malone, Dumas. *Jefferson and His Time*. New York: Little, Brown and Company, 6 volumes, 1967–1982.

Markovits, Daniel. *The Meritocracy Trap: How America's Foundational Myth Feeds Inequality, Dismantles the Middle Class, and Devours the Elite*. New York: Penguin Press, 2019.

Marx, Karl, and Friedrich Engels. *The Communist Manifesto*. New York, Penguin Classics, 1967.

Mason, Lilliana. *Uncivil Agreement: How Politics Became Our Identity*. Chicago: University of Chicago Press, 2018.

Matthewson, Tim. "Jefferson and the Nonrecognition of Haiti." *Proceedings of the American Philosophical Society* 140, no. 1 (1996): 22–48.

McCormick, Thomas J. *America's Half-Century: United States Foreign Policy in the Cold War*. Baltimore: Johns Hopkins University Press, c. 1989.

McCullough, David. *John Adams*. New York: Simon & Schuster, 2001.

Meacham, Jon. *Thomas Jefferson: The Art of Power*. New York: Random House, 2012.

Meatto, Keith. "Still Separate, Still Unequal: Teaching about School Segregation and Educational Inequality." *The New York Times*, May 2, 2019, section: The Learning Network. https://www.nytimes.com/2019/05/02/learning/lesson-plans/still-separate-still-unequal-teaching-about-school-segregation-and-educational-inequality.html.

Miller, John C. *The Federalist Era 1979–1801*. New York: Harper & Brothers, 1960. http://archive.org/details/federalistera197000675mbp.

Montesquieu, Charles de Secondat, Thomas Nugent, and Jean Le Rond d'Alembert. *The Spirit of Laws*. New York: The Colonial Press, c. 1899. http://archive.org/details/spiritoflaws01montuoft.

Nadler, Steven. "Baruch Spinoza." In *The Stanford Encyclopedia of Philosophy*, edited by Edward N. Zalta, Summer 2020. Metaphysics Research Lab, Stanford University, 2020. https://plato.stanford.edu/archives/sum2020/entries/spinoza/.

Nagourney, Adam. "Obama Wins Election." *The New York Times*, November 4, 2008.

National Archives, "Declaration of Independence: A Transcription." America's Founding Documents. https://www.archives.gov/founding-docs/declaration-transcript.

Newkirk, Vann R. II. "Voter Suppression Is the New Old Normal." *The Atlantic*, October 24, 2018. https://www.theatlantic.com/politics/archive/2018/10/2018-midterms-and-specter-voter-suppression/573826/.

Onishi, Norimitsu. "George Floyd Protests Stir a Difficult Debate on Race in France." *The New York Times*, June 16, 2020.

Onishi, Norimitsu. "A Racial Awakening in France, Where Race Is a Taboo Topic." *The New York Times*, July 14, 2020.

Online Library of Liberty. *The Writings of James Madison*, Vol. 5 (1787–1790). https://oll.libertyfund.org/titles/madison-the-writings-vol-5-1787-1790, accessed September 22, 2020.

Packer, George. "The President Is Winning His War on American Institutions: How Trump is destroying the civil service and bending the government to his will," *The Atlantic,* April 2020. https://www.theatlantic.com/magazine/archive/2020/04/how-to-destroy-a-government/606793.

Packer, George. *The Unwinding: An Inner History of the New America.* New York: Farrar, Straus & Giroux, 2013.

Padgett, John F. and Paul D. McLean. "Economic Credit in Renaissance Florence." *The Journal of Modern History* 83, no. 1 (2011): 1–47. https://doi.org/10.1086/658247.

Paine, Thomas. *Agrarian Justice.* Cabin John, Maryland: Wildside Press, 2010.

Paine, Thomas. *Common Sense, Rights of Man, and Other Essential Writings.* Digireads, Amazon Kindle edition, 2017.

Painter, Nell Irvin. *The History of White People.* New York: W.W. Norton, 2010.

Parramore, Lynn. "Baby Bonds: A Plan for Black/White Wealth Equality Conservatives Could Love?" Institute for New Economic Thinking, October 25, 2016. https://www.ineteconomics.org/perspectives/blog/baby-bonds-a-plan-for-black-white-wealth-equality-conservatives-could-love-1.

Pennsylvania Historical & Museum Commission. "Pennsylvania Constitution of 1776." http://www.phmc.state.pa.us/portal/communities/documents1776-1865/pennsylvania-constitution-1776.html.

Peterson, Merrill D. *The Jefferson Image in the American Mind.* Charlottesville, Virginia: University of Virginia Press, 1960.

Piketty, Thomas. *Capital in the Twenty-First Century.* Translated by Arthur Goldhammer. Cambridge, Massachusetts: Harvard University Press, 2013.

Postel, Charles. *The Populist Vision.* New York: Oxford University Press, 2007.

Prasad, Monica. "The Popular Origins of Neoliberalism in the Reagan Tax Cut of 1981." *Journal of Policy History* 24, no. 3 (2012): 351–356.

"Project MUSE — The Popular Origins of Neoliberalism in the Reagan Tax Cut of 1981." http://muse.jhu.edu/article/479639, accessed September 26, 2020.

Psillos, Stathis, and Martin Curd. *The Routledge Companion to Philosophy of Science* (first published in paperback edition). London: Routledge, 2010.

Rauch, Jonathan. "The Constitution of Knowledge." *National Affairs,* Fall 2018. https://www.nationalaffairs.com/publications/detail/the-constitution-of-knowledge.

Rawls, John. *A Theory of Justice.* Cambridge, Massachusetts: Harvard University Press, 1971.

Ro, Hyun Kyoung, and Inger Bergom. "Why Don't STEM Majors Vote as Much as Others?" The Conversation. http://theconversation.com/why-dont-stem-majors-vote-as-much-as-others-89015, accessed September 22, 2020.

Robinson, Marilynne. "Don't Give Up on America." *The New York Times*, October 9, 2020.

Rodrik, Dani, and Charles Sabel. "Building a Good Jobs Economy." November 2019. HKS Working Paper No. RWP20-001. https://ssrn.com/abstract =3533430 or http://dx.doi.org/10.2139/ssrn.3533430.

Roemer, John E. "What Is Socialism Today? Conceptions of a Cooperative Economy." Cowles Foundation Discussion Paper, No. 2220, January 21, 2020.

Rothstein, Richard. *The Color of Law: A Forgotten History of How Our Government Segregated America*. London: Liveright Publishing Corporation, a division of W.W. Norton & Company, 2017.

Rousseau, Jean-Jacques. *Discourse on Political Economy and The Social Contract*. Translation by Christopher Betts. New York: Oxford World Classics, 1994.

Routley, Nick. "Visualizing the Extreme Concentration of Global Wealth." *Visual Capitalist* (blog), December 26, 2018. https://www.visualcapitalist.com/ global-wealth-concentration/.

Sachs, Jeffrey. "Keynes and the Good Life." *The American Prospect*, May 18, 2020. https://prospect.org/culture/books/keynes-and-the-good-life.

Samuelson, Richard. "Jefferson and religion: private belief, public policy," In *The Cambridge Companion to Thomas Jefferson*, edited by Frank Shuffelton, pp. 143–154. Cambridge Companions to American Studies. New York: Cambridge University Press, 2009.

Schlesinger, Arthur M. *The Disuniting of America*. New York: Norton, 1992.

Schwartz, Mattathias. "William Barr's State of Emergency." *New York Times Magazine*, June 1, 2020. https://www.nytimes.com/2020/06/01/magazine/ william-barr-attorney-general.html.

Sentencing Project, The. "Trends in U.S. Corrections: Fact Sheet." https://www. sentencingproject.org/wp-content/uploads/2020/08/Trends-in-US-Corrections. pdf.

Shuffelton, Frank, ed. *The Cambridge Companion to Thomas Jefferson*. Cambridge Companions to American Studies. New York: Cambridge University Press, 2009.

Snyder, Timothy. *On Tyranny: Twenty Lessons from the Twentieth Century*. New York: Tim Duggan Books, 2017.

Social Security Administration. "Thomas Paine." In-Depth Research, Social Security Administration. https://www.ssa.gov/history/tpaine3.html.

Spinoza, Benedict de. *Theological-Political Treatise*, edited by Jonathan Israel. New York: Cambridge University Press, 2007.

Steward, David O. (2016). *Madison's Gift: Five Partnerships That Built America*. New York: Simon and Schuster, 2016.

Sullivan, Andrew. "America Desperately Needs a Healthy Conservatism." *New York Intelligencer,* September 14, 2018. https://nymag.com/intelligencer/2018/09/gop-destroying-conservatism.html.

Sullivan, Andrew. *Andrew Sullivan and I Work Out Our Differences.* Ezra Klein Podcast, February 19, 2019.

Swanson, Ian. "Trump Says Mail Ballots Greater Election Threat than Foreign Interference." Text. *The Hill,* September 16, 2020. https://thehill.com/homenews/administration/516793-trump-says-mail-ballots-greater-election-threat-than-foreign.

Taylor, Steven L., Matthew S. Shugart, Arend Lijphart, and Bernard Grofman. *A Different Democracy: American Government in a Thirty-One-Country Perspective.* New Haven: Yale University Press, 2014.

United States, Continental Congress, 1775. *The "Olive Branch" Petition to King George III of England From the Second Continental Congress, Signed by Forty-Six of Its Members.* New York: American Art Association, 1932.

U.S. Department of State, Office of the Historian. "The United States and the Haitian Revolution, 1791–1804." https://history.state.gov/milestones/1784-1800/haitian-rev.

Verschraegen, Gert and Michael Schiltz. *Knowledge as a Global Public Good: The Role and Importance of Open Access.* Societies Without Borders, Vol 2, Issue 2, 2007.

Vitiello, Domenic and Thomas J. Sugrue, eds. *Immigration and Metropolitan Revitalization in the United States. The City in the Twenty-First Century.* Philadelphia: PENN University of Pennsylvania Press, 2017.

Voltaire. *An Essay on Universal History, the Manners, and Spirit of Nations, from the Reign of Charlemaign to the Age of Lewis XIV.* 2nd ed., London, 1759. http://hdl.handle.net/2027/hvd.hwnhrv.

Walker, William. "Nuclear Enlightenment and Counter-Enlightenment." *International Affairs,* Royal Institute of International Affairs, 83, no. 3 (2007): 431–433.

Wall Street Journal Editorial Board. "Opinion | Limiting Too Big to Fail." *Wall Street Journal,* March 18, 2019, Opinion section. https://www.wsj.com/articles/limiting-too-big-to-fail-11552951166.

Wallace, Mike. *Greater Gotham: A History of New York City from 1898 to 1919.* New York: Oxford University Press, 2017.

Wesberry, James P. Jr. et al., Appellants, v. Carl E. Sanders, etc., et al. 376 U.S. 1, 84 S.Ct. 526, 11 L.Ed.2d 481. https://www.law.cornell.edu/supremecourt/text/376/1.

White House. "The Inaugural Address." January 20, 2017. https://www.whitehouse.gov/briefings-statements/the-inaugural-address.

"Why George Floyd's Death In Minneapolis Hit A Nerve In France." NPR.org. https://www.npr.org/2020/06/12/875548045/why-george-floyds-death-in-minneapolis-hit-a-nerve-in-france, accessed September 22, 2020.

"Why So Many Young People Don't Vote." https://today.duke.edu/2018/10/why-so-many-young-people-don%E2%80%99t-vote, accessed September 23, 2020.

Wills, Gary. *Inventing America: Jefferson's Declaration of Independence*. Garden City, New York: Doubleday, 1978.

Wills, Gary. *Lincoln at Gettysburg: The Words That Remade America*. New York: Simon & Schuster, 1992.

Winkler, Adam. "'Corporations Are People' Is Built on an Incredible 19th-Century Lie." *The Atlantic*, March 5, 2018. https://www.theatlantic.com/business/archive/2018/03/corporations-people-adam-winkler/554852/.

"With Latest Nativist Rhetoric, Trump Takes America Back To Where It Came From." NPR.org. https://www.npr.org/2019/07/16/742000247/with-latest-nativist-rhetoric-trump-takes-america-back-to-where-it-came-from, accessed September 26, 2020.

Woodward, C. Vann. *Origins of the New South, 1877–1913*. Electronic Resource. Baton Rouge: Louisiana State University Press, 1971.

The Writings of James Madison, Vol. 5 (Correspondence, 1787–1790). Online Library of Liberty. https://oll.libertyfund.org/titles/madison-the-writings-vol-5-1787-1790, accessed September 22, 2020.

The Writings of James Madison, Vol. 6 (Correspondence, 1790–1802). Online Library of Liberty. https://oll.libertyfund.org/titles/madison-the-writings-vol-6-1790-1802, accessed September 22, 2020.

Wu, Ellen D. *The Color of Success: Asian Americans and the Origins of the Model Minority*. 1st Edition. Princeton, New Jersey: Princeton University Press, 2013.

Zinn, Howard. *A People's History of the United States*. New York: Harper Collins, 1999.

INDEX

ABOUT THE AUTHOR

SETH DAVID RADWELL is an internationally known business executive and thought leader in consumer marketing.

A common thread across all his leadership and business endeavors has been his passion for our shared democratic values and his interest in American public policy.

Mr. Radwell served as president of e-Scholastic, the digital arm of the global children's publishing and education conglomerate. In an earlier role he was president at Bookspan/ Bertelsmann, where he was responsible for all editorial, marketing, media, and digital functions for such iconic brands as Book of the Month Club, Doubleday Book Club, and Literary Guild.

Until 2018, Mr. Radwell served as the CEO of The Proactiv Company, the leading skincare brand for acne. Previously, he served as president and chief revenue officer of Guthy-Renker, the worldwide leading direct-to-consumer beauty company. Prior to his publishing career, Radwell served as senior vice president, content, for Prodigy Services Company, where he pioneered new ecommerce revenue streams for the online service business. Before that, he spent six years with management consulting firm McKinsey & Company.

Seth David Radwell received a master's degree in public policy from Harvard University's Kennedy School of Government. He holds a bachelor of arts degree, summa cum laude from Columbia College, Columbia University. He currently divides his time between New York, Los Angeles, and Paris.